U.S. ARMY INFANTRY DIVISIONS
1943–45
VOLUME 1
Organization, Doctrine, Equipment

Yves J. Bellanger

HELION & COMPANY

This book is dedicated to all those who served with a U.S. Army Infantry Division in the Second World War.

Helion & Company Limited
26 Willow Road
Solihull
West Midlands
B91 1UE
England
Tel. 0121 705 3393
Fax. 0121 711 4075
Email: publishing@helion.co.uk
Website: http://www.helion.co.uk

Published by Helion and Company Limited, 2002

Designed and typeset by Carnegie Publishing Ltd, Lancaster, Lancashire
Printed by The Cromwell Press, Trowbridge, Wiltshire

© Helion and Company 2002

ISBN 1 874622 95 7

British Library Cataloguing-in-Publication Data.
A catalogue record for this book is available from the British Library.

For details of other military history titles published by Helion & Company contact the above address, or visit our website: http://www.helion.co.uk.

We always welcome receiving book proposals from prospective authors.

The front cover shows unit badges of the following U.S. Army divisions (reading clockwise) – 1st, 32nd, 77th, 34th, 79th and 4th infantry divisions. All badges are from the collection of the author.

All charts drawn by the author.

CONTENTS

List of charts   v
Publishers' note and acknowledgements   vii
Introduction   viii
Background   ix
    Mobilization   ix
    The United States Army   ix
    The Army Reorganization of 1940–43   ix
    The Table of Organization & Equipment   xi

CHAPTER 1 – INFANTRY DIVISION, DIVISION HEADQUARTERS, HEADQUARTERS COMPANY,
            RECONNAISSANCE TROOP   1
    1.1 – Infantry Division, Organization and General Doctrine   1
    1.2 – Headquarters, Infantry Division   4
    1.3 – Division, Headquarters Company   13
    1.4 – Cavalry Reconnaissance Troop, Mechanized   16

CHAPTER 2 – INFANTRY REGIMENT   25
    2.1 – Regimental Headquarters   25
    2.2 – Regimental Headquarters Company   27
    2.3 – Service Company, Infantry Regiment   33
    2.4 – Infantry Cannon Company   39
    2.5 – Infantry Anti-tank Company   42
    2.6 – Medical Detachment, Infantry Regiment   45
    2.7 – Command Post, Infantry Regiment   49
    2.8 – Train Bivouac, Infantry Regiment   50

CHAPTER 3 – INFANTRY BATTALION   53
    3.1 – Headquarters Company, Infantry Battalion   54
    3.2 – Infantry Rifle Company   61
    3.3 – Infantry Heavy Weapons Company   66
    3.4 – Command Post, Infantry Battalion   71

CHAPTER 4 – INFANTRY DOCTRINE   74
    4.1 – Security missions   74
    4.2 – Defensive combat   80
    4.3 – Offensive combat   87

CHAPTER 5 – DIVISION ARTILLERY, MOTORIZED   95
    5.1 – Artillery Doctrine   96
    5.2 – Headquarters & Headquarters Battery, Division Artillery   98
    5.3 – Field Artillery Battalions, 105mm, 155mm   104
    5.4 – Headquarters Battery, Motorized, Field Artillery Battalion   106
    5.5 – Field Artillery Battery Motorized, Field Artillery Battalion   114
    5.6 – Service Battery, Motorized, Field Artillery Battalion   121

CHAPTER 6 – ENGINEER COMBAT BATTALION   125
    6.1 – Engineer Doctrine   126
    6.2 – Headquarters & Headquarters Service Company, Engineer Combat Battalion   129
    6.3 – Engineer Combat Company   136

CHAPTER 7 – SPECIAL TROOPS, INFANTRY DIVISION   140
    7.1 – Headquarters, Special Troops   141
    7.2 – Ordnance Light Maintenance Company, Infantry Division   142
    7.3 – Quartermaster Company, Infantry Division   148
    7.4 – Signal Company, Infantry Division   152
    7.5 – Signal Doctrine, Signal Company, Infantry Division   162
    7.6 – Military Police Platoon, Infantry Division   175
    7.7 – Band, Infantry Division   179

CHAPTER 8 – MEDICAL BATTALION, INFANTRY DIVISION   181
    8.1 – Headquarters & Headquarters Detachment, Medical Battalion   182
    8.2 – Collecting Company, Medical Battalion   186
    8.3 – Clearing Company, Medical Battalion   189

CHAPTER 9 – EQUIPMENT   193
    9.1 – Company standard equipment   194
    9.2 – Equipment issued with vehicles and weapons   195
    9.3 – Individual equipment   198
    9.4 – Clothing and smaller items of equipment   207
    9.5 – Attached units   211

APPENDICES
    I – US Army Ranks   213
    II – US Army Unit Symbols   215
    III – US Army Abbreviations   216
    IV – Example of casualties and replacements in an infantry regiment (10th Infantry Regiment)   219
    V – Organization of the 5th Infantry Division, 6 June 1944   221
    VI – Command Roster of the 5th Infantry Division, 1943-45   223
    VII – Command Roster of the 11th Infantry Regiment, 31 January 1945   236
Bibliography   241

LIST OF CHARTS

See charts 31 and 74 for keys to many of the symbols used.

1. Infantry Division, 1943–1945   1
2. Headquarters, Infantry Division   4
3. Headquarters Company, Infanty Division   13
4. Cavalry Reconnaissance Troop, Infantry Division   17
5. Headquarters Section, Cavalry Reconnaissance Troop   19
6. Armored Car Section, Cavalry Reconnaissance Troop   23
7. Scout Section, Reconnaissance Platoon, Cavalry Reconnaissance Troop   24
8. Infantry Regiment   25
9. Headquarters Company, Infantry Regiment   28
10. Intelligence & Reconnaissance Platoon, Headquarters Company, Infantry Regiment   32
11. Service Company, Infantry Regiment   33
12. Infantry Cannon Company, Infantry Regiment   39
13. Infantry Anti-tank Company, Infantry Regiment   42
14. Medical Detachment, Infantry Regiment   45
15. Command Post, Infantry Regiment   49
16. Train Bivouac, Infantry Regiment   51
17. Infantry Battalion   53
18. Headquarters & Headquarters Company, Infantry Battalion   54
19. Infantry Rifle Company, Infantry Battalion   62
20. Infantry Heavy Weapons Company, Infantry Battalion   66
21. Command Post, Infantry Battalion   72
22. Advance Guard   75
23. Flank Guard on a route parallel to the Main Body   76
24. Disposition of an Outpost for a Bivouac   77
25. Position of an Outguard and of the Sentinels, day and night   78
26. Combat Outpost of a Battalion, with a General Outpost   79
27. Combat Outpost   80
28. Emplacement of a Platoon   81
29. Emplacement of a Squad   83
30. Emplacement of frontline Platoons   84
31. Chart symbols   86
32. The different methods by which Squads were to be utilised   87
33. The Support Echelon as manoeuvring force (1)   93
34. The Support Echelon as manoeuvring force (2)   93
35. Division Artillery, Motorized, Infantry Division   95
36. Headquarters & Headquarters Battery, Motorized, Divisional Artillery   98
37. Field Artillery Battalions, 105mm, 155mm   105
38. Headquarters & Headquarters Battery, Field Artillery Battalion 105mm   107
39. Headquarters & Headquarters Battery, Field Artillery Battalion 155mm   107
40. Field Artillery Battery, Field Artillery Battalion, 105mm   115
41. Field Artillery Battery, Field Artillery Battalion, 155mm   115
42. Positioning of 105mm Howitzers   118
43. Service Battery, Motorized, Field Artillery Battalion   121
44. Engineer Combat Battalion   125
45. Headquarters, and Headquarters & Service Company, Engineer Combat Battalion   130
46. Engineer Combat Company, Engineer Combat Battalion   136
47. Special Troops, Infantry Division   140

48. Ordnance Company, Infantry Division   142
49. Quartermaster Company, Infantry Division   148
50. Signal Company, Infantry Division   152
51. Division Command Net   170
52. Division Reconnaissance Net   170
53. Division Warning Net   170
54. Wire Net, Infantry Division   171
55. Division Artillery Net   171
56. Division Artillery Air Ground Channels   172
57. Field Artillery Battalion Radio Net   172
58. Cavalry Reconnaissance Troop Radio Net   172
59. Infantry Regiment Radio Net   173
60. Infantry Battalion Radio Net   173
61. Message Center Section, Team organization   173
62. Telephone & Telegraph Section, Team organization   174
63. Radio Section, Team organization   174
64. Construction Platoon, Team organization   174
65. Military Police Platoon, Infantry Division   175
66. Medical Battalion, Infantry Division   181
67. The evacuation of the wounded   182
68. Headquarters & Headquarters Detachment, Medical Battalion   183
69. Collecting Company, Medical Battalion   186
70. Clearing Company, Medical Battalion   189
71. Bivouac of an Infantry Battalion, in combat area   195
72. Enlisted Men's rank insignia   213
73. Officers' & Warrant Officers' rank insignia   214
74. Organization chart symbols   215

PUBLISHERS' NOTE & ACKNOWLEDGEMENTS

Publishers' Note

This book is the first in a two-volume set that, once complete, will offer an extremely detailed treatment of the organization and doctrine of U.S. Army infantry divisions during the 1943–45 period. Volume 2, already in preparation, will provide a vast assemblage of order-of-battle data – notes on corps and armies including constituent divisions, lists of commanders, and a detailed record of each infantry division, including organizational diagrams, component units, command rosters, assignments to higher formations, and a combat diary.

Author's Acknowledgements

Any work in military history needs research, any research needs assistance, any assistance requires acknowledgement.

I am grateful to all the people who helped me in my researches undertaken to write this book. I am also grateful to those who supported me in this undertaking. I thank:-

Those who provided me with the necessary documents:

National Archives and Records Administration, Washington, D.C.

Center for Legislative Archives, particularly Rodney A. Ross and William H. Davis.

Suitland Reference Branch.

U.S. Army Military History Institute, Carlisle Barracks, particularly John J. Slonaker and Louise Arnold-Friend.

Those who helped me:

Center of Military History, U.S. Army, Washington, D.C.

The Society of the 5th Division, U.S. Army (of which I am a Honorary Life Member).

The veterans of the 5th Infantry Division whom I mention in the bibliography. I corresponded with some, and met a certain number of them in my town, Angers, France, during ceremonies, or at Orlando, Florida during their Annual Reunion.

The U.S. Army officers who encouraged and sometimes helped me: LTC Daniel Perron, Corps of Engineers; Captain (ret) Michael E. Travis, Corps of Engineers; LTC Brian A. Jost, Corps of Engineers; Major Mike Maklary, Corps of Engineers; LTC John Moncure, Cavalry.

Special thanks for their precious help to:

Charles Laborie, Guy Stéfanini, Brian A. Jost, Dick Durst and Herb Williams.

Finally, I have a particular thought for my wife, Cathy, and my children, Jérémie, Florian, Maëlle and Clément, for their support while I wrote this book.

Yves J. Bellanger
Angers, France, 13 January 1999

INTRODUCTION

This book was born because I wanted to buy it but nobody had written it. I searched for a long time to learn the organization of U.S. Army units. When I read in histories the terms 'regiment', 'battalion', 'division', I did not know what they meant. I found that I missed the human element. The term 'division' without the knowledge of the real division represents nothing. Knowing the units within a division is the beginning of knowledge. What was important to me, was to find the position and role of men within the organization. Now, with this book, I have realized my dream. I know how men functioned in this organization, what equipment they used, what doctrine influenced how they fought. The dream changed into reality when I met, for the first time, veterans who served in U.S. Army divisions. By this time, I knew what the soldiers' duties were and who performed them.

From lack of knowledge, I was conscience of a lack of memory. If I began this book with the goal of knowing, I ended it with the hope of serving human memory and paying tribute to those who served in an infantry division. I know many of them and I like to meet them.

However, this book does not show the individuals, the men, who made up each division; it shows, from the major general to the basic, from the mess sergeant to the machine gunner, who fought, and sometimes died, within it. It shows all that was the infantry division, from duties to ranks, from vehicles to minor items of equipment, weapons, and clothing, but does not show all that is hidden behind such terms.

Many books that describe equipment and uniforms exist; in this book I only note what equipment was issued and to whom it was issued. Doctrine and organization are not explained in other books, however, except in military manuals. This book describes how the units of the infantry division worked and fought.

This book reveals an organization in which men often lived through the most difficult time of their life, and in which some lost their lives. After learning, through its organization, what made up an infantry division in the Second World War, do not forget to recall that such a unit is only a means to serve a goal. The goal of the Second World War, as it must remain today, was freedom.

BACKGROUND

Mobilization

In September 1939, the U.S. Army counted only 190,000 men in its active component, the Regular Army and 225,000 men, all volunteers, in the National Guard. The U.S. Army was formed from professionals, men who often due to patriotism pursued a military career in the Army. On July 11 1940, President Roosevelt asked Congress to vote a budget of 4.5 billion dollars, to equip a 1,200,000 men army and to assure a supplementary reserve of 800,000 men. This would rise to become a 2,000,000-strong army.

On September 16 1940, the Congress of the United States approved the Selective Service Act by 232 against 124 votes in the House of the Representatives, and 47 against 25 votes in the Senate. About 16 million Americans had to be registered, 75,000 were to be drafted before 1st November, 400,000 by January and 900,000 by the spring of 1941. Military service was, in principle, for one year, soldiers could serve only in the Continental United States, and the wage was $30 a month ($50 by 1944). For receiving all draftees, the government constructed military camps. These were virtually self-sufficient towns, with their barracks, training grounds and hospital.

In 1941, the threat became more pressing. In order to be ready to answer all acts of aggression, the President proclaimed a national emergency on May 27 1941. In June, the Federal Government asked for one million draftees but the Armed Forces could not attain this until 1943. On July 21, Franklin D. Roosevelt requested the military services to prepare as rapidly as possible. After the Japanese attack on Pearl Harbor, on December 7 1941, the United States went to war against Germany and Japan. Following this, men from eighteen to thirty-eight years old were to be inducted for the length of the war plus six months.

On April 30 1945, the U.S. Armed Forces numbered 12,000,000 personnel, of whom 8,290,993 were in the U.S. Army. The United States Army included 1,194,569 men in 89 divisions, 779,882 in non-divisional combat units, 259,403 in the anti-aircraft artillery, 1,638,214 in non-divisional service units and 2,307,501 in the Army Air Forces.

The United States Army

The U.S. Army had three components during World War II: the Regular Army, the National Guard and the National Army.

The Regular Army [1] was the permanent army maintained in peace, as in war, and was the main component of the United States Army. In July 1940, the Regular Army numbered 243,095 men, of whom 14,000 were officers.

The National Guard was a reserve component organized by a State or a Territory of the United States. The guardsmen were not professional. They performed a civilian job and become soldiers during training periods. The units of the National Guard were financed and controlled by their State. The 226,837 men of the National Guard did not enable its 18 divisions to be operational. The President of the United States could, in a state of emergency, induct National Guard units into Federal service. The guardsmen's motto was 'Civilian in Peace, Soldier in War'.

The National Guard of the United States was a reserve component of the United States Army, including Federally-recognized National Guard organizations and persons appointed, commissioned, or enlisted therein. The 18 infantry divisions of the National Guard were inducted and reorganized between September 1940 and March 1941.

The National Army included the units formed from the Organized Reserve and organized with draftees.

The Organized Reserves (called the Army Reserve since 1952) were a component of the U.S. Army consisting of personnel and units organized and maintained to provide military training in peacetime and a reservoir of trained reservists to be ordered to active duty in the event of a national emergency. In 1940, the reserve units were only listed on mobilisation plans and not activated, the Organized Reserves being just a reservoir of 104,288 trained officers.

In 1941, the units activated without a mission of mobilisation, and were classified Army of the United States (AUS). The AUS included 28 divisions in 1945 (12 Infantry, 12 Armored, 4 Airborne). Today, this distinction no longer exists and Army of the United States is synonymous with United States Army.

The Army Reorganization of 1940–43

The armed conflict which started in Europe, on September 3 1939 with the invasion of Poland by the German Army, found the U.S. Army in a situation of doctrinal and organizational weakness. At this time it was ranked 17th in the armies of the

---

1. The definition of the terms proceeds from, Army Regulations, AR 320-5, *Dictionary of the United States Army Terms*, HQ Department of the Army, November 1958 (hereafter referred to as AR 320-5).

world. In the Regular Army, 3 infantry divisions existed at the half of their strength, 6 other divisions were just a skeleton, with cadres only. The 18 divisions of the National Guard existed due to their enlisted cadres.

Limited changes, such as the reduction in strength of the engineer unit, were made to the division after the First World War. However, the division, called a 'Square Division', essentially preserved its organization of 1918. It was composed of 2 brigade headquarters with 4 infantry regiments and included 22,000 men. The Square Division had been obsolete since the 1930s and was unable to play the role assigned to it in a modern war.

A new organization was developed in 1935, and approved on August 13 1936 to be tested in the field. From 1937 to 1939 the 2nd Infantry Division was designated to test the new organization as well as the new doctrine. On January 1 1939, the new organization (T/O 70, Triangular Division) was adopted, the brigade headquarters were cancelled and the number of regiments was reduced to 3. The strength of the division was only 15,000 men. The organization of three regiments, with, at each level, three units of manoeuvre, ensured that the new division was named a 'Triangular Division'.

In the spring of 1940, the first Triangular Divisions, the 1st, 5th and 6th infantry divisions, conducted the first manoeuvres in the IV Corps. The infantry division underwent many changes before the 1943 organization. The division approved to test involved 13,552 men. In the T/O 70 dated 1 June 1941, the Triangular Division was composed of 15,245 men. The new infantry division organization, T/O 7, dated 1 August 1942 called for a divisional strength of 15,514 men. In 1941, each regiment, as well as those in artillery divisions, received a band of 29 musicians. In July 1943, all bands were cancelled and the infantry division was issued with a new 58-strong band. A cannon company was assigned to each infantry regiment in 1942, but because of lack of men and equipment, it was not present in the majority of the divisions before July 1943.

The U.S. Army observed the battles of 1940 in Europe with great interest and studied the German doctrine of Blitzkrieg. The German doctrine was founded on the use of Panzer corps, composed of Panzer divisions and Panzergrenadier divisions, which gave the German army a firepower and mobility hitherto unknown.

The U.S. Army began to create an armored corps. The first was activated on July 15 1940 at Fort Knox, Kentucky. The armored corps was to receive the newly-designated armored divisions and motorized divisions. Between January and September 1942, Army Ground Forces constituted the II, III, and IV armored corps, serving to train all tank battalions. I Armored Corps was the only one to see action using this organization.

On November 1 1940, the U.S. Army adopted a new organization of division, the motorized division. This was an entirely motorized infantry division, able to displace all its units at one time. The Commander of Army Ground Forces, Lieutenant-General Lesley J. McNair was opposed to this type of unit from its inception. A motorized division and 2 armored divisions formed an armored corps. From April 1942, the 6th, 7th, 8th and 9th divisions were reorganized as motorized divisions. The 4th and 90th divisions would be transformed shortly later. The motorized division organization was modified on August 1 1942; at this date it included: 755 officers, 49 warrant officers and 16,085 enlisted men. It was issued with the impressive number of 2,790 vehicles among which were: 17 light tanks, 44 motorcycles, 553 ¼-ton trucks (jeeps), 667 ¾-ton trucks of all types, 889 2½-ton trucks of all types, 30 half-tracks, 3 scout cars, 18 75mm self-propelled howitzers, 6 105mm self-propelled howitzers, and 496 trailers of all types. [2]

The 4th Motorized Division was the only one to become operational. In August 1942, it was placed on alert for departure overseas. The transportation of a motorized division occupied as many boats as an armored division, without offering the same firepower, consequently no Theater of Operations Commander requested it. It possessed 1,000 more vehicles than an infantry division, consuming tons of rubber for the tyres of its vehicles. It needed twice the shipping tonnage for its transportation overseas. Army Ground Forces examined the problem and Lt. Gen. Lesley J. McNair decided to de-activate the motorized divisions. [3]

A procedure (SOP) to motorize the infantry divisions, if needed, was developed. Reinforced by 6 quartermaster truck companies, each with 48 2½-ton trucks, the infantry division was able to transport all its men and equipment in one go. Only the 3 infantry regiments had no organic transportation, although they consisted of more than 60% of the division (9,999 men of the 15,514 in the division on 1 August 1942; 9,354 of the 14,253 in the division on 15 July 1943). All motorized divisions were reorganized into infantry divisions from July 1943, according to T/O&Es dated 15 July 1943. The quartermaster truck companies were assigned to corps to be attached, not simultaneously, to several divisions, following specific needs.

The U.S. Army tried to lighten its logistics whilst trying to answer the claims of the new doctrine. It reorganized its divisions, armored divisions and infantry divisions in 1943, with the goal of saving personnel and vehicles, having failed to achieve this in 1942. Armored divisions were reorganized as light armored divisions in order to activate, using the excess tanks, more independent tank battalions. The abandonment of the motorized divisions called for the cancellation of the armored corps. The I Armored Corps was de-activated in Sicily in July 1943 and re-designated 7th Army. On October 10 1943 other armored corps were de-activated, the II was re-designated XVIII Corps, the III and the IV were re-designated XIX and XX Corps respectively.

The infantry division was reorganized to save on personnel. Army Ground Forces wanted to conserve a replacement force in order to maintain all units at their T/O&E strength throughout the war, in spite of battle losses. Army Ground Forces decided to cancel driver specialties and to assign to these tasks personnel who already had another specialty. The reorganization

---

2. T/O 77, *Motorized Division*, August 1, 1942, War Department.

3. Army Ground Forces, *Letter on Revised Organization*, 21 July 1943. Published in: Kent Roberts Greenfield, Robert R. Palmer & Bell I. Wiley *The Army Ground Forces, The Organization of Ground Combat Troops*, U.S. Army in WWII, U.S. Army Center of Military History, Government Printing Office, 1947, p 374–382.

also aimed at decreasing the number of vehicles by providing the units the minimum transportation they needed for supply. The ¼-ton trucks replaced the ¾-ton, and the 1½-ton the 2½-ton trucks. This reorganization materialized in the infantry division with the new T/O&E dated 15 July 1943.

In 1945, forecasting the victory in Europe and the commitment of those units at this time in Europe, against Japan, a new organization was designated. In part it reflected the combat unit experiences and wishes of army, corps and division commanders. The infantry division was the first to be reorganized; the new tables were dated 1 June 1945. The War Department initially thought to organize the divisions before their departure from Europe to the United States. It then preferred sending the required personnel and equipment to the Pacific Theater of Operations to reorganize the units already on the field. Finally, the capitulation of Japan occurred more quickly than had been foreseen; no division were reorganized according to the new tables dated 1 June 1945, the reorganization was submitted to the authorisation of the War Department. The first reorganizations were authorized in October 1945, and involved the 2nd and 4th infantry divisions.[4]

The Table of Organization & Equipment

A unit is organized according to defined criteria. A unit organization is elaborated from a unit doctrine. To be able to perform the role determined in the doctrine, a unit must have an organization that is a function of this doctrine. Organizations, like doctrine, have rules, they are written as texts, to which the commanders refer to organize, equip and use their units.

The organization of a unit was described in the 'Tables of Organization' (T/O), the material necessary and sufficient to equip a unit listed in the 'Tables of Equipment' (T/E). From 1943, both were consolidated in a new document called 'Tables of Organization and Equipment' (T/O&E).

A T/O&E[5] prescribed the number of officers and men, the duties, ranks and specialties (Military Occupational Specialty, MOS). It determined the necessary means for transportation, maintenance, supply, medical care, communications, and weapons. It allowed the determination of the MOS in men and to prepare their training before their assignment in a unit. A T/O&E is an authorisation to require men and equipment for the unit it describes.[6]

A T/O&E described the unit without regard to its zone of operations, however the Theater of Operations Commanders could be authorized by the War Department to make some modifications to the units. These modifications were generally noted in the tables with the sentence: "When authorized by the Commander of the Theater of Operations". Improvements wished for by units, following their battle experience, were transmitted to the agencies (Infantry, Cavalry, Armored, Engineer, Artillery) who studied the requests, and if needed, published a change to the T/O&E. A table of a unit could undergo many changes between 1943 and 1945.

For example, T/O&E 7-17, 'Infantry Rifle Company' was issued on 15 July 1943, replacing the organization dated 1 April 1942. It required a change, C1, on 29 October 1943, and a second change, C2, on 4 December 1943. A new table was issued on February 26 1944, under the same number, which required a change, C1, on June 30 1944, a second change, C2, on January 30 1945, and a third change, C3, on June 1 1945. Changes were not always important, sometimes they were concerned with the organization, sometimes the equipment, sometimes both. Because a new organization was issued on June 1 1945, with the same numbers, all T/O&Es were renamed 'Out of Service' (OS), e.g.: T/O&E 7-17-OS. However, the new T/O&Es, requiring the authorisation of the War Department, were not utilized before the end of WWII and many units would remain in wartime organizations until their de-activation in 1946.

A T/O&E was listed with a number, such as 7-17 or 2-15. Each sequence of digits was significant. The first represented the branch of service, for example, the 7 represented the infantry and the 2 represented the cavalry. The second number designated the unit described in the table, but in its number the last digit is again a reference mark. For example, the last number of 17, therefore the 7, denotes that it is a company (or a troop in the cavalry), and the 5 from 15 denotes that it is a battalion (or a squadron in the cavalry).

All data presented in this book is based on U.S. Army sources, these sources including the T/O&Es of all units studied, T/E, particularly the T/E 21 – Clothing and Individual Equipment, Army Regulations (AR), Field Manuals (FM) and booklets published by Command and General Staff College (CGSC), and the Training Bulletins of the Infantry School published in 1943.[7] References are indicated in the footnotes and in the bibliography at the end of the book.

I hope by this book to answer the readers' expectations in providing data which is not easily accessible and which has hitherto never been compiled so completely.

Before beginning to study the organization of the infantry division, one should mention two paragraphs from chapter 3, 'Leadership', of the Field Manual 100-5, *Field Service Regulations, Operations*. It seems very important to understand the doctrine and to let the reader see that the main force in the U.S. Army was (and is) man.

"Man is the fundamental instrument in war; other instruments may change but he remains relatively constant. Unless his behaviour and elemental attributes are understood, gross mistakes will be made in planning operations and in troop leading.

"In the training of the individual soldier, the essential considerations are to integrate individuals into a group and to

4. Greenfield, Palmer, Wiley, op. cit., p. 477.
5. The acronym of Table of Organization and Equipment is not currently T/O&E, but simply TOE.
6. Greenfield, Palmer, Wiley, op. cit.; correspondence with Brigadier General (Ret) William H. Birdsong, who commanded the 3rd Battalion, 11th Infantry, and with Robert H. Williams, who commanded L Company, before becoming Ex-O of the 1st Battalion, 11th Infantry.
7. See bibliography for more details.

establish for that group a high standard of military conduct and performance of duty without destroying the initiative of the individual." [8]

"In spite of the advances in technology, the worth of the individual man is still decisive. The open order of combat accentuates his importance. Every individual must be trained to exploit a situation with energy and boldness and must imbued with the idea that success will depend upon his initiative and action." [9]

8. FM 100-5, *Field Service Regulations, Operations*, May 22, 1941, War Department, p. 18, no. 98.
9. FM 100-5, op. cit., p. 18, no. 100.

CHAPTER 1

INFANTRY DIVISION, DIVISION HEADQUARTERS, HEADQUARTERS COMPANY, RECONNAISANCE TROOP

1.1 ORGANIZATION & GENERAL DOCTRINE

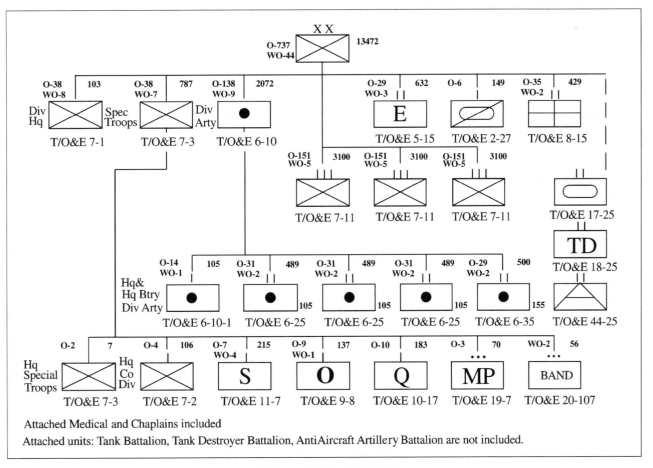

1. Infantry Division, 1943–1945

The division was the basis of the organization of the ground forces. It was the basic large unit, the largest units being corps and armies, but it was the smallest U.S. Army unit that was composed of all essential arms and services. The division possessed its own support and was capable of independent operations for a limited period. However, it generally fought as part of a higher unit, usually a corps. It could strike and penetrate efficiently, manoeuvre quickly and absorb reinforcements easily. The combat value of the infantry division derived from its ability to combine the action of the different arms and services to maintain combat over a considerable period of time. During sustained operations, the corps could provide services and additional supports. [1]

The U.S. Army doctrine of 1941 determined that the first arm to seize terrain would be the infantry. It could seize and

1. Field Manual, FM 100-5, *Field Service Regulations, Operations,* May 22 1941, War Department (hereafter referred to as FM 100-5 1941), p. 253.

hold a main objective. However, "no one arm wins battles", [2] victory results from the combined action of all arms. The other arms increased the offensive power of the infantry to seize hostile well-defended positions. Each arm developed a doctrine, which allowed it to support infantry actions. The infantry was capable of independent limited actions by using its own weapons.

Its offensive power decreased appreciably when its freedom of manoeuvre was limited or when it was confronted by an organized defensive position. Under these conditions, or against a combined force, the limited firepower of infantry had to be reinforced by artillery support, tanks, ground attack aviation and other arms. [3] In order to keep the light structure of the division, Army Ground Forces refused to assign a tank battalion to the organization of the infantry division. The U.S. Army constituted independent tank battalions (General Headquarters Tank Units) that were assigned to corps and armies. These could, depending upon the situation, attach tank battalions to infantry divisions, or concentrate them into a powerful armored fist. In Europe, a tank battalion, a tank destroyer battalion and an anti-aircraft artillery battalion were systematically attached to each infantry division.

INFANTRY DIVISION GENERAL ORGANIZATION (Chart 1)

Division Headquarters (T/O&E 7-1, chapter 1)
Headquarters Company (T/O&E 7-2)
Reconnaissance Troop (T/O&E 2-27)
3 Infantry Regiments (T/O&E 7-11, chapter 2)
   3 Infantry Battalions (T/O&E 7-15, chapter 3)
Division Artillery (T/O&E 6-10, chapter 5)
   3 Field Artillery Battalions, 105mm (T/O&E 6-25)
   1 Field Artillery Battalion, 155mm (T/O&E 6-35)
Engineer Combat Battalion (T/O&E 5-15, chapter 6)
Special Troops (T/O&E 7-3, chapter 7)
   Signal Company (T/O&E 11-7)
   Ordnance Company (T/O&E 9-8)
   Quartermaster Company (T/O&E 10-17)
   Military Police Platoon (T/O&E 19-7)
   Division Band (T/O&E 20-107)
Medical Battalion (T/O&E 8-15, chapter 8)

The infantry division involved three types of units: combat, combat support and combat service support. These were classified as follows:

Combat units:
   Cavalry Reconnaissance Troop
   3 Infantry Regiments
Combat support units:
   Divisional Artillery units
   Engineer Combat Battalion.
Combat service support units:
   Special Troops units
   Medical Battalion

The combat units achieved the mission of the division. The combat support units sustained combat units by their actions. The role of service support units was to make and to keep the division operational, and to provide for its needs during a determined period. We will study in detail the role of each unit of the division.

The infantry division was called a "Triangular Division" by reference to its organization. It included 3 infantry regiments. Each regiment included 3 infantry battalions and each battalion, 3 rifle companies. A rifle company contained 3 rifle platoons with 3 rifle squads in each. The doctrine anticipated a triangular use of the units, two in the attacking echelon and the third as the support echelon.

Field Manual 100-5, *Field Service Regulations, Operations* classified manoeuvres into two categories: envelopments and penetrations: [4]

"In an envelopment, the main attack is directed against the flank or rear of the initial disposition of the enemy's main forces and toward an objective in rear of his front lines. It seeks to surround that portion of the enemy's forces in front of the objective. It is assisted usually by a secondary attack directed against the enemy's front. The success depends largely on the degree of surprise attained and on the ability of the secondary attack to contain the bulk of the enemy's forces. An envelopment avoids attacking on ground chosen by the enemy, and forces him to fight in two or more directions to meet the converging efforts of the attack."

"In a penetration the main attack passes through some portion of the area occupied by the enemy's main forces and is directed on an objective in his rear. It is characterized by the complete rupture of the enemy's dispositions; the seizure of

---

2. FM 100-5 1941, p. 5.
3. FM 100-5 1941, p. 5.
4. FM 100-5 1941. This manual replaced the tentative edition of 1939 which aimed at revising the previous issue of FM 100-5 in 1923. It was the doctrinal guide to a modern and mechanized army, which increased in size from month to month. It was replaced by an updated edition in June 1944. The envelopment is described on p. 99 (no. 462), the penetration on p. 101 (nos 468–470).

the objective by operations through the gap; and the envelopment of one or both flanks created by the breakthrough. The essential conditions for success are surprise, sufficient fire power, especially combat aviation and artillery, to neutralize the front of the penetration, favourable terrain within the hostile position for advance of the attacking troops, and strength to carry the attack through to its objective."

"When the situation does not favour an envelopment, the main attack is directed to penetrate the hostile front." A penetration can often be organized more rapidly than an envelopment. "In the penetration of a defensive position, the main attack is launched on a front wider than that of the contemplated break-through in order to hold the enemy in place on the flanks of the penetration. The attack on the remainder of the hostile front is designed to contain the enemy and prevent him from moving his reserves."

When orders were issued to a regiment to seize an objective, the regimental commander designated a main objective to which he committed a battalion, a secondary objective to which he committed the second battalion, whilst he kept the third in reserve. The reserve battalion served as the attacking regiment's anti-aircraft protection. It also supported the attacking battalions by firing in the direction of the enemy. As a support, it could be committed to help a battalion in difficulty, to repel a hostile counter-attack or to exploit a breakthrough in hostile lines. When the regiment had to commit all its battalions, the protection of the regiment was assured by the engineer company (from the engineer combat battalion) attached to the regiment (if in a combat team). Engineers were trained to fight as infantrymen.

Although the infantry division was not, when compared to the armored division, a combined arms unit, the U.S. Army foresaw in the former a tactical organization that permitted combined arms action as a means of securing success.[5] This organization was the combat team (CT), officially designated a regimental combat team (RCT). The term 'combat team' was first assigned to this organization by the 5th Infantry Division in its Standing Operating Procedure (SOP)[6] upon being notified in a report of 3 March 1940 about the SOP of the 2nd Division.[7] The 2nd Division had tested the new triangular organization concept, and had used, in its SOP, the term 'echelon'.

A RCT consisted of the regiment with attachments from all combat support and service support units of the division:
    Infantry Regiment
    Field Artillery Battalion (105mm)
    Company, Engineer Battalion
    Company, Medical Battalion
and from units attached to the division:
    Company, Tank Battalion
    Company, Tank Destroyer Battalion
    Battery, Anti-aircraft Artillery Automatic Weapons Battalion

For a particular task, another force could be organized at regimental or divisional-level. This force was a combined arms team and was called a 'task force' (TF). The task force was a "temporary grouping of units under one commander, formed for the purpose of carrying out a specific operation or mission." It could also be described as a "semi-permanent organization of units under one commander for the purpose of carrying out a continuing specific task."[8]

A RCT always had the same organization, and was under control of the regimental headquarters. A task force was organized for a defined task. It could have a battalion or a company as its main component. The task force was controlled by the commander of the main unit.

Chart 1 shows the organization of the infantry division according to the T/O&E 7, dated 15 July 1943. See Appendix II for a key to the symbols. T/O&E numbers are given for each unit; these appear under the headings of the respective unit throughout the book, e.g. see section 1.2, 'Headquarters, Infantry Division (T/O&E 7-1)'. Alongside the symbol for each unit, numbers indicate the personnel, for example in the case of the infantry regiment: 'O-151', where 'O' represents officers and 151 gives number of officers; 'WO-5', represents 5 warrant officers; '3100', represents the number of enlisted men. The number of personnel varied a lot from 1943 to 1945 and it is not possible to give all changes in this particular chart, although these can be found noted in the succeeding chapters. The actual organization of the infantry division as shown in chart 1 did not see a major change before June 1 1945, when the military police platoon became a company.

Before continuing this survey, important terms used by the U.S. Army should be explained, thus:[9]
    Infantry: branch of the army trained, equipped, and organized to fight on foot.
    Mobile unit: a unit equipped with sufficient organic vehicles for the purpose of transporting all assigned personnel and equipment from one location to another at one time.
    Motorized unit: a unit equipped with complete motor transportation that enables all of its personnel, weapons, and

5. FM 100-5 1941, p. 5 (no. 26): "The combined action of all arms and services is essential to success."
6. The Standing Operating Procedure (SOP) was a set of instructions having the force of orders, covering those features of operations that lent themselves to a definite or standardised procedure without loss of effectiveness. The procedure was applicable unless prescribed otherwise in a particular case. Thus, the flexibility necessary in special situations was retained. (AR 320-5, p. 465). Prior to 1941, SOP denoted Standard Operating Procedure.
7. AG 370.2 – 5th Division, *Preliminary Report on 'Standard Operating Procedure, 2nd Division*, 3 March 1940, HQ 5th Division, Fort McClellan, Alabama. This report, concerning the procedure used during the testing of the new organization in the 2nd Division, states in paragraph 2b, "our S. O. P. uses the term 'Combat Team (reinforced)' because the chance of confusion is lessened thereby. 'Echelon' already has two or more generally-accepted military meanings."
8. AR 320-5, p. 497.
9. AR 320-5, p. 240, 303, 306 and 287 respectively.

equipment to be moved at the same time without assistance from other sources.

Mechanized unit: a unit that is transported by, and that fights from, armed and armored motor vehicles.

The infantry division included a mechanized unit, the cavalry reconnaissance troop, and motorized units, divisional artillery units. All other units of the division, particularly the 3 infantry regiments, did not have sufficient transportation, their means of displacement being by marching on foot. The infantry division could be motorized by the attachment of 6 quartermaster truck companies, T/O&E 10-57, assigned to the corps.

1.2 HEADQUARTERS, INFANTRY DIVISION
T/O&E 7-1

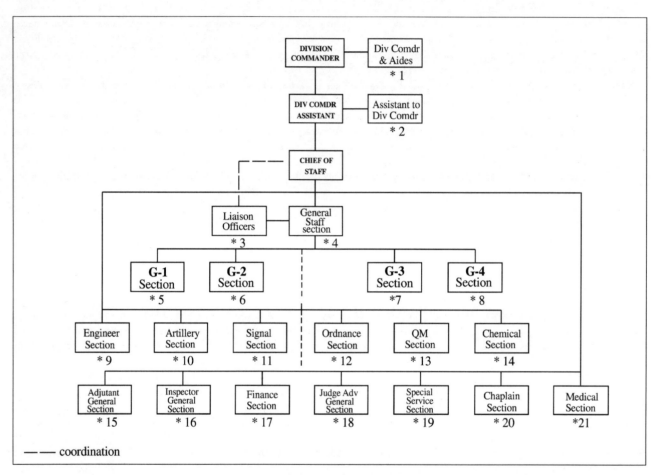

2. Headquarters, Infantry Division

Chart 2 shows the division headquarters. Each section is numbered to allow the reader to refer to the relevant text below.

Division headquarters included the division commander, the staff officers and the necessary personnel to make and keep the division operational. In the division headquarters, the commander played the central role. He was to clearly establish and communicate his intentions. The commander had his vision of the battle, of the manner in which he considered it necessary to fight and how he planned to accomplish the mission. The duties of the commander were as follows:

command the forces
know the situation
assign the missions
allow means
take decisions
direct and synchronize the forces
support committed forces
motivate subordinates

The second in the chain of command was the assistant commander. He assumed command in the absence of the commander. Otherwise, he executed the tasks as directed by the commander.

The third was the chief of staff; he supervised and coordinated the actions of the general staff and liaison officers.

The commander was assisted by staff officers. These were classified into four categories: general staff officers, special staff officers, personal staff officers and liaison officers. Staff officers could not, either individually or in a group, exercise command.

The command and the responsibility inherent to this function remained with the division commander and could not be delegated. [10]

The general staff was a group of officers who planned, coordinated and supervised. The members of the general staff were the chief of staff, who coordinated and supervised the entire headquarters, and four assistant chiefs of staff: personnel officer (G-1), intelligence officer (G-2), operations and training officer (G-3), supply officer (G-4), and their respective assistants.

The special staff covers all personnel who were included neither in the general staff nor in the personal staff, i.e. sections numbered from 9 to 21 in chart 2.

The personal staff was constituted by the aides of the commander. [11]

The following now reviews in detail all sections of the headquarters, infantry division, using the same sequence of numbers as in chart 2.

*1 – DIVISION COMMANDER AND AIDES

1 Major General, Division Commander-P [12]
1 Captain, Aide-C
1 1st Lt, Aide-C
1 Techn 5th, Stenographer-C

*2 – ASSISTANT TO DIVISION COMMANDER

1 Brigadier General, Division Commander Assistant-P
1 1st Lt, Aide-C
1 2nd Lt, Aide-C
1 Techn 5th, Stenographer-C

*3 – LIAISON OFFICERS

3 Captains, Liaison-C

The liaison officers were representatives of the commander. They worked under the direction of the chief of staff, the G-3, or other designated officers.

*4 – GENERAL STAFF SECTION

1 Colonel, Chief of Staff-P
1 Major, Air Ground Liaison-P (added T/O&E 7-1, 13 January 45)
1 Tech Sgt, Photo Interpreter-C
2 Techns 4th, Stenographer-C

The chief of staff was responsible for formulating and announcing staff operating policies, ensuring that the commander and the staff were informed on matters affecting the command, representing the commander when authorized, maintaining the master policy file and monitoring the SOP, ensuring that required liaison was established, and exercising direct supervision of the main command post and its operations.

The following sections each had a speciality. However, they are included in the general staff section. The division headquarters was, at this time, both a composition of specialized subsets and a framework for co-ordinating these.

*5 – PERSONNEL SECTION, G-1

1 Lt Col, Personnel, G-1-P
1 Major, Personnel, G-1 Assistant-P
1 WO, Administration-C
1 Mr Sgt, Chief Clerk-C
1 Techn 5th, Typist-C
1 Techn 4th, Stenographer-C

The G-1 was responsible for unit strength maintenance, personnel service support, discipline, law and order, civilian personnel, administrative support for other personnel, safety and accident prevention, and headquarters management.

---

10. Field Manual FM 101-5 *Staff Organization and Procedures*, 25 May 1984, HQ DA (for divisional headquarters core doctrine), Field Manual FM 5-6, *Operations of Engineer Troop Units*, 23 April 1943 with Changes, War Department (hereafter referred to as FM 5-6 1943), and FM 5-6, 25 August 1954, HQ DA (hereafter referred to as FM 5-6 1954).

11. FM 5-6 1954.

12. A breakdown of personnel listings is as follows:- example, '10 Pvts, Basic-R'. '10' indicates the number of men sharing the same rank and duty; 'Pvt' indicates rank, in this case, 'Private' (see Appendix I for more information about ranks); 'Basic' indicates the duty of the role – basic means that soldier had no determined duty or speciality, and could be employed for different duties when the unit had suffered losses (chapter 2 will provide more information concerning details of the different duties); 'R' indicates the weapon carried by that individual, weapon abbreviations are, P – pistol, C – carbine, R – rifle, S – submachine-gun.

*6 – INTELLIGENCE SECTION, G-2

1 Lt Col, Intelligence, G-2-P
1 Major, Intelligence, G-2 Assistant-P
1 Captain, Intelligence, G-2 Assistant-C
1 Mr Sgt, Chief Clerk-C
1 Techn 4th, Intelligence-R
1 Techn 5th, Intelligence-R
1 Techn 3rd, Photo Interpreter-C
1 Techn 4th, Stenographer-C

The G-2 was responsible for the production and exploitation of intelligence, counter-intelligence, and intelligence training.

*7 – OPERATIONS AND TRAINING SECTION, G-3

1 Lt Col, Operations and Training, G-3-P (Colonel on 13 January 1945, Lt Col again with C2 dated 24 May 1945)
1 Major, Operations and Training, G-3 Assistant-P (Lt Col on 13 January 1945, Major again with C2 dated 24 May 1945)
1 Capt, Information-Education, G-3 Assistant-P (Major on 13 January 1945, Capt again with C2 dated 24 May 1945)
1 Mr Sgt, Chief Clerk-C
1 Mr Sgt, Operations-C
1 S Sgt, Operations-C
2 Sgts, Operations-C
3 Techns 4th, Draftsman-R
2 Techns 4th, Orientation-C
1 Techn 5th, Orientation-C
1 Techn 4th, Stenographer-C

The G-3 was responsible for the operations, the organization and the training. He maintained a current operational estimate of the situation, prepared the SOPs, operation plans and orders. He maintained lists of troops, organized and equipped the units. He assigned, attached and detached units, detachments or teams. He identified training needs and prepared programs, directives and training orders.

*8 – SUPPLY SECTION, G-4

1 Lt Col, Supply, G-4-P
1 WO, Motor-C
1 Major, Supply, G-4 Assistant-P
1 Mr Sgt, Chief Clerk-C
1 S Sgt, Supply-C
1 Techn 5th, Typist-C
1 Techn 4th, Stenographer-C

The G-4 was responsible for supply[13], maintenance, transportation and services. He worked in constant coordination with the commander of special troops and the G-3.

Special Staff

The following sections detail the special staff. This contained all staff officers who were not included in the general (coordinating) staff or in the personal staff group. The special staff included technical specialists and officers in charge of units, such as the quartermaster officer and the transportation officer.

*9 – DIVISION ENGINEER SECTION

Lt Col, Division Engineer

He provided engineer advice, information and assistance to the division commander and staff. He was also the commander of the divisional engineer battalion (T/O&E 5-15, chapter 6). This section does not include personnel in the T/O&E 7-1. The personnel came from the divisional engineer section of the engineer battalion headquarters (T/O&E 5-16). However, members of this section worked in close collaboration with the divisional staff, and were located at the division headquarters, engineer section.[14]

---

13. Supply – procurement, distribution, maintenance and salvage of supplies. In army usage, also includes the determination of kind and quantity of supplies, thus – all items necessary for the equipment, maintenance, and operations of a military command, including food, clothing, equipment, arms, ammunition, fuel, forage, materials and machinery of all kinds. AR 320-5, p. 479.
14. FM 5-6, p. 34.

*10 – ARTILLERY SECTION

Brigadier General, Division Artillery Commander

He assisted the division commander with the questions pertaining to the artillery. He planned and coordinated the use of artillery units and worked in collaboration with G-3. He was also the commander of division artillery (T/O&E 6-10). All personnel of the artillery section came from headquarters, division artillery (T/O&E 6-10-1, chapter 5, section 5.2).

*11 – SIGNAL SECTION

Lt Col, Division Signal

He advised the division commander on technical matters relating to communications. He organized and coordinated the installation and the operations of the communications within the division. He was in charge of the signal company (T/O&E 11-7, chapter 7, section 7.4) and the personnel of the signal section came from the division signal officer's section of this company.

*12 – ORDNANCE SECTION

Lt Col, Division Ordnance

He advised the division commander on technical matters of ordnance. The ordnance was the military material, such as combat weapons of all kinds, with ammunition and equipment used by them, vehicles, and repair tools and machinery. [15] The division ordnance officer was also the commander of the ordnance company. The personnel of the ordnance section came from the division ordnance officer's section (T/O&E 9-8, chapter 7, section 7.2).

*13 – QUARTERMASTER SECTION

Lt Col, Division Quartermaster

He advised the division commander on logistics. The quartermaster had the responsibility of the technical supervision of supply, for the following items: supply of subsistence, clothing and textiles, petroleum, and general supplies and equipment. He also organized and operated commissaries, laundry and dry-cleaning plants. [16] The division quartermaster was also the commander of the quartermaster company. The personnel of the section came from the office of the division quartermaster within this company (T/O&E 10-17, chapter 7, section 7.3).

*14 – CHEMICAL SECTION

1 Lt Col, Division Chemical-P
1 Captain, Division Chemical Assistant-C
1 Mr Sgt, Chief Clerk-C
2 Sgts, Operations-C
1 Techn 5th, Clerk, Typist

The division chemical section assisted the commander and his staff in all matters concerning the operations, offensive and defensive, where chemical matters were involved.

*15 – ADJUTANT GENERAL SECTION

1 Lt Col, Adjutant General-P
1 Major, Adjutant General Assistant-P
1 Captain, Adjutant General Assistant-C
1 1st Lt, Adjutant General Assistant-C
1 Mr Sgt, Chief Clerk-C

A – Administrative Section

1 WO, Administrative-C
1 Tech Sgt, Chief Clerk-C
1 Techn 3rd, Clerk, Typist-C
3 Techns 4th, Clerk, Typist-C
1 Techn 3rd, Stenographer-C

B – Personnel Section

1 WO, Administrative-C
1 Tech Sgt, Chief Clerk-C
1 Techn 3rd, Clerk, Typist-C
3 Techns 4th, Clerk, Typist-C
1 Techn 3rd, Stenographer-C
1 Techn 5th, Clerk, General-R

15. AR 320-5, p. 331.
16. AR 320-5, p. 380.

C – Classification Section

1 WO, Administrative-C
1 Tech Sgt, Chief Clerk-C
1 Techn 4th, Classification Specialist-C
3 Techns 4th, Clerk, Typist-C
1 Techn 5th, Clerk, Typist-R
1 Techn 3rd, Stenographer-C
1 Techn 3rd, Statistician-C

D – Postal Section

1 1st Lt, Postal-C (Capt, on a Theater of Operations)
1 S Sgt, Clerk, Postal-C
1 Sgt, Clerk, Postal-C
1 Cpl, Clerk, Postal-C
4 Techns 4th, Clerk, Postal-C
4 Techns 5th, Clerk, Postal-R
3 Pvts, Clerk, Postal-C

E – Morale Support Section

1 Tech Sgt, Chief Clerk-C
3 Techns 5th, Clerk, Typist-R

This section was responsible for:
strength accounting
replacement operations
casualty reporting
promotions and reductions (Personnel Section)
correspondence and distribution management
printing and reproduction services
classified document control
publication management (Administrative Section)
personnel classification and reclassification (Classification Section)
postal services (Postal Section)
morale support activities including the band (Morale Support Section)

*16 – INSPECTOR GENERAL'S SECTION

1 Lt Col, Inspector General-P
1 Captain, Inspector General Assistant-C
1 WO, Auditing-C
1 Mr Sgt, Chief Clerk-C
1 Techn 4th, Stenographer-C
1 Techn 5th, Stenographer-C

The inspector general was in charge, under the supervision of the division commander and according to laws and regulations, of inquiring and reporting on matters about the performance of the mission, the state of discipline, efficiency and economy, by conducting inspections and studies.

*17 – FINANCE SECTION

1 Lt Col, Division Finance-P
1 Captain, Finance Disbursing-C
1 WO, Budget and Fiscal-C
1 Mr Sgt, Clerk, Financial-C
1 Tech Sgt, Clerk, Financial-C
3 Techns 3rd, Clerk, Financial-C
5 Techns 4th, Clerk, Financial-C
5 Techns 5th, Clerk, Typist-R
1 Techn 5th, Clerk, Typist-C
1 Techn 4th, Stenographer-C

The division finance officer advised the division commander on matters relating to reports of survey and report of loss of funds, and banking facilities, civilian and military, within the division area of responsibilities. He worked with G-1.

*18 – JUDGE ADVOCATE GENERAL'S SECTION

1 Lt Col, Judge Advocate General-P
1 Captain, Judge Advocate General Assistant-C
1 WO, Judge Advocate General Assistant-C
1 S Sgt, Clerk, Record-C
1 Techn 5th, Clerk, Typist-C

The officer in charge of this section advised the commander, the staff and the subordinate commanders on matters involving military laws (War Department directives, army regulations and command regulations), domestic laws (US statutes, Federal regulations, states and local laws), foreign law, international law and the law of armed conflict. He supervised the administration of military justice and other legal matters in the command.

*19 – SPECIAL SERVICE SECTION

1 Major, Athletic and Recreation-P
1 Techn 4th, Athletic Instructor-C
1 Techn 5th, Clerk, Typist-R
1 Techn 4th, Entertainment Director-C

The Special Service was responsible for a program designed to stimulate, develop and maintain physical and mental well-being of military personnel, through voluntary participation in planned recreation activities. [17]

*20 – CHAPLAIN'S SECTION

1 Lt Col, Chaplain
1 Major, Chaplain Assistant
1 Sgt, Clerk, Record-C
2 Techns 5th, Clerk, Typists-C (drove the ¼-ton trucks)

The chaplain advised the commander and staff on matters about religion, morals, and morale affected by religion. He was the pastor of his own unit and provided pastoral ministry for unit personnel and attached elements which had no assigned chaplain, and to casualties, hospitalized, and confined personnel. He supervised chaplains of assigned units, and all individual and organized religious activities. He provided functional training guidance for chaplains to meet religious needs within a military environment.

*21 – MEDICAL SECTION

1 Lt Col, Division Surgeon
1 Major, Dental
1 Major, Medical Inspector
1 Major or Capt, Division Neuropsychiatrist (added C2, 13 October 1943)
1 Captain, Medical Assistant (MAC) (C3 dated 5 January 1944)
1 Mr Sgt, Chief Clerk
1 Techn 3rd, Clerk, Typist
2 Techns 5th, Clerk, Typist
1 Techn 5th, Stenographer

The division surgeon advised the commander on matters pertaining to medical activities, to preserve the combat strength of the division. He was responsible for health services and for preventive and curative actions. The dental surgeon coordinated dental activities with the division surgeon. He exercised staff supervision and technical control over command dental activities.

The change no. 3 dated 6 June 1945 to the T/O&E dated 13 January 1945 added the following personnel, when required by the commander of the Theater of Operations:

TRANSPORT QUARTERMASTER'S TEAM

1 Lt Col, Division Transport Quartermaster-P
1 Major, Artillery Transport Quartermaster-P
1 Major, Division Transport Quartermaster Assistant-P
10 Captains, Division Transport Quartermaster Assistant-C (1 for special troops, 3 per infantry regiment)
1 Mr Sgt, Administrative-C
1 Techn 3rd, Clerk, General-C
11 Techns 4th, Checker, Cargo-C (1 for the artillery transport quartermaster, 1 for special troops, 1 for each regiment)
1 Techn 4th, Draftsman-C

With change no. 4 dated 7 June 1945, the T/O&E was redesignated T/O&E 7-1-OS on 1 June 1945.

---

17. AR 320-5, p. 457.

Command Post

The organization of a headquarters for combat operations was made by regrouping the staff sections, or some elements of these, in order to improve their efficiency and coordination. The resultant grouping was designated the command post. For convenience of operations on campaign, the division headquarters was divided into a forward and a rear echelon. The forward echelon consisted of the staff sections immediately required by the commander to assist him in tactical operations. The rear echelon consisted of the remaining staff, those sections having administrative duties.

The command post was the location of the forward echelon of the headquarters. All signals communications centred on the command post. On the march, the post could move by bounds along a designated road, or it could move at a designated place in a column of march. In battle, the division command post was preferably installed next to a suitable landing field. [18]

The forward echelon (command post) consisted of:

Command:
    Division Commander and Aides (*1)
    Chief of Staff
    Liaison Officers (*3)
Operations:
    Col, G-3 (*7)
    Lt Col, G-2 (*6)
    Lt Col, G-3 Assistant (*7)
    Major, Air Ground Liaison (*4)
    S Sgt, Operations (*7)
    Tech Sgt, Photo Interpreter (*4)
    2 Techns 4th, Stenographer (*4)
    Division Engineer Assistant (*9)
    Division Signal Assistant (*11)
    Division Chemical (*14)
Plans:
    Major, Information and Education (*7)
    Mr Sgt, Operations (*7)
    Sgt, Operations (*7)
    Techn 4th, Draftsman (*7)
    Techn 4th, Stenographer (*7)
    Techn 4th, Orientation (*7)
Intelligence:
    Major, Intelligence, G-2 Assistant (*6)
    Mr Sgt, Chief Clerk (*6)
    Techn 4th, Intelligence (*6)
    Techn 5th, Intelligence (*6)
    Techn 3rd, Photo Interpreter (*6)
Fire support:
    Division Artillery Officer (*10)
    Personnel from the Artillery Section (*10)
    Combat Service Support:
    Lt Col, G-4 (*8)
    Techn 4th, Stenographer (*8)
    Lt Col, G-1 (*5)
    Techn 4th, Stenographer (*5)
The rear echelon consisted of:
Command:
    Assistant Division Commander and Aides (*2)
Operations:
    Captain, Intelligence, G-2 Assistant (*6)
    Division Chemical Assistant (*14)
    Sgt, Operations (*7)
    Techn 4th, Stenographer (*7)
    2 Techns 4th, Draftsman (*7)
    2 Techns 4th, Orientation (*7)
Special Staff Section:
    G-1 Section (*5)
    G-4 Section (*8)

18. FM 100-5 1941, p. 33.

      Ordnance Section (*12)
      Quartermaster Section (*13)
      Adjutant General Section (*15)
      Inspector General Section (*16)
      Finance Section (*17)
      Judge Advocate Section (*18)
      Special Service Section (*19)
      Chaplain Section (*20)
      Medical Section (*21)

Equipment

To describe the entire equipment inventory of the T/O&E for each unit would become tedious. For a standard inventory list for a company, see chapter 9, section 9.1. Specialized equipment for each unit will be listed within the relevant place throughout the book.

    The division headquarters equipment section is not in the T/O&E 7-1 but in the T/O&E 7-2, headquarters company, infantry division.

DIVISION HEADQUARTERS EQUIPMENT

    8 gas proof curtains, M1

    1 alarm, gas, M1

    22 luminous dial compasses (1 per Off, Tech Sgt Int, Sgt Int, Cpl Int) (19 on 5 January 1944, 1 per Off) (23 on 13 January 1945, 1 per Off, Comdr, Asst Comdr Section, General Staff and Chemical Sections)

    19 transparent map templates, M2 (1 per Off) (23 on 13 January 1945)

    22 binoculars, M13 (1 per Off, Tech Sgt Int, Sgt Int, Cpl Int) (19 on 5 January 1944, 1 per Off) (23 M13A1 on 13 January 1945)

    1 drafting and duplicating equipment, set no. 1

    1 sketching equipment, set no. 1

    2 magnifying stereoscopes, mirror, with binoculars and case

    2 magnifying self illuminated glasses (C3, dated 5 January 1944)

    3 pocket watches, 15 jewels

    18 wristwatches, 7 jewels (Mr Sgt, Tech Sgt, S Sgt, Sgt, Cpl)

    15 grenade launchers, M7

    7 leather brief cases (for Div HQ)

    24 canvas dispatch cases (Off, WO)

    25 whistles, thunderer (Off, WO, Mr Sgt Opns)

    40 folding chairs, wooden

    2 record chests, fibre

    16 empty field desks, headquarters

    1 distinguishing flag

    33 hand-portable electric lanterns

    19 gasoline, two-mantle, commercial lanterns (cancelled 15 June 1944, C5 to the T/O&E dated 15 July 1943), replaced by: hand-portable electric lantern, command post (1 per CP tent)

    3 duplicating machines, spirit process, military field

    2 duplicating machines, stencil surface, hand-operated, 8 × 13″

    1 embossing machine, complete with plate and roller, hand-operated

    6 paper-fastening machines, lever or plunger type, wire staple

    10 officers' mess outfits, complete, M1941 (chest including tableware for the officers' mess, 1 per 6 officers) (substitute standard in January 1944 but still in the catalogue in April 1947)

    2 adjustable perforators, 3-hole

    5 field safes, key-lock, changed by combination-lock (C5, 15 June 1944)

    3 latrine screens, complete with pins and poles

    3 official rubber stamps

    1 shoe stretcher, new type (sizes 0, 1 and 2)

    40 folding tables, camp

    24 flashlights TL-122 (Off, S Sgt Supply)

    19 command post tents, complete; changed 6 April 1945, (C2 to the T/O&E dated 13 January 1945) by: command post tents, M1945

    3 small wall tents (1 per Officer General, per Chaplain Section)

    22 tent stoves M1941 with grate

    22 oil burners for tent stove M1941

    16 typewriters, non-portable; T/O&E dated 13 January 1945 furnishes the following detail:
       7 with 11″ carriage (9, C2, 6 June 1945)

7 with 14" carriage
1 with 18" carriage
1 with 26" carriage
19 portable typewriters, 1 per desk (21 typewriters 13 January 1945)
1 Flag set M-133
1 Radio Set SCR-506-( ) [19] for M20 Armored Car Utility, added 13 January 1945
1 Radio Set SCR-608-( ) for M20 Armored Car Utility, added 13 January 1945
1 tool equipment, TE-33, for radio set (C4, 5 November 1945)
1 wood maul, reinforced head (1 per 6 tents C2, 13 October 1943)
2 photographic interpreter kits type F-2 (C5, 15 June 1944)
1 land odograph, 6-volts, M1 (C5, 15 June 1944)
3 electric lighting equipments, set no. 3, 3-kw (C5, 15 June 1944, outside the U.S.A., if authorized by the Commander of the Theater of Operations)
2 electric lighting equipments, set no. 4, 5-kw (C5, 15 June 1944, outside the U.S.A., if authorized by the Commander of the Theater of Operations)
24 luminous radioactive markers, type I (13 January 1945)
24 luminous radioactive markers, type II (13 January 1945)

POSTAL SECTION, ADJUTANT GENERAL SECTION EQUIPMENT

2 mail bags, with leather bottom, top, and locking strap
2 leather money bags
1 canvas dispatch case (Off)
1 flashlight TL-122-( ) (Off)
1 whistle, thunderer (Off)
3 mail baskets, canvas, 28" × 17" × 10"
1 wood storage cabinet, K.D. Type, 5-section
3 mail distribution cases, canvas, portable, 77 separations
1 mail distribution desk, wood, portable
1 empty field desk, company
1 locker box
1 adjustable perforator, 3-hole
6 mail bag racks, K.D. type, 6-bag capacity
1 field safe, key-lock, changed by combination-lock (C5, 15 June 1944)
3 boxes, cash and stamp (C3 dated 5 January 1944)
1 stamping-cancelling hand machine, model K (C5)
2 large canvas paulins (tarpaulin) (C5)

FINANCE SECTION EQUIPMENT

2 leather money bags
2 locker boxes
3 canvas dispatch cases (Off, WO)
2 flashlights TL-122-( ) (Off)
3 whistles, thunderer (Off, WO)
1 coin-counting machine, hand-operated
4 computing, listing machines
2 numbering machines
7 field safe, key-lock, changed by combination-lock (C5, 15 June 1944)
3 payroll machines, denominator, 11-unit (C5)

MEDICAL SECTION EQUIPMENT

10 brassards, Geneva Convention (Red Cross)
5 canvas dispatch cases (Off)
6 flashlights TL-122-( ) (Off, chest MD No. 2, C5)
1 small wall tent
1 tent stove M1941 with grate
1 oil burner for tent stove M1941
1 dental kit, officer
1 dental kit, private
2 medical kits, NCO (Tech Sgt, Sgt)

19. The open parenthesis indicates that the designated equipment existed in several variants.

11 medical kits, private (Med Techn, Surg Techn, basic)
2 small blanket sets
1 tent pin case
2 chests, MD No. 1
1 chest, MD No. 2
1 chest, MD No. 4
1 chest, MD No. 60
1 gas casualty first aid kit
2 suction kits, snake-bite
12 steel pole litters
2 imprinting machines
12 litter bar splints (6 per splint set)
2 splint sets
1 aneroid sphygmomanometer (13 January 1945)
1 tuning fork set (set of 5) (C2, 13 October 1943, for Neuropsychiatrist)
1 percussion hammer (C2, 13 October 1943, for Neuropsychiatrist)
1 electric ophthalmoscope (C2, 13 October 1943, for Neuropsychiatrist)
1 mercurial sphygmomanometer (C2, 13 October 1943, for Neuropsychiatrist)
1 otoscope and ophthalmoscope, combined, electric (C2, 6 June 1945 for Neuropsychiatrist)
1 stethoscope (C2, 6 June 1945 for Neuropsychiatrist)

The lists of equipment, unless noted otherwise, are dated 15 July 1943. The modifications, following the changes to the T/O&E, or according to the new table of 13 January 1945 and its own changes, are mentioned in the lists by the number and the date of change, for example: (C5, 15 June 1944).

Individual equipment lists are in chapter 9. The division headquarters company furnished transportation to the division headquarters. This is described in the following section.

1.3 DIVISION, HEADQUARTERS COMPANY
T/O&E 7-2

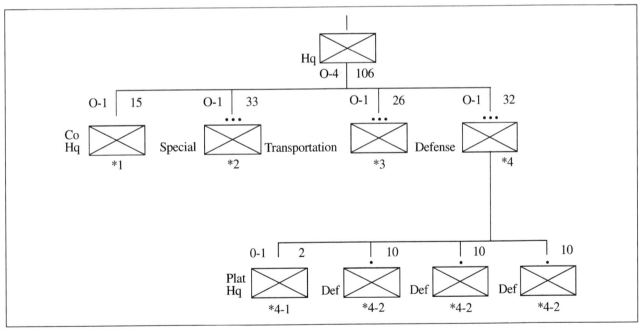

3. Headquarters Company, Infantry Division

The headquarters company, infantry division is shown in chart 3. This type of unit, the headquarters company, will be encountered regularly in this book. All units larger than a company, i.e. battalion, squadron, group, regiment, brigade, division, corps, army, had a headquarters company. The headquarters companies, having a role less glorious than combat companies, are generally forgotten in most accounts. Nevertheless, their activities were very important in maintaining the operational status of the unit and for administrative duties. The headquarters company provided for the transportation, communications, services, and sometimes the protection of the headquarters.

As can be seen, the headquarters company furnished not only mess, administration, drivers and orderlies for staff officers, transportation and vehicle maintenance to the division headquarters, but anti-tank defense, too.

*1 – COMPANY HEADQUARTERS (1 Officer, 15 Enlisted Men)

1 Captain, Company Commander-C
1 1st Sgt-C
1 S Sgt, Supply-C
1 Cpl, Co Clerk-C
1 Techn 5th, Armorer – artificer, drove the ¾-ton truck, command-R
1 Techn 5th, Clerk, Supply-C
6 Pvts, Basic-C
4 Pvts, Basic-R

Vehicles:

1 Truck, ¾-ton, Command with winch, replaced by:
2 Trucks, ¼-ton (13 January 1945)

Equipment:

1 luminous dial, compass (Off)
2 wrist compasses, liquid-filled (1st Sgt, driver)
1 transparent map template, M2 (Off)
1 grenade launcher, M7
1 grenade launcher, M8
2 hand pyrotechnic projectors, M9
2 wristwatches, 7 jewels (1st Sgt, S Sgt)
2 canvas dispatch cases (Off, 1st Sgt)
1 goggles, M1943, clear lens (driver)
4 flashlights TL-122-( ) (Off, 1st Sgt, Sgt Sup, driver)
3 whistles, thunderer (Off, 1st Sgt, S Sgt)
6 panel sets AP-50-A

*2 – SPECIAL PLATOON (1 Officer, 33 Enlisted Men)

1 Captain-C
1 Tech Sgt, Mess-C
1 S Sgt, Mess-C
1 S Sgt, Platoon-C
2 Sgts, Duty-C
5 Techns 4th, Cook-C
5 Techns 5th, Cook-C
6 Pvts, Cook's helper-R
2 Techns 5th, Light truck driver-R
10 Pvts, Orderly-C

Vehicles:

2 Trucks, 1½-ton, cargo, replaced by:
2 Trucks, 2½-ton, cargo (C1, 13 October 1943)
2 Trailers, 1-ton

Equipment:

1 luminous dial, compass (Off)
1 transparent map template, M2 (Off)
1 canvas dispatch case (Off)
2 grenade launchers, M7
2 grenade launchers, M8
2 goggles M1943, clear lens (driver)
1 commissary roll, complete (rolled up cover containing all material to prepare food rations)
17 insulated round containers M1941, with inserts (4 per other company see chapter 9, section 9.1)
14 hair clippers (1 per other company)
3 flies, tent, wall, large (1 per other company)
3 field ranges, M1937, 3-unit (1 per other company)
9 heaters, immersion type for corrugated cans (3 per field range M1937)
3 corrugated cans, nesting, galvanized, with cover, 10-gal
3 corrugated cans, nesting, galvanized, with cover, 16-gal
3 corrugated cans, nesting, galvanized, with cover, 24-gal
3 corrugated cans, nesting, galvanized, with cover, 32-gal
4 flashlights, TL-122-( ) (Off, S Sgt Mess, driver)
6 whistles, thunderer (Off, T Sgt, S Sgt, Sgt)

4 panel sets AP-50-A (2 per truck)

The remainder of the equipment of this company was similar to that listed in chapter 9, section 9.1.

*3 – TRANSPORTATION PLATOON (1 Officer, 26 Enlisted Men)

1st Lt-C
1 S Sgt, Motor-C
1 Techn 4th, Chauffeur-P [20]
4 Techns 5th, Messenger, Light truck driver-R
18 Techns 5th, Light truck driver-R
1 Techn 4th, Mechanic, Automobile-C
1 Techn 5th, Mechanic, Automobile, drove the ¾-ton truck, WC-C

Vehicles:
1 Car, 5-passenger, medium, Sedan
15 Trucks, ¼-ton
5 Trucks, ¾-ton, Command
1 Truck, ¾-ton, Weapons Carrier (WC)
2 Trucks, 1½-ton, Cargo
2 Trailers, 1-ton
1 Armored Car, Utility, M20 (13 January 1945)

The ¾-ton trucks, Command, were replaced in all units, from March 1944, by ¾-ton trucks, Weapons Carrier. The replacement was not systematic and was done when the first type was no longer available. In the divisional headquarters company's case, the T/O&E dated 13 January 1945 shows one ¾-ton truck, WC, because the 'command car' was replaced by ¼-ton trucks.

Equipment:
1 luminous dial, compass (Off)
1 wrist compass, liquid-filled (S Sgt motor)
1 transparent map template, M2 (Off)
1 canvas dispatch case (Off)
2 flashlights TL-122-( ) (Off, S Sgt)
2 whistles, thunderer (Off, S Sgt)
1 grenade launcher, M8
15 mounts M48, for LMG, caliber .30 (cancelled by C3, 5 January 1944)
1 unit equipment tool set, 2nd echelon, set no. 1
1 unit equipment tool set, 2nd echelon, set no. 6
2 motor vehicles mechanics' tool sets (1 per mechanic)
1 tool kit, carpenters' and wheelwrights'

*4 – DEFENSE PLATOON (1 Officer, 32 Enlisted men; 29 Enlisted Men following C2, 5 January 1944)

The defense platoon consisted of:
Platoon Headquarters
3 Defense Squads

*4-1 – Platoon Headquarters

1 2nd Lt, Platoon Leader-C
1 S Sgt, Platoon-C
1 Pvt, Messenger, drove the ¼-ton truck-R

Vehicles:
1 Truck, ¼-ton

Equipment:
3 luminous dial, compasses (Off, 2 per platoon)
3 transparent map templates, M2 (Off, platoon)
1 canvas dispatch case (Off)
2 flashlights TL-122-( ) (Off, S Sgt)
2 whistles, thunderer (Off, S Sgt)
1 grenade launcher, M7 (1 per M1 rifle)
1 mount M48, per LMG, Cal. .30 (cancelled by C3, 5 January 1944)

---

20. Before 1943, motor vehicle drivers (SSN 345) were called 'chauffeur'. From 1943, they were called driver (SSN 345), only the major general's driver retained the designation 'chauffeur'.

*4-2 – Defense Squad (×3)

1 Cpl, Squad Leader-R
3 Pvts, Ammunition-bearers-R
5 Pvts, Cannoneers-P (only 4, from C2, 5 January 1944)
1 Techn 5th, Light truck driver, ammunition-bearer-R

Weapons:

1 Gun, 57 mm, M1, with Carriage M1A3
2 Rocket launchers, AT, 2.36", M1
1 MG, HB, Cal .50, M2, flexible

Vehicles:

1 Truck 1 ½-ton, cargo, with ring mount

Equipment:

1 camouflage net, twine, fabric garnished, 29 × 29" (1 per gun)
1 protractor semicircular, plastic, MG, 10", graduated in mm
3 grenade launchers, M7 (per M1 rifle)
4 rocket carrying bag, M6 (2 per Rocket launcher)
2 goggles, M1943, red lens (per 57 mm gun)

For the remainder of the equipment see chapter 9, section 9.1.

With change 3 dated 7 June 1945, the T/O&E was redesignated T/O&E 7-1-OS on 1 June 1945.

Change 4, dated 5 November 1945, added a new section to the division headquarters, and personnel to the headquarters company. This change was submitted for the authorisation of the War Department. This section is shown below, although it is not represented on chart 3, being a late change.

Air Section

1 Captain, Pilot, Ground Forces-P
2 1st Lt, Pilot, Ground Forces-P
1 Techn 3rd, Mechanic, Airplane and Engine-C
1 Techn 4th, Mechanic, Airplane and Engine-C
1 Techn 5th, Mechanic, Airplane and Engine-C

Vehicles:

3 Airplanes, Liaison
1 Truck, ¼-ton
1 Trailer, ¼-ton
1 Truck, 2½-ton, cargo
1 Trailer, 1-ton

To cater for the air section's mess, the special platoon (*2) received:

1 Techn 4th, Cook-C
1 Pvt, Cook's helper-C

For division headquarters, air section transportation (see the previous section) the transportation platoon (*3) received:

1 Truck, ¼-ton
1 Trailer, ¼-ton

1.4 CAVALRY RECONNAISSANCE TROOP, MECHANIZED
T/O&E 2-27

The reconnaissance troop was the only one combat unit included in the division base. The division commander needed information concerning the enemy. With intelligence he could plan, make his decisions and formulate his orders. The cavalry led reconnaissance operations, observing the battlefield in order to reduce the uncertainties of battle, such as terrain, effects of weather, and the presence or the absence of the enemy. The reconnaissance was necessary to avoid the division's main force entering battle without information and without a complete picture of the battlefield. So that the firepower of combat units (infantry, armor) was not weakened by the necessity to undertake these missions (reconnaissance, security), the cavalry was used.

The cavalry troop was not the only unit to receive reconnaissance missions. Every commander was responsible for his intelligence and had to undertake his own reconnaissance in his unit's area of action. The infantry regiment undertook its reconnaissance via its intelligence and reconnaissance platoon, the infantry battalion used its scouts (see battalion HQ section, chapter 3, section 3.1) and every company organized patrols. The cavalry troop was more specifically the division commander's eyes and ears.

A reconnaissance unit performed three types of mission – road reconnaissance, zone reconnaissance and area reconnaissance

The reconnaissance of the division's routes of advance was done by the cavalry reconnaissance troop, infantry division, as

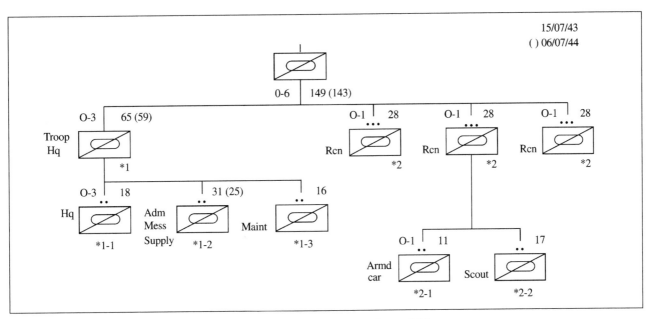

4. Cavalry Reconnaissance Troop, Infantry Division

well as by patrols sent forward by the advance guard of the division when in motion. [21]

A zone reconnaissance was undertaken when a doubt existed concerning the presence of the enemy, and it was performed within a cover operation of the divisions committed in its zone. A cavalry group from the army corps was in charge of these operations. A cavalry squadron, cavalry group was responsible for collecting information regarding a zone. All roads and all terrain had to be inspected and all the hostile forces pinpointed.

The reconnaissance of a specific area, a city or a crossroad, could be executed by a cavalry squadron of a cavalry group, or by the reconnaissance troop, infantry division, when this area lay on the division's route of advance.

The second mission of the cavalry was to perform security missions. These were of three types: screen, guard and cover missions.

A screen mission was aimed at countering enemy reconnaissance elements and to alert friendly units to their presence. It was done when few troops were available or when the positions were static. The mission was to make contact with the enemy, maintain this contact, and destroy or repel hostile patrols encountered.

A guard mission was conducted to procure early warning, reaction time and manoeuvre space to the front, flanks or rear of a moving or stationary force. The cavalry reconnaissance troop of the infantry division was responsible for these operations, which consisted of defending selected battle positions, generally situated in the most terrain, and keeping in touch with supporting forces. The division commander could specify as battle positions the zones that he considered to be those by which the enemy would approach. The battle positions were located at least at 3,000m from the division's main body.

A cover mission was designed to secure for the division's main body the same advantages as those for guard missions, but was undertaken at a considerable distance to the front, flank or rear of the unit. The mission was to rapidly develop a contact situation and defeat the enemy. [22]

General Rules of Reconnaissance

All reconnaissance was obtained by a continuous operation of movement and observation. Movement had to be fast, accurate and based on a preconceived plan. In those situations where contact was not immediately imminent, observation was to be subordinated to movement. However, when contact with the enemy was imminent, observation became the rule and movement became subordinate to it.

It was essential in all reconnaissance that observation was maintained all around and on all occasions, even in small units. Observation sectors were assigned to members of each vehicle. Generally, the leading vehicle was in charge of the observation to the front. The even vehicles observed the right flank, the odd vehicles observed the left flank and the last vehicle the rear. The rule could be extended to the platoon, by assigning sectors to sections based upon their number and by assigning to the support section the role of rear observation.

The reconnaissance vehicles worked in twos, one covered the advance of the other and reconnoitred ('point'), while the other remained on guard to cover the withdrawal or assist in the attack ('point support'). When it was possible, the vehicle that reconnoitred moved in a zigzag. The vehicle in cover directed its gun towards the suspected enemy position. A member of the reconnoitring vehicle observed the rear to watch for signals from the vehicle in support.

If the advance was conducted over open terrain where no cover was available for the vehicles on reconnaissance, two

21. See also chapter 4, section 4.2 for security missions.
22. Security missions performed by the cavalry were nearly identical to those of the infantry, the difference being that they were done more in advance of the division's main body, whereas the infantry undertook security missions to protect the main body.

vehicles, or more, were sent on reconnaissance by different routes and at different speeds. Two vehicles deployed on 'point support' covered them.

The approach to a village or town that had not been reconnoitred was done via different routes and followed the same method as that previously described.

The reconnaissance units, committed to any type of mission, had to give at all times a complete report concerning the terrain over which the unit operated, and on contacts with the enemy situated either between the unit and hostile forces, or between adjacent friendly forces and hostile forces.

Reports on terrain included:
  roads and bridges, their types and condition and load limit
  location of possible landing fields
  location and the condition of communication systems, both military and commercial
  location of contaminated areas
  location and type of supplies, both civil and military, particularly gas, oil, and subsistence
  location of high ground and the routes thereto
  location of railroads, spurs, switches, crossings, turntable, repair shops, and rolling stock
  location of streams, including information on depth, width, and current, and possibilities of crossing them by means
    of available boats and rafts
Reports on contacts with the enemy had to cover the following information:
  emplacement, time, and direction of movement of the first enemy contact
  information on the movements, contacts and observations which had been gathered since the last visit to friendly
    troops, and which could not be sent for lack of means of communication
  movements of friendly troops that were cut off from their own headquarters
  information on enemy movements, transports, vehicles, troops was to be gleaned from the local population
  location, type and the direction of movement of enemy planes should they appear
  each message concerning hostile troops had to answer the following questions: What were they? Where were they?
    What time were they observed?
Reconnaissance units were to avoid battle unless it was necessary for the success of their mission. Their mission was observing and reporting. Time spent fighting the enemy was lost time. In a zone patrolled by the enemy, the reconnaissance unit was to stay at a sufficient distance to reduce the effect of hostile fire. However, the unit was always to be ready for action, and was to have its weapons loaded and available.

Once hostile forces were discovered, they were to be kept under surveillance until they entered battle. A reconnaissance unit was to maintain a constant liaison with units on its left and on its right. It had to know where they were and what they were doing. This prevented gaps in reconnaissance screens to appear through which hostile patrols could infiltrate.

Before starting a reconnaissance mission, a unit had to know:
  the situation of its own forces
  the situation of the enemy
  its mission and the mission of the higher formation of which it was part
  the zone in which it was to operate
  the adjacent friendly forces and the direction of their movement
  the contacts that it planned to make with its own forces
  its axis of movement
  how long it would be away from a supply base
  the initial location of the command post, the axis of movement of the commander of the unit and his command post
The section commander of a reconnaissance section was to know the axis of movement and the initial command posts of his platoon commander, troop commander and division commander.

Before starting a mission, the unit destroyed its reconnaissance notes, its orders and annotated maps. A reconnaissance unit was trained to perform any mission at any moment.

When the reconnaissance unit met resistance, it took cover. When the vehicles and their crews were under cover, the reconnaissance was to discover the size, strength, and disposition of the enemy that had opened fire on the unit. It was necessary to detect types of weapons used, presence, and if so caliber, of machine guns, and type of artillery support. It was also tasked with discovering the enemy unit's branch of service and exact identification (division, regiment, company). As soon as possible this information was to be sent to the rear.

If resistance became stronger, or its patrols more aggressive, the reconnaissance unit could enter combat. The enemy would be engaged for two main reasons, either to force him to reveal his dispositions, or to break the enemy security screen and thus to continue the reconnaissance more deeply into his territory. The support elements, infantry, armor, artillery, were committed quickly, and would be attached to a designated commander or to the commander of the reconnaissance unit.

If the hostile position was too strong, the reconnaissance unit was to be prepared to break combat and to withdraw, leaving one or two patrols for observation purposes. The enemy would be obliged to fight, revealing his positions and strength. These actions were aimed at permitting the reconnaissance unit to provide the information requested on the enemy force.

In the presence of the enemy reconnaissance was done on foot. Vehicular reconnaissance was necessary when reconnoitring farther distances, although little information could be gleaned by remaining in the vehicles.

The reconnaissance unit of the infantry division was called a reconnaissance troop up to 6 July 1944 (C2 to T/O&E dated

15 July 43), on which date it was redesignated a cavalry reconnaissance troop.

The cavalry reconnaissance troop, mechanized, included (see chart 4):

Troop Headquarters:
> Headquarters section
> Administrative, Supply and Mess sections
> Maintenance section

3 Reconnaissance Platoons, each:
> Armored Car section
> Scout section

The cavalry reconnaissance troop assigned to an infantry division was stronger than that assigned to a cavalry squadron. The reconnaissance troop of the infantry division is studied below.

*1 – TROOP HEADQUARTERS (3 Officers, 61 Enlisted Men (55 EM, C2, 6 July 1944)

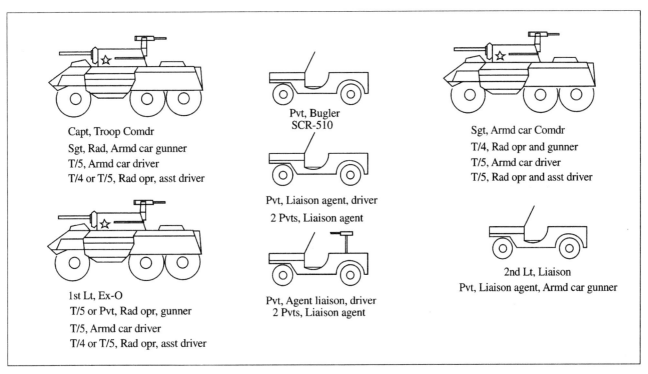

Capt, Troop Comdr

Sgt, Rad, Armd car gunner

T/5, Armd car driver

T/4 or T/5, Rad opr, asst driver

Pvt, Bugler
SCR-510

Pvt, Liaison agent, driver

2 Pvts, Liaison agent

Pvt, Agent liaison, driver
2 Pvts, Liaison agent

Sgt, Armd car Comdr

T/4, Rad opr and gunner

T/5, Armd car driver

T/5, Rad opr and asst driver

2nd Lt, Liaison
Pvt, Liaison agent, Armd car gunner

1st Lt, Ex-O

T/5 or Pvt, Rad opr, gunner

T/5, Armd car driver

T/4 or T/5, Rad opr, asst driver

5. Headquarters Section, Troop Headquarters, Reconnaissance Troop

*1-1 – Headquarters Section

1 Captain, Troop commander-C
1 1st or 2nd Lt, Ex-O, Motor Officer-C
1 2nd Lt, Liaison-C
1 Sgt, Communication Chief (542) and Armored car gunner-C replaced, C2, 6 July 1944 by:
(1) Sgt, Radio (740), Armored car gunner-C
1 Sgt, Car commander-C
4 Pvts, Liaison agent-C
2 Pvts, Liaison agent (345), drove the ¼-ton trucks-S
1 Pvt, Bugler, drove a ¼-ton truck-S
2 Techns 5th, Armored car driver-C
1 Techn 5th, Armored car driver-S
2 Techns 4th or 5th, Radio operator and assistant driver (776)-C became (C2):
(1) Techn 4th or 5th, Radio operator and assistant driver (740)-C
(1) Techn 4th, Radio operator and assistant driver (776)-C
1 Techn 4th, Radio operator and gunner (776)-C (T/5, by C2) (mounted in armored car)
1 Techn 5th, Radio operator and assistant driver (776)-C (T/4 (740), by C2)
1 Pvt or Techn 5th, Radio operator and gunner (776)-C (T/5, C1, 15 September 1843)
1 Pvt, Liaison agent, Armored car gunner-S

Weapons:
1 Light Machine Gun, caliber .30, M1919A4, flexible (mounted on ¼-ton truck)

Vehicles:
    4 Trucks, ¼-ton (1 with Radio set SCR-510)
    3 Armored cars, light, M8

Equipment:
    3 luminous dial compasses (Off)
    155 dust respirators, M2 (1 per individual in the troop)
    6 reconnaissance boats, with paddles, replaced by 6 reconnaissance boats, pneumatic, canvas, 2-man (C2, 6 July 1944)
    6 wrist compasses, liquid-filled (Sgt Car Comdr, Agent liaison)
    3 demolition equipments, set no. 4 cavalry (1 per armored car), replaced by set no. 5 individual (C2, 6 July 1944)
    1 magnifying glass, self-illuminated
    1 pioneer equipment, set no. 1 cavalry
    1 plastic coordinate scale, graduated in yards (1/20,000 and 1/62,500), and metres (1/25,000 and 1/50,000)
    8 transparent map templates, M2 (1 per off, 5 per troop)
    4 binoculars, M13 (Off, Sgt Car Comdr) replaced by M17 (C3, 1 December 1944)
    8 grenade launchers, M7 (1 per 3 rifles)
    33 grenade launchers, M8 (1 per 3 carbines)
    1 truck mount, pedestal, M31 per ¼-ton truck
    4 pocket watches, 15 jewels (Sgt com, 1 per SCR-510 in armored car)
    12 combat winter suits (winter combat, jacket, trousers, helmet) (4 per armored car)
    19 ammunition-carrying bags (1 per SMG, 1 per 2 grenade launchers)
    3 canvas dispatch cases (Off)
    2 empty field desks, company
    5 hand-portable electric lanterns (replaced by lanterns MX-290/GV, C3, 1 December 1944)
    3 lanterns, kerosene, Army
    43 cooking outfits, 1-burner (gasoline cooking stove, M1942, 1-burner with mountain cookset) (1 per vehicle in troop)
    4 scabbards, SMG, M1940 (1 per SMG)
    2 portable typewriters, with carrying case (1 per desk)
    37 tool equipments, TE-33 (knife TL-29, pliers TL-13) (1 per radio set)
    3 belts LC-23-( )
    1 chest BC-5 (general purpose chest)
    3 climbers LC-6-( )
    13 converters M-209 (cipher and decipher machine, printing on strip) (1 per SCR-506)
    3 detector set SCR-625-( ) (mine detector)
    16 flag sets M-113, (2 flags M-44 with case CS-16, hand signal) (1 per combat vehicle, armored car, half-track) cancelled C1, 15 September 1943
    25 flag sets M-238 tank (3 coloured flags M-273, M-274, M-275, poles MC-270, case CS-90) (1 per vehicle except combat vehicles) (43, 1 per vehicle, C2, 6 July 1944)
    47 flashlights, TL-122-( ) (Off, NCO, mech, vehicles)
    1 frequency metre set SCR-211
    3 holders M-167 (1 per SCR-506) (for documents)
    3 interphone equipments RC-99 (1 per armored car) cancelled by C1, 15 September 1943
    3 radio sets SCR-506-( ) (older models SCR-245 or SCR-583)
    1 radio set SCR-508 (armored car)
    1 radio set SCR-510-( ) (¼-ton truck)
    2 radio sets SCR-528-( ) (armored car) C2, 6 July 1944
    1 asbestos mittens, M 1942 (MG, caliber .50)
    1 panel set AP-30-C (13 panels AL-122, case CS-18)
    1 panel set AP-30-D (13 panels AL-121, case CS-18)
    6 panel sets AP-50-A (1 panel AL-140 and 1 panel AL-141,[23] 1 case) (1 per 4 vehicles except combat vehicles)
    24 panel sets AP-50-A (C3, 1 December 1944, 1 per 4 vehicles including combat vehicles)
    1 observation telescope M4 (C1, 15 September 1943, cancelled by C2, 6 July 1944)
    1 interpreter scales, transparent, 12-in, graduated in 1/1000' and 1/10"
    9 mine probes, M1 (C2, 6 July 1944)
    16 camouflage nets, twine, fabric garnished, 15 × 15' (1 per MG, caliber .30, MG, caliber .50, ground) (C2, 6 July 1944)
    8 binoculars, M16 or M17 (C2); M17 (C3, 1 December 1944)
    2 compasses M6 (C2, 6 July 1944)
    3 whistles, thunderer (Off)

23. AL-121: white cotton panel 1.11×0.22'; AL-122: black cotton panel (same size); AL-140:panel with one white side, one red side, 0.93×0.24'; AL-141: one white side, one fluorescent yellow side (same size as AL-140).

3 wristwatches, 15 jewels or more (Off, if authorized by the Commander of the Theater of Operations); 6 watches (1 per Off, if authorized by the Commander of the Theater of Operations, C3, 1 December 1944)

1 alignment equipment ME-73-( ) (C2)

1 stencil outfit, complete, with figures and letters, ½" and 1" (C3, 1 December 1944)

2 installation kits MC-538 (C3, 6 July 1944)

1 power unit PE-210-( ), (C3)

1 spool DR-8, (C3)

1 vibrator pack PP-68-( )/U, (C2)

*1-2 – Administration, Supply & Mess Section

1 1st Sgt-C (¼-ton truck)

1 S Sgt, Mess-C

1 S Sgt, Supply-C (¼-ton truck)

3 Cpls, Ammunition agent-C

1 Cpl, Troop clerk, drove the ¼-ton truck-S

2 Techns 4th, Cook-C

1 Techn 5th, Cook-C

1 Pvt, Cook's helper-R

3 Techns 5th, Half-track driver-S

1 Techn 5th or Pvt, Light truck driver-S

3 Pvts, Ammunition handler, machine gunner-R

8 Pvts, Basic-C (2 Pvts, Basic, C2, 6 July 1944)

5 Pvts, Basic-R

Weapons:

2 LMG, caliber .30, M1919A4, flexible (mounted on half-track and 2½-ton)

3 MG, HB, M2, caliber .50, flexible (mounted on half-track)

3 Rocket launchers, AT, 2.36"

Vehicles:

1 Truck, ¼-ton

1 Truck, 2½-ton, cargo, kitchen & equipment

3 Half-tracks, M3A1 [24]

1 Trailer, 1-ton

Equipment:

6 wrist compasses, liquid-filled (1st Sgt, S Sgt, Cpl Agent am)

3 demolition equipments, set no. 4, cavalry (1 per half-track)

2 carbon tetrachloride fire extinguishers, 4-quart, pressure type

1 binocular, M13 (1st Sgt)

1 wristwatch, 7 jewels (1st Sgt)

5 ammunition-carrying bags (1 per SMG)

1 canvas dispatch case (1st Sgt)

3 flashlights TL-122-( ) (1st Sgt, S Sgt)

1 whistle, thunderer (1st Sgt)

5 scabbards, SMG, M1940 (1 per SMG)

8 asbestos mittens, M1942 (1 per MG, caliber .30; 2 per MG, caliber .50)

*1-3 – Maintenance Section

1 Tech Sgt, Motor-C

1 S Sgt, Mechanic chief-C

1 Sgt, Car commander-C

2 Techns 5th, Armorer-R

1 Techn 5th, Armored car driver-C

1 Techn 4th, Mechanic, automobile, reinforced Rcn plat-C

1 Techn 4th, Mechanic, automobile, drove the half-track-S

2 Techns 5th, Mechanic, automobile, reinforce Rcn plat-C

1 Techn 4th or 5th, Radio operator, assistant driver (776)-C (T/4, C2, 6 July 1944)

1 Techn 4th, Radio repairman, drove the ¼-ton truck-S

---

24. In the T/O&E dated 15 July 1943 the half-track was designated 'half-track personnel carrier M3A1'; change 2, dated 6 July 1944, renamed it 'car, half-track'. The M3A1 version had a ring mount for a MG caliber .50 and two panel-mounts for LMG caliber .30 added. From 15 July 1943 it replaced the M3 version, although supplies of the M3 were to be exhausted. Change 2 dated 6 July 1944 saw the M3A2 version replace the M3A1, the use of the M3 being cancelled.

1 Cpl, Supply motor, Machine gunner-S (Inf Div only)
2 Techn 4th, Mechanic, automobile-C (Inf Div only)
1 Techn 5th, Mechanic, automobile, drove the 2½-ton truck-C (Inf Div only)

Weapons:

1 LMG, caliber .30, M1919A4, flexible, mounted on half-track
2 Rocket launchers, AT, 2.36"

Vehicles:

1 Truck, ¼-ton
1 Armored car, light, M8
1 Half-track, M3A1, with winch, replaced by:
1 Truck, 2½-ton, cargo, with winch, and
1 Trailer, 1-ton (C3, 1 December 1944)

Equipment:

2 wrist compasses, liquid-filled (T Sgt, Sgt Car Comdr)
3 demolition equipments, set no. 4, cavalry (1 per armored car, half-track) (2 equipments, 1 December 1944, when half-track was replaced by 2½-ton truck)
1 binocular, M13 (Sgt Car Comdr)
2 armorers' tools sets, Tank Destroyer Bn (1 per Armorer)
2 wristwatches, 7 jewels (Sgt Car Comdr, SCR-506 in armored car)
1 towing bar, universal type
1 spare parts cabinet, type I, M1940
1 tool set, complete, Half-tracks, no. 5 (cancelled, C2, 6 July 1944)
7 motor vehicle mechanics' tool sets, (general mechanics' tool sets, C2) (1 per mechanic)
1 unit equipment tool set, 2nd echelon, set no. 1 (cancelled C3, 1 October 1944)
1 unit equipment tool set, 2nd echelon, set no. 2, common (added, C3, 1 December 1944)
1 unit equipment tool set, 2nd echelon, set no. 4
1 unit equipment tool set, 2nd echelon, set no. 6
1 unit equipment tool set, 2nd echelon, set no. 7, hoist and towing (added, C3)
4 winter combat suits (combat winter, helmet, jacket, trousers) (4 per armored car)
3 ammunition-carrying bags (1 per SMG)
2 wrecking bars, type D, gooseneck, ¾" × 24"
3 scabbards per SMG, M1940 (1 per SMG)
1 carpenters' tool kit, complete, no. 2
1 carpenters' tool kit, complete, no. 1 (C3, 1 October 1944)
1 holder M-167 (1 per SCR-506, to hold documents)
1 interphone equipment RC-99 (1 per armored car) (cancelled, C1, 15 September 1943)
1 radio set SCR-506-( ) (earlier models SCR-245 or SCR-583)
1 maintenance equipment ME-13 [25] (radio repairman)
1 radio set SCR-528-( ) (half-track)
1 radio set SCR-508-( ) (armored car)
1 test set I-56-( ) (tube testers, voltmeters and voltmeters) (radio repairman)
9 flashlights, TL-122-( ) (T Sgt, S Sgt, mech)
1 tool equipment TE-41 (pliers, screwdrivers, soldering iron) (radio repairman)
3 asbestos mittens, M1942 (1 per Armorer; MG, caliber .50)

*2 – RECONNAISSANCE PLATOON (× 3) (1 Officer, 28 Enlisted Men)

*2-1 – Armored Car Section

1 1st or 2nd Lt, Platoon commander-C (mounted in armored car or other platoon vehicle)
1 S Sgt, Platoon-C
1 Sgt, Car commander-C
3 Techns 5th, Armored car driver-C
(2) Techns 4th, Radio operator (776) and assistant driver-C

Vehicles:

3 Armored cars, light, M8

Equipment:

1 wrist compass, liquid-filled (Sgt Car Comdr)
3 demolition equipments, set no. 4, cavalry (1 per armored car)

25. For SCR-509, 510, 609, 610 maintenance including 1 signal generator HF VO-4-C, 1 voltmeter 1-107-C, 1 adaptor and accessories.

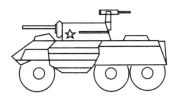 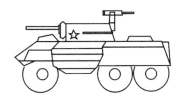 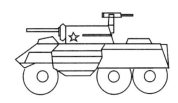

1st or 2nd Lt, Platoon Comdr	S Sgt, Platoon	Sgt, Car Comdr
T/5, Armored car driver	T/5, Armored car driver	T/5, Armored car driver
T/4 or T/5, Rad opr, asst driver	T/4 or T/5, Rad opr, asst driver	T/4 or T/5, Rad opr, asst driver
T/4 or T/5, Rad opr, Gunner	T/4 or T/5, Rad opr, Gunner	T/4 or T/5, Rad opr, Gunner

6. Armored Car Section, Cavalry Reconnaissance Troop

1 transparent map template, M2 (Off)
3 binoculars, M13 (Off, S Sgt, Sgt Car Comdr)
5 wristwatches, 7 jewels (S Sgt plat, Sgt Car Comdr, SCR-506, armored car)
12 winter combat suits (combat winter, helmet, jacket, trousers) (4 per armored car)
2 canvas dispatch cases (Off, S Sgt Plat)
2 whistles, thunderer (Off, S Sgt)
2 flashlights, TL-122-( ) (Off, S Sgt)
3 holders M-167 (1 per SCR-506, to hold documents)
3 interphone equipments RC-99 (1 per armored car), cancelled, C1, 15 September 1943
3 radio sets SCR-506, earlier models: SCR-245 or SCR-583 (armored car)
3 radio sets SCR-508 (armored car)
1 observation telescope, M4 (C1, 15 September 1943, cancelled C2)
3 observation telescopes, M48 or M49 (C2, 6 July 1944)
1 wristwatch, 15 jewels or more (Off, if authorized by the Commander of the Theater of Operations)

The replacement, dependent upon availability, of the armored cars, M8, by scout cars, M3A1 and of half-tracks, M3A1 with ring mount M3, was no longer authorized by the time of C2. Prior to this, two M8s could be replaced by two M3A1s and a 37mm anti-tank gun. The half-track M3A1A could be replaced by the M3 version. From 6 July 1944, the standard model of half-track was the M3A2.

The winter combat suits, (winter combat jacket, trousers and helmet), were replaced on 1 December 1944 by:
52 pile field jackets, OD (field jacket M1943)
52 cotton field trousers, OD (trousers M1943)
52 wool field trousers, OD, (wool trousers M1943) (4 per armored car).

Pending availability, winter combat suits were issued. The cotton field trousers were not available before May 1945.

*2-2 – Scout Section

1 Sgt, Section leader-R
2 Cpl, Squad leader-R
6 Techns 5th or Pvts, Light truck driver-S
6 Pvts, Gunner, Mortar-C
2 Pvts, Rifleman, Radio operator-R

Weapons:
3 LMG, cal. .30, M1919A4, flexible, mounted on ¼-ton trucks
3 Mortars, 60 mm, M2, with mount M2 (C2, 6 July 1944, mount M3)

Vehicles:
6 Trucks, ¼-ton

Equipment:
2 wrist compasses, liquid-filled (Cpl, Squad Leader)
3 binoculars, M13 (Sgt, Cpl)
3 truck mounts, pedestal, M31 per ¼-ton truck
3 wristwatches, 7 jewels (Sgt, Cpl)
9 ammunition-carrying bags (1 per mortar 60 mm, SMG)
6 scabbards SMG, M1940 (1 per SMG)
3 radio sets SCR-510-( ) (¼-ton truck)
9 asbestos mittens, M1942 (2 per mortar, 3 per MG, caliber .30)

Sgt, Section Ldr

T/5 or Pvt, Light truck driver

SCR-510
LMG, M1919A4

Cpl, Squad Ldr

T/5 or Pvt, Light truck driver

Pvt, Rifleman, Rad Opr

SCR-510
LMG, M1919A4

Cpl, Squad Ldr

T/5 or Pvt, Light truck driver

Pvt, Rifleman, Rad opr

SCR-510
LMG, M1919A4

T/5 or Pvt, Light truck driver

2 Pvts, Mortar gunner

Mortar, 60mm, M2

T/5 or Pvt, Light truck driver

2 Pvts, Mortar gunner

Mortar, 60mm, M2

T/5 or Pvt, Light truck driver

2 Pvts, Mortar gunner

Mortar, 60m, M2

7. Scout Section, Reconnaissance Platoon, Cavalry Reconnaissance Troop

1 reel equipment, CE-11 (C 2, 6 July 1944) (included: 1 spool DR-8, 1 connector M-221, 3 straps (1 ST-33, 1 ST-34, 1 ST-35), 1 handset TS-10)

½ mile of wire W-130- on spool DR-8 (C2)

1 handset TS-10 (C3, 1 December 1944)

The term 'mechanized' used by the cavalry was synonymous with that of 'armored'. By the National Defense Act of 1920, all tanks of the U.S. Army were assigned to the Infantry. During testing of an experimental armored force, at the beginning of the 1930s, the cavalry designated its tanks 'combat cars'. The first experimental unit was called 'mechanized' (7th Cavalry Brigade, Mechanized) to distinguish it from horsed units. In spring 1940, General Adna R. Chaffee, Brig. Gen. Bruce Magruder, Colonel George S. Patton and Brig. Gen. Frank Andrew recommended the creation of an independent armored force. To avoid using the terms of the cavalry (mechanized) and of the infantry (tank), they chose the term 'armored'. The armored forces were created on 10 July 1940.

The cavalry reconnaissance troop completes our survey of the first part of the division's 'base'. The remainder of the divisional base, i.e. the support units, will be studied in chapter 7, Special Troops, because they were assigned under this command. The engineer battalion and the medical battalion are studied in chapters 6 and 8 respectively.

INFANTRY REGIMENT
T/O&E 7-11

The infantry regiment was, during WWII, the combat unit of the infantry division. It was an administrative and tactical unit of a command level lower than a division or brigade but higher than a battalion. The infantry regiment contained 3 infantry battalions. All units that formed the infantry regiment were administratively and tactically under the authority of the regimental commander. The infantry division's 3 infantry regiments, taken together, comprised 9,753 of the 14,253 men theoretically in the division, i.e. more than 60% of the division's total force. The infantry regiment, which was at the heart of the division is also at the heart of this book. Chart 8 shows the infantry regiment. It was composed of the following units:

Regimental Headquarters
Medical Detachment
Attached Chaplains
Headquarters Company
Service Company
Cannon Company
Anti-Tank Company
3 Infantry Battalions

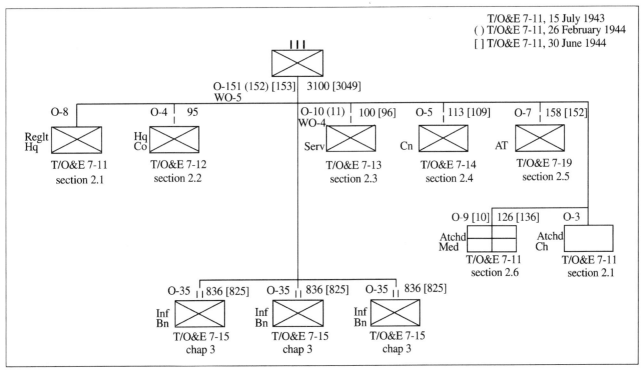

8. Infantry Regiment

2.1 REGIMENTAL HEADQUARTERS

The regimental headquarters included the regimental commander, his staff, and some assistants, warrant officers and enlisted men. These personnel were assigned to:
a command echelon, which operated in the regimental command post
an administrative echelon, which operated in the train bivouac
Following the survey of the regimental units, the command post will be examined in section 2.7 and the train bivouac in section 2.8.

A – Command Group

The command group was composed of the headquarters (8 officers), and the regimental staff members who were in command of other units of the regiment, but who also had duties as staff officers.

    1 Colonel, Regimental commander-P
    1 Lt Col, Executive-P
    1 Major, Intelligence, S-2-P
    1 Major, Operations and training, S-3-P
    1 Captain, Adjutant and S-1-C
    3 1st Lts, Liaison-C

The intelligence officer (S-2) planned and supervised intelligence activities within the regiment.

The plans and training officer (S-3) planned the training and tactical operations of the Regiment. He was assisted by personnel from the staff section, regimental headquarters platoon, service company (T/O&E 7-13, *2-11).

The adjutant (S-1) supervised the execution of administrative arrangements pertaining to personnel. He was assisted by the assistant regimental adjutant from the staff section, regimental headquarters platoon, service company.

The staff members described below were not assigned to the regimental headquarters but assigned to other organizations within the regiment. They had two duties, one in their organizations, another as staff officers. They will be encountered again in their respective organizations.

The supply officer (S-4) commanded the regimental supply service. He was carried in the table of organization of the company headquarters, service company (T/O&E 7-13). His principal assistant was the service company commander. He was also assisted by the assistant supply officer from company headquarters, service company, and by personnel from supply section, regimental headquarters platoon, service company (T/O&E 7-13,*2-2).

The surgeon commanded the regimental medical detachment and supervised the medical service of the regiment. His assistants were provided by the headquarters section, medical detachment (T/O&E 7-11, section 2.6).

The headquarters commandant was also the company commander of the regimental headquarters company (T/O&E 7-12). He was assisted by personnel from his company headquarters group (T/O&E 7-12, *1-1). He worked in close collaboration with the S-1.

The communication officer commanded the communication platoon, headquarters company (T/O&E 7-12, *2). He was assisted in his duties by a warrant officer from the communication platoon, headquarters company (T/O&E 7-12, *3-1). He advised the regimental commander and staff on matters of communication technique.

The gas officer was also the executive officer (Ex-O) of the regimental headquarters company (T/O&E 7-12, *1). He was the adviser of the regimental commander and staff in all matters involving the use of gas and smoke, and in defence against chemicals.

The anti-tank officer was the commander of the anti-tank company (T/O&E 7-19). He advised the staff on matters concerning defense against armored vehicles.

The howitzer officer was the commander of the cannon company (T/O&E 7-14). He advised the regimental commander and his staff about the tactical use of the cannon company.

B – Administration Group

The personnel officer commanded the administration group (*2-12), staff section (*2-1), regimental headquarters platoon (*2), service company (T/O&E 7-13). He headed the personnel officer's group of the S-1 section. He was assisted by personnel from the staff section (T/O&E 7-13, *2-1) and by the company clerks of every company. In the field his section could operate at division headquarters or a higher headquarters.

The attached chaplains (T/O&E 7-11, section 2.1, C) were the advisers of the regimental commander and his staff on matters dealing with the spiritual and moral welfare of the command.

The munition officer was from the supply section (*2-2), regimental headquarters platoon (*2), service company (T/O&E 7-13). He was responsible, under the direction of the S-4, for the ammunition supply of the regiment. He was assisted by the assistant munition officer and by the ammunition sergeant from the munition group of the supply section (T/O&E 7-13, *2-23).

The motor officer was from the maintenance section (*3-6), transportation platoon (*3), service company (T/O&E 7-13). He was the adviser to the regimental commander and his staff on technical matters pertaining to the operation and maintenance of motor vehicles.

The special service officer was from the special service group (*2-13), staff section (*2-1), regimental headquarters platoon (*2), service company (T/O&E 7-13). He was responsible for morale and recreational activities. He was assisted by the athletic instructor and entertainment director (*2-13).

Equipment of the Regimental Headquarters:
    8 luminous dial compasses, with case (Off)
    4 gas proof curtains, M1
    1 reading glass, 4½", with case
    1 drafting and duplicating equipment, set no. 1
    2 plastic semicircular protractors, Machine Gun

1 sketching equipment, set no. 1
2 magnifying stereoscopes, pocket
8 transparent map templates, M2 (1 per Off)
8 wristwatches, 15 jewels (1 per Off)
1 observation telescope, M4, M48 or M49
3 gasoline lanterns, two mantle, commercial, 1 per tent CP, replaced by 3 hand-portable electric lanterns (C1, 30 June 1944)
1 duplicating machine, spirit process, military field
1 latrine screen, complete (with pins and poles)
2 official rubber stamps
1 organization flag, color, silk [1]
1 national colors flag, silk
3 Command Post (CP) tents, complete
3 tent stoves M1941, for tent
3 oil burners for tent stove M1941, 1 per stove
3 empty field desk, headquarters (in T/O&E 7-13)
2 non-portable typewriters (in T/O&E 7-13)
3 portable typewriters, with carrying case
1 photographic interpreter kit, type F2 (C1, 30 June 1944)
1 interpreter's scales, 12-in
8 hand-portable electric lanterns; 5 (C1, 30 June 1944) the 3 others were replaced by gasoline lantern, two mantle, commercial
8 flashlights, TL-122-( )
8 whistles, thunderer

Attached Chaplains

3 Captains or 1st Lts, Chaplain

Vehicles:
3 Trucks, ¼-ton
3 Trailers, ¼-ton, driven by Chaplain's assistants (T/O&E 7-13, *2-12)

Equipment:
3 wrist compasses, liquid-filled
3 brassards, Geneva Convention
3 Chaplain outfits (including: 1 steel chest for music edition, hymnal; 1 empty field desk, HQ; 2 chaplain's flags, one Christian and one Jewish; 1 music book set, hymnal, song-and-service (150); 1 folding organ)
1 portable typewriter, with carrying case
3 flashlights, TL-122-( )

For personal equipment and the equipment of vehicles, see chapter 9.

2.2 REGIMENTAL HEADQUARTERS COMPANY
T/O&E 7-12

The regimental headquarters company provided the necessary personnel for working at regimental headquarters. The headquarters company was organized to give the higher formation the means by which it could perform effectively. We can compare the regimental headquarters company with the division headquarters company. The division headquarters company provided anti-tank protection because the division did not possess it. It provided neither a communications unit because the division possessed a signal company nor a reconnaissance unit because the division possessed a reconnaissance troop. The regiment had an anti-tank unit (the anti-tank company), but it did not possess a signal unit or a reconnaissance unit. These means were thus provided by the headquarters company in the form of the communication platoon and the intelligence and reconnaissance platoon. The composition of the regimental headquarters company is shown chart 9.

*1 – COMPANY HEADQUARTERS (2 Officers, 24 Enlisted Men (20 EM, C1, 30 June 1944 to the table dated 26 February 1944)

*1-1 – Command Group

1 Captain, Company Commander, HQ Commandant-C
1 1st Lt, Executive-Officer, Regimental Gas Officer-C

1. The different flags of the U.S. Army were: standard – the flag of a mounted or motorized unit; color – the flag of a dismounted (infantry) unit; guidon – the flag carried by a unit for identification (had swallow-tailed end).

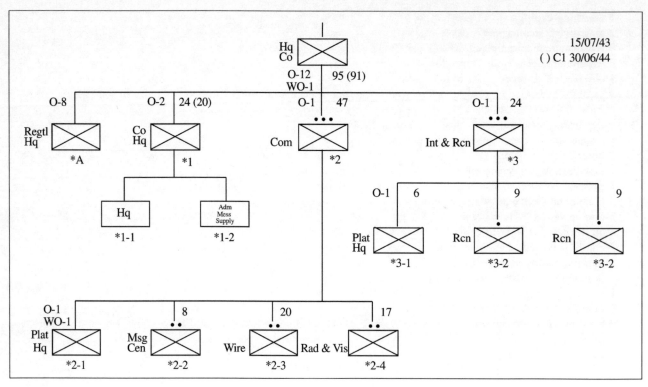

9. Headquarters Company, Infantry Regiment

1 1st Sgt-C
1 S Sgt, Transportation-C
1 Pvt, Bugler, drove the ¼-ton truck-C
1 Techn 5th, Light truck driver-R
1 Techn 4th, Mechanic, automobile, drove the ¾-ton truck-R
2 Pvts, Orderly, drove the ¼-ton trucks-C
9 Pvts, Basic-R (5 Basics, C1, 30 June 1944)

*1-2 – Administration Group

1 S Sgt, Mess-C
1 S Sgt, Supply-C
1 Cpl, Company clerk, classification specialist-R
1 Techn 5th, Armorer-artificer-R
1 Techn 4th, Cook (Officer Mess)-R
1 Techn 4th, Cook-R
1 Techn 5th, Cook-R
1 Pvt, Cook's helper-R

Weapons:
1 MG, HB, M2, caliber .50, flexible
4 Rocket launchers, AT, 2.36″ M1 (15 July 1943), M9 (26 February 1944), M9A1 (30 June 1944)
3 Submachine Guns, caliber .45, M3 (added C1, 30 June 1944)

Vehicles:
4 Trucks, ¼-ton
1 Truck, ¾-ton, WC

Equipment:
2 luminous dial compasses, with case (Off)
7 wrist compasses, liquid-filled (1st Sgt, S Sgt T, bglr, driver, mech, orderly)
2 transparent map templates, M2 (Off)
3 binoculars, M13 (Off, 1st Sgt)
1 grenade launcher, M7 (driver)
3 grenade launchers, M8 (bglr, odly)
1 truck mount, pedestal, M31 for ¼-ton truck (mount for MG, caliber .50)
3 hand pyrotechnic projectors, M9
1 wristwatch, 7 jewels (1st Sgt)

2 wristwatches, 15 jewels (Off)
1 motor vehicles mechanics' tool set (mech)
1 unit equipment tool set, 2nd echelon, set no. 1
3 asbestos mittens, M1942 (1 per Armr-Artif, 2 per MG, caliber .50)
3 packboards, plywood
3 packboard attachments, cargo (6, C1, 30 June 1944, 2 per packboard)
6 packboard quick-release straps (2 per packboard)
4 ammunition-carrying bags (1 per grenade launcher)
8 rocket-carrying bags, M6 (2 per Rocket launcher)
3 canvas dispatch cases (Off, 1st Sgt)
1 flag, guidon
2 gasoline lanterns, two mantle, commercial
3 officers' mess outfits, M1941 (1 per 6 officers)
1 carpenters' tool set, no. 2
6 whistles, thunderer (Off, 1st Sgt, S Sgt)
10 flashlights, TL-122-( ) (Off, 1st Sgt, S Sgt, bglr, mech, odly)
3 hand-portable electric lanterns

Outside the U.S.A., if authorized by the Commander of the Theater of Operations, it can be added (C1, 30 June 1944):

10 packboards, plywood
20 packboard attachments, cargo
20 packboard quick-release straps

The personnel quoted above were assigned to every company, although sometimes distributed in different groups or sections. We are now going to examine in more detail the duties of each member of the headquarters of the company; the reader wanting to remember these duties when studying the other companies should refer to this section.

The company commander was responsible for the administration, discipline, basic training and supply of the company. The company commander of the headquarters company was also the headquarters commandant of the regimental headquarters.

The executive officer was the second-in-command. The executive officer of the headquarters company was also the regimental gas officer.

The first sergeant assisted the company commander in the administration of the company and in the performance of his duties as headquarters commandant (only for the headquarters company).

The transportation sergeant was responsible for maintenance, loading and movement of all motor vehicles assigned to the company. This role did not exist in companies having few vehicles.

The bugler was trained as a messenger and drove a jeep.

The light truck driver drove a vehicle ranging from ¼ to 2½-tons.

The automobile mechanic, as automotive repair technician, performed company maintenance. He drove the Dodge ¾-ton Weapons Carrier.

The orderlies assisted the regimental commander and his staff and drove jeeps.

The basics did not have a specific duty in the organization, but replaced casualties. With change no. 1 (C1) dated 30 June 1944 to the table dated 26 February 1944, the number of basics was reduced by 50% in the infantry regiment; in the headquarters company it decreased from 9 to 5. Replacement soldiers arriving in the unit were assigned as basics. They were used as messengers, ammunition bearers and for secondary duties. They undertook training whenever possible. When units asked for replacements, basics were assigned to those duties. New replacements would then arrive to replace these basics. The reduction of the number of basics on 30 June occurred due to the fact that newly-arrived soldiers were sometimes assigned directly to the units without passing by the basic step, and without additional training in small unit tactics, due to urgent demand for replacements.

The mess sergeant was responsible for the company mess.

The supply sergeant procured and issued supplies for the company. During combat he performed his duties in the regimental train bivouac where he could be in charge of the preparation of shelters and other installations.

The company clerk kept the records of the company, under the supervision of the personnel officer.

The armorer-artificer made minor repairs to weapons and performed simple carpentry tasks. He helped in handling and procuring supplies.

The cooks prepared the meals. They were assisted by a cook's helper. One cook was designated for the officers' mess.

*2 – COMMUNICATION PLATOON (1 Officer, 1 WO, 47 Enlisted Men)

*2-1 – Platoon Headquarters

1 Captain, Platoon leader, Communication Officer-C
1 WO, Assistant Communication Officer-C
1 Mr Sgt, Communication chief-C
1 Techn 5th, Light truck driver-R

Vehicles:
- 1 Truck, ¼-ton
- 1 Truck, 2½-ton
- 1 Trailer, 1-ton

Equipment:
- 1 panel set AP-30-C
- 1 panel set AP-30-D
- 2 luminous dial compasses, with case (Off, Com Plat)
- 1 wrist compass, liquid-filled (driver)
- 1 transparent map template, M2 (Off)
- 1 binocular, M13 (Off)
- 1 grenade launcher, M7 (driver)
- 1 ammunition-carrying bag (driver)
- 1 wristwatch, 7 jewels (Mr Sgt)
- 2 wristwatches, 15 jewels (Off, WO)
- 12 flashlights, TL-122-( ) (Off, WO, Mr Sgt, 8 for platoon)
- 3 whistles, thunderer (Off, WO, Mr Sgt)
- 2 tool equipments, TE-33 (1 knife TL-29 and 1 pliers TL-13) (1 per man in the platoon)

*2-2 – Regimental Message Center Section

- 1 S Sgt, Message center chief-C
- 1 Techn 4th, Clerk, code-R
- 1 Techn 5th, Clerk, code-R
- 2 Pvts, Clerk, code-R
- 3 Pvts, Messenger-C

Vehicles:
- 2 Trucks, ¼-ton

Equipment:
- 1 wristwatch, 7 jewels (S Sgt)
- 1 whistle, thunderer (S Sgt)
- 1 flashlight, TL-122-( ) (S Sgt)
- 8 tool equipments, TE-33

*2-3 – Regimental Wire Section

- 1 S Sgt, Wire chief-C
- 1 Techn 5th, Switchboard operator-R
- 4 Techns 5th, Lineman telephone & telegraph-R
- 11 Pvts, Lineman telephone & telegraph-R
- 3 Pvts, Switchboard operator-R

Vehicles:
- 2 Trucks, ¼-ton
- 2 Trailers, ¼-ton (26 February 1944)

Equipment:
- 6 axles RL-27-( ) (to unwind reel DR-4)
- 4 chests BC-5
- 8 chest sets TD-3 (to use with T-45, 1 per 2 EE-8, 1 per BD-72)
- 8 flashlights, TL-122-( )
- 8 headsets HS-30 (1 per 2 EE-8, 1 per BD-72)
- 5 lineman's equipments TE-21 (including: 1 belt LC-23, 1 climbers LC-5, 1 hatchet LC-1, 1 pliers TL-107, 1 pliers LC-24, 1 screwdriver TL-106, 1 wrench LC-25, 1 hammer HM-1)
- 8 microphones T-45 (1 per 2 EE-8, 1 per BD-72)
- 8 reel equipments CE-11
- 4 reel units RL-31 (for 1 reel DR-5 or 2 reels DR-4)
- 2 switchboards BD-72
- 4 telegraph sets TG-5-( )
- 12 telephones EE-8-( )
- 20 miles of wire W-110-B on reel DR-4
- 5 miles of wire W-130-A on reel DR-4
- 2 miles of wire W-130-A on spool DR-8, may be issued on DR-4; the wire W-130-A may be replaced in the order of preference by: wire WD-3/TT or wire W-130

2 pikes MC-123
15 wrist compasses, liquid-filled (1 per Lineman)
4 wristwatches, 7 jewels (1 per Switchboard operator)
1 grenade launcher, M7 (1 per 4 Techns 5th, Lineman)
1 ammunition-carrying bag (1 per lance-grenades)
18 flashlights, TL-122-( ) (S Sgt, Lineman, Sb)
1 whistle (thunderer) (S Sgt)
5 wristwatches (S Sgt, Sb operator)
20 tool equipments, TE-33

*2-4 – Regimental Radio & Visual Section

1 Tech Sgt, Section leader, Radio & Visual chief-C
5 Techns 4th, Radio operator-R
1 Techn 4th, Radio repairman-R
5 Techns 5th, Radio operator-R
5 Pvts, Radio operator-R (become Techn 5th with the table dated 26 February 1944)

Vehicles:
3 Trucks, ¼-ton
2 Trailers, ¼-ton (26 February 1944)

Equipment:
2 converters M-209 (cypher and decypher machines)
1 frequency conversion kit MC-518
1 frequency metre set SCR-211-( ) (frequency metre BC-221-( ), case BG-81-B, 1 feeding)
8 holders M-167 (for documents)
2 maintenance equipments ME-40-( ) (for SCR-300 maintenance)
1 maintenance kit ME-36 (for SCR-536 maintenance)
2 maintenance kits ME-53, 1 per ME-40-( ) (spare parts)
8 radio sets SCR-300-( ), replaced SCR-511 (26 February 1944)
6 radio sets SCR-694-( ), replaced SCR-284-( ) (26 February 1944)
6 converters M-209, for SCR-694 (C1, 30 June 1944)
6 remote control units RM-29, 1 per SCR-694 or SCR-284 replaced by remote control equipment RC-290 (C1, 30 June 1944)
1 test equipment IE-17-( ) (tuning of the SCR-536)
1 test set I-56-( )
17 tool equipments, TE-33
1 tool equipment, TE-41
1 vibrator pack PP-68-( )/U
1 voltammeter I-50
15 wristwatches, 7 jewels (1 per Radio operator)

*3 – INTELLIGENCE & RECONNAISSANCE PLATOON (1 Officer, 24 Enlisted Men)

*3-1 – Platoon Headquarters

1 1st Lt, Platoon Commander-C
1 S Sgt, Platoon-C; became Tech Sgt, Platoon Intelligence† (table of 26 February 1944)
1 Techn 5th, Draftsman, topographic-R†
1 Pvt, Light truck driver-R
1 Techn 5th, Radio operator-R
2 Pvts, Scout, observer, Intelligence-R†

† The platoon sergeant (Tech Sgt), the topographic draftsman (T/5) and both scouts (privates) assigned to the reconnaissance platoon headquarters were attached to the S-2 section of the regimental headquarters (see section 2.7, Command Post, Infantry Regiment).

Weapons:
1 MG, HB, M2, caliber .50, flexible

Vehicles:
1 Truck, ¼-ton

Equipment:
4 luminous dial compasses, with case (Off, S Sgt, scout)
2 wrist compasses, liquid-filled (driver, Radio operator)
1 transparent map template, M2 (Off)

*3-1 Platoon Headquarters   *3-2 1st Reconnaissance Squad   *3-2 2nd Rcn Squad

1st Lt, Platoon Commander
Techn 5th, Light Truck Driver
Techn 4th, Radio operator

Sgt, Squad Leader
Techn 5th, Light Truck Driver
Techn 4th, Radio operator

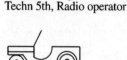

Sgt, Squad Leader
Techn 5th, Light Truck Driver
Techn 5th, Radio operator

Corporal, Assistant Squad Leader
Techn 5th, Light Truck Driver
Pvt, Scout, Observer, Intelligence

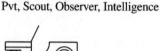

Corporal, Assistant Squad Leader
Techn 5th, Light Truck Driver
Pvt, Scout, Observer, Intelligence

Pvt, Light Truck Driver
Pvt, Scout, Observer, Intelligence
Pvt, Scout, Observer, Intelligence

Pvt, Light Truck Driver
Pvt, Scout, Observer, Intelligence
Pvt, Scout, Observer, Intelligence

10. Intelligence and Reconnaissance Platoon, Headquarters Company, Infantry Regiment

2 binoculars, M13 (Off, S Sgt)
1 grenade launcher, M7 (driver)
1 truck mount, pedestal, M31 per MG, caliber .50 (¼-ton truck)
1 wristwatch, 15 jewels (Off)
2 whistles, thunderer (Off, S Sgt)
1 tool equipment, TE-33 (Radio operator)
1 lineman's equipment TE-21 (lineman)
2 radio sets SCR-300-( ) (replaced SCR-511, 26 February 1944)
4 flashlights, TL-122-( ) (Off, S Sgt, driver, Rad opr)

*3-2 Reconnaissance Squad (× 2)

1 Sgt, Squad Leader-R
1 Cpl, Squad Leader assistant-R
2 Techns 5th, Light truck driver-R
1 Pvt, Light truck driver-R
1 Techn 4th, Radio operator-R
3 Pvts, Scout, observer, intelligence-R

Vehicles:
3 Trucks, ¼-ton

Equipment:
1 lineman's equipment TE-21 (lineman)
1 radio set SCR-300 (replaced SCR-511, 26 February 1944)
1 tool equipment, TE-33 (Radio operator)
2 wrist compasses, liquid-filled (1 per driver, Radio operator)
5 luminous dial compasses, with case (1 per Sgt, Cpl, Scout)
2 binoculars, M13
1 wristwatch, 7 jewels (Radio operator)

The composition of the headquarters company was little altered between 15 July 1943 and 1 June 1945. At this date, the table was renamed T/O&E 7-12-OS.

2.3 SERVICE COMPANY, INFANTRY REGIMENT
T/O&E 7-13

The service company is shown in chart 11. It was complementary to the headquarters company in regiments and in independent battalions. Some battalions, such as the engineer combat battalion, had a company that combined both roles, and was named headquarters and headquarters & service company. The regimental service company gathered together those services that were not included in the headquarters company.

The company consisted of:

Company Headquarters (as in every company)

Regimental Headquarters Platoon (it contained all services necessary to the regimental headquarters as well those for administration, supply, and regimental operations)

Transportation Platoon (responsible for the maintenance of all vehicles of the regiment, and for the transportation of the regiment, including those of the infantry battalions)

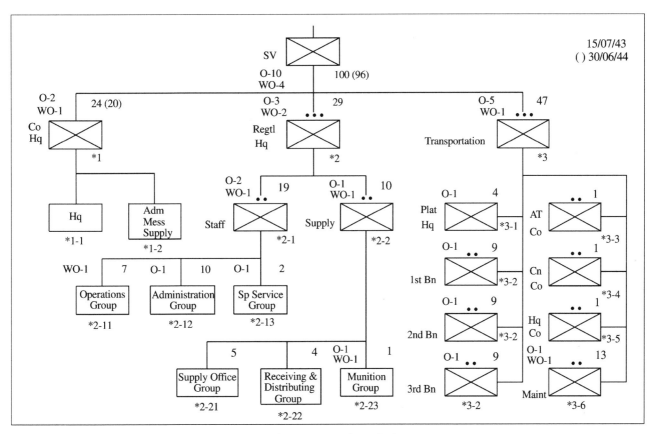

11. Service Company, Infantry Regiment

*1 – COMPANY HEADQUARTERS (2 Officers, 24 Enlisted Men (20 EM, C1, 30 June 1944)

*1-1 – Command Group

1 Major, Supply, S-4-P
1 Captain, Company Commander-C
1 WO, Supply administrative-C
1 1st Sgt-C
1 Pvt, Bugler, drove a ¼-ton truck-C
1 Pvt, Messenger, drove a ¼-ton truck-C
9 Pvts, Basic-R (5 Basics, C1, 30 June 1944)

The major (regimental supply officer) commanded the regimental supply service and was responsible to the regimental commander. The service company commander was his principal assistant. He was also assisted by the munition officer and by certain members of the supply section (*2-2), regimental headquarters platoon (*2).

The captain, besides his duties as company commander, was the principal assistant of the S-4, and commanded the train bivouac.

*1-2 – Administration Group

1 S Sgt, Mess-C
1 S Sgt, Supply-C
1 Cpl, Company clerk, classification specialist-R
1 Techn 5th, Armorer-artificer-R
1 Pvt, Carpenter general-R
1 Techn 4th, Cook-R
1 Techn 5th, Cook-R
1 Pvt, Cook's helper-R
1 Techn 5th, Light truck driver-R
2 Techns 4th, Mechanic, automobile, one drove a ¾-ton truck-R
1 Techn 5th, Mechanic, automobile, drove a ¾-ton truck-R

Weapons:
8 Rocket launchers, AT, 2.36″

Vehicles:
2 Trucks, ¼-ton
2 Trucks, ¾-ton, WC
1 Truck, 2½-ton, cargo
1 Trailer, 1-ton

Equipment:
2 luminous dial compasses, with case (Off)
3 wrist compasses, liquid-filled (1st Sgt, bugler, driver)
2 transparent map templates, M2 (Off)
3 binoculars, M13 (Off, 1st Sgt)
3 wristwatches, 15 jewels (Off, WO, on Theater of Operations)
3 wristwatches, 7 jewels (1st Sgt, S Sgt mess, S Sgt supply)
2 canvas dispatch cases (Off)
3 grenade launchers, M7 (individual driving, armed with a rifle)
16 rocket-carrying bags, M6 (2 per Rocket launcher)
3 ammunition-carrying bags (1 per grenade launcher)
144 radioactive luminous markers, type I, replaced C1, 30 June 1944 by:
36 radioactive luminous markers, type II
1 unit equipment tool set, 2nd echelon, set no. 1
1 carpenters' tool set no. 1 (carpenter)
3 motor vehicle mechanics' tool sets (1 per mech)
2 large canvas paulins (tarpaulin)
6 small canvas paulins
1 panel set AP-50-A
1 panel set AP-34 (including 10 panels AL-125 white) (C1, 30 June 1944)
11 flashlights, TL-122-( ) (Off, mech, driver, S Sgt, 1st Sgt, bugler, messenger)
6 whistles, thunderer (Off, WO, 1st Sgt, S Sgt)
6 hand-portable electric lanterns (per company)

*2 – REGIMENTAL HEADQUARTERS PLATOON (3 Officers, 4 WO, 29 Enlisted Men)

The regimental headquarters platoon included all personnel necessary to keep the regimental headquarters functioning (T/O&E 7-11, *A). It was composed of the following sections.

*2-1 – Staff Section (2 Officers, 1 Warrant Officer, 19 Enlisted Men)

The staff section was composed of three independently-operating groups:
Operations Group (worked in the regimental command post)
Administration Group (worked in the train bivouac but could also, when in the field, stay in the rear echelon with the divisional staff or even corps staff)
Special Service Group (worked in installations provided by the regimental commander)

*2-11 – Operations Group

1 WO, Adjutant & S-1 assistant-C
1 Mr Sgt, Operations-C
1 Mr Sgt, Sergeant Major-C-1 Techn 4th, Headquarters clerk-R
1 Techn 5th, Headquarters clerk-R
1 Pvt, Headquarters clerk-R

1 Pvt, Messenger-C
1 Techn 4th, Stenographer-R

*2-12 – Administration Group
1 Captain, Personnel Officer-C
1 Tech Sgt, Personnel-C
3 Techns 5th, Chaplain's assistant, drove the ¼-ton trucks assigned to Chaplains-R
1 Techn 4th, Headquarters clerk-R
1 Techn 4th, Personnel clerk, classification specialist-R
1 Techn 4th, Record clerk-R
1 Techn 4th, Mail clerk-R
2 Techns 5th, Mail clerk-R

*2-13 – Special Service Group
1 Captain, Special Service, Orientation, Assistant S-3-C
1 1st Lt, Athletic & Recreation, Assistant S-1-C (added, 26 February 1944)
1 Techn 5th, Athletic instructor-R
1 Techn 5th, Entertainment director-R

Equipment of the Staff Section:
3 luminous dial compasses, with case (Off)
3 transparent map templates, M2 (Off)
3 binoculars, M13 (Off)
1 wristwatch, 7 jewels (Mr Sgt, Sgt Major)
4 wristwatches, 15 jewels (Off, WO, on Theater of Operations)
3 canvas dispatch cases (Off)
7 whistles, thunderer (Off, WO, Mr Sgt, T Sgt)
4 qualification cards selectors
2 empty field desks, headquarters
1 non-portable typewriter
2 portable typewriters, with carrying case
2 Command Post tents, complete, (added, C1, 30 June 1944)
2 tent stoves, M1941 (C1, 30 June 1944)
2 gasoline lanterns, two-mantle, commercial
2 hand-portable electric lanterns
2 oil burners for tent stove M1941 (C1, 30 June 1944)
4 flashlights, TL-122-( ) (Off, Sgt Maj)

*2-2 – Supply Section (1 Officer, 1 Warrant Officer, 10 Enlisted Men)
The supply section worked in the train bivouac, and consisted of the following groups:

*2-21 – Supply Office Group
1 S Sgt, Supply assistant-C
1 Techn 4th, Stock clerk-R
1 Techn 5th, Headquarters clerk-R
1 Pvt, Headquarters clerk-R
1 Pvt, Messenger-C
This group maintained all of the supply reports of the regiment, prepared and consolidated requisitions, records and receipts, and compiled the operating records and reports required by the supply officer. It worked under the direction of the staff sergeant, supply assistant, and, in the train bivouac, under the control of the service company commander. However one clerk (sometimes two) worked in the S-4 section of the regimental command post.

*2-22 – Receiving & Distributing Group
1 Mr Sgt, Supply-C
2 Pvts, Record clerk-R
1 Pvt, Light truck driver-R

Vehicles:
1 Truck, 2½-ton, cargo

*2-23 – Munition Group
1 Captain, Munition Officer-C
1 WO, Munition Assistant-C
1 Sgt, Ammunition-R

The captain, munition officer, was the assistant of the S-4 for all class V supplies. The class V supplies were ammunitions of all types, including chemicals, explosives, anti-tank and anti-personnel mines, fuses and detonators, and pyrotechnics. [2]

This group operated the regimental ammunition distributing point, and was charged to prepare and execute the ammunition plan. It could be furnished with a ¾-ton truck, WC, and an automobile mechanic as truck driver, assigned to company headquarters (*1-2).

Equipment of the Supply Section:

    1 luminous dial compass, with case (Off)
    1 binocular, M13 (Off)
    1 transparent map template, M2 (Off)
    1 grenade launcher, M7 (driver, *2-22)
    2 wristwatches, 7 jewels (Mr Sgt Sup, S Sgt Sup)
    2 wristwatches, 15 jewels (Off, WO on Theater of Operations)
    1 ammunition-carrying bag (grenade launcher)
    1 canvas dispatch case (Off)
    5 whistles, thunderer (Off, WO, Mr Sgt, S Sgt)
    1 stencil equipment with figures and letters, ½" and 1"
    1 shoe stretcher, new type (sizes 0, 1 and 2)
    1 commissary roll, complete (rolled up cover containing all material to prepare food rations)
    1 men's foot measuring outfit, M1943
    1 empty field desk, headquarters
    1 non-portable typewriter
    1 portable typewriter, with carrying case
    1 Command Post tent, complete, (added by C1, 30 June 1944)
    1 tent stove, M1941 (C1, 30 June 1944)
    1 oil burner for tent stove M1941 (C1, 30 June 1944)
    2 gasoline lanterns, two-mantle, commercial
    2 hand-portable electric lanterns
    1 panel set AP-50-A
    4 flashlights, TL-122-( ), (Off, Mr Sgt Supply, S Sgt, Light truck driver)

*3 – TRANSPORTATION PLATOON (5 Officers, 1 WO, 47 Enlisted Men)

The transportation platoon consisted of:
    Platoon Headquarters
    6 Transportation Sections, 1 per unit, i.e.: – 1 per Infantry Battalion
    1 for Headquarters Company
    1 for Cannon Company
    1 for Anti-tank Company.
    Maintenance Section (provided maintenance for all vehicles of the regiment)

The transportation platoon provided the vehicles that the units of the regiment needed for supply, these units possessing for themselves only those vehicles necessary for combat. For regimental supplies, it acted as the link between the higher-level formation (division) and subordinate units, particularly the 3 infantry battalions.

*3-1 – Platoon Headquarters

    1 Captain, Motor transport, Platoon Commander-C
    1 1st Lt, Platoon Commander assistant-C
    1 Mr Sgt, Motor-C
    1 Sgt, Ammunition-R
    1 Sgt, Truckmaster-R
    1 Pvt, Light truck driver-R

Vehicles:
    1 Truck, 2½-ton, cargo

Equipment:
    2 luminous dial compasses, with case (Off)
    2 wrist compasses, liquid-filled (Mr Sgt, driver)
    2 transparent map templates, M2 (Off)
    2 binoculars, M13 (Off)
    2 canvas dispatch cases (Off)
    1 grenade launcher, M7 (driver)
    2 wristwatches, 7 jewels (Mr Sgt Motor, Sgt Truckmaster)

2. AR 320-5, p. 479 (supplies).

2 wristwatches, 15 jewels (Off)
1 ammunition-carrying bag (grenade launcher)
1 panel set AP-50-A
1 crosscut saw, type L, 2-man, 6 feet
5 flashlights, TL-122-( ) (Off, Mr Sgt Motor, Sgt Truckmaster, driver)

The ammunition sergeant accompanied those parts of the ammunition train that were under regimental control, and carried out the orders of the munitions officer.

The truckmaster sergeant assisted in controlling the movement and operation of the regimental train. He accompanied parts of the kitchen and baggage train while they were under regimental control.

*3-2 – Battalion Section (× 3)

The transportation platoon had a transportation section for each infantry battalion within the regiment, i.e., the 1st, 2nd, 3rd battalion sections, which corresponded to the 1st, 2nd, and 3rd infantry battalions.

1 1st Lt, Supply, S-4-C
1 S Sgt, Supply-C
1 Cpl, Truckmaster, drove the ¼-ton truck-R
7 Pvts or Techns 5th, Light truck driver-R

Weapons:
2 MG, HB, M2, caliber .50, flexible

Vehicles:
1 Truck, ¼-ton
5 Trucks, 2½-ton, cargo, with winch
2 Trucks, 2½-ton, cargo, with winch and ring mount
5 Trailers, 1-ton

Equipment:
1 luminous dial compass, with case (Off)
8 wrist compasses, liquid-filled (Cpl Truckmaster, driver)
1 transparent map template, M2 (Off)
1 binocular, M13 (Off)
8 grenade launchers, M7 (1 per individual driving)
8 ammunition-carrying bags (1 per grenade launcher)
1 wristwatch, 7 jewels (S Sgt Sup)
1 wristwatch, 15 jewels (Off)
1 canvas dispatch case (Off)
2 panel sets AP-50-A
9 flashlights, TL-122-( ) (Off, Cpl Truckmaster, driver)

For the equipment of vehicles and drivers see the sections concerning vehicle equipment (9.2) and individual equipment (9.4).

The 1st lieutenant, section leader, was also the battalion supply officer, S-4, of the relevant infantry battalion. He prepared and executed the supply plan for the battalion and attached units.

The corporal, truckmaster, normally drove the ¼-ton truck. However, when the echelon of supply of the battalion was operating, the battalion supply sergeant could drive this vehicle.

*3-3 – Anti-tank Company Section

1 Techn 5th, Light truck driver-R

Weapons:
1 MG, HB, M2, caliber .50, flexible

Vehicles:
1 Truck, 2½-ton, cargo, with winch and ring mount
1 Trailer, 1-ton

Equipment:
1 wrist compass, liquid-filled
1 grenade launcher, M7
1 ammunition-carrying bag
1 panel set AP-50-A
1 flashlight, TL-122-( )

*3-4 – Cannon Company Section

1 Techn 5th or Pvt, Light truck driver-R

Weapons:
>   1 MG, HB, M2, caliber .50, flexible

Vehicles:
>   1 Truck, 2½-ton, cargo, with winch and ring mount
>   1 Trailer, 1-ton

Equipment:
>   1 wrist compass, liquid-filled
>   1 grenade launcher, M7
>   1 ammunition-carrying bag
>   1 panel set AP-50-A
>   1 flashlight, TL-122-( )

*3-5 – Headquarters Company Section

>   1 Techn 5th or Pvt, Light truck driver-R

Weapons:
>   1 MG, HB, M, caliber .50, flexible

Vehicles:
>   1 Truck, 2½-ton, cargo, with winch and ring mount

Equipment:
>   1 wrist compass, liquid-filled
>   1 grenade launcher, M7
>   1 ammunition-carrying bag
>   1 panel set AP-50-A
>   1 flashlight, TL-122-( )

*3-6 – Maintenance Section

>   1 WO, Motor transport-C
>   1 Techn 5th, Record clerk-R
>   5 Techns 4th, Mechanic, automobile-R
>   6 Techns 5th, Mechanic, automobile, 3 were drivers-R
>   1 Techn 4th, Welder general-R

Weapons:
>   1 MG, HB, M2, caliber .50, flexible

Vehicles:
>   1 Truck, ¼-ton
>   1 Truck, 2½-ton, cargo, with winch
>   1 Truck, 2½-ton, cargo, with winch and ring mount

Equipment:
>   3 wrist compasses, liquid-filled (Mech driving)
>   3 grenade launchers, M7 (1 per individual driving)
>   3 ammunition-carrying bags (1 per grenade launcher)
>   1 wristwatch, 15 jewels (WO, on Theater of Operations)
>   3 spare parts cabinets, type I, M1940
>   12 motor vehicles mechanics' tool set, (1 per Mechanic)
>   1 unit equipment tool set, 2nd echelon, set no. 2
>   1 unit equipment tool set, 2nd echelon, set no. 5
>   1 unit equipment tool set, 2nd echelon, set no. 7
>   1 Welders' tool set
>   11 flashlights, TL-122-( ), (Mechanic)

The warrant officer, assistant motor officer, was answerable to the motor officer (*3-1) for regimental maintenance of all motor vehicles of the regiment. This included maintenance of company transport not performed by companies (2nd echelon). The assistant motor officer could command the maintenance section on the orders of the captain, motor officer.

2.4 INFANTRY CANNON COMPANY
T/O&E 7-14

The cannon company was the direct artillery support of the infantry regiment. It was equipped with the same 105mm howitzers as the field artillery batteries (105mm) of the division's artillery that will be encountered later in this study. However, this company was organized by the infantry and was not identical to the artillery batteries. The cannon company was issued with six 105mm Howitzers, M3 (with M3 carriage), towed by 1½-ton cargo trucks, while a field artillery battery (T/O&E 6-27), had four 105mm howitzers, M2A1 (with M2A2 carriage), towed by 2½-ton trucks, short wheel base.

The cannon company was added to the triangular division on 1 April 1942, in order to reinforce the regiment with its own artillery support, and to assist the regiment when that artillery support furnished by the division artillery was unavailable. Army Ground Forces wanted to cancel it in March 1943, and instead add three cannon platoons to the regimental headquarters company. However, it remained, but with a different cannon (self-propelled guns in 1942, replaced by towed howitzers in 1943). Few divisions received their cannon companies before the reorganization of July 1943.

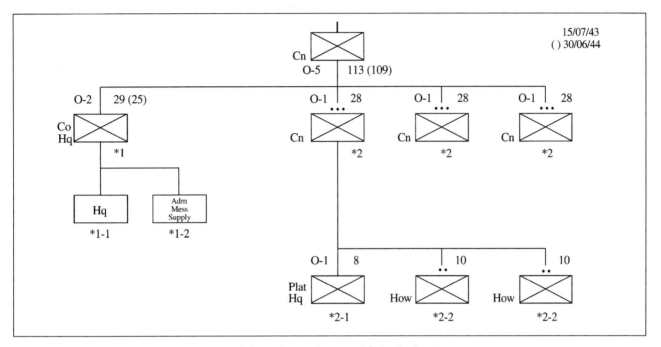

12. Infantry Cannon Company, Infantry Regiment

The cannon company consisted of:
    Company Headquarters
    3 Cannon Platoons
        2 Howitzer Sections

*1 – COMPANY HEADQUARTERS (2 Officers, 29 Enlisted Men)

*1-1 – Command Group

    1 Captain, Company Commander-C
    1 1st Lt, Reconnaissance, Second-in-Command-C
    1 1st Sgt-C
    1 S Sgt, Reconnaissance-C
    1 Sgt, Communication-C
    1 Sgt, Transportation-C
    1 Pvt, Bugler, drove a ¼-ton truck-C
    2 Pvts, Messenger, drove a ¼-ton truck-C
    1 Techn 5th, Light truck driver-R
    1 Techn 4th, Mechanic, automobile, drove the ¾-ton truck
    2 Pvts, Radiotelephone operator-C
    10 Pvts, Basic-R, (6 basics, C2, 30 June 1944)

*1-2 – Administration Group

  1 S Sgt, Mess-R
  1 S Sgt, Supply-R
  1 Cpl, Company clerk-R
  1 Techn 5th, Armorer-artificer-R
  1 Techn 4th, Cook-R
  1 Techn 5th, Cook-R
  2 Pvts, Cook's helper-R

Weapons:
  1 Rocket launcher, AT, 2.36″

Vehicles:
  3 Trucks, ¼-ton
  1 Truck, ¾-ton, WC
  1 Truck, 1½-ton, cargo

Equipment:
  1 drawing board, MG, with canvas case
  3 luminous dial compasses, with case (Off, S Sgt Rcn)
  7 wrist compasses, liquid-filled (1st Sgt, Sgt Trans, bugler, driver, mech, msgr)
  2 plastic semicircular protractors, MG, 10″ diameter, 1-mil graduation
  1 magnifying stereoscope, pocket
  2 transparent map templates, M2 (Off)
  4 binoculars, M13 (1 per Off, 1st Sgt, S Sgt Rcn)
  4 binoculars, M16 or M17
  11 ammunition-carrying bags (per grenade launcher and S Sgt Rcn)
  2 grenade launchers, M7 (1 per driver, per mechanic driving)
  8 grenade launchers, M8 (1 per Sgt Rcn, Sgt Com, bugler, messenger)
  1 truck mount, pedestal, M24A2, for MG (for ¾-ton truck, WC)
  1 hand pyrotechnic projector, M9
  8 wristwatches, 7 jewels (1st Sgt, S Sgt, Sgt, radiotelephone operator)
  2 wristwatches, 15 jewels (Off)
  1 motor vehicles mechanics' tool set (for Mechanic, auto)
  1 unit equipment tool set, 2nd echelon, set no. 1
  3 rocket-carrying bags, M6 (1 per Rocket launcher)
  3 axles RL-27-( )
  4 chest sets TD-3 (1 per 2 EE-8, 1 per BD-71)
  20 flashlights, TL-122-( ) (Off, 1st Sgt, S Sgt Mess, S Sgt Sup, Sgt Trans, bugler, driver, mech, msgr, radio set)
  4 headsets HS-30 (1 per 2 EE-8, 1 per BD-71)
  2 hand-portable electric lanterns
  1 maintenance equipment ME-40-( )
  1 maintenance kit ME-53 (per ME-40)
  4 microphones T-45 (1 per 2 EE-8, 1 per BD-71)
  13 panel sets AP-50-A (3 per company, 1 per 1½-ton and 2½-ton truck)
  2 radio sets SCR-300 (replace the SCR-511)
  12 reel equipments CE-11
  1 reel unit RL-31
  1 switchboard BD-71
  6 telephones EE-8-( )[3]
  14 tool equipments, TE-33 (knife TL-29, pliers TL-13) (1 pair Radio operator, CE-11)
  8 miles of wire W-130-A on reel DR-4
  3 miles of wire W-130-A on spool DR-8 (for use with equipment CE-11). The wire (wire W-130-A) could be replaced by WD-3-TT or W-130.

*2 – CANNON PLATOON (× 3) (1 Officer, 28 Enlisted Men)

*2-1 – Platoon Headquarters

  1 1st or 2nd Lt, Platoon Commander-C
  1 S Sgt (becomes Tech Sgt on 26 February 1944), Platoon-C
  1 Cpl, Agent-R (during combat, he was liaison with supported units; he assisted the Platoon Commander during

---

3. The parenthesis situated at the end of the designation of Signal Corps equipment signifies that it existed in several models. For example, EE-8 ( ) indicates that the equipment issued could be an EE-8-A or an EE-8-B.

his reconnaissance)
1 Pvt, Ammunition handler-C
1 Techn 4th, Mechanic, Artillery-R
1 Pvt, Messenger, drove the ¼-ton truck-C
1 Pvt (became Cpl with C1, 19 May 1944), Instrument operator-C (operated the fire-control equipment)
1 Pvt, Radiotelephone operator-C

Weapons:
1 MG, HB, M2, caliber .50, flexible
1 Rocket launcher, AT, 2.36"

Vehicles:
1 Truck, ¼-ton
1 Truck, 1½-ton, cargo
1 Trailer, 1-ton

Equipment:
1 drawing board, MG, with canvas case
3 luminous dial compasses, with case (1 per Off, Tech Sgt, Cpl Instrument)
1 wrist compass, liquid-filled (driver)
1 transparent map template, M2 (Off)
2 plastic semicircular protractors, MG, 10" diameter, 1-mil graduation
1 magnifying stereoscope, pocket
2 binoculars, M13 (1 per Off, Tech Sgt) 3 binoculars (C1, 19 May 1944, 1 added for the Cpl Instrument)
1 aiming circle, M1
1 rangefinder, M9A1
1 grenade launcher, M7
1 ammunition-carrying bag (grenade launcher)
1 truck mount, pedestal, M31, for MG, M2 (for ¼-ton truck)
1 hand pyrotechnic projector, M9
1 observation telescope, M4, M48 or M49
2 wristwatches, 7 jewels (1 per Tech Sgt, Radio operator)
1 wristwatch, 15 jewels (Off)
3 rocket-carrying bags, M6 (for Rocket launcher)
2 whistles, thunderer (Off, S Sgt)
6 flashlights, TL-122-( ) (1 per Officer, Tech Sgt, driver and radio set)
1 radio set SCR-300-( ) (replaced SCR-511), 2 radio sets (C1, 19 May 1944)
1 tool equipment, TE-33 (knife TL-29, pliers TL-13) (for Radio operator)

*2-2 – Howitzer Section (× 2)

1 Sgt, Chief of Section-R
1 Cpl, Gunner-C
7 Pvts, Cannoneers-C
1 Techn 5th, Light truck driver-R

Weapons:
1 Howitzer 105 mm M3, with carriage M3

Vehicles:
1 Truck, 1½-ton, cargo

Equipment:
2 luminous dial compasses, with case (Sgt, Cpl)
1 wrist compass, liquid-filled (driver)
1 camouflage net, twine, fabric garnished, 29 × 29' (for howitzer)
2 binoculars, M13 (Sgt, Cpl)
1 grenade launcher, M7 (driver)
1 ammunition-carrying bag (grenade launcher)
1 wristwatch, 7 jewels (Sgt)
1 single bit axe, handled, standard guard, weight 4 lbs
1 handled pick, railroad, 6 to 7 lbs
1 round point shovel, no. 2, D-handled, GP
1 whistle, thunderer (Sgt)
2 flashlights, TL-122-( ) (Chief of Section, driver)
On 1 June 1945, this table was renamed T/O&E 7-14-OS.

2.5 INFANTRY ANTI-TANK COMPANY
T/O&E 7-19

The anti-tank defence of the regiment was provided mainly by the infantry anti-tank company. Each infantry battalion had, for its own protection, an anti-tank platoon, which was assigned to the battalion headquarters company. The other means of protection against tanks was the rocket launcher (bazooka), with which all units were equipped.

In March 1943, Army Ground Forces had requested the removal of the mine platoon in its proposed reorganization. The War Department decided to preserve it. Instead of losing one-third of its strength from the table of 1 August 1942, the company lost only four men in the reorganization of July 1943. The 57mm anti-tank guns replaced the 37mm from this date.

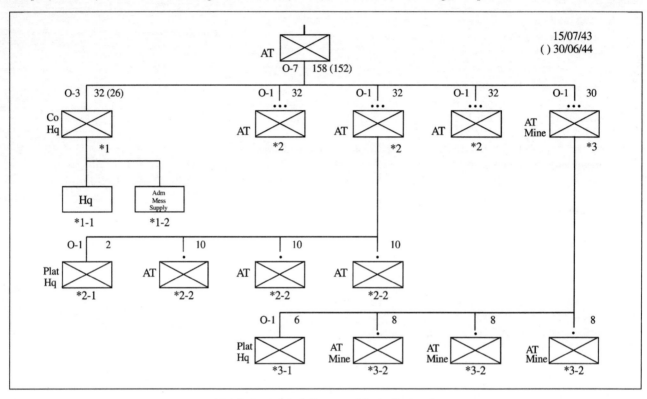

13. Infantry Anti-tank Company, Infantry Regiment

The anti-tank company consisted of:
    Company Headquarters
    3 Anti-tank Platoons
        Platoon Headquarters
        3 Anti-tank Squads
    1 Anti-tank Mine Platoon
        Platoon Headquarters
        3 Anti-tank Mine Squads

*1 – COMPANY HEADQUARTERS (3 Officers, 32 Enlisted Men (26 EM, C1, 30 June 1944)

*1-1 – Command Group

    1 Captain, Company Commander-C
    1 1st Lt, Executive-C
    1 2nd Lt, Reconnaissance-C
    1 1st Sgt-C
    1 Sgt, Communication-C
    1 Sgt, Reconnaissance-C
    1 Pvt, Bugler, drove the ¾-ton truck, WC, radio-C
    1 Techn 4th, Mechanic, automobile, drove the ¾-ton truck, WC, maintenance-R
    2 Pvts, Messenger, drove the ¼-ton trucks-C
    1 Techn 4th, Radio operator (740)-R
    1 Techn 5th, Radio operator (776)-R
    14 Pvts, Basic-R (8 Basics, C1, 30 June 1944)

*1-2 – Administration Group

1 S Sgt, Mess-C
1 S Sgt, Supply-C
1 Sgt, Transportation-R
1 Cpl, Company clerk, classification specialist-R
1 Techn 5th, Armorer-artificer-R
1 Techn 4th, Cook-R
2 Techns 5th, Cook-R
1 Pvt, Cook's helper-R

Vehicles:
2 Trucks, ¼-ton
1 Truck, ¾-ton, WC, with winch (Maintenance)
1 Truck, ¾-ton, WC, without winch (Radio)
1 Truck, 1½-ton, cargo (added to the table dated 26 February 1944). A member of an anti-tank platoon, designated by the company commander, drove it.

Equipment:
4 luminous dial compasses, with case (1 per Off, Sgt Rcn)
6 wrist compasses, liquid-filled (1st Sgt, Sgt T, bugler, driver, mech, msgr)
1 plastic semicircular protractor, MG
1 magnifying stereoscope, pocket
5 binoculars, M13 (Off, 1st Sgt, Sgt Rcn)
3 binoculars, M16 or M17 (M17, C2, 29 January 1945)
3 transparent map templates, M2 (1 per Off)
24 radioactive luminous markers, type II (C1, 30 June 1944)
1 grenade launcher, M7 (mech)
5 grenade launchers, M8 (Sgt Rcn, Sgt Com, bglr, msgr)
6 ammunition-carrying bags (1 per grenade launcher)
2 truck mounts, pedestal, M24A2 (1 per ¾-ton truck)
1 hand pyrotechnic projector, M9
8 wristwatches, 7 jewels (1st Sgt, Sgt Mess, Sgt Supply, Sgt Com, Sgt Rcn, Sgt T, Rad Opr)
3 wristwatches, 15 jewels (Off)
1 motor vehicles mechanics' tool set (mech)
1 unit equipment tool set, 2nd echelon, set no. 1
1 carpenters' tool set, complete, no. 2
1 gasoline lantern, two mantle, commercial
17 flashlights, TL-122-( ) (Off, 1st Sgt, S Sgt, Sgt T, bugler, cook's helper, driver, mech, messenger, 1 per radio set)
9 whistles, thunderer (Off, 1st Sgt, S Sgt, Sgt)
1 holder M-167 (per radio set SCR-694 or SCR-284)
1 maintenance equipment ME-40-( )
1 maintenance kit ME-53 (per ME-40)
3 panel sets AP-50-A
1 radio set SCR-300-( ) (replaces SCR-511)
1 radio set SCR-694-( ) (replaces SCR-284)
12 reel equipments CE-11
1 remote control unit RM-29 (for radio set SCR-694), replaced by remote control equipment RC-290 (C1, 30 June 1944)
14 tool equipments, TE-33 (knife TL-29, pliers TL-13) (1 per reel equipment CE-11, Rad Opr)
3 miles of wire W-130-A on spool DR-8 (for use with equipments CE-11)
1 converter M-209 (C1, 30 June 1944)
1 demolition equipment, set no. 5 (C2, 29 January 1945)
5 vibrator power supplies PE-212-( ) (1 per SCR-300) (C2, 29/01/45)

*2 – ANTI-TANK PLATOON (× 3) (1 Officer, 32 Enlisted Men)

*2-1 – Platoon Headquarters

1 1st or 2nd Lt, Platoon Commander-C
1 S Sgt, Platoon-C (became Tech Sgt, T/O&E dated 26 February 1944)
1 Pvt, Messenger, drove the ¼-ton truck-R

Weapons:
1 MG, HB, M2, caliber .50, flexible

Vehicles:

    1 Truck, ¼-ton

Equipment:

    2 luminous dial compasses, with case (Off, Techn Sgt)

    1 wrist compass, liquid-filled (messenger)

    1 transparent map template, M2 (Off)

    2 plastic semicircular protractors, MG, 10″ diameter, 1-mil graduation

    1 magnifying stereoscope, pocket

    2 binoculars, M13 (Off, T Sgt)

    1 hand pyrotechnic projector, M9

    1 wristwatch, 7 jewels (Techn Sgt)

    1 wristwatch, 15 jewels (Off)

    2 whistles, thunderer (Off, Techn Sgt)

    4 flashlights, TL-122-( ) (1 per individual, radio set)

    1 radio set SCR-300-( )

*2-2 – Anti-tank Squad (×3)

    1 Sgt (S Sgt, 26 February 1944), Squad Leader-R

    1 Cpl, Gunner-P

    3 Pvts, Ammunition bearer-C

    4 Pvts, Cannoneer-P

    1 Techn 5th, Light truck driver, Ammunition bearer-R

Weapons:

    1 Gun, AT, 57mm, M1, towed, with carriage M1A3

    1 Rocket launcher, AT, 2.36″

Vehicles:

    1 Truck, 1½-ton, cargo, with winch

Equipment:

    2 goggles (red lens) M1943, replaced amber lens M1 or red M2

    1 binocular, M13 (S Sgt)

    1 grenade launcher, M7 (driver)

    1 ammunition-carrying bag (grenade launcher)

    1 handled pick, railroad, 6-7lbs

    5 drag ropes, with shoulder strap, M1918 (6 ropes, C1, 30 June 1944)

    1 crosscut saw, type L, 2-man, 6-feet

    1 round point shovel, no. 2, D-handled, GP

    2 flashlights, TL-122-( ) (Squad Leader, driver)

    1 whistle, thunderer (S Sgt)

*3 – ANTI-TANK MINE PLATOON (1 Officer, 30 Enlisted Men)

*3-1 – Platoon Headquarters

    1 1st or 2nd Lt, Platoon Commander-C

    1 S Sgt (Techn Sgt, 26 February 1944), Platoon-C

    1 Techn 5th, Topographic Draftsman-C

    3 Techns 5th or Pvt, Light truck driver-R

    1 Techn 4th, Surveyor-C

Vehicles:

    1 Truck, ¼-ton

    2 Trucks, 1½-ton, cargo, with winch

    2 Trailers, 1-ton

Equipment:

    4 luminous dial compasses, with case (1 per Off, 3 per Platoon)

    3 wrist compasses, liquid-filled, (drivers)

    9 mine probes, M1

    2 plastic semicircular protractors, MG, 10″ diameter, 1-mil graduation

    1 sketching equipment, set no. 1

    1 metallic woven tape, U.S., 50′

    2 binoculars, M13 (Officer, T Sgt)

    1 aiming circle, M1

3 grenade launchers, M7 (drivers)
1 hand pyrotechnic projector, M9
1 wristwatch, 7 jewels (Techn Sgt)
1 wristwatch, 15 jewels (Officer)
1 transparent map template, M2 (Off)
3 ammunition-carrying bags (1 per grenade launcher)
6 flashlights, TL-122-( ) (Off, T Sgt, driver, radio posts)
1 radio set SCR-300-( )
2 whistles, thunderer (Off, S Sgt)

*3-2 – Anti-tank Mine Squad (× 3)

1 Sgt, Squad leader-R
7 Pvts, Pioneer-R

Equipment:

1 single-bit axe, handled, chopping, standard grade, 4lb
1 handled pick, railroad, 6-7lbs
12 round point shovels, no. 2, D-handled, GP
3 detector sets, SCR-625-( )
1 flashlight, TL-122-( ) (Squad Leader)
1 whistle, thunderer (Sgt)

Data drawn from the tables dated 15 July 1943 and 26 February 1944, and from changes no. 1 (C1) dated 30 June 1944, and no. 2 (C2) dated 29 January 1945. The table was renamed, on 1 June 1945: T/O&E 7-19-OS.

2.6 MEDICAL DETACHMENT, INFANTRY REGIMENT
T/O&E 7-11

The medical detachment, infantry regiment, was a unit of the Medical Corps attached to the infantry regiment.

The division had two medical echelons. The medical detachment or attached medical (both terms were used) of a unit was the first echelon. Thus, the medical detachment, which is examined in this section, was the first echelon, i.e., first aid. Each battalion that did not belong to a regiment (i.e. was independent), had a medical detachment (the engineer battalion and all field artillery battalions). Division artillery also had a medical detachment. The medical detachments were attached to units before departing overseas. In the Continental U.S. they were attached to units only if the personnel was available.

The second echelon was the medical battalion assigned to the division (division level). It will be examined in chapter 8. It undertook the evacuation of casualties from unit aid stations to a higher level of medical support.

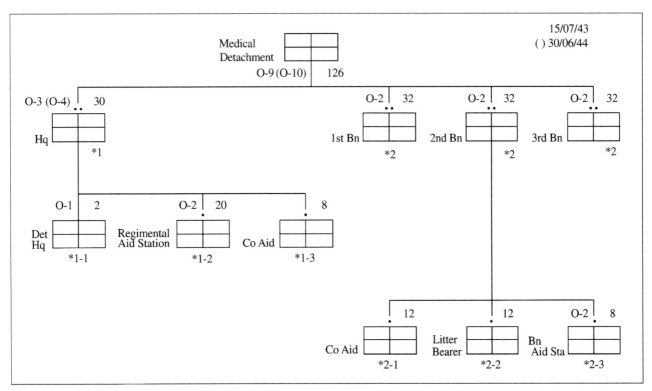

14. Medical Detachment, Infantry Regiment

The first echelon medical support (unit-level medical support), undertook:
>   preventive medicinal activities within the unit
>   acquisition of the sick and wounded
>   emergency medical treatments
>   evacuation to the nearest aid station

These were the capabilities of the medics or aid men who were with the combat platoons, and the soldiers who manned the battalion aid stations.

The first echelon medical support was often accomplished under enemy fire and would be the first medical treatment received by a wounded soldier.

The medical detachment, infantry regiment, was composed of:
>   Headquarters Section
>   3 Battalion Sections

The battalion sections were subordinate to the medical detachment. However, on the march, in bivouac, in combat and as soon as the battalion operated independently, they were attached to their respective battalion.

When the battalion sections joined their respective battalions, they were under the command of the battalion surgeon who was answerable to the battalion commander (see T/O&E 7-15, *1). As a member of the regimental headquarters, the regimental surgeon exercised only technical supervision over the battalion sections when they were attached to their battalions; on the other hand he retained the control of the headquarters section.

*1 – HEADQUARTERS SECTION (3 Officers, 30 Enlisted Men)

*1-1 – Detachment Headquarters

>   1 Major, MC, Detachment Commander, Regimental Surgeon
>   1 Captain, Medical General Duty (C1, 30 June 1944)
>   1 Tech Sgt, Medical (acting as 1st Sgt)
>   1 Techn 5th, Record clerk, drove the ¼-ton truck

Vehicles:
>   1 Truck, ¼-ton
>   1 Trailer, ¼-ton

*1-2 – Regimental Aid Station Squad

>   1 Captain or 1st Lt, DC, commanded the Headquarters Section, Regimental Dental Surgeon
>   1 Captain or 1st Lt, DC, Regimental Dental Surgeon Assistant
>   1 Sgt, Medical
>   1 Techn 4th, Podiatrist
>   2 Techns 5th, Dental technician
>   1 Techn 5th, Medical technician
>   2 Techns 3rd, Surgical technician
>   1 Techn 5th, Light truck driver
>   1 Pvt, Sanitary technician
>   11 Pvts, Basics

Vehicles:
>   1 Truck, 2½-ton, cargo

The regimental aid station squad took care of all regimental units that did not belong to a battalion, or did not serve in its zone of action. It was used frequently to provide first aid to the units held in regimental reserve until they were committed. It permitted the battalion section (* 2) of the reserve battalion to preserve its mobility.

The personnel of the regimental aid station squad could be assigned to battalion sections (* 2) as reinforcements or replacements.

*1-3 – Company Aid Squad

The squad contained 8 company aid men, also called medics when in the field:
>   1 Techn 3rd, Surgical technician
>   3 Techns 4th, Surgical technician
>   2 Techns 5th, Surgical technician
>   2 Pvts, Surgical technician.

The squad detached:
>   3 company aid men to the anti-tank company
>   3 company aid men to the cannon company
>   1 company aid man to the headquarters company
>   1 company aid man to the service company

The company aid men were to maintain contact with the company to which they were assigned. They were to give first aid to the injured and wounded soldiers, and place them in a position so as to be found by litter bearers. Then, they were to inform the nearest aid station regarding the wounded who were sent to it. They were to show the walking wounded the location of the aid station and the route to take to it. They sent to the surgeon of the aid station responsible for the wounded that were to be evacuated, information about the combat zone, the number of losses and the locations where the wounded could be found. These messages were routed by the litter bearers or by walking wounded.

Equipment of the Headquarters Section:
    1 gas proof curtain, M1
    5 wrist compasses, liquid-filled, with case (1 per Off, Tech Sgt, Sgt) (6 compasses with C1, 30 June 1944)
    3 transparent map templates, M2 (Off) (4 with C1, 30 June 1944)
    33 brassards, Geneva Convention, Red Cross (1 per individual)
    2 dental kits, Officer (1 per Dental Officer)
    2 dental kits, Private (1 per Dental technician)
    2 medical kits, NCO (1 per Tech Sgt, Sgt)
    1 medical kit, Officer (Major); 2 medical kits, Officer with C1, 30 June 1944 (Major, Captain)
    26 medical kits, Private (Privates technicians, except Dental technicians)
    1 tent pin case
    1 chest, MD, no. 1 (MD: Medical Department Field Equipment)
    1 chest, MD, no. 2
    1 chest, MD, no. 4
    1 chest, MD, no. 60 (for Dental Officer)
    6 straight steel litters
    2 imprinting machines
    1 small blanket set
    1 gas casualties' equipment, M2
    1 lantern set
    1 splint set
    1 binocular, M13
    3 packboard attachments, cargo (6 attachments with C1, 30 June 1944)
    1 canvas water sterilizing bag, complete with cover and hanger (+2, if authorized by the Commander of the Theater of Operations)
    3 galvanized buckets, General Purpose, without lip, 14-qt
    1 oil burners for tent stove M1941
    1 canvas dispatch case (Off)
    1 flag, Geneva Convention, Red Cross
    1 gasoline lantern, two-mantle, commercial
    3 packboards, plywood (C1, 30 June 1944, if authorized by the Commander of the Theater of Operations)
    1 tent stove M1941
    6 packboard quick-release straps (2 per packboard), (+2, C1, 30 June 1944, if authorized)
    1 Command Post tent, complete
    2 hand-portable electric lanterns (1 lantern with C1, 30 June 1944)
    2 cooking outfits, 1-burner (1 per 12 men)
    7 flashlights, TL-122-( ) (Officers, Tech Sgt, Sgt, drivers, chest MD no. 2) (8 flashlights, TL-122, C1, 30 June 1944)
    5 whistles, thunderer (Off, T Sgt, S Sgt, Sgt) (6 whistles, C1, 30 June 1944)
    1 hand-portable electric lantern, CP (C1, 30 June 1944)
    1 sphygmomanometer (C1, 30 June 1944)
    2 goggles with clear lens, M1943 (drivers, outside the U.S.A., if authorized by the Commander of the Theater of Operations)
    31 goggles with green lens, M1943 (other personnel, outside the U.S.A., if authorized by the Commander of the Theater of Operations) (32 goggles, C1, 30 June 1944)
Each chest, MD, included medicines, bandaging and technical equipment. This equipment was sufficient to provide essential medical, dental and surgical care, for one day of combat.

Tents provided, for every aid station, the necessary protection against the inclement weather. They were employed only when they could be concealed from ground and air view.

*2 – BATTALION SECTION (× 3, 1 per Infantry Battalion) (2 Officers, 32 Enlisted Men)

*2-1 – Company Aid Squad
The squad comprised 12 company aid men:
    2 Techns 4th, Surgical technician
    5 Techns 5th, Surgical technician
    5 Pvts, Surgical technician

The squad detached:

    1 company aid man per rifle platoon of each rifle company
    1 company aid man per platoon of the heavy weapons company.

The company aid men were attached to the company when it was on the march, in bivouac, or in combat. These men carried two bags with suspenders, which contained the equipment for emergency treatments: bandaging, tourniquets and instruments (medical kit). They were not provided with a litter.

*2-2 – Litter Bearer Squad

    12 Pvts, Litter bearer (organized into three teams of 4)

The litter bearers were sent to join the company aid men when the combat began, to bring back seriously wounded soldiers within the zone under the responsibility of the aid station. They gave first aid to the wounded whom the company aid men overlooked. The litter bearer squad was also used to help the aid station squad to transport its equipment when necessary.

Casualties were numerous in the litter bearer squads. Replacement and reinforcement during combat was essential. It was one of the duties of the regimental surgeon to provide replacements and reinforcements to the battalion sections. The regimental surgeon used, as reinforcements, the personnel of the headquarters section; he could also request additional reinforcements from the regimental commander. The regimental commander would consider the immediate needs of the men in combat and compared it with the need for a fast evacuation of wounded. He decided whether it would possible, or not, to send infantrymen as reinforcements to the medical detachment, to help evacuate wounded from the battlefield.

According to the international laws of war, prisoners of war could be requisitioned to transport their own wounded toward the aid station.

*2-3 – Battalion Aid Station

    1 Captain or 1st Lt, Medical General Duty
    1 Captain or 1st Lt, Medical General Duty (cancelled by C1, 30 June 1944) replaced by: 1st Lt, Medical Assistant, MAC
    1 S Sgt, Medical
    1 Cpl, Medical
    2 Techns 3rd, Surgical technician
    1 Techn 4th, Medical technician
    1 Techn 5th, Medical technician
    2 Pvts, Medical technician, drove the ¼-ton trucks

Vehicles:

    2 Trucks, ¼-ton (1 truck, C1, 30 June 1944)
    2 Trailers, ¼-ton (1 Trailer, C1)
    1 Truck, ¾-ton, WC (C1)

The captain, Medical Corps (MC), was the battalion surgeon, his duties being identical to those of the regimental surgeon. Before combat, he recommended the location of the battalion aid station to the battalion commander. When combat began and casualties accumulated, he supervised the battalion aid station and assisted in the care of casualties. He was also to keep himself constantly informed of changes in the tactical situation, maintaining close contact with the infantry battalion.

The captain or first lieutenant, MC, was the battalion surgeon assistant. His first duty was to take care of non-combat illnesses and injuries. This duty was cancelled by the C1 dated 30 June 1944, to the T/O&E dated 26 February 1944. He was replaced by a first lieutenant, Medical Administration Corps, whose duties were different, as he was not a physician. [4]

The staff sergeant, medical, supervised all enlisted personnel of the battalion section and was also the section supply sergeant. He assisted in the care of the casualties.

The corporal, medical, was in charge of sterilizing instruments, and administering hypodermic medications. He also assisted in the treatment of casualties.

Equipment of the Battalion Section:

    1 gas proof curtain, M1
    3 wrist compasses, liquid-filled (Off, S Sgt)
    2 transparent map templates, M2 (Off)
    34 brassards, Geneva Convention, Red Cross (1 per individual)

---

4. When the 1st Lt, MAC, were assigned to the divisions in July and August 1944, they did not have a well-defined duty. Fred P. Body, who was one of them, relates, "In July, 1944, I was transferred from a hospital to a replacement unit to be assigned to an infantry division as a MAC officer. There were about 30 of us who were assigned to various divisions at that time. I was assigned to the 2nd Battalion, 2nd Infantry Aid Station. At that time there were two doctors, both captains. There was no written list of duties available for a 2nd Lt. MAC assigned to a battalion aid station. As a result, it was decided that I could be of most assistance by leading the driver and litter bearers in picking up the wounded from the battlefield. Shortly thereafter, captains Stevenson and Dion were re-assigned and replace by Captain Richard Snipes (consistent with T/O&E 7-11). As time went on, in addition to my duties in collecting the casualties from the battlefield, I would precede the unit and find a location for our next aid station." (Letter of 17 October 1995 from Fred P. Body, at this time National Secretary of The Society of the Fifth Division).

2 medical kits, NCO (S Sgt, Cpl)

2 medical kits, Officer (1 per Officer)

30 medical kits, Privates

1 chest, MD, no. 2

12 straight steel litters

2 imprinting machines

1 gas casualties set, M2

2 unit medical equipment packs, the pack comprised 1 tent pin case, 2 small blanket sets, 2 chests, MD, no. 1, 2 splint sets

1 canvas water sterilizing bag, complete with cover and hanger

2 galvanized buckets, General Purpose, without lip, 14-qt

1 oil burner for tent stove M1941 (for tent)

1 canvas dispatch case

2 flags, Geneva Convention, Red Cross

1 gasoline lantern, two-mantle, commercial

1 tent stove, M1941, for tent

1 tent, Command Post, complete

2 hand-portable electric lanterns (1 lantern, C1, 30 June 1944)

3 cooking outfits, 1-burner (gasoline cooking stove, M1942, 1-burner with mountain cookset, 1 per 12 men)

6 flashlights, TL-122-( ) (Off, drivers, S Sgt, Cpl, 1 per chest MD no. 2)

3 whistles, thunderer (Off, S Sgt)

2 portable electric lamps, Command Post (1 lamp, C1)

1 sphygmomanometer, aneroid (C1)

2 goggles, M1943, clear lens (drivers, outside the U.S.A., if authorized by the Commander of the Theater of Operations)

32 goggles, M1943, green lens (other personnel, outside the U.S.A., if authorized by the Commander of the Theater of Operations)

With the medical detachment, we finish the survey of the support and service units of the infantry regiment. Chapter 3 discusses the combat units, the infantry battalions. The following sections give the organization of the personnel of the infantry regiment and of the infantry battalions within the command post and the train bivouac.

2.7 COMMAND POST, INFANTRY REGIMENT

The command post, infantry regiment, had the same function within the regiment, as the divisional command post already encountered in chapter 1, section 1.2, had within the division. Like this, the regimental command post had two echelons, a forward and a rear echelon. Administration and supply were located in the train bivouac, of which administrative elements worked in the rear echelon, at divisional level.

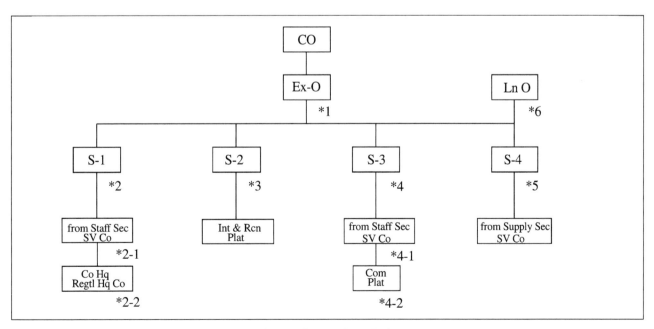

15. Command Post, Infantry Regiment

The following sections formed the command post, infantry regiment:

*1 COMMAND (T/O&E 7-11, *A)
Regimental Commander, Commanding Officer (CO) of the Command Post
Executive-Officer (Ex-O)
S-1, S-2, S-3, S-4 (each of them commanded a section)

*2 S-1 SECTION

*2-1: from the Staff Section, Service Company (T/O&E 7-13, *2-1)
Regimental Adjutant Assistant, WO (*2-11)
Regimental Sergeant Major, Mr Sgt (*2-11)
2 Headquarters clerks, Techn 4th, Techn 5th (*2-11)
1 Messenger, Pvt (*2-11)

*2-2: from the Company Headquarters (*1), Regimental Headquarters Company (T/O&E 7-12)
The Command Group (*1-1)
Supply Sergeant, S Sgt (*1-2)

*3 S-2 SECTION [5]
Intelligence & Reconnaissance Platoon (*3), Regimental Headquarters Company (T/O&E 7-12)
The platoon undertook reconnaissance in the field except for the following personnel who remained at the headquarters.
Platoon Intelligence Sergeant, Tech Sgt
Topographic Draftsman, Techn 5th
2 Scouts, observer, intelligence, Pvts

*4 S-3 SECTION
*4-1 from the Staff Section (*2-1), Service Company T/O&E 7-13)
Operations Sergeant, Mr Sgt (*2-11)
1 Headquarters clerk, Techn 4th (*2-11)
Stenographer, Techn 4th (*2-11)
*4-2 The Communication Platoon (*3), Regimental Headquarters Company

*5 S-4 SECTION
Assistant Supply Officer, WO (T/O&E 7-13, *1-1)
2 Headquarters clerks, techn 5th, Pvt (T/O&E 7-13, *2-21)

*6 LIAISON OFFICERS
3 Liaison Officers (T/O&E 7-11, *A)

For equipment, see the section concerning the relevant unit.

2.8   TRAIN BIVOUAC, INFANTRY REGIMENT

The train bivouac gathered all personnel who were neither combatants, nor necessary for command post duties. It included the necessary personnel for administration, supply, mess, and regimental transportation. The personnel came, as we shall see, from all units of the regiment.

The train bivouac was commanded by the company commander of the service company (T/O&E 7-13), and consisted of:

*1 from Company Headquarters, Regimental Headquarters Company (T/O&E 7-12, *1-2):
Mess Sergeant, S Sgt
Company clerk, Cpl
Armorer-artificer, Techn 5th
3 Cooks, Techn 4th, 2 Techns 5th
1 Cook's helper, Pvt

*2 from Company Headquarters, Cannon Company (T/O&E 7-14, *1-2):
Mess Sergeant, S Sgt
Company clerk, Cpl
Armorer-artificer, Techn 5th
2 Cooks, 1 Techn 4th, 1 Techn 5th
2 Cook's helpers, Pvt

*3 from Company Headquarters, Anti-tank Company (T/O&E 7-19, *1-2):
Mess Sergeant, S Sgt
Company clerk, Cpl

---

5. Correspondence with Leo H. Eberhardt, in command of the Intelligence & Reconnaissance Platoon, 11th Infantry Regiment, then of the Headquarters Company, 11th Infantry.

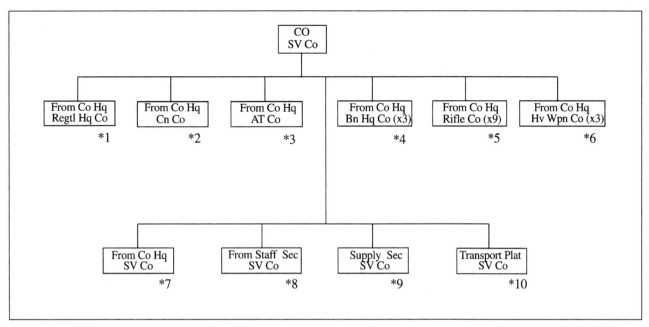

16. Train Bivouac, Infantry Regiment

Armorer-artificer, Techn 5th
3 Cooks, 1 Techn 4th, 2 Techns 5th
2 Cook's helpers, Pvt

*4 from Company Headquarters, Battalion Headquarters Company (TO&E 7-16, *2-2), from each battalion:
Mess Sergeant, S Sgt
Company clerk, Cpl
Armorer-artificer, Techn 5th
3 Cooks, 2 Techns 4th, Techn 5th
1 Cook's helper, Pvt

*5 from Company Headquarters, Rifle Company (T/O&E 7-17, *1-2), from each company (9 companies – A, B, C, E, F, G, I, K, L):
Mess Sergeant, S Sgt
Company Clerk, Cpl
Armorer-artificer, Techn 5th
4 Cooks, 2 Techns 4th, 2 Techns 5th
1 Cook's helper, Pvt

*6 from Company Headquarters, Heavy Weapons Company (T/O&E 7-18, *1-2), from each company (3 companies – D, H, M):
Mess Sergeant, S Sgt
Company clerk, Cpl
Armorer-artificer, Techn 5th
3 Cooks, 2 Techns 4th, 1 Techn 5th
2 Cook's helpers, Pvt

*7 from Company Headquarters, Service Company (TO&E 7-13, *1-1):
Company Commander, Captain, Commanding Officer of the Train Bivouac
First Sergeant
Bugler, Pvt
Messenger, Pvt
9 Basics, Pvt
These personnel were from the command group (*1-1) of the service company and organized the command group within the train bivouac. The following personnel were from the administration group (*1-2) and had the same duties as the personnel of the train bivouac (*1 to *6, above):
Mess Sergeant, S Sgt
Company clerk, Cpl
Armorer-artificer, Techn 5th
Carpenter, Pvt
2 Cooks, 1 Techn 4th, 1 Techn 5th

Light truck driver, Pvt
3 Automobile mechanics, 2 Techns 4th, 1 Techn 5th

*8 from Staff Section, Service Company (T/O&E 7-13, *2-1)

*8-1 The entire Administration Group (*2-12), i.e.:
Personnel Officer, Captain †
Personnel Sergeant, Tech Sgt †
3 Assistants to Chaplains, Techns 5th †
Headquarters clerk, Techn 4th †
Personnel clerk, Techn 4th †
Record clerk, Techn 4th †
3 Mail clerks, 1 Techn 4th, 2 Techns 5th

*8-2 from Special Service Group (*2-13):
Special Service Officer, Captain
Athletic instructor, Techn 5th
Entertainment director, Techn 5th

The personnel denoted with a †, were in the personnel section, which could be concentrated at division level, under the supervision of the adjutant general (G-1). The personnel of the mail section could operate with, or next to, the personnel section.

*9 The entire Supply Section (*2-2), from Regimental Headquarters Platoon (*2), of the Service Company (T/O&E 7-13). The Supply Section included:
Supply Office Group (*2-21)
Receiving & Distributing Group (*2-22)
Munition Group (*2-23)

*10 included the entire Transportation Platoon (*3), Service Company (T/O&E 7-13). The Transportation Platoon comprised:
Platoon Headquarters (*3-1)
Battalion Section (*3-2), 1 section per Infantry Battalion †
Anti-tank Company Section (*3-3)
Cannon Company Section (*3-4)
Headquarters Company Section (*3-5)
Maintenance Section (*3-6)

† The battalion section commander (*3-2), who was also S-4 of the infantry battalion, and his assistant, the battalion supply sergeant, operated from the command post, infantry battalion (chapter 3, section 3.4).

To locate the personnel in the relevant unit, the number of the T/O&E and the sub-unit number within all sections of the command post and the train bivouac has been given.

CHAPTER 3

INFANTRY BATTALION
T/O&E 7-15

The infantry battalion was the manoeuvre unit of the infantry regiment. The division contained nine infantry battalions assigned to three infantry regiments (see charts 1 and 8).

In chapter 1 it was noted that the envelopment was considered by the U.S. Army as the best method of attack, but for a battalion-sized unit the method generally employed was the penetration. The unity of the battalion was seldom broken on the part of the front to which it was assigned. The battalion fought intact, with all of its companies.

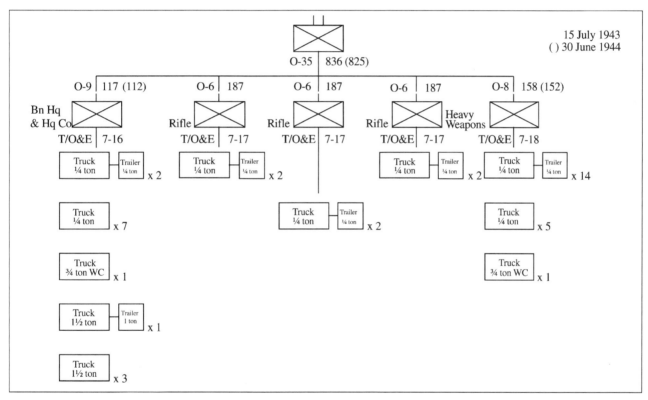

17. Infantry Battalion

Two companies formed the attacking echelon, the remainder made up the support echelon, at least during the initial phase of the attack. One of the three battalions was initially kept as regimental reserve. If the action undertaken did not justify the commitment of this entire reserve battalion, one or two companies could be attached to one battalion of the attacking echelon.

In the part of the front to which it was assigned, a battalion seldom had the necessary space for an attack by envelopment to be conducted by its companies. The battalion commander would therefore choose a penetration. When an envelopment was necessary, it would be made only in coordination with the adjacent units, so that operations could be undertaken in their zones of action.

After a survey of the battalion, chapter 4 will discuss the doctrine of the infantry, one of the sections treating of the attack by the rifle platoons of the rifle company.

The infantry battalion is shown in chart 17; the type and the number of vehicles in each part of the battalion are indicated. It can be seen that the number of vehicles did not permit the unit to be mobile, even less motorized. A battalion disposed of only 40 vehicles for 871 men. In particular, the rifle companies had only two ¼-ton trucks with trailers. These vehicles served mainly for transporting the company ammunition and food supply. The heavy weapons company possessed more vehicles. These were used to supply its heavy weapons and transport them quickly in case of need. The supplies of the battalion were transported by the 2½-ton cargo trucks of the battalion section (*3-2), of the transportation platoon (*3), service company (T/O&E 7-13).

Data concerning the battalion's units comes from the T/O&Es dated 15 July 1943 and 26 February 1944. Changes are shown in the text as previously noted. All tables were renamed on 1 June 1945, -OS, e.g.: for the infantry battalion: T/O&E 7-15-OS. This is valid for sections 3.1, 3.2 and 3.3 of this chapter.

3.1   HEADQUARTERS AND HEADQUARTERS COMPANY, INFANTRY BATTALION
T/O&E 7-16

The headquarters company of the infantry battalion also included the battalion headquarters. The headquarters was not considered important enough to be differentiated from the headquarters company. The company was designated 'headquarters and headquarters company', the first headquarters designated representing the battalion staff. The headquarters company, infantry battalion is shown in chart 18. It included:

Battalion Headquarters
Company Headquarters
Battalion Headquarters Section
Ammunition & Pioneer Platoon
Communication Platoon
Anti-tank Platoon

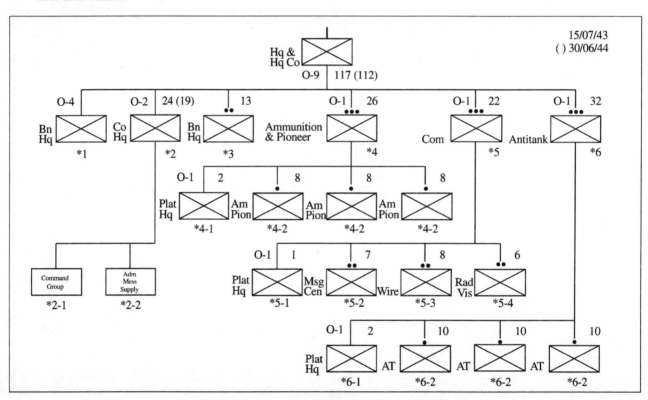

18. Headquarters & Headquarters Company, Infantry Battalion

Again, the personnel necessary for company duties in company headquarters and those necessary for operating the battalion command post and the battalion observation post in the battalion headquarters section are represented. The communication platoon was also a usual component of a headquarters company, except in the case of the division headquarters company. As in the latter, an anti-tank platoon was assigned to the infantry battalion headquarters company. This was the anti-tank unit of the battalion. If the battalion needed to increase its anti-tank defence, in particular at company level, the regiment could attach one or several platoons from the anti-tank company to the battalion or provide a tank destroyer platoon from the tank destroyer battalion attached to the division. For tactical operations, the headquarters company was divided into a command group and an administration group.

*1 – BATTALION HEADQUARTERS (4 Officers)

1 Lt Col, Battalion Commander-P
1 Major, Executive Officer-P
1 Captain, Operations & Training, S-3-C
1 1st Lt, Intelligence, S-2-C (became Captain, C2, 1 June 1945 to the table dated 26 February 1944)

The S-3 was the equivalent of the G-3.[1] He was responsible for battalion tactical operations and training.

The S-2 was the equivalent of the G-2. He planned and supervised intelligence activities within the battalion.

The S-1, battalion adjutant, was the company commander of the headquarters company. He was assigned to company headquarters and not to battalion headquarters (*2-1).

The battalion motor officer was the second-in-command of the headquarters company. He was also assigned to company headquarters (*2-1).

The following staff members were neither in battalion headquarters, nor in company headquarters, but in other organizations within the infantry battalion; they will be encountered later in the book:

the battalion supply officer, S-4, commanded the battalion section, transportation platoon, service company (T/O&E 7-13, *3-2) and was responsible for battalion supply (chapter 2, section 2.3).

the battalion surgeon commanded the battalion section (*2), of the regimental medical detachment (T/O&E 7-11, *B) (chapter 2, section 2.6).

the battalion communication officer commanded the communication platoon (*5), of the headquarters company (T/O&E 7-16).

the company commander of the heavy weapons company (T/O&E 7-18), advised staff officers about heavy weapons employment.

the battalion anti-tank officer commanded the anti-tank platoon (*6) of the headquarters company (T/O&E 7-16).

the battalion ammunition & pioneer officer commanded the ammunition & pioneer platoon (*4) of the headquarters company (T/O&E 7-16). He was also the battalion gas officer.

Equipment:

2 gas proof curtains, M1
1 chemical agent detection kit, M9
4 luminous dial compasses (1 per Off)
4 transparent map template, M2 (Off)
4 canvas dispatch cases (Off)
4 binoculars, M13 (Off)
4 wristwatches, 15 jewels (Off)
4 goggles, M1943, with green lens, cancelled (C2, 19 February 1945)
2 plastic semicircular protractors, MG, 10" diameter, 1-mil graduation
1 magnifying stereoscope, pocket
1 hand pyrotechnic projector, M9
1 observation telescope, M4 or M48 or M49
1 flag, national colours, service
1 latrine screen, complete
1 colour sling, web, olive drab
1 tent, Command Post, complete
1 oil burner for tent stove M1941
1 tent stove M1941 for tent
1 non-portable typewriter (not taken in the combat zone)
1 portable typewriter, with carrying case
1 transparent scale, interpreters, 12-in, 1/1000-ft and 1/10-in graduations (C1, 30 June 1944 to the table dated 26 February 1944)
1 portable electric lamp, Command Post (C1, 30 June 1944)
4 flashlights, TL-122-( ) (Off)
4 whistles, thunderer (Off)

*2 – COMPANY HEADQUARTERS (2 Officers, 24 Enlisted Men (19 EM, C1)

*2-1 – Command Group

1 Captain, Adjutant & S-1, Company Commander-C
1 1st Lt, Motor Transport, Second-in-Command-C
1 1st Sgt-C-1 Sgt, Motor-R
1 Pvt, Bugler-C
1 Techn 4th, Mechanic, Automobile, drove the ¾-ton truck, WC, maintenance-R
1 Pvt, Orderly, drove the ¼-ton truck-C
11 Pvts, Basic-R (6 Basics, C1)

The command group comprised the personnel whose duty in the field was directly associated with the battalion headquarters and was, for a large part, performed at the battalion command post, ammunition distributing point, or in the train bivouac.

1. The duties of the staff officers were represented by a number, e.g. '3' for the chief of operations. 'G' represented the staff of a general, 'S' for another staff of which the commanding officer was not a general.

*2-2 – Administration Group

1 S Sgt, Mess-C
1 S Sgt, Supply-C
1 Cpl, Company clerk, classification specialist-R
1 Techn 5th, Armorer-artificer-R
1 Techn 4th, Cook-R (for Officers' mess)
1 Techn 4th, Cook-R
1 Techn 5th, Cook-R
1 Pvt, Cook's helper-R

The administration group comprised the personnel whose duty was related to the mess, or the supply and the administration of the headquarters company.

Weapons:
2 Rocket launchers, AT, 2.36″
6 LMGs, caliber .30, M1919A6, flexible (C1, 30 June 1944)
2 SMGs, caliber .45, M3 (C1)

Vehicles:
1 Truck, ¼-ton
1 Truck, ¾-ton, WC, with winch

Equipment:
2 luminous dial compasses (Off)
5 wrist compasses, liquid-filled (1st Sgt, Sgt Motor, bugler, driver, mechanic, messenger)
1 compass, M6 (C1)
2 transparent map templates, M2 (Off)
3 binoculars, M13 (Off, 1st Sgt)
4 wristwatches, 7 jewels (1st Sgt, S Sgt mess, S Sgt Sup, Sgt Motor)
2 wristwatches, 15 jewels (Off)
1 canvas dispatch case (Off)
2 grenade launchers, M8
2 grenade launchers, M7 (driver, mechanic)
1 truck mount, pedestal, M24A2 (truck ¾-ton)
1 motor vehicles mechanics' tool set (for Auto Mechanic)
1 unit equipment tool set, 2nd echelon, set no. 1
3 packboards, plywood
3 packboard attachments, cargo (6 attachments, C1)
6 packboard quick-release straps
6 shoulder pads, for packboard (C2, 19 February 1945)
10 hand carts, M3A4 (per battalion, for use in landing operations when authorized by the Theater of Operations Commander)
1 carpenters' tool set, no. 2, complete
2 goggles, clear lens (orderly, mechanic), cancelled by C2, replaced by goggles, M1944 (2 per truck)
24 goggles, green lens (cancelled by C2)
6 whistles, thunderer (Off, 1st Sgt, Tech Sgt, S Sgt, Sgt)
8 flashlights, TL-122-( )
24 luminous markers, radioactive, type I (C1, 30 June 1944)
24 luminous markers, radioactive, type II (C1)

Items below were added, if authorized by the Commander of the Theater of Operations.
14 packboards, plywood (C1)
28 packboard attachments, cargo (C1)
28 packboard quick-release straps (C1)
28 shoulder pads, 2 per packboard (C2, 19 February 1945)

*3 – BATTALION HEADQUARTERS SECTION (13 Enlisted Men)

1 Techn Sgt, Sgt major-C
1 S Sgt, Intelligence-C
1 S Sgt, Operations-C
1 Cpl, Gas-R
1 Techn 5th, Headquarters clerk-R
1 Techn 5th, Light truck driver-R
1 Pvt, Light truck driver-R
6 Pvts, Scout, Observer, Intelligence-R

Vehicles:
    2 Trucks, ¼-ton

Equipment:
    1 luminous dial compass (S Sgt, Int) 7 compasses (S Sgt Int, scouts, C2, 19 February 1945)
    8 wrist compasses, liquid-filled (drivers, scouts) 2 compasses (drivers, C2)
    7 binoculars, M13 (S Sgt Int, scouts)
    1 wristwatch, 7 jewels (Tech Sgt)
    1 reading glass, 4½″ with case
    1 empty field desk, headquarters
    1 portable typewriter, with carrying case
    1 arm brassard, gas (Cpl, Gas)
    2 goggles, M1943, clear lens (drivers) (cancelled by C2, 19 February 1945)
    11 goggles, M1943, green lens (cancelled by C2)
    4 goggles, M1944 (2 per truck, C2)
    2 grenade launchers, M7 (drivers)
    2 ammunition-carrying bags (1 per grenade launcher)
    3 whistles, thunderer (Off, Tech Sgt, S Sgt)
    3 flashlights, TL-122-( ) (Off, Tech Sgt, S Sgt)

The intelligence sergeant was in charge of the battalion observation post and the scouts. He worked either in the observation post, or with the patrols. He could assist the operation sergeant if the latter was working with the S-2. The scouts operated in the battalion command post or accompanied the frontline units, the patrols, the reconnaissance parties and the security detachments as intelligence scouts.

In the field, the intelligence officer (S-2), the intelligence sergeant and the six scouts formed the S-2 section in the command post (see chapter 3, section 3.4). This section, when operating in the field, was often called the battalion reconnaissance platoon. Some unit histories, such as *The History of the Eleventh Infantry Regiment* discuss the activities of this platoon. Robert H. Williams corroborated, after conversations with Charles Bartley and Perry Teegarden, that all units in the battalion command post were organized like platoons.

The operation sergeant kept the situation maps and assisted the S-2 and S-3.

The sergeant major supervised the duties of the enlisted personnel of the battalion headquarters section and assisted the executive officer and S-1, as well as carrying messages.

The gas corporal assisted the battalion gas officer (*1).

*4 – AMMUNITION & PIONEER PLATOON (1 Officer, 26 Enlisted Men)

*4-1 – Platoon Headquarters

    1 1st Lt, Munitions-C
    1 S Sgt, Platoon-C (became Tech Sgt, 26 February 1944)
    1 Pvt or Techn 5th, Light truck driver-R

Weapons:
    1 MG, HB, M2, caliber .50, flexible
    2 Rocket launchers, AT, 2.36″

Vehicles:
    1 Truck, 1½-ton, cargo, with winch

Equipment:
    1 luminous dial compass (Off)
    1 wrist compass, liquid-filled (driver)
    1 wristwatch, 7 jewels (Tech Sgt)
    1 wristwatch, 15 jewels (Off)
    2 binoculars, M13 (Off, S Sgt)
    1 transparent map template, M2 (Off)
    1 goggles, M1943, green lens (driver) (cancelled by C2, 19 February 1945)
    2 goggles, M1944 (per truck, C2)
    2 flashlights, TL-122-( ) (Off, T Sgt)
    1 hand pyrotechnic projector, M9
    2 whistles, thunderer (Off, Tech Sgt)

For the entire Platoon:
    1 carpenters' equipment, set no. 1, Pioneer Squad
    2 demolition equipments, set no. 5, individual (+1, if authorized by the Commander of the Theater of Operations, C2)

1 demolition equipment, set no. 7, electrical (if authorized, C2)
1 intrenching equipment, set no. 1, infantry
1 pioneer equipment, set no. 1, Pioneer Squad
1 goggles, M1943, red lens (MG, caliber .50) (cancelled by C2)
3 goggles, M1943, green lens (cancelled by C2)
2 detector sets, SCR-625-( )

*4-2 – Ammunition & Pioneer Squad (× 3)

1 Cpl, Squad Leader-R (became Sgt, 26 February 1944)
7 Pvts, Ammunition bearer-C

Equipment:
3 mine probes, M1
8 ammunition bags, M2
8 shoulder pads, M2
64 gauntlets, for barbed wire
7 packboards, plywood
7 packboard attachments, cargo (14 attachments, C1, 30 June 1944, 2 per packboard)
14 packboard quick-release straps
14 shoulder pads, 2 per packboard (C2, 19 February 1945)
8 goggles, M1943, green lens (cancelled by C2)
1 whistle, thunderer (Sgt)
1 flashlight, TL-122-( ) (Squad Leader)

*5 – COMMUNICATION PLATOON (1 Officer, 22 Enlisted Men)

*5-1 – Platoon Headquarters

1 1st Lt, Communication-C
1 S Sgt, Communication chief-C

Vehicles:
1 Truck, ¼-ton

Equipment:
2 luminous dial compasses (Off, plat)
5 wrist compasses, liquid-filled (for the platoon)
1 transparent map template, M2 (Off)
1 binocular, M13 (Off)
1 wristwatch, 15 jewels (Off)
10 wristwatches, 7 jewels (S Sgt Rad, Sgt Wire, Sb Op, Rad Op)
1 hand pyrotechnic projector, M9
1 panel set, AP-30-C
1 panel set, AP-30-D
10 packboards, plywood (for the entire Platoon)
10 packboard attachments, cargo (20 attachments, C1, 30 June 1944)
20 packboard quick-release straps
20 shoulder pads for packboard (C2, 19 February 1945)
2 goggles, M1943, green lens (cancelled, C2)
2 goggles, M1944 (2 per truck, C2)
2 whistles, thunderer (Off, S Sgt)
7 flashlights, TL-122-( ) (Off, S Sgt, 5 per platoon)

*5-2 – Message Center Section

1 Sgt, Message Center Chief-R
1 Techn 5th, Code clerk-R
1 Pvt, Code clerk-R
4 Pvts, Messenger-C

Vehicles:
2 Trucks, ¼-ton

Equipment:
4 wrist compasses, liquid-filled (messengers)
1 wristwatch, 7 jewels (Sgt Msg Cen chief)

7 goggles, M1943, green lens (cancelled, C2)
4 goggles, M1944 (2 per truck, C2)
1 whistle, thunderer (Sgt)
1 flashlight, TL-122-( ) (Sgt)

*5-3 – Wire Section

1 Sgt, Wire chief-R
1 Techn 5th, Telephone & Telegraph lineman-R
4 Pvts, Telephone & Telegraph linemen-R
1 Techn 5th, Telephone switchboard operator-R
1 Pvt, telephone switchboard operator-R

Vehicles:
1 Truck, ¼-ton
1 Trailer, ¼-ton

Equipment:
1 grenade launcher, M7 (Techn 5th, lineman)
5 wrist compasses, liquid-filled (per Platoon)
8 wristwatches, 7 jewels (Sgt Wire, Sb Op, Rad Op)
5 goggles, M1943, clear lens (Linemen)
3 goggles, M1943, green lens (cancelled, C2, 19 February 1945)
2 goggles, M1944 (2 per truck, C2)
3 axles RL-27-( )
3 chests BC-5
5 chest sets, TD-3 (1 per 2 EE-8, 1 per BD-71), replaced by H-12 ( )/GT (C2)
5 headsets HS-30 (1 per 2 EE-8, 1 per BD-71)
8 flashlights, TL-122-( ) (Sgt, linemen, Switchboards)
2 lineman equipments TE-21
5 microphones T-45 (1 per 2 EE-8, 1 per BD-71)
1 whistle, thunderer (Sgt)
8 reel equipments CE-11
1 reel unit RL-31
1 telephone switchboard BD-71 (+1, if authorized, C2)
1 telegraph set TG-5-( )
8 telephones EE-8-( )
2 emergency switchboards SB-18/GT (C2)
4 miles of wire W-110-B on reel DR-4
4 miles of wire W-130-A on reel DR-4
2 miles of wire W-130-A on spool DR-8 or reel DR-4 (for use with reel equipment CE-11)
1 wire pike MC-123

*5-4 – Radio & Visual Section

1 S Sgt, Radio & Visual chief-R
1 Techn 4th, Radio operator (740)-R
1 Techn 4th, Radio operator (776)-R
2 Techns 5th, Radio operator (776)-R
1 Techn 4th, Radio repairman-R

Vehicles:
1 Truck, ¼-ton
1 Trailer, ¼-ton

Equipment:
1 grenade launcher, M7 (S Sgt, Radio)
1 wristwatch, 7 jewels (S Sgt Rad)
6 goggles, M1943, green lens (cancelled, C2)
2 goggles, M1944 (2 per truck, C2)
1 coil C-161
2 converters M-209 (3, C1, 30 June 1944) (+1 for SCR-694)
3 holders M-167 (1 per radio set SCR-694)
1 maintenance equipment ME-40-( )
1 maintenance kit ME-36-( )
1 maintenance kit ME-53 (cancelled by C2)

6 radio sets, SCR-300 (replaced the SCR-511, which was definitely cancelled from tables as substitution on 19 February 1945) [2]

1 radio set SCR-694-( ) (replaced the SCR-284, which remained a possible substitution for SCR-694 after 19 February 1945 and was to be issued until exhausted)

1 test equipment IE-17-( ) (replaced by IE-75, C2, only if IE-17 was not more serviceable)

1 test set I-56-( )

22 tool equipments TE-33 (per enlisted personnel)

1 tool equipment, TE-41

8 flashlights, TL-122-( ) (S Sgt, radio set)

1 vibrator pack PP-68( )/U

1 voltammeter I-50

1 remote control unit RM-29 (1 per SCR-694 replaced by remote control equipment RC-290, C1, 30 June 1944)

1 whistle, thunderer (S Sgt)

*6 – ANTI-TANK PLATOON (1 Officer, 23 Enlisted Men)

*6-1 – Platoon Headquarters

1 2nd Lt, Platoon Commander-C

1 S Sgt, Platoon-C (became Tech Sgt, 26 February 1944)

1 Pvt, Messenger, drove the ¼-ton truck-C

Weapons:

1 MG, HB, M2, caliber .50, flexible

Vehicles:

1 Truck, ¼-ton

Equipment:

2 luminous dial compasses (Off, 1 for the Platoon)

2 plastic semicircular protractors, MG, 10″ diameter, 1-mil graduation

1 magnifying stereoscope, pocket

1 wrist compass, liquid-filled (driver)

1 transparent map template, M2

2 binoculars, M13 (Off, Tech Sgt)

1 hand pyrotechnic projector, M9

1 wristwatch, 7 jewels (Tech Sgt)

1 wristwatch, 15 jewels (Off)

1 goggles, clear lens (driver, cancelled C2)

2 goggles, green lens (cancelled C2)

1 goggles, red lens (MG, caliber .50, cancelled C2)

2 goggles, M1944 (2 per truck, added C2)

*6-2 – Anti-tank Squad (× 3)

1 Sgt, Squad leader-R (became S Sgt, 26 February 1944)

1 Cpl, Gunner-P

3 Pvts, Ammunition bearer-C

4 Pvts, Cannoneer-P

1 Pvt, Light truck driver, Ammunition bearer-R

Weapons:

1 Gun, 57mm, M1, towed, with Carriage M1A3

1 Rocket launcher, AT, 2.36″

Vehicles:

1 Truck, 1½-ton, cargo, with winch

Equipment:

1 camouflage net, twine, fabric garnished, 29 × 29-ft (57mm Gun, M1)

1 handled pick, railroad, 6-7 lbs

5 drag ropes, with shoulder strap, M1918 (6 ropes, C1, 30 June 1944)

1 crosscut saw, type L, 2-man, 6-feet

---

2. Of the 6 radio sets SCR-300, 2 remained at battalion headquarters, the others were distributed to companies, 1 per company (rifle company and heavy weapons company). They utilised the battalion radio net (battalion headquarters and companies headquarters). See also relevant footnote in section 3.2 of this chapter. Correspondence with Richard Durst, 20 November 1995 and 7 March 1996, and conversation with Richard Nowling, 14 June 1996.

1 round point shovel, no. 2, D handled, GP
1 wrist compass, liquid-filled, compass (driver)
1 binoculars, M13 (Squad Leader)
1 goggles, clear lens (driver, cancelled C2)
9 goggles, green lens (cancelled C2)
2 goggles, red lens (57mm Gun, cancelled C2)
2 goggles, M1944 (2 per truck, C2)

Like the regiment, the battalion established a command post. Inside it, one could again find the units of the headquarters company. The battalion command post will be discussed in section 3.4 of this chapter.

The infantry battalion, like all units within the infantry regiment, was scarcely motorized. Army Ground Forces had considered the motorization of the infantry division by adding six quartermaster truck companies. In chapter 7, section 7.3, Quartermaster Company, Infantry Division, it can be seen that this company could transport tactically one infantry battalion. In Europe, following the Avranches breakthrough, when divisions moved forward quickly, the quartermaster truck companies were not available to all divisions. In order to motorize their units, regimental commanders had to have new ideas. One idea was to mount riflemen without their own transportation onto vehicles from motorized units.

Robert H. Williams wrote in his diary: "At 1400 hours the I & R Platoon, 11th Infantry, crossed the IP and the advance on Angers began. Infantry was loaded on organic trucks, top of tanks, top of tank-destroyers, artillery and engineer trucks. More crowded than the day before. We had discovered we were motorized with only the organic transportation of the combat team. The military planners never dreamed such could be possible. It certainly was not taught at Command and General Staff School. Wars are not won by just following the book but by innovation, desire and confidence on the part of all levels of a trained army following the well-founded principles of war."

These comments from Herb Williams, who was the commander of L Company, 11th Infantry, then Executive-Officer, 1st Battalion, 11th Infantry, need some explanations. The 'IP' was the 'Initial Point', or point of departure of a motorized march. Before the IP, troops loaded into trucks at the 'EP' (Entrucking Point); after arriving they unloaded from vehicles at the 'DP' (Detrucking Point). Herb discusses organic transportation of the combat team, not only of the regiment. The combat team was the infantry regiment with attached field artillery battalion, engineer company, tank company, and tank destroyer company. The U.S. Army Command and General staff School is now the Command and General Staff College, Fort Leavenworth, Kansas. [3]

3.2 INFANTRY RIFLE COMPANY
T/O&E 7-17

The rifle company was the combat unit of the infantry battalion. The mission of other units was to support it in combat. The division contained 27 rifle companies (3 in each battalion, 9 within each regiment). These companies, along with the heavy weapons companies (see the following section) were those that suffered the most casualties.

The infantry division was the unit that had the highest percentage of battle losses (93%). Of these losses, 16.5% were killed in action, 70% wounded in action and 13.5% missing or captured. The total of casualties from battle, for the personnel (infantrymen and heavy weapons crew) of the rifle and heavy weapons companies, reached 87.4%. A typical infantry division lost, each month, 10% of its strength in battle, and 8% for other reasons (non-battle casualties). [4] A comparison by branch of service reveals the following percentages losses in the combat zone: infantry, 81.9%; field artillery, 3.6%; armor, 6.6% (armored forces, 2.9; tank destroyer, 1.4; cavalry, 2.3); corps of engineers, 3.2%; medical service, 2.8% and signal corps, 0.2%.

Chart 19 shows the infantry rifle company. It consisted of the following units:
    Company Headquarters
    Weapons Platoon, which contained:
        60mm Mortar Section with 3 Mortar Squads
        Light Machine Gun Section with 2 LMG Squads
    3 Rifle Platoons, each containing 3 Rifle Squads.

*1 – COMPANY HEADQUARTERS (2 Officers, 33 Enlisted Men)

*1-1 – Command Group

1 Captain, Company Commander-C
1 1st Lt, Executive-Officer-C
1 1st Sgt-C
1 Sgt, Communication-R
1 Pvt, Bugler-C

---

3. Email from Herb Williams to the author, 23 January 1997.
4. Field Manual, FM 101-10-1. Staff Officers Field Manual, Organizational, Technical and Logistical Data, Dept of the Army, 1976. The percentage figures given are the field battle loss distribution as reported through data processing unit channels, European Theater of Operations, for the period 6 June 1944 through to 31 March 1945.

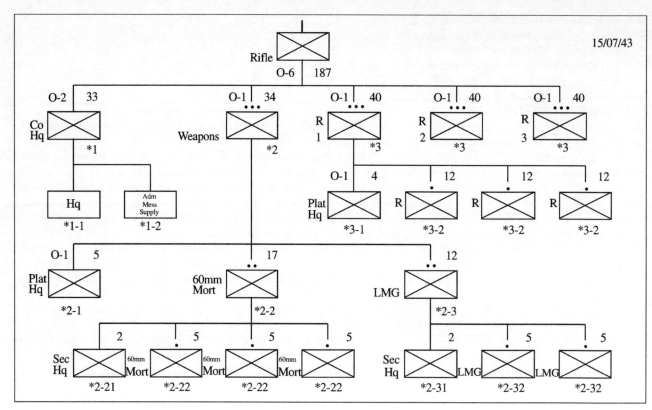

19. Infantry Rifle Company, Infantry Battalion

3 Pvts, Messenger-C
17 Pvts, Basic-C

The communication sergeant was trained in the use of the telephones and visual signals, in the preparation of sketches and in observation.[5] He controlled the internal and external communications of the company and assisted in organizing observation over the company front.

*1-2 – Administration Group

1 S Sgt, Mess-C
1 S Sgt, Supply-C
1 Cpl, Company clerk, classification specialist-R
1 Techn 5th, Armorer-artificer-R
2 Techns 4th, Cook-R
2 Techns 5th, Cook-R
2 Pvts, Cook's helper-R

Weapons:
5 Rocket launchers, AT, 2.36" (26 February 1944)
6 SMGs, caliber .45, M3 (C1, 30 June 1944)
6 Automatic Rifles, caliber .30, BAR, M1918A2 (C1, outside continental US, when authorized by the Commander of the Theater of Operations)

Equipment:
3 binoculars, M13 (Off, 1st Sgt)
5 wrist compasses, liquid-filled (1st Sgt, Messenger, bugler)
2 transparent map templates, M2 (Off)
1 grenade launcher, M8 (bugler)
1 grenade launcher, M7 (Sgt, Communication)
4 wristwatches, 7 jewels (1st Sgt, S Sgt Mess, S Sgt Supply, Sgt Communication)
2 wristwatches, 15 jewels (Off)

5. Although the SCR-300 was not issued to the rifle company in the T/O&E, each company had a radio set in its headquarters. The battalion commander would allot a SCR-300 (from the HQ and HQ Company) to the HQ of each rifle company and to the heavy weapons company, although no radio operator would be provided. The communication sergeant was responsible for the operation of the radio set in the battalion communication net. However, he was not necessarily the operator of the SCR-300. Information via correspondence with Richard Durst and Richard Nowling.

3 packboard attachments, cargo (6, C1, 30 June 1944)
2 ammunition-carrying bags (Sgt Communication, bugler)
3 packboards, plywood
6 packboard quick-release straps (2 per packboard)
6 shoulder pads (2 per packboard, C2, 30 January 1945)
7 flashlights, TL-122-( ) (1 per Off, 1st Sgt, S Sgt Mess, S Sgt Supply, per radio set)
2 radio sets SCR-536 [walkie-talkie] (3 SCR-536, including 1 for the Field Artillery Observer, C2)
2 hand-portable electric lanterns (cancelled, C2)
2 electric lanterns, MX-290/GV (C2)
3 panel sets, AP-50-A
2 reel equipments, CE-11
2 tool equipments, TE-33 (1 per CE-11)
½ mile of W-130-A wire on spool DR-8 or reel DR-4 (for use with CE-11)
8 packboards, plywood (outside the U.S.A., if authorized by the Commander of the Theater of Operations, C1)
16 packboard quick-release straps (C1)
16 packboard attachments, cargo (C1)
16 shoulder pads (C2)
1 demolition equipment, set no. 5, individual (C2)
35 goggles, M1943, green lens (cancelled, C2)
5 whistles, thunderer (Off, 1st Sgt, S Sgt)
33 three-pocket grenade carriers (1 per individual not issued ammunition carrying bag, C2, 30 January 1945)

*2 – WEAPONS PLATOON (1 Officer, 34 Enlisted Men)

*2-1 – Platoon Headquarters

1 1st Lt, Platoon Commander-C
1 S Sgt, Platoon-C (became Tech Sgt, 26 February 1944)
2 Techns 5th or Pvt, Light truck driver-R
2 Pvts, Messenger-C (One messenger was to be assigned to the company commander, the other remained with the platoon commander.) [6]

Weapons:
1 MG, HB, M2, caliber .50, flexible
3 Rocket launchers, AT, 2.36" (cancelled, 26 February 1944)

Vehicles:
2 Trucks, ¼-ton
2 Trailers, ¼-ton
The maintenance of vehicles was undertaken by the headquarters company, infantry battalion (T/O&E 7-16), the service company providing regimental-level maintenance (T/O&E 7-13).

Equipment:
2 binoculars, M13 (Off, Techn Sgt)
2 grenade launchers, M7 (drivers)
1 truck mount, pedestal, M31 (for ¼-ton truck)
1 hand pyrotechnic projector, M9
1 wristwatch, 7 jewels (Tech Sgt)
4 wrist compasses, liquid filled (messenger, driver)
1 transparent map template, M2 (Off)
2 goggles, M1943, clear lens (driver, cancelled, C2)
4 goggles, M1943, green lens (cancelled, C2)
1 goggles, M1943, red lens (MG, caliber .50, cancelled, C2)
4 goggles, M1944 (added, C2, 2 per truck)
1 wristwatch, 15 jewels (Officer)
13 packboard attachments, cargo
13 packboards, plywood
2 ammunition-carrying bags (1 per grenade launcher)
26 packboard quick-release straps
5 flashlights, TL-122-( ) (Off, Tech Sgt, Drivers, 1 per radio set)
1 radio set, SCR-536
2 whistles, thunderer (Off, Tech Sgt)

---

6. If a company was understrength, messengers were frequently not provided. Any trained infantryman could be used as a messenger. Information via conversation with Richard Nowling, 14 June 1996.

*2-2 – 60mm Mortar Section (17 Enlisted men)
*2-21 – Section Headquarters
1 Sgt, Section Leader-R (became S Sgt, 26 February 1944)
1 Pvt, Messenger-C

Equipment:
1 luminous dial compass
1 binocular, M13 (Section Leader)
1 wrist compass, liquid-filled (messenger)
2 goggles, M1943, green lens (cancelled, C2)
1 wristwatch, 7 jewels (Sec Leader)
1 flashlight, TL-122-( ) (Sec Leader)
1 whistle, thunderer (S Sgt)

*2-22 – 60mm Mortar Squad (× 3)
1 Cpl, Squad Leader-R (became Sgt, 26 February 1944)
1 Pvt, Mortar Gunner-P
1 Pvt, Mortar Gunner assistant-P
2 Pvts, Ammunition bearer-C

Weapons:
1 Mortar 60mm, M2, with mount, M2

Equipment:
1 luminous dial compass
1 camouflage net, twine, fabric garnished, 15 × 15′ (per mortar)
1 packboard attachment, Mortar 60mm (cancelled, C1, 30 June 1944)
2 packboard attachments, cargo (added, C1)
1 packboard, plywood
2 packboard quick-release straps
1 binocular, M13 (Sgt, Squad leader, C2, 30 January 1945)
1 whistle, thunderer (Sgt)
5 goggles, M1943, green lens (cancelled, C2)

*2-3 – Light Machine Gun Section (12 Enlisted Men)
*2-31 – Section Headquarters
1 Sgt, Section Leader-R (became S Sgt, 26 February 1944)
1 Pvt, Messenger-C

Equipment:
1 luminous dial compass
1 wrist compass, liquid filled (messenger)
1 binocular, M13 (Section Leader)
1 grenade launcher, M7 (Sec Leader)
1 wristwatch, 7 jewels (sec Leader)
1 ammunition-carrying bag (Sec Leader)
1 flashlight, TL-122-( ) (Sec Leader)
2 goggles, M1943, green lens (cancelled, C2)
1 whistle, thunderer (Sgt)

*2-32 – Light Machine Gun Squad (× 2)
1 Cpl, Squad Leader-R (became Sgt, 26 February 1944)
1 Pvt, Machine Gunner-P
1 Pvt, Machine Gunner assistant-P
2 Pvts, Ammunition bearer-C

Weapons:
1 Light Machine Gun, caliber .30, M1919A6, flexible

Equipment:
1 luminous dial compass
1 camouflage net, twine, fabric garnished, (per LMG)
1 packboard attachment, Machine Gun caliber .30 (cancelled, C1)
2 packboard attachments, cargo (added C1, 30 June 1944)
1 packboard, plywood
2 packboard quick-release straps

1 ammunition-carrying bag (Squad Leader)
5 goggles, M1943, green lens (cancelled, C2)
1 whistle, thunderer (Sgt)

*3 – RIFLE PLATOON (× 3) (1 Officer, 40 Enlisted Men)

*3-1 – Platoon Headquarters

1 1st Lt, Platoon Commander-C
1 S Sgt, Platoon-R (became Tech Sgt, 26 February 1944)
1 Sgt, Platoon Guide-R (became S Sgt, 26 February 1944)
2 Pvts, Messenger-R

The platoon guide prevented straggling and enforced orders concerning cover, concealment and discipline.
When the company began operational movements, one messenger reported to the company commander, the other remained with the platoon commander.[7]

The platoon commander designated, from among the members of the rifle squads, a rifleman as sharpshooter of the platoon. He was then armed with the Springfield rifle, caliber .30, M1903A4 (Snipers). The Garand rifle, caliber. 30, M1C replaced the Springfield rifle (Snipers) with C2, dated 30 January 1945.

Equipment:
1 luminous dial compass
2 wrist compasses, liquid-filled (messengers)
2 binoculars, M13 (Officer, Tech Sgt)
1 transparent map template, M2 (Off)
1 grenade launcher, M7 (Platoon Guide)
1 hand pyrotechnic projector, M9
1 wristwatch, 7 jewels (Tech Sgt)
1 wristwatch, 15 jewels (Off)
1 ammunition-carrying bag (grenade launcher)
5 goggles, M1943, green lens (cancelled, C2)
3 flashlights, TL-122-( ) (1 per Off, Tech Sgt, radio set)
1 radio set, SCR-536
3 whistles, thunderer (Off, Tech Sgt, S Sgt)

*3-2 – Rifle Squad (× 3)

1 Sgt, Squad Leader-R (became S Sgt, 26 February 1944)
1 Cpl, Squad Leader Assistant-R (became Sgt, 26 February 1944)
1 Pvt, Automatic Rifleman-BAR
1 Pvt, Automatic Rifleman Assistant-R
1 Pvt, Ammunition bearer-R
7 Pvts, Rifleman-R

The role of the rifle squad will be explained in detail in chapter 4. The squad was articulated around the BAR Team. This consisted of: the automatic rifleman (BAR), the automatic rifleman assistant and the ammunition-bearer. Two of the riflemen were designated as scouts. The three men in the BAR team were each issued with a Belt, magazine, M1937, BAR, until C1 dated 30 June 1944. From that date only one such belt was issued amongst the three; this change also affected the six weapons in the company headquarters.

Equipment:
2 wrist compasses, liquid-filled (Sqd Ldr, Asst Sqd Ldr)
3 grenade launchers, M7 (1 with Sgt Asst Sqd Ldr, 2 per Squad)
13 ammunition-carrying bags (1 per individual, 2 with Ammunition bearer), (20 bags, C2 dated 30 January 1945,
   2 per Rifleman)
12 goggles, M1943, green lens (cancelled, C2)
2 whistles, thunderer (S Sgt, Sgt)

The organization of the rifle company underwent no modifications between 15 July 1943 and 1 June 1945. It was the only sub-unit within the infantry regiment that did not see its number of Basics decrease on 30 June 1944. However, this did not prevent rifle companies becoming understrength due to losses. In real terms, the rifle squad numbered ten men in combat. The squad remained a combat unit as long as there remained a man able to take command of it, another to fire rifle grenades and a third, able to serve the automatic rifle. If these conditions could not be met, the men from the squad would be distributed amongst other squads, the original squad remaining out of combat until replacement.[7]

---

7. Robert J. Hamilton was wounded on August 9 1944 at Angers and was evacuated to England. After he recovered from his wounds, he joined his unit (1st Platoon, E Company, 2nd Bn/ 10th Infantry, 5th Infantry Division) in Germany, in January 1945, as Staff Sergeant, Squad Leader; he found he did not know anybody in his platoon (conversation of 8 June 1989). At the battle of San Pietro, Italy, Richard Nowling's platoon include less than 12 men able to fight. His company (I Company, 143rd Infantry) formed one

3.3 INFANTRY HEAVY WEAPONS COMPANY
T/O&E 7-18

The rifle company had to be equipped with weapons that could allow an equivalent mobility to the rifle. Nevertheless, the battalion needed support from heavy weapons. In 1939, a heavy weapons company was created within the infantry battalion. This company gathered together all infantry heavy weapons which could not be assigned to the rifle company because of their poor mobility and ammunition requirements. In the original T/O&E (7-18, 1 January 1939), the company included a machine gun platoon (caliber .50) that served in an anti-tank role. This was discontinued in 1942.

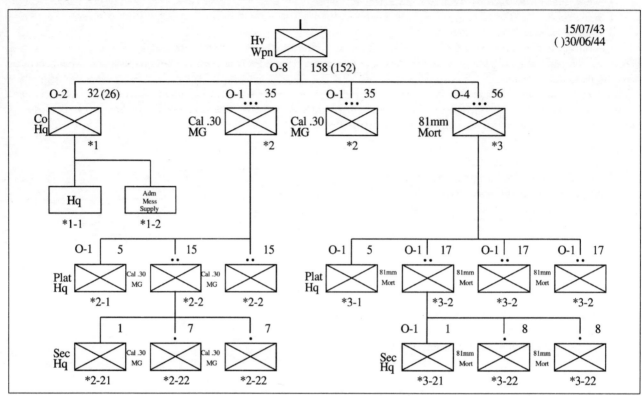

20. Infantry Heavy Weapons Company, Infantry Battalion

The battalion commander was responsible for the tactical employment of the company. He could give specific instructions concerning the employment of the platoons, but generally, he would direct the company commander to submit plans for the employment of his men.

If one or several platoons were detached to support the action of a rifle unit, the heavy weapons company commander remained in charge of those platoons. If a platoon was attached to a rifle company, it came under the command of the rifle company commander.

The main functions of the company command group were:

1. Obtaining information,
2. Maintaining communication within the company, with the supported unit's commanders and with the battalion headquarters,
3. Controlling the actions and the movements of the company.

The company commander was responsible for the administration, supply, and employment of the unit according to the battalion commander's tactical plans. He had to keep abreast of the situation through personal reconnaissance and prepare plans for the platoons operating under company control. The plans could include:

issuing of orders to all platoons, including initial positions and specific missions
responsibility for the computation of fire data and the conduct of this fire
ammunition supply
communication with supported units
reconnaissance of the forward positions
deployment and movement

Besides the normal duties of a company commander, he would be frequently called upon to perform the functions of a

Note 7 continued

composite platoon from the survivors of all platoons (conversation with Richard Nowling, Platoon Sergeant, I Company, 143rd Infantry at Angers, 14 June 1996).

battalion staff officer. As a staff officer, he advised the battalion commander concerning the employment of the platoons, or would be directed to coordinate the fire of his heavy weapons with the fire of the rifles companies and the supporting artillery.

The second-in-command had the following duties:

he would replace the company commander or any other company officer wounded or killed

he obtained information. He reconnoitred the initial and secondary positions, the routes of advance and of supply. He assisted in computing the fire data and went on reconnaissance with the company commander. He conducted the platoons toward their firing positions. He controlled one or more platoons directly or acted as liaison officer between the company and the battalion commander.

The first sergeant was usually with the forward echelon of the company. He assisted the company commander.

The reconnaissance sergeant assisted the reconnaissance officer in the collection and computation of fire data.

The communication sergeant supervised communications and the messengers at company headquarters.

The command post of the heavy weapons company was generally located near the battalion command post. The company commander would send a messenger to the battalion commander. The remaining messengers would be employed to communicate with the platoons or the rear echelon, or to accompany the reconnaissance officer. The bugler remained with the first sergeant at the company command post.

The battalion commander could ask the heavy weapons company commander and the reconnaissance officer to accompany him on reconnaissance. During this time, he could give his orders concerning the disposition of the company. The company commander would consult with, and receive orders frequently from the battalion commander. He could also receive individual orders via messengers.

When a machine-gun platoon was in direct support of a rifle company, the platoon commander would send a messenger or the corporal to the rifle company's company commander. If the platoon was in a general supporting role, the corporal, or a messenger, would be sent to the battalion command post. The remaining messenger stayed with the platoon commander in order to communicate with the sections or with the company headquarters. The mortar platoon commander retained his messengers to communicate with his squads or with the company headquarters.

Because of the diversity of the weapons in the company, their different tactical employment, and characteristics, and the difficulty for a single commander to exercise adequate supervision, the company was not employed as a single cohesive unit in the attack. Great latitude and initiative was given to the platoon leaders.

Doctrine for the employment of the Machine Gun Platoon

in the general support of a battalion. This method was appropriate when the entire battalion zone was visible from a single favourable firing position. It was frequently used at the beginning of the attack.

a platoon in direct support of each rifle company in an assault. This method provided faster and more effective support, but the company commander would lose partial control of his company.

one platoon in direct support of the assaulting company and the other in general support. The platoon in direct support assisted by supporting the lead assaulting company with its fire.

attached to assault companies. This was used only when the rifle companies were operating semi-independently during a pursuit, when they were acting as security elements, or when they were operating in very difficult terrain.

Besides its role as support, the heavy weapons company also had to undertake the protection of the flanks of the battalion.

Doctrine for the employment of the Mortar Platoon

The mortar platoon always remained under direct battalion control (in general support).

Organization

The heavy weapons company, shown in chart 20, comprised:

Company Headquarters
2 Machine Gun Platoons including each:
Platoon Headquarters
2 Machine Gun Sections
Section Headquarters
2 Machine Gun Squads
1 Mortar Platoon including:
Platoon Headquarters
3 Mortar Sections
Section Headquarters
2 Mortar Squads

*1 – COMPANY HEADQUARTERS (2 Officers, 32 Enlisted Men (26 EM, C1, 30 June 1944)

*1-1 – Command Group

1 Captain, Company Commander-C
1 1st Lt, Executive Officer, Reconnaissance Officer-C

1 1st Sgt-C
1 Sgt, Communication-C
1 Sgt, Reconnaissance-C
1 Sgt, Transportation-R
1 Pvt, Bugler-C
3 Pvts, Messenger-C (2 drove the ¼-ton trucks)
14 Pvts, Basics-R (8 basics, C1, 30 June 1944)

The reconnaissance officer assisted the company commander in the reconnaissance of firing position areas and unloading carrier positions, in locating the targets, in computing fire data, and in ammunition supply. He was assisted by the reconnaissance sergeant.

*1-2 – Administration Group

1 S Sgt, Mess-C
1 S Sgt, Supply-C
1 Cpl, Company clerk, classification specialist-R
1 Techn 5th, Armorer-artificer-R
2 Techns 4th, Cook-R
1 Techn 5th, Cook-R
2 Pvts, Cook's helper-R
1 Techn 4th, Mechanic, Automobile, drove the ¾-ton truck, WC, maintenance-R

Weapons:
1 MG, HB, M2, caliber .50, flexible

Vehicles:
2 Trucks, ¼-ton
1 Truck, ¾-ton

Equipment:
2 transparent map templates, M2 (Off)
6 binoculars, M16 or M17
6 ammunition-carrying bags (1 per grenade launcher)
2 goggles, M1943, clear lens (drivers)
34 goggles, M1943, green lens
1 goggles, M1943, red lens (1 per MG, caliber .50) [8]
1 drawing board, MG, with case
3 luminous dial compasses (1 per Off, Sgt Rcn)
7 wrist compasses, liquid-filled (1st Sgt, Sgt Transport, bugler, mech, msgr)
2 plastic semicircular protractors, MG, 10″ diameter, 1-mil graduation
1 magnifying stereoscope, pocket
4 binoculars, M13 (Off, 1st Sgt, Sgt Rcn)
1 aiming circle, M1
1 range finder, M9A1
1 grenade launcher, M7 (Mechanic)
5 grenade launchers, M8 (Sgt Rcn, Sgt Com, bugler, messengers drivers)
1 truck mount, pedestal, M31 (for ¼-ton truck)
6 wristwatches, 7 jewels (1st Sgt, S Sgt Mess, S Sgt Supply, Sgt Com, Sgt Rcn, Sgt Transportation)
2 wristwatches, 15 jewels (Off)
1 motor vehicles mechanics' tool set (Mech)
1 unit equipment tool set, 2nd echelon, set no. 1
6 packboard attachments, cargo
6 packboards, plywood
12 packboard quick-release straps
2 hand-portable electric lanterns
11 flashlights, TL-122-( ) (Off, 1st Sgt, S Sgt, messengers, mech, radio)
6 whistles, thunderer (Off, 1st Sgt, Sgt)
3 panel sets AP-50-A
3 radio sets SCR-536 (handy-talkie)
20 reel equipments CE-11
20 tool equipments TE-33 (1 per CE-11)
5 miles of wire W-130-A on reel DR-8 (or DR-4) for use with CE-11 (may be replaced by WD-3/TT or W-130)

8. T/O&E 7-18 contained new changes until the publication of a new table on 1 June 1945. The replacement of M1943 goggles by M1944 ones was not indicated for this unit, unlike others. However, as soon as the M44 goggles were in the chain of supply they were certainly issued to the heavy weapons company.

*2 – CALIBER .30 MACHINE GUN PLATOON (× 2) (1 Officer, 35 Enlisted Men)

*2-1 – Platoon Headquarters

1 1st Lt, Platoon Commander-C
1 S Sgt, Platoon-C (becomes Tech Sgt, 26 February 1944)
1 Cpl, Instrument-R
1 Cpl, Transportation-R
2 Pvts, Messenger-C (1 drove the ¼-ton truck)

Weapons:

2 Rocket launchers, AT, 2.36" (26 February 1944)

Vehicles:

1 Truck, ¼-ton

The instrument corporal assisted the platoon commander in reconnaissance for positions and in computing fire data. He installed and supervised the platoon observation post and helped with liaison.

The transportation corporal directed platoon transportation (for transporting weapons before the combat) and ammunition supply when the platoon was engaged. He supervised the concealment and the camouflage of transport in position, and during halts.

One messenger reported to the company commander when the company manoeuvred, the other remained with the platoon commander.

Equipment:

1 transparent map template, M2 (Off)
3 binoculars, M13 (Off, Tech Sgt, Cpl Instr.)
1 wristwatch, 7 jewels (Tech Sgt)
1 wristwatch, 15 jewels (Off)
1 drawing board, MG, with case
3 luminous dial compasses (Off, Cpl Instrument, Platoon)
2 wrist compasses, liquid-filled, compasses (messengers)
2 plastic semicircular protractors, MG, 10" diameter, 1-mil graduation
1 grenade launcher, M8 (driver)
1 ammunition-carrying bag (grenade launcher)
6 rocket-carrying bags, M6 (3 per Rocket launcher)
1 hand pyrotechnic projector, M9
1 magnifying stereoscope, pocket
1 goggles, M1943, clear lens (driver)
5 goggles, M1943, green lens
2 whistles, thunderer (Off, Tech Sgt)
4 flashlights, TL-122-( ) (Off, Tech Sgt, radio, driver)
1 radio set SCR-536

*2-2 – Caliber .30 Machine Gun Section (× 2) (15 Enlisted Men)

*2-21 – Section Headquarters

1 Sgt, Section Leader-R (became S Sgt, 26 February 1944)

Equipment:

1 luminous dial compass (Section Leader)
1 binocular, M13 (Sec Ldr)
1 wristwatch, 7 jewels (Sec Ldr)
1 goggles, M1943, green lens
1 whistle, thunderer (S Sgt)
1 flashlight, TL-122-( ) (S Sgt)

*2-22 – Caliber .30 Machine Gun Squad (× 2)

1 Cpl, Squad Leader-R (became Sgt, 26 February 1944)
1 Pvt, Machine Gunner-P
1 Pvt, Machine Gunner Assistant-P
4 Pvts, Ammunition bearer-C (1 drove the ¼-ton truck)

Weapons:

1 MG, caliber .30, Heavy, M1917A1, flexible

Vehicles:

1 Truck, ¼-ton
1 Trailer, ¼-ton

Equipment:

    1 goggles, M1943, clear lens (driver)
    6 goggles, M1943, green lens
    1 whistle, thunderer (Sgt)
    1 flashlight, TL-122-( ) (Sgt)
    1 luminous dial compass
    1 wrist compass, liquid-filled, compass (Am bearer and driver)
    1 camouflage net, twine, fabric garnished, 15 × 15′ (for MG)
    1 grenade launcher, M7 (Squad Leader)
    1 grenade launcher, M8 (Am bearer and driver)
    1 Machine Gun mount, M48, for MG caliber .30, (per ¼ ton truck)
    1 Machine Gun tripod for MG caliber .30, M1917A1
    1 packboard attachment, MG cal .30, M1917A1, for packboard
    1 packboard attachment, tripod MG caliber .30, M1917A1, for packboard
    5 packboards, plywood
    3 packboard attachments, cargo
    10 packboard quick-release straps
    13 ammunition-carrying bags (2 per Am bearer, 2 for the Squad, 1 per grenade launcher, 1 for the Squad Leader)
    1 machete, 18″ blade, M1942
    1 sharpening stone, pocket (for machete)
    1 machete sheath, 18″ blade, M1942

*3 – 81mm MORTAR PLATOON (4 Officers, 56 Enlisted Men)

*3-1 – Platoon Headquarters

    1 1st Lt, Platoon Commander-C
    1 S Sgt, Platoon-C (became Tech Sgt, 26 February 1944)
    1 Cpl, Instrument-R
    1 Cpl, Transportation-R
    2 Pvts, Messenger-C (1 drove the ¼-ton truck)

Weapons:

    2 Rocket launchers, AT, 2.36″ (26 February 1944)

Vehicles:

    1 Truck, ¼-ton

Equipment:

    1 transparent map template, M2 (Off)
    1 grenade launcher, M8 (messenger and driver)
    1 ammunition-carrying bag (1 per grenade launcher)
    1 goggles, M1943, clear lens (driver)
    5 goggles, M1943, green lens
    6 rocket-carrying bags, M6 (3 per Rocket launcher)
    2 whistles, thunderer (Off, Tech Sgt)
    4 flashlights, TL-122-( ) (Off, Tech Sgt, radio, driver)
    1 drawing board, MG, with case
    3 luminous dial compasses (Off, Cpl Instr, 1 for the Platoon)
    2 wrist compasses, liquid-filled (messengers)
    2 plastic semicircular protractors, MG, 10″ diameter, 1-mil graduation
    1 magnifying stereoscope, pocket
    3 binoculars, M13 (Off, Tech Sgt, Cpl Instr)
    1 wristwatch, 7 jewels (Tech Sgt)
    1 wristwatch, 15 jewels (Off)
    1 hand pyrotechnic projector, M9
    1 radio set SCR-536

*3-2 – 81mm Mortar Section (× 3) (1 Officer, 17 Enlisted Men)

*3-21 – Section Headquarters

    1 2nd Lt, Section Commander-C
    1 Sgt, Section Leader-R (became S Sgt, 26 February 1944)

Equipment:

    1 transparent map template, M2 (Off)
    2 goggles, M1943, green lens

2 whistles, thunderer (Off, S Sgt)
2 flashlights, TL-122-( ) (Off, S Sgt)
2 luminous dial compasses
2 binoculars, M13 (Off, S Sgt)
1 wristwatch, 7 jewels (S Sgt)
1 wristwatch, 15 jewels (Off)

*3-22 – 81mm Mortar Squad (× 2)

1 Sgt, Squad Leader-R (became S Sgt, 26 February 1944)
1 Cpl, Mortar Gunner-P
1 Pvt, Mortar Gunner assistant-P
1 Pvt, Ammunition bearer-P
4 Pvts, Ammunition bearer-C (1 drove the ¼-ton truck)

Weapons:
1 Mortar 81mm, M1, with mount M1

Vehicles:
1 Truck, ¼-ton
1 Trailer, ¼-ton

A mortar team included:
Mortar Gunner
Mortar Gunner Assistant
Ammunition bearer (with pistol)

Equipment:
1 goggles, M1943, clear lens (driver)
7 goggles, M1943, green lens
1 whistle, thunderer (Sgt)
2 flashlights, TL-122-( ) (Sgt, driver)
1 luminous dial compass
1 wrist compass, liquid-filled (ammunition bearer and driver)
1 camouflage net, twine, fabric garnished, 15 × 15' (per mortar)
1 grenade launcher, M8 (Ammunition bearer and driver)
1 ammunition-carrying bag (grenade launcher)
1 packboard attachment, 81mm mortar base plate
1 packboard attachment, 81mm mortar bipod
1 packboard attachment, 81mm mortar tube
2 packboard attachments, cargo
5 packboards, plywood
10 packboard quick-release straps

3.4 COMMAND POST, INFANTRY BATTALION

In the field, the battalion headquarters was called the command post. All the battalion's means of command and control were concentrated at the command post – the battalion commander, the staff, and other officers required by the commander to operate at, and from, the command post. The command post was organized to assist them in their duties. It had to be concealed from air and ground observation. The different installations had to be separated by more than 50 yards to avoid total destruction of the command post by a single artillery shell.

On the march, the battalion command group moved near the head of the battalion. The number of vehicles was held to a minimum. Those vehicles not necessary for the staff moved at the head of the motor echelon. A part of the communication platoon (messengers and radios) would be prepared to furnish means of communication, and marched near the command group.

During combat, the location of the initial command post was usually designated by the regimental commander, and would be located to facilitate battalion control. The considerations that influenced this choice were: the tactical situation (attack or defence), the communication routes toward the regimental command post and to subordinate units, cover and concealment, the proximity of a good observation point for communicating with the observation post, and obstacles preventing mechanized attacks. After the general location of the command post had been chosen, the S-1, accompanied by the communication officer, selected the exact site of the command post. He would also decide the interior arrangement of it, and designate the emplacement of the installations. The communication officer directed the installation of communications. A wire would be laid to the battalion observation post. The motor vehicles would be parked in a concealed location as far as possible from the command post to avoid its disclosure.

The command post was organized for continuous operations. To ensure the necessary rest, each staff officer relieved one other or the battalion commander as necessary. Enlisted men worked in a shift. All means of communication were used for

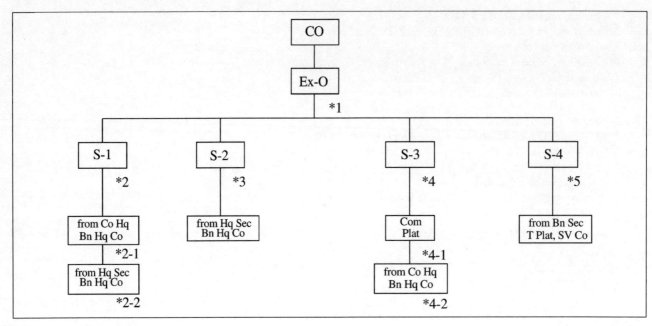

21. Command Post, Infantry Battalion

transmitting messages or orders. All incoming messages passed through the message center. The battalion sergeant major supervised delivery of messages to their addresses, their circulation to interested officers and their return for entry in the unit journal. Outgoing messages were sent through the message center. After the message center chief received notification that a message had been delivered, he placed the duplicate copy in his dead file, which was periodically turned over to the S-1 for entry into the unit journal. All officers had to see that a synopsis of each message or order sent or received, orally, by telephone or radio-telephone, were sent for registering in the unit journal.

During the offensive, the battalion command post would be kept close to the attacking echelon to facilitate the communication between it and the troops, and to afford it protection. The displacement of the command post would be anticipated, and the communication officer kept the wire head pushed close to the advancing troops in order that wire communication could be available whenever the command post moved. In combat, the companies selected the location of their command posts, and informed the battalion commander accordingly. The security of the battalion command post was ensured by the frontline units and the battalion reserve. The headquarters company commander (S-1) was responsible for the security of the command post in combat. Observers and small patrols could be employed to cover all approaching routes. Foxholes would be dug to provide individual protection.

The command post included the following sections:

*1 – COMMAND (T/O&E 7-16, *1)

> Battalion Commander, CP Commanding Officer
> Executive-Officer
> S-1
> S-2
> S-3
> S-4 (each was in charge of a Section of the Headquarters)

*2 – S-1 SECTION

*2-1 (from Company Headquarters (*2), Battalion Headquarters Company, T/O&E 7-16)

> Adjutant & S-1, Company Commander, Captain
> Motor Transport Officer, Second-in-Command, 1st Lt
> 1st Sgt
> Motor Sgt
> Bugler, Pvt
> Mechanic, Techn 4th
> Orderly, Pvt
> Basics

*2-2 (from Battalion Headquarters Section (*3), Battalion Headquarters Company T/O&E 7-16)

> Sergeant Major, Tech Sgt
> Gas Corporal, Cpl

Headquarters clerk, Techn 5th
2 Light truck drivers, Techns 5th or Pvts

*3 – S-2 SECTION (also called Battalion Reconnaissance Platoon)

(from Battalion Headquarters Section (*3), Battalion Headquarters Company T/O&E 7-16)
Intelligence Officer, S-2, 1st Lt
Intelligence Sergeant, S Sgt
6 Scouts, Pvts

*4 – S-3 SECTION

*4-1: (from Battalion Headquarters Section (*3), Battalion Headquarters Company (T/O&E 7-16)
Operations Sergeant, S Sgt

*4-2: Communication Platoon (*5), Battalion Headquarters Company (T/O&E 7-16)
Communication Officer, 1st Lt
Communication Chief, S Sgt
Message Center Section
Message Center Chief, Sgt
Code Clerk, Techn 5th – Messengers, Pvts
Wire Section
Wire Chief, Sgt
Telephone & Telegraph Lineman, Techn 5th
Telephone & Telegraph Linemen, Pvts
Telephone switchboard Operator, Techn 5th
Telephone switchboard Operators, Pvt
Radio & Visual section
Radio & Visual Chief, Sgt
Radio Operator (740), Techn 4th
Radio Operator (776), Techn 4th
Radio Operators (776), Techn 5th
Radio repairman, Techn 4th

*5 – S-4 SECTION (from Battalion Section (*3-2), Transportation Platoon (*3), Service Company T/O&E 7-13)

Battalion Supply Officer, S-4
Battalion Supply Sergeant, S Sgt
Equipment for the above is given in the corresponding section of the book.

CHAPTER 4

INFANTRY DOCTRINE

In chapter 1 we surveyed the general doctrine of the U.S. Army concerning the infantry division. This chapter now explains infantry doctrine in detail. The doctrine of employment of the sub-units of the rifle company, the platoons and the squads, will be examined.

The principal missions of the rifle companies were the following:

security missions, which consisted of reconnoitring and protecting a unit on the march from the actions of the enemy

defensive missions, which included all actions undertaken to protect a unit from enemy attack and to retain terrain seized from the enemy

offensive missions planned to seize terrain from the enemy and to hold it. After the attack had achieved its objective(s), to protect them from enemy counterattacks, the units shifted from attack to defence.

In chapter 1, it was noted that with its triangular organization, a U.S. Army unit could be divided into three parts, one of the elements being generally kept in reserve. The same applies to the rifle company (see chapter 3, section 3.2). A unit would be divided into two or three echelons, the last echelon always being the reserve echelon, sometimes called support echelon.

During the attack two echelons were organized. In the rifle company, the first echelon contained platoons, the second echelon one platoon.

During defensive missions, the company was organized into three echelons, each echelon containing one platoon. These were:

a security echelon

a garrison echelon

a reserve echelon

All data concerning infantry doctrine is taken from:

Training Bulletins GT-20, a pictorial supplement to FM 7-10 (Rifle Company, Infantry Regiment), published by The Infantry School, Fort Benning, Georgia:

Security Missions, 30 June 1943

Defensive Combat, 1 October 1943

The Attack, 15 May 1943

Field Manual, FM-7-20, Rifle Battalion, 28 September 1942.

4.1 SECURITY MISSIONS

1 – Advance Guard

A security detachment preceded a unit on the march and protected it. This detachment was called an advance guard. When the unit on the march was a regiment, a battalion constituted the advance guard and its leading company would be designated as the support.

The support (company) detached one of its platoons forward. This one was called the advance party. The advance party (platoon), in turn, sent forward a small security group, generally a squad, called a point. Chart 22 shows, on the road, the positions of the different components of the advance guard.

For providing security to the support (company), the advance party (platoon) manoeuvred rapidly to determine hostile dispositions, and fired upon any enemy encountered. The advance party marched in columns of twos with one file on each side of the road. The members of each squad of the advance party marched on the same side of the road.

The commander of the advance party (platoon commander) was to ensure that the assigned route or direction was followed, and was charged with maintaining the prescribed rate of march. He marched at the head of the detachment, or between the point and the detachment. However, he moved where he could best observe the terrain and direct the action if resistance was encountered.

The support commander (company commander) designated the patrolling to be undertaken by the advance party. In the absence of orders, the advance party commander (platoon commander) was to ask about patrols to be sent out.

As advance party, the platoon could furnish two or three patrols of a few men each to oversee each flank to a distance of 200 or 300 yards. The patrols maintained a visual contact with the platoon commander. This commander examined the ground in the front of the platoon, particularly noting locations which would afford a good ambush site to the enemy.

Men were sent forward from the support (rifle company), to maintain contact with the advance party (platoon), and forward from the advance party, to maintain contact with the point. They were called connecting files.

When a man acted as a connecting file, he had to closely oversee visual signals from the rear and from the front. When

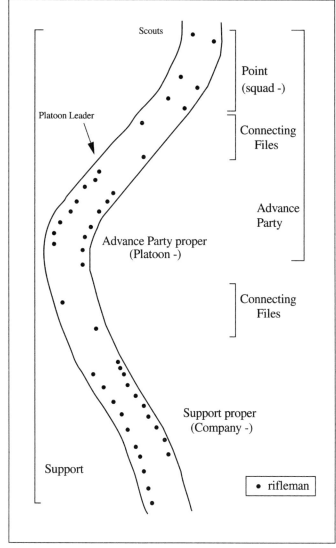

22. Advance Guard

there were two men, one looked to the rear for signal and the other to the front. They would stay near to each other to communicate by voice.

The connecting files would pass forward the orders, messages and signals received from the unit, which sent them. They halted only on orders or signals from that unit or when the small unit stops (point for the advance party, advance party for the support). They passed back no signals except 'enemy in sight' or previously-agreed signals.

The point preceded the advance party at a distance prescribed by the platoon commander (advance party commander). This distance varied with terrain and visibility, in open terrain it varied between 150 and 300 yards. In wooded terrain and at night, that distance would be considerably reduced. The point observed toward the front and the flanks, but did not execute flank reconnaissance.

To permit prompt fire action toward the front or the flanks and reduce the danger from enemy small arms fire, the point moved along the route of advance in a column of two, one file on each side of the road with a minimum of five steps between each man. Two scouts precede the point by 50 to 100 yards.

The leader of the point (squad leader) usually marched near its head, but could go wherever his presence was requested.

The mission of the point was to warn the support of any enemy who had not been discovered by the mechanized (Cavalry Troop, T/O&E 2-27) or motorized covering forces (Reconnaissance Platoon, T/O&E 7-12, *3).

When the enemy was detected but was beyond the effective range of weapons, his presence was reported by the signal 'enemy in sight'. The point continued its advance while the signal was relayed to the advance party by the connecting files. When the point reached within the effective range of its weapons, it opened fire on the enemy.

The point could undertake an aggressive action not only against a small enemy group, but could also assist the advance party by forcing a large enemy group to disclose its positions.

Resistance that the point was unable to overcome was attacked without hesitation, or special reconnaissance, by the advance party. Every effort was made to clear the way for the remainder of the regiment.

Civilians were not authorized to precede the advance party or the point. If any were found to be acting suspiciously, they were arrested and turned over to the support commander (company commander).

When the support (company) halted, a march outpost was formed by the advance party (platoon). The march outpost sent observers to nearby vantage points, to observe to the front and the flanks. Those members of the platoon who were not detailed as observers remained under. They did not remove their equipment.

When it stopped, the point sent one or two observers to vantage points, to prevent an enemy attack. Except to open fire, the point (squad) halted only when ordered by the advance party commander (platoon commander). [1]

2 – Rearguard

The rearguard provided the protection for the rear of a foot or motorized column on the march, when it was marching away from the enemy or when it was marching toward the enemy if attack or harassing actions were expected.

A company assigned as support of a rearguard usually employed a platoon as rear party to provide security at the rear. The rear party sent, in turn, to the rear a small covering force called a rear point.

The distance between the support and the rear party was prescribed by the support commander. He sent back connecting files to maintain contact with the rear party. The rear party marched in column of twos, one file on each side of the road.

The platoon employed as rear party was organized and directed in the same manner as the advance party previously

1. Platoon commander: this appellation appears with the T/O&E dated 26 February 1944, and replaced 'platoon leader'. Before 26 February 1944, the commanders at company level had the title of 'commander', at lower levels (platoon, section, squad), they had the title 'leader'. From 26 February 1944, all officers received the title of 'commander' and enlisted cadres (NCO) who were in charge of a unit (section, squad) had the title of 'leader'. It seems that the appellation 'platoon leader' was retained throughout the war.

discussed. Patrols to the flanks were rarely undertaken by a rear party about the size of a platoon. The rearguard patrols sent out by the support rejoined the rear party as it passed them by.

The rear party commander (platoon commander) normally marched behind the rear party, so he could make a quick decision and undertake any action when the rear point was attacked. The rear party commander stated, in his orders, the distance at which the rear point had to follow the detachment, usually not more than 200 yards in open terrain, and less than 200 yards in close terrain. He sent back connecting files to maintain contact with the rear point.

The rear point, sent by the rear party, consisted of a half-squad, sometimes of an entire squad. The rear point's dispositions were similar to those of the point of an advance party, but in reverse order. The rear point signalled to the detachment commander when the enemy was observed.

The rear point would stop to open fire only when enemy action threatened to interfere with the march. It could expect no reinforcement. When it was forced to withdraw, it did so via a flank, or by a designated route so it did not mask the fire of rear troops.

When the rear party commander decided that it was necessary to fight in a certain location, he selected a firing position that provided long fields of fire and was well to the rear of the position occupied by the rear point. He sent a messenger to the rear point leader (squad leader) to indicate the position and to lead the rear point in its withdrawal. The rear support covered the withdrawal of the rear party.

When the rear support halted and immediately formed a march outpost, it sent observers nearby the rear point to provide observation of the flanks. The rear point stopped when the rear party halted. It placed one or more observers in position to prevent a surprise attack by the enemy.

3 – Flank Guard

The flank guard was a detachment for security purposes sent out by a column on the march to protect its flanks against observation, surprise and attack. The flank guard of a battalion seldom exceeded a reinforced platoon. Its commander was instructed as to what he was to do and when and for how long was to do it. The flank guard was responsible for its own security.

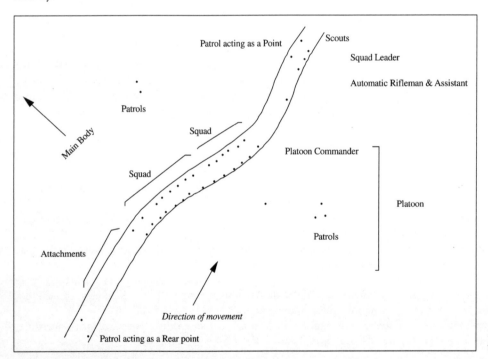

23. Flank guard on a route parallel to the main body

The flank guard could be ordered to:
a) move on a route parallel to the main body (regiment)
b) occupy simultaneously a series of flank positions
c) occupy a single flank position
a) When the platoon as flank guard marched on a route parallel to the main body, the platoon commander provided for the security for its unit by employing a small advance point and rear point, and by using flank patrols. [2]
b) If the flank guard occupied a series of positions to protect the main body, it generally did so ahead of its march. The platoon would preferably be motorized, so as to form motorized detachments used to block each avenue of approach. When the end of the main body reached a point on the route where it could be covered by the flank guard at the second occupied position, the flank guard elements at the first position move to a previously reconnoitred position toward the front. As long as the terrain and the situation allowed, this leapfrog method continued. Roadblocks were

2. Main body: this was the unit (regiment, division, etc.) less the advance guard and the rearguard.

established and demolitions ordered. When the intent was to offer anti-tank protection to the main body, anti-tank guns were attached to the flank guard.

c) When, on a threatened flank, there was only one avenue of approach, the platoon commander would be directed to occupy a single key position, which would afford the necessary protection to the main body. The key positions were those that commanded the enemy's routes of approach. A platoon without transportation had to begin its march before the main body reached its position in time to accomplish its mission.

The flank guard's commander kept in touch with the main body, not only to transmit information but also to keep informed of its progress. Contact with the main body was maintained by patrols sent to points of observation and by motor messengers or radiotelephones, if available.

The platoon commander notified the main body commander immediately in case of attack and delayed the advance of the enemy until the main body was ready for action, or until the tail of the column passed a designated point. The platoon reassembled after the end of the column had passed a prescribed emplacement, or at a specified time. If operating on foot, it rejoined its company at the earliest opportunity.

4 – March Outpost

A march outpost was a point of security established by a marching unit making a temporary halt. It was organized by occupying critical terrain features that controlled the approaches to the column at rest. Advance, flank and rear guards were established.

When a platoon was detached as a march outpost, it received specific instructions from the company commander. Usually, it operated according to the methods prescribed for the support of an outpost for a bivouac (see section 5 below).

The strength of a march outpost varied from a single squad to a company reinforced with attached weapons (from a heavy weapons company) in support. Its size depended on:

a) the size of the main body
b) the duration of the temporary halt
c) proximity of the enemy and probability of contact
d) nature of the terrain

5 – Outpost

An outpost was a security or covering force sent out:

      to protect a command at rest, or troops in battle position, against surprise enemy attack

      to screen from enemy observation

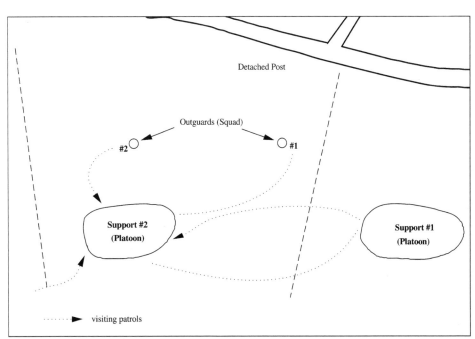

24. Disposition of an outpost for a bivouac

·······► visiting patrols

A – DISPOSITION OF AN OUTPOST FOR A BIVOUAC

A support was a security element on the outpost line of resistance. It furnished outguards and patrols, and was responsible for a specifically-assigned area. It was prepared for close combat. Within the outpost, the supports were numbered from right to left.

An outguard was a security element sent forward by the support. The outguards established the outpost observation line and were responsible for specifically-assigned zones. They discovered enemy activity and gave the alarm in case of attack. Each outguard furnished at least one, but sometimes more, sentinels. The outguards were numbered from right to left within the support.

A detached post was an outguard situated outside the limits of the outpost proper, for a special mission, or to observe or guard a position of importance.

A rifle platoon could be detailed as part or all of the support or as an outguard. A squad, or a part of it, could be detailed as an outguard. If the support was a rifle company, the outguard would be a rifle platoon; if the support was a rifle platoon, the outguard would be a rifle squad. A platoon assigned as support of an outpost for a bivouac was assigned an area on the line of resistance of the outpost and a sector of surveillance. Rifle company crew-served weapons, and the heavy machine guns and 81mm mortars of the heavy weapons company could be attached to a rifle platoon.

B – ACTIONS OF THE SUPPORT COMMANDER (A PLATOON BEING SUPPORT)

After he received his orders, the platoon commander made a quick map reconnaissance, if a map was available. He informed his second-in-command of his tentative plans and directed him to move the platoon to the assigned area. He preceded his unit to the area, if practicable, and made a reconnaissance of the terrain as detailed as conditions permitted.

The platoon commander would inform the outpost commander about the situation and the ground. He decided how he would organize the ground, designate the location and the mission of each squad, and the positions of attached support weapons. As soon as contact was established with the adjacent supports, he would confer with their commanders. When it moves to its location as outpost, the platoon would be responsible for its own security, so would adopt a suitable formation.

The platoon commander issued orders to his subordinates, if possible, concerning the situation. These orders included:
1) information about the enemy and adjacent units
2) the mission of the platoon
3) the composition, the mission, the location of each outguard
4) patrols to be conducted
5) the password, or the call-and-answer system to be used
6) the location and the mission of each of the attached weapons
7) the route of withdrawal
8) ammunition supply, the Battalion Aid Station
9) location of the Command Post

C – ORGANIZATION OF THE GROUND

The platoon commander organized his position as for defence on a broad front. The position should provide for long-range and for close-range defensive fire. The gaps between the squads were to be covered by fire, and if possible, by obstacles.

The attached light machine guns were positioned so as to provide direct and flanking fire; the 60mm mortars (attached from the weapons platoon) covered the approaches, which could not be covered by flat-trajectory weapons.

Immediately after the arrival of the platoon at its positions, the commander posted the outguards, pointed out fields of fire and foxholes were dug. Camouflage was executed as the work progressed. Communications with the adjacent supports and outguards were maintained by patrols, radiotelephone or telephone. The outguards occupied day positions, habitually 400 yards ahead of the line of resistance of the outpost, affording extensive views, good fields of fire, and a covered route of withdrawal.

The support commander fixed the posts of the outguards and the number of sentinels. He designated the action to be undertaken if the enemy attacked. The members of the outguard who were not posted as sentinels rested nearby under natural cover (or in foxholes), but stayed fully equipped and with their weapons to hand. If the outpost occupied a position for

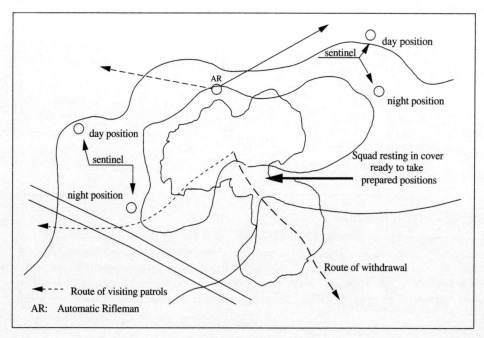

25. Position of an outguard and of the sentinels, day and night

several days in close proximity to the enemy, the positions of the outguards had to be changed frequently, to avoid capture by enemy raids.

The commander of the outguard selected the posts of the sentinels that covered his sector of observation. During the day, the sentinels were posted primarily to observe. An outguard usually posted a single sentinel in the day. To each sentinel the following information was given:

a) about the enemy:
   direction
   patrols or other activities in the area
   special sector of observation
b) about friendly troops:
   the number of outguards and of supports
   the location of the support and of the
      adjacent outguards
   the patrols sent out that would return
      through this outpost
   where the prisoners were to be taken and the
      location to which messages were to be sent
c) special signals, such as 'gas alarm' or countersigns
d) names of the principal geographic features, such as
      villages, roads, streams

The support commander inspected the positions as soon as the support was posted. He made any changes necessary and reported the dispositions to the outpost commander; a sketch was to accompany his report. The support commander made frequent visits to the outguards. The outguards were to be located within visual communication distance of each other. If this was not practicable, contact was to be maintained by patrols, radiotelephones, and telephones.

The support could be required to execute patrols beyond the outguards, to the front and the flanks, using vehicles

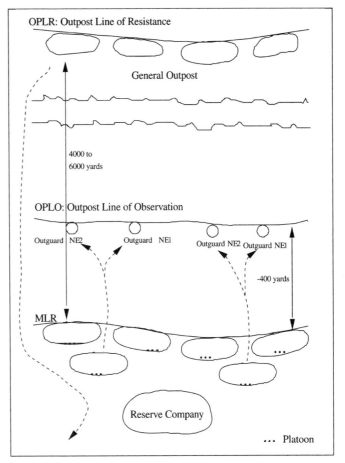

26. Combat outpost of a battalion with a general outpost to provide security

when available. The patrol routes were frequently changed to avoid enemy ambushes. Two-man visiting patrols were used between outguards to cover the terrain at night and during periods of reduced visibility. The information gathered was transmitted to the support commander.

At night, the outguards were posted to cover the routes of approach of the enemy. The sentinels were placed primarily to listen, and had the means to identify friendly personnel. These means were not be conspicuous, but had to be easily recognizable at a few yards distance.

Patrols were increased at night. The patrols detached from the support covered only their front and the gaps between the outguards, unless they received other specific instructions. Patrols were to go over their route during daylight.

D – DETACHED POST

A platoon detailed as a detached post organized for all-around defence, posted observers and executed the patrolling necessary for its own security. Roadblocks were established and explosives placed according to orders. The roadblocks were kept under constant surveillance and covered by fire. A roadblock had to be within the effective range of the rifles of the defending platoon. It had to be sufficiently distant (200 yards) to prevent artillery fire or bombing aimed at the roadblock reaching the platoon's position.

When the area covered by the patrols was too broad, or obscured, a detached post could be established as a patrol base beyond the line of the outguards. This method facilitated the flow of information, prevented excessive fatigue and provided for better reconnaissance of the sector

Inhabitants were not authorized to pass through the outpost. They were conducted, under guard, to the outpost commander. When a large number of refugees were encountered, a higher authority issued orders for their collection and disposal.

6 – General Outpost

The general outpost was a security force that had the goal of holding its positions until a specified time or until orders were received, or of conducting a delaying action. It consisted of an infantry battalion, or larger unit.

A company, on the outpost line of resistance, organized a defensive area and could be directed to conduct delaying actions. In the general outpost, the platoon organized a defensive area as part of the company area.

If necessary, the attacking units, like the defensive units, established combat outposts.

7 – Combat Outpost

Combat outposts were sent toward the front to screen and protect an organization that had halted during combat. A combat outpost operated habitually from several alternate positions. It opened fire on the enemy at long range.

When an enemy advance threatened it, it withdrew via routes that did not interfere with the fields of fire of the unit that fired on the enemy from the rear.

A frontline battalion organized its own security by designating and posting a line of combat outposts. With a general outpost in position, the combat outpost consisted of observation groups. When there was no general outpost, the combat outpost had to be stronger. A platoon from the reserve company was frequently detailed as all or part of a combat outpost.

The combat outpost was organized as a series of outguards. The outguards organized defensive areas on positions permitting observation, and giving fields of fire, as well as providing close protection to support weapons. Combat outposts were informed of the action to take if they were attacked. Communication with the battalion command post was maintained by wire, radiotelephones or messengers.

If the order given to the outpost stated that the line of resistance of the outpost must hold for a definite time or until other orders were received, the platoon area, on this line, would be organized for a protracted defence. In the organization of the ground, deception would be accentuated. Dummy emplacements would be constructed. Additional foxholes would be dug and partly camouflaged to deceive the enemy and disperse his fire.

The observation groups, outguards, and the patrols covered the front of the general outpost as for a bivouac outpost. The observation posts were placed to observe the front and the flanks.

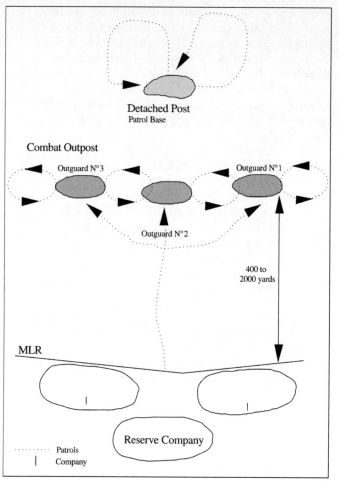

27. Combat outpost

When the combat outposts were forced or ordered to withdraw, they withdrew along designated and reconnoitred routes. If the distance from the battle position was short, there were, usually, no intermediate delaying positions, and the withdrawal was made directly to the company assembly area. The battalion commander was informed when the combat outpost was assembled.

8 – Defence Of The Obstacles

Security could be reinforced by artificial obstacles, such as anti-tank mines and roadblocks, even when natural obstacles existed.

A reinforced rifle squad was frequently detached to protect obstacles. The location of the squad permitted flanking fire over the outer edge of the obstacle. When the squad protected a minefield, the squad leader organizes a warning patrol over the minefield area to inform the drivers of friendly vehicles.

The following section discusses defensive combat. Many actions were similar to the security missions. However, the targets were different. The goal of the security missions was to protect a unit that was neither on the frontline, nor in contact with the enemy. However, in a war of movement, security had to provide for an encounter with an enemy far from the frontline, particularly with the reconnaissance units. Defensive combat included tactics to repulse an attack or a counterattack on the main line of resistance, while the security missions aimed to prevent an enemy action from occurring.

4.2 DEFENSIVE COMBAT

The mission of the infantry in defence was, with the support of other arms, to stop the enemy by fire in front of the battle position; if the enemy reached the positions, to repel his assault by close combat; if he succeeded in entering it, to eject him by a counterattack.

The goal of defensive combat was to gain time pending the development of more favourable conditions to undertake an offensive, or to economize the forces on one front, to concentrate superior forces for a decision elsewhere. A commander could assume the defensive pending the arrival of reinforcements. He could be forced onto the defensive because of numerical inferiority. He could take a defensive position to hold up a vital zone during the manoeuvre of other forces or to contain the enemy while an offensive was conducted elsewhere.

The organization of defensive positions may be classified into two categories, the hastily-occupied defensive position (hasty), and the more strongly fortified position (deliberate). The terms hasty and deliberate are relative because it is difficult to indicate a definite line of demarcation between the two. Usually, a hasty position was organized in eight hours or less with organic equipment and materials. A deliberate position required more time to complete. Only the hasty defence will be described.

A hasty defence could have to be assumed at any time and from any type of combat. It was one of the means used by the security detachments to protect the main body (chapter 4, section 4.1). When it became necessary to prepare a hasty defence, the ground was evaluated and the defence prepared. The extent to which the defence was prepared was limited only by available time and facilities.

A part of the platoon maintains its firepower, while the remainder dug the foxholes. All weapons were kept loaded and close at hand. The automatic rifles (BAR) and the crew-served weapons were placed to cover the most probable route of approach of the enemy. Every advantage was taken of natural cover and concealment. The area was improved as time permitted.

Unless the offensive was resumed almost immediately, when an objective was taken security detachments were posted and the platoon dug-in and prepared to repel a counterattack.

The combat elements were distributed in the defence in three echelons: security forces, holding garrisons and the reserve. The rifle platoon, as part of the company, could be assigned to any of these echelons. The battle position was the position of principal resistance in defence. It consisted of a number of mutually supporting areas disposed in width and depth. Each was organized for all-around defence. The rifle platoon of a frontline company could be employed to organize and defend an area on the main line of resistance or to organize and defend the company support area. It occupied, normally, one defence area. When it occupied more than one, each area was independently-commanded and operated directly under the company commander.

The line joining the forward edges of the more advanced organized defence areas in the battle position was called the main line of resistance (MLR).

The front assigned to a frontline platoon varied according to the natural defences and the importance of the defensive area. General limits were a frontage of 250-500 yards and a depth of not more than 200 yards. The area physically occupied should not exceed 300 yards. The frontage could exceed 55 yards when the terrain was open and flat, or when an obstacle made the enemy attack very difficult. The platoon covered by fire the part of its front which was not occupied.

1 – Actions by the Platoon Commander

After he had received his orders from the company, the platoon commander had to:

a) study his notes. If a map was available, a hasty map study had to be made. Reconnaissance was to be planned, and a vantage point overlooking his area selected.

b) order the platoon to move forward, meet his subordinate leaders at the vantage point, or other point, and give the defensive orders

c) make his reconnaissance.

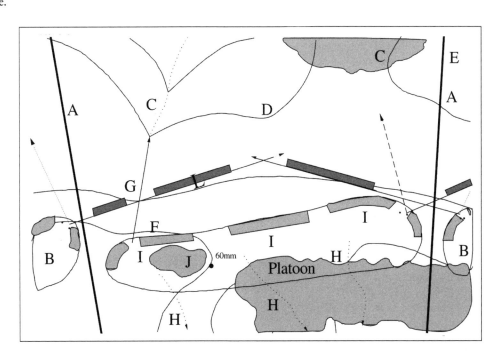

28. Emplacement of the platoon, reconnaissance by the platoon commander

The reconnaissance by the platoon commander was to be as detailed as the time and the situation permitted. He was to plan how to make best use of the ground to employ his firepower to accomplish the mission. He had to keep in mind an all-around defence.

During his reconnaissance, the platoon commander was to consider (see chart 28, letters correspond to those of the drawing):

a) limits of the defended area
b) emplacements of adjacent units
c) areas which permitted the enemy to approach closely
d) natural obstacles and exposed areas over which the enemy must pass
e) commanding terrain features which could be used by the enemy as observation points
f) areas of the proposed position which were exposed to enemy observation
g) emplacements which permitted early detection of the enemy by the observers of the platoon
h) covered routes to the rear
i) location of the squads (tentative at this stage) and of the attached weapons,
j) location of the platoon commander's command and observation post.

During his reconnaissance, the platoon commander contacted the commanders of the supporting weapons in his area and the commanders of the adjacent units, to organize the flanking fires before he decided definitively upon the emplacements of his squads and of the attached weapons. At the same time, he determined the best fields of fire for all weapons. The trace of the platoon's dispositions was coordinated with the fire of the supporting weapons and that of the adjacent units.

When the platoon commander of a frontline platoon had assigned positions to the rifle squads and to the supporting weapons, the platoon dug its foxholes. The platoon commander would again contact the commanders of the adjacent platoons. They exchanged information about the final dispositions and the fire plans. By such coordination, mutual support was assured. The fire plans within the entire company defence area were coordinated by the company commander.

The platoon commander planned to distribute his fire to cover the front and the flanks of his platoon and the fronts of the adjacent platoons. To each rifle squad a sector of fire was assigned. The responsibility for an enemy route of approach was specifically assigned to one leader. The sectors of fire of the squads overlapped to assure complete coverage. The sectors of fire of the flank squads include the area in front of the adjacent platoons.

The platoon commander disposed the squads to cover the front of the platoon area, the gaps on the flanks, and to furnish supporting fire to adjacent platoons.

The rifle squads could be positioned abreast when the assigned frontage was so narrow that there were few or no gaps between the frontline platoons.

The flanks of the platoon were drawn back, to provide better fire to the flank and mutual supporting fire with the adjacent units when the frontage is wide. In this case, there would be gaps between the platoons.

The platoon could occupy two defence areas. The platoon sergeant was in charge of one of them, and the integrity of the squads was maintained.

When company control and observation of the 60mm mortars was difficult, or when a platoon defensive area could not be effectively supported by mortars under company control, a mortar squad (weapons platoon) could be attached to that platoon. The platoon commander directed the squad in action, but the company commander assigned the primary targets (final protective fire) which took precedence over other fire. The mortars covered the gaps in the final protective line and defiladed positions.

2 – Organization of the Ground

The primary consideration was to get the men dug-in when the locations of the weapon emplacements had been fixed. The positions were to be concealed to the maximum extent from both air and ground observation, and the foreground cleared sufficiently to permit effective fire. The extent of the organization of the platoon defence area was only limited by the time and the available facilities. Supplementary positions were constructed to permit an all-around defence of the area. Whenever possible, natural cover was used to move to the supplementary positions.

After having established his plans, the platoon commander issued his orders to the squad leaders, if possible in position. He conducted the squad leaders to the various squad areas and showed each squad leader his specific area, the sectors of fire and the locations for the automatic rifleman (BAR) and the rifle grenadier (with grenade-launcher M7, usually the assistant squad leader). He also showed the adjacent areas, the supporting weapons and their sectors of fire.

A platoon commander's orders for defence should have included:

a) information about the enemy, including the direction of the attack and if known, the time of the attack
b) information on supporting and adjacent units
c) mission of the Platoon
d) location and mission of each squad, sectors of fire, the location and the primary missions of the automatic rifleman (BAR) and of the rifle grenadier
e) location and mission of the attached 60mm mortars, the primary and the secondary target areas being assigned by the company commander
f) security measures
g) priority of work
h) ammunition supply, the battalion aid station, and other administrative details
i) location of the platoon command post

After he issued his plans, the platoon commander indicated to his squad leaders where the platoon was laid out, guided by messengers. Each squad leader had the opportunity to study his own area and dispositions before the arrival of his men.

A good observation, permitting command and control of the fire was a vital necessity to the defenders. The attacker had to be denied possession of terrain features that would be favourable for observation.

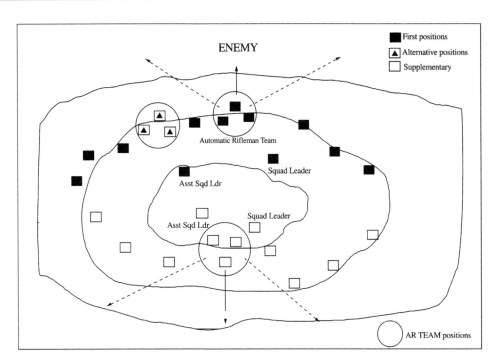

First positions
Alternative positions
Supplementary

ENEMY

Automatic Rifleman Team

Squad Leader

Asst Sqd Ldr

Asst Sqd Ldr

Squad Leader

AR TEAM positions

29. Emplacement of a squad, primary and supplementary positions

Each platoon, or subordinate defence area, provided its own security, despite measures taken by higher units. When the platoon arrived on the position, at least one observer was posted to give warning of enemy ground or air approach and of gas. In the same way, an observer was posted in each subordinate area. These sentinels were relieved regularly, at least every two hours; more frequent relief was advised. The automatic riflemen were posted to give immediate protection and to cover enemy approaches.

The squad defence order included:

a) new information about the enemy or the situation
b) emplacements of adjacent squads and support weapons
c) mission of the squad, the extent of the area and the sectors of fire, and the approximate location of each member of the squad
d) information concerning ammunition, aid station location
e) location of the platoon and company command posts

After he received the platoon defence order, the squad leader:

a) carefully examined his area to determine the best place to defend
b) noted the location of the adjacent squads and of the supporting weapons for which he must furnish protection
c) decided where he must place each member of his squad

When the squad arrived, the squad leader:

a) placed the automatic rifleman at the emplacement designated by the platoon commander and indicated his sector of fire. This measure also furnished to the squad its immediate protection and observation.
b) issued the squad orders. He positioned each man in position and assigned to each a sector of fire.
c) supervised the preparation of the squad defence area including an alternate position for the automatic rifleman and supplementary positions for the squad.
d) if time and duties permitted, he prepared a rough sketch of the sector of fire of the squad in duplicate showing terrain characteristics and ranges. He submitted one copy to the platoon commander and kept the other.

The squad leader selected the positions for himself and for the assistant squad leader, from which they could best command and control the squad, and observe. The position of the assistant squad leader was determined, too, by his duty as rifle grenadier.

The automatic rifleman was positioned so as to accomplish the mission defined by the platoon commander. He was assigned a principal direction of fire to cover the specific terrain features or the gaps in the defensive fire of the supporting weapons, or other approaches. The sector of fire of the automatic rifleman included the sector of the squad and the front of the adjacent squads.

The order of priority of the construction:

a) clear fields of fire, at least 100 yards
b) dig foxholes and the emplacements
c) place or erect obstacles and mines

To be most effective, camouflage was to be executed with the other work.

The command and observation post consisted initially of a foxhole for each member of the platoon headquarters. The position of the platoon commander had to provide cover for the messengers and defiladed routes to the company command post. The platoon sergeant was to be near the platoon commander.

Each member of the squad was assigned an emplacement situated at least five yards from the next emplacement. Each man took up a firing position in his assigned emplacement. He was positioned primarily to assure effective fire, and secondarily to take advantage of the cover and the concealment available.

The squad leader controlled and adjusted each individual position to ensure that the sectors of fire overlapped. Each rifleman was to know the sectors of fire on his left and right.

The clearing of the fields of fire was undertaken. The field of fire of each flank of the squad included the front of the adjacent squad. The characteristics of the ground were disturbed as little as possible, only brush, tall grass and low hanging limbs of trees, which interfered with the observation, were removed.

3 – The Foxhole

The foxhole was an entrenchment dug for individual protection, when contact with the enemy was imminent or expected. The foxhole was dug with its longer side parallel to the most likely enemy route of approach. It had to stay small, 2 feet by 3½ feet, to provide the maximum protection.

The turf, the sod, the leaves or the topsoil were removed over an area extending about 4 feet. They were set aside to be used later to camouflage the excavated earth. In some situations, the soldier could remove the spoil entirely and improvise a cover for his foxhole. In this manner, a foxhole could become practically invisible from air and ground observation. In other cases, the soil could be excavated from the foxhole and piled around the hole to form a 3-foot wide parapet. That was then covered with the removed sod or topsoil as camouflage. The camouflage had to be continuous. If the earth showed the likelihood of caving-in, the sides of the foxhole were to be sloped or revetted.

An additional depth or sump was dug for the soldier's feet. The remaining portion was called the fire step. The foxhole had to be dug deep enough so that the soldier could fire when standing on the fire step and observe when standing in the sump. It was to be deep enough so that when the man leant forward, there was at least 2 feet of clearance above his body.

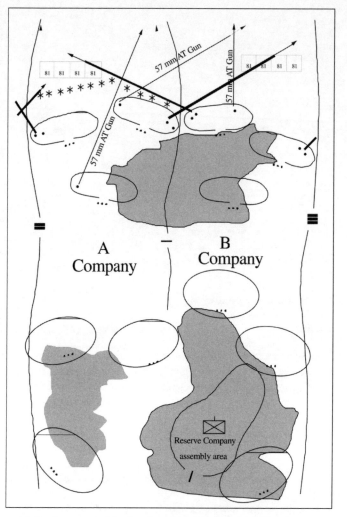

30. Emplacement of the frontline platoons and the reserve platoons

The turf, the sod, the leaves, or the topsoil which had been set aside for camouflage were placed over the newly removed soil as the foxhole was prepared.

The squad leader would examine the squad area from the direction of the enemy to control its appearance and camouflage. A camouflage cover, if prepared to conceal the foxhole, had to match the surrounding terrain.

Chart 29 shows an arrangement of foxholes in an independent squad defence area on flat terrain. The riflemen could shift their fire to the flank or the rear of their primary emplacement. The ranges were estimates to landmarks and each soldier was informed of them. This procedure facilitated target designation and accurate fire.

4 – Camouflage

Camouflage was an important consideration during the organization of a defensive position and during the occupation of the position. The new paths, the freshly-dug earth, the felled trees and all signs of occupation had be avoided as they communicated information to the enemy ground and air observers. One of the best means of protection against enemy fire was good camouflage.

The measures to take for concealment from enemy air and ground observations were planned and constantly improved while the positions were being prepared and as long as the position was occupied. Natural concealment and camouflage went hand in hand.

The dummy works served to mislead the enemy and to disperse or direct his fire. To be effective, they had to look closely like real works. They had to be easily recognizable, so as to give to the enemy valuable misinformation. They were to show evidence of an attempt at camouflaging them. The distances from the real positions were to be enough to protect the latter from the natural dispersion of artillery fire

Dummy foxholes needed to be dug only one foot deep and to be only partially camouflaged. To be effective, they had to be realistic, dark foliage being placed into the bottom to increase the illusion of depth.

Enemy planes could strafe the positions anytime. The guards had to always be on the alert to give immediate warning of the approach of enemy aircraft.

The dispersion and camouflage of the foxholes was the best individual protection against enemy aircraft. The defending soldiers used all available weapons to fire against enemy planes which attacked them. However, if they were not attacked, the frontline troops were not to disclose their positions by firing at them.

The enemy would try to find by ruses the platoon areas on the battle position. Enemy patrols would try to pass through the outguards at night, or in fog, and attempt to draw their fire. The local security had to deal with such attempts. The battle positions must not be disclosed; silence and concealment had to be observed. Discipline and camouflage would prevent their untimely disclosure.

A frontline platoon could occupy night defence positions different from its day positions. These positions were to be reconnoitred during the day, and prepared as time permitted. During night, smoke or fog, double sentinels were posted. They were supplemented by patrols.

5 – The Conduct of the Defence

Success in defence depended upon each platoon, squad, and soldier holding in place and repulsing or killing the attackers. The platoon withdrew only on a verified order from a higher authority.

During preparatory enemy artillery shelling, the platoon took cover in its foxholes. When the bombardment or the artillery fires stopped, the firing positions were taken. The observers were to keep the foreground under a constant observation.

The platoon took advantage of all passive means of defence. Natural obstacles were improved, and mines were used when available. The mines were covered by fire. The guards posted over minefields, in front of the main line of resistance, were withdrawn when the outpost or other covering fire positions withdrew.

The anti-tank rifle grenadiers sought to destroy all tanks or armoured vehicles that came within effective range of their weapons. The soldiers who were armed with machine guns, mortars, or rifles, did not fire at tanks. They took cover in their foxholes or emplacements to prevent themselves being crushed as the tank reached their position. They engaged the infantry accompanying or closely following the tanks. They prevented the tank crews from opening their hatches and throwing grenades into the foxholes.

Artificial obstacles were positioned to direct the movements of the enemy toward an exposed area and to hold him under fire. The obstacles were placed in tall grass, bushes, or hidden if possible. They were to be covered all the time by fire, to avoid that the enemy removing or destroying them

Tactical obstacles, usually a double-apron fence, were placed to hold the enemy in an area covered by defensive fire, particularly on the line of final protective fire of the machine guns.

Protective obstacles, usually a single 4-strand barbed-wire fence, had to surround the platoon defence area. They were placed between 50 and 100 yards beyond the platoon defence area. Anti-personnel mines were hidden near the tactical wires and the obstacles.

The members of the squad opened fire on the words of their commander, who complied with the platoon commander's orders. Fire was withheld until the enemy was within the effective range of the rifles (500 yards). The company was kept informed of the situation.

The accuracy of fire and the close combat skills of the riflemen and the automatic riflemen was the deciding issue of the battle. If enemy infantry entered the area, they were to be driven out by fire, hand grenades, and the bayonet. A stubborn defence in situ by the frontline squads broke up the enemy attack formation and made him vulnerable to counterattack by higher units. A unit entrusted with the defence of a tactical position, under no circumstances abandoned it unless authorized to do so by higher authority. The vital positions on the main line of resistance (MLR) were to be held to the last man.

When an adjacent area was penetrated, fire was directed such as to prevent the hostile forces from widening the breach and enveloping nearby platoons. If a squad area was overrun, the same action was undertaken. If a platoon was threatened with envelopment, its leader made changes in the disposition of his personnel and of the supporting weapons in his area, to ensure an all-around defence of his perimeter.

Prisoners were disarmed and searched upon capture. They were divided in three groups, officers, non-commissioned officers, privates, and were taken to the platoon commander or the company commander as ordered. The questioning of the prisoners by the platoon or the company was limited to obtaining information of immediate importance. The information habitually searched for was:
a) identification of the unit to which the prisoners belonged
b) strength of the enemy in the immediate vicinity
c) emplacement of automatic weapons in the immediate vicinity
Language difficulties generally prevented frontline units from obtaining more information.

6 – Ammunition Supply

The impulse for supply was from rear to front. Loaded trucks were delivered by the battalion to the company ammunition point. The loads were usually dumped at this point. Distribution to the platoons was effected by hand. If the vehicles could move directly to the platoon defence areas, the company ammunition point was purely a control point. The ammunition was delivered as closely as possible to the platoon area. The platoon commander was responsible for the delivery to weapons and to individual soldiers. If necessary, he could demand help from the company commander.

After contact with the enemy was made, ammunition replenishment within the company was made after dark. The platoon commander then informed the company commander of the status of ammunition.

7 – The Dispositions for Mess

The platoon commander sent carrying parties to the company mess location when the kitchen truck arrived. The food was carried by these parties to their own platoon. At a specified time, the empty containers were returned to the company.

The platoon commander could also send his platoon to eat at the company mess area. Regardless of the method employed, the platoon was always fed in relays so the positions were always manned and defence thus continually maintained.

8 – Aid to Wounded

During an enemy attack, the riflemen were not to stop fighting to aid the wounded. The company aid men administered first aid and tagged the wounded. The litter bearers carried the non-walking wounded to the battalion aid station. The wounded would be helped most by driving the enemy back.

9 – The Support Platoon

Usually, a frontline rifle company placed two rifle platoons on the main line of resistance (MLR) and one in support. The support platoon organized a position from which it was capable of firing towards the flanks of the forward platoon defence areas, in the gaps between the platoons, and within the forward areas in case they were overrun by the enemy.

The mission of the support platoon was to assist the frontline platoons by firing, to limit penetrations within the company area, to execute local counterattacks and to protect the flanks and the rear of the company.

The support could be be required to organize more than one platoon area. It was then held mobile in a concealed assembly area, ready either to occupy prepared positions or to counterattack as decided by the company commander.

In the assembly area, the squads were segregated and the foxholes dug. All men were kept up-to-date with covered routes to the prepared positions and with their positions and missions in each area. The terrain could require that the support platoon occupy two defence areas; the platoon sergeant commanded the second area although the squad integrity was maintained.

If the enemy succeeded in penetrating the positions, his advance was to be limited by the support platoon, either by firing from its prepared positions or by a counterattack. The decision to counterattack rested with the company commander. A counterattack had to be delivered quickly if it was to be successful, and before the enemy had a chance to organize his defences.

Each plan was fully explained to all men of the platoon and if time permitted, rehearsed. The platoon did not pursue the enemy beyond the main line of resistance (MLR), except by fire.

A counterattack would be launched against:

a) the flank of the enemy elements which had overrun a frontline defence area or...

b) enemy elements effecting an infiltration that threatened to envelop a forward area

The platoon commander of a support platoon assigned to a counterattack mission was told the objective and direction of the counterattack. The counterattack of a support platoon was a bayonet assault delivered quickly before the enemy had had time to take over the area or to reorganize.

10 – The Reserve Platoons

The platoons of a reserve rifle company in defence were assigned defensive areas similar to those of the frontline platoons. The fire and the positions were coordinated with those of the heavy machine gun in the battalion reserve area. The automatic rifles (BAR) were situated in the company assembly area for anti-aircraft defence. The working parties could be detailed to the forward areas to assist in clearing fields of fire, erecting obstacles, laying anti-tank mine fields, constructing emplacements and entrenchments, executing camouflage, and performing other similar tasks.

31. Symbols of the charts

11 – The Withdrawal

A platoon withdrew only if ordered by a higher authority. The company commander personally informed the platoon commander of:

    a) reconnaissance to be made

    b) time of withdrawal

    c) platoon and company assembly areas

    d) the covering force to leave behind, usually a squad per platoon.

NIGHT WITHDRAWAL

The rearward movement of the frontline rifle units, less the covering force, began at the hour designated by the company commander. The soldiers moved straight to the rear to the squad assembly individually, where the squad leader regained control of his men. The squads moved to the designated platoon assembly area. The platoons then moved to the company assembly area. To facilitate control, small column formations were adopted.

DAYLIGHT WITHDRAWAL

The company order for the withdrawal of a frontline platoon was habitually brief, oral and fragmentary. The squad leaders would be informed by the platoon commander for the reason of the withdrawal, when it must begin and where the squads were to assemble.

The rifle squad would be thinned out as rapidly as possible by the squad leader who sent the soldiers to a specified nearby area at the rear. The remaining soldiers covered the withdrawal. The soldiers retired taking advantage of concealed and covered routes. The squad leader withdrew with his last man, normally the automatic rifleman.

The platoon commander withdrew with his last element. The assistant squad leader, or a designated member of the squad, assembled the men as rapidly as possible at the platoon assembly area.

The support platoon covered the withdrawal of the frontline platoons. When the last elements of the frontline platoons had passed, the support platoon, under the protection of the battalion reserve, withdrew. The covering force consisted of a squad with support weapons placed in the platoon area. Before the withdrawal, the squad leader of the covering force received orders from the commander of the company acting as a covering force about the redistribution of the squad to provide observation and protection for supporting weapons. Not less than two men were situated in any one position.

The support platoon withdrew in the same manner as a frontline platoon. The squad left in the support platoon area was generally kept intact for local patrolling, or to repel enemy patrols which may have succeeded in entering the position.

Defensive combat was temporary. It was only performed to allow the time necessary to prepare the offensive.

4.3 OFFENSIVE COMBAT

1 – Reconnaissance, Plans and Orders

To prepare for the attack, the platoon as part of the company, halted generally in a designated portion of the company assembly area. However, the platoon could also attack directly from the approach march, if ammunition had been issued beforehand. As this procedure left little opportunity for reconnaissance and coordination of plans, it was adopted only when the situation demanded an immediate attack.

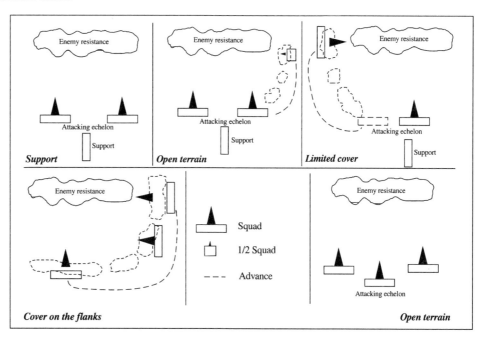

32. Different methods of utilising the squads of a platoon dependent upon the terrain

The company orders prescribed whether the platoon was to be initially in the attacking (leading) echelon or support echelon. Each platoon in the attacking echelon was assigned to a zone of action. A zone was defined by the assignment of the platoon to:

a particular section of the line of departure (LD) or an area from which to start its attack

a direction of attack

a defined objective on the terrain or series of objectives to capture

The platoon was responsible for driving forward and gaining the objectives assigned to its zone of action. The boundaries between the platoons were rarely defined as the platoon often took advantage of covered routes in the adjacent platoon zones of action to manoeuvre against enemy resistance.

Each platoon was assigned, as its initial objective, the nearest terrain feature or enemy position within its zone of action whose capture was essential for the further advance of the company as a whole. It had to continue its attack after the initial objective had been captured, either in a given direction, or against another defined objective.

When he received the company attack order, the commander of a platoon assigned to the attacking echelon made the necessary preparations to have his platoon ready to attack. He planned his reconnaissance, selected a vantage point, making the former as extensive as possible, and issued attack orders to his squad leaders.

The platoon commander selected a location from which he could point out the important terrain features, whilst he issued his attack orders. The location of this vantage point was shown to the messenger who returned to the platoon and guided the squad leaders to it to receive their attack orders.

During his reconnaissance, the platoon commander had to picture the situation as it existed on the ground over which the platoon was to attack. He considered the possible methods of attack and made plans to use his weapons and men to the best advantage to accomplish the assigned mission with the least practicable delay and with the fewest casualties.

Frequently, to save time, the platoon commander required the movement forward of the platoon whilst he performed his reconnaissance and issued his orders.

During the brief time available to plan his attack, the platoon commander had to consider the following:

a) How the terrain offered the enemy observation and fields of fire against the platoon or the adjacent platoons, and concealment, from which he could launch surprise counterattacks. As knowledge of the enemy strength and his exact dispositions was usually incomplete or nonexistent, the platoon commander had to determine not only where the enemy guns and men were, but also where the camouflaged and concealed positions were.

b) How the terrain offered the squads the opportunity for movement. The platoon commander would try to select a favourable approach: ditches, brushes, wooded draws leading toward his objective.

c) He decided whether his flanks would be exposed or protected by the action or location of other friendly troops.

d) He considered the positions where smoke or supporting fire would be provided by higher units.

e) He identified the positions where he had to place his rifles and automatic rifles (BAR), and any attached mortar or machine gun in order to coordinate their fire with the fire provided by higher units, and to support the advance of any part of the platoon.

f) He determined the firing positions provided by the terrain and the covered routes to these positions.

The 60mm mortars and the machine guns (Light Machine Gun caliber .30) from the weapons platoon were normally employed under company command. The attachment of one of these weapons to the rifle platoon was seldom desirable, particularly the light machine guns. This placed the burden of control and the supervision of ammunition supply on the platoon commander.

When an attacking rifle platoon could not be effectively supported by mortar fire under company command, a mortar squad could be attached to the platoon, the other mortars remaining under company control. The 60mm mortars were used against defined targets that could not be reached by flat-trajectory weapons.

The attachment of a machine gun to the rifle platoon was exceptional; if done, it was employed to add to the covering fire provided by the automatic rifles for the movement of elements of the platoon. The characteristics of the machine guns made them valuable for flanking fire. If possible, flanking or oblique fire was to be employed in short, concentrated bursts on groups of enemy soldiers.

Large flank movements were rarely possible using a platoon. Each unit was responsible for the protection of its own flanks. Surprise being an essential element of a successful attack, the platoon commander had to avoid stereotyped procedures. Deception, manoeuvre, the screening of dispositions by cover or concealment, all aided in effecting surprise.

The platoon commander initially kept one squad in support for use as a manoeuvre element. The BAR team of the support squad assisted the attacking echelon by fire. In exceptional circumstances, if the enemy's frontal strength was considerable, or if the zone of action was wide, all the firepower of the platoon could be required at the beginning of the attack.

The ground and the nature of the enemy resistance sometimes favoured a frontal assault with one or two squads, while the third manoeuvred to a suitable position on the flank. From this flank position, the manoeuvre element assisted by firing to support the advance of the other elements. When the situation permitted, the platoon commander could attack the enemy flank with the entire attacking echelon of the platoon. To be more effective, the fire delivered from the flank had to be surprise fire. This manoeuvre was most likely to succeed if the enemy was immobilized by fire from the support echelon.

The platoon could launch a frontal attack, all squads in line, by employing fire and movement. The soldiers in each squad moved forward, one or two at a time, as directed by the squad leader. They took advantage of shell holes, small folds in the ground, and if available, cover and concealment. This method provided the maximum firepower in the minimum time but left no support.

The platoon commander met his squad leaders at the selected point after he had decided his plan of attack. He oriented his squad leaders by pointing out the important characteristics of the terrain and issued his order for the attack.

The platoon commander's attack orders would include:

1) new information about the enemy, friendly troops, and supporting fire
2) the mission of the platoon, time or signal for attack, the line of departure (LD)
3) the role of each squad
4) the location of the battalion aid station;
5) the positions and expected movement of the platoon commander

The platoon commander ensured that all squad leaders understood his order. He repeated them when necessary. He allowed his squad leaders necessary time to inform the soldiers of the platoon about the mission. It must be remembered that the initial attack orders did not cover the entire attack of the platoon. As the advance progressed, the situation changed and the platoon commander issued subsequent orders. Each squad had to be in its assigned place, ready to commence firing or moving forward at the prescribed time. When the assembly of the squad leaders and the issuing of complete order were not permitted by time or circumstances, the platoon commander issued fragmentary orders.

Each squad leader had to know the platoon's mission, the plans to accomplish it and other details as time was available. When the squad was engaged with the enemy, the squad leader did not leave his unit, orders or instructions being delivered to him by messengers.

The squad leader would observe the terrain as he moved to the vantage point to receive orders from the platoon commander. After receiving the platoon attack orders, the squad leader reconnoitred the ground over which the squad must attack, as far as time permitted. During this brief reconnaissance, he decided where and how he would employ his automatic rifle team (AR team or BAR team). The squad leader then returned to his unit to issue the squad's orders. After receiving the platoon order, if little time remained, the squad leader would lead his squad directly into position, selecting a route of advance during his return to the squad. When he issued certain parts of his orders, he preceded his squad and continued his reconnaissance as he advanced. The squad leader never exposed his squad in an area subject to enemy small arms fire without prior reconnaissance.

The squad's attack orders included:

1) new information about the enemy, the adjacent units and the supporting weapons
2) objectives of the squad, and plans for achieving these
3) objectives for each soldier, or all
4) location of the aid station
5) location of the squad leader

The squad leader issued his attack orders to all soldiers of his squad. He ascertained that the orders had been understood, and that all men knew the squad's mission and the plans to accomplish it.

2 – The Advance to and across the Line of Departure

The movement of a platoon of the attacking echelon from the assembly area across the line of departure had to be conducted in order to preserve the secrecy of the attack. The platoon sometimes might have to fight to reach or cross the line of departure (LD).

The terrain and the probability of coming under enemy observation or fire determined the particular formation used. Before arriving at the line of departure, the platoon took up its attack formation. The scouts from the leading squad preceded the platoon to protect its advance. The platoon commander followed and observed the conduct of the scouts. He changed the platoon formation if necessary. A patrol, or several observers, could be sent to a dangerous or an exposed area.

The platoon would be held under cover a short distance to the rear of the designated line of departure, until just before the time of the attack. At the prescribed time, the squads had to be in their assigned place, ready to move forward or to commence firing. However, a squad was sometimes directed to cross a road or another line of departure at or on a designated time or signal. In this situation, the squad would be held under cover in the rear of the designated line until just before the time of the attack. The squad crossed the line of departure in squad column or in diamond formation and did not deploy further until obliged to fire on the enemy.

3 – The beginning of the Firefight

Fire was usually opened on the orders of the platoon commander. However, the company commander could reserve to himself the authority for opening fire to gain surprise. At the first firing position, the attacking echelon sought to suppress the fire superiority of the enemy by accurate and intense fire to its enemy front.

When the platoon came under the effective fire of small arms, further advances were undertaken by fire and movement. The enemy would be pinned down by frontal and flanking fire under the cover of which the other elements of the platoon would manoeuvre forward, using all available cover to protect themselves against enemy fire. The first manoeuvre element of the platoon having moved forward, it would occupy, in turn, firing positions and cover the advance of the former covering element. This combination of movement and fire was used even with a few men or a small group.

To manoeuvre in the adjacent platoon area was often the only feasible method to a squad or a small group if it was to reach the enemy positions. The platoon commander would use such a route without hesitation. Its use did not interfere with the action of the adjacent unit. When the two units were abreast, the commander of the adjacent unit would be advised of the envisaged action.

The platoon commander would follow his attacking echelon closely. He went where he could best observe the development and influence the action of the platoon. He watched the development of the enemy's fire and the location of its main force. To use his support, he noted where the enemy was weakest and where his attacking echelon made the most progress.

The platoon protected its flanks by sending connecting groups of two or three men toward each flank to maintain the contact with the adjacent units. When a gap developed between the platoon and an adjacent unit, the connecting group fanned out to maintain contact and notified the platoon commander. He verified the report by a personal reconnaissance, reinforced the connecting group, and reported the fact and the actions undertaken to the company commander.

During the attack, the squad leader's duties were varied. His primary duty was, during the firefight, to place the fire of his squad on target. During this time, he kept in mind the firepower of his automatic rifle team and used it to support the advance of the other members of the squad.

The squad leader took up a position from which he could best control his men and observe the effects of their fire. In selecting his position, he considered the necessity to maintain contact with the platoon commander. Whenever the majority or all of the squad advanced, he led the way.

Unless otherwise ordered by the platoon commander, the squad leader permitted his squad to open fire only when it was necessary to cover a further advance. At its first firing position, the squad sought to gain firepower superiority over the enemy.

The position of the assistant squad leader was not fixed, he took up position where he could best assist the squad leader, and be prepared to protect the squad against a tank attack. He assisted the squad leader in enforcing fire, discipline, controlling the fire, supervising ammunition supply and maintaining contact with the platoon commander.

When the squad leader could not maintain personally-effective control over the fire of the squad as a whole, he could temporarily delegate the control of part of the squad to the assistant squad leader.

4 – The Automatic Rifle Team

The automatic rifleman, the assistant automatic rifleman and the ammunition bearer operated as a team to keep the automatic rifle ready for action. Except when they needed to keep the automatic rifle in action, the assistant automatic rifleman and the ammunition bearer paid particular attention to targets which threatened the automatic rifle.

The squad leader sought a position for his automatic rifleman from which he could deliver effective fire on any target holding up the squad. Practically, this position had to permit fire across the entire front of the squad. The chosen position was usually the one that offered the best field of fire, although tactical considerations could require that fields of fire be given secondary consideration. The firepower of the automatic rifle was especially used to maintain or gain the fire superiority of the squad.

Under the cover of the automatic rifle team's fire, riflemen of the squad would move forward to take firing positions near the enemy. They covered, in turn, the advance of the remainder of the squad.

5 – The Squad's Fire Orders

Whenever possible, the preliminary fire orders would be issued under cover before the skirmishers occupied the firing positions. When the target could not be easily identified, the squad leader sent his men creeping or crawling close to the crest to see the foreground. He completed the fire orders when the men had finished their reconnaissance. Details included in the fire order depended on the time, available cover and nature of the target.

Targets are generally indistinct on a battlefield. They had to be designated promptly with such accuracy and simplicity as not to be mistaken. The squad leader announced the range, designated the targets and gave the order to open fire. If a target was at close range and unmistakable, the fire order could be limited to the command 'commence firing'.

Fire control allowed the squad leader to open fire when he wished, adjusted the fire of his squad upon the target, regulated the rate of fire, shifted the fire whenever necessary to new targets, and to cease fire at will. The squad leader controlled the fire as long as possible, by the use of signals or by requiring riflemen to transmit oral orders from one to another.

At times, because of the noise and confusion of the battle, the squad leader had to go to the firing line and move from man to man to give instructions.

When the squad began firing, the method for its further advance was determined by the effectiveness of the enemy fire and by the characteristics of the terrain, affording cover and concealment. The squad leader was constantly on the alert, looking ahead for new firing positions that his squad could use as the platoon moved forward.

Once gained fire superiority had to be maintained. Unless supporting units or other units could maintain the fire superiority without any help from the squad, some members of it had to stay in position and continue firing to maintain it. When available cover permitted, the squad leader could lead forward a large part of the squad, leaving the remaining men under the control of the assistant squad leader to move further. When available cover allowed only a few men to advance, the squad leader could direct the assistant squad leader to control the advance of the first few soldiers. The squad leader remained with the majority of his squad in the firing position.

The squad generally moved forward by irregular or successive rushes, from cover to cover. Each soldier moved individually or in a small group. A new position had to be selected before a rush. To leave a covered position, make a short rush and drop into a position that afforded no protection from enemy fire served only to increase casualties. Even in very open terrain, a well-trained rifleman could find and use all kinds of limited cover. An aggressive action by one soldier who had been able to work his way forward could sometimes aid the advance of the entire squad.

When the advance to a new firing position was necessary, the squad leader made the signal 'forward' to individuals or groups, then left it up to the leading element to select the new firing position.

After dropping into a new covered or concealed position from the run, a rifleman had to roll quickly a few yards to the right or left to deceive the enemy about his exact emplacement.

The squad increased its rate of fire during periods when any part of it or of an adjacent squad was in movement. It could advance as a unit only when it was completely defiladed or when the enemy fire was kept neutralized by friendly fire. Its advance was led by the squad leader.

If, when moving from one firing position to another, a defiladed area could be found in the rear of the new firing position, the soldiers were halted in the defiladed area.

a) The squad leader crept forward quickly to localize and observe the target. He decided where he would place the members of his squad.

b) He would select a position for the automatic rifleman, then decided how and where he would employ his riflemen. He designated men to move forward and observe the target with a minimum of exposure and gave his preliminary fire order (sight setting and description of the target).

c) Then, he would issue the command 'fire position'. His men would crawl to a position from which they could open fire on the target at the signal. The squad leader then ordered or signalled 'commence firing'.

When the method described above could not be followed, the squad leader could designate a new firing position to which the first soldiers should advance. He sent them forward and after that built up the new firing line with other men as they arrived. The squad leader was to resist, by fire, a sudden attack on its flanks. Each unit, despite its size, was responsible of its own security.

Without instructions from the platoon commander, particularly during the last stages of the firefight, the squad leader frequently had to attack important or dangerous targets without orders.

During the lulls in the fight, the squad leader was to check ammunition and remove all unexpended ammunition from the dead and the wounded.

The squad leader was to observe the units on his flanks and inform the platoon commander whenever wide gaps occurred between the units of the attacking echelon. The squad leader prevented the members of his squad from becoming so widely separated that he lost control. He was to concentrates the fire of the squad on the assigned target.

A squad of even five men remained an effective fighting unit or team if it included a competent leader, an automatic rifleman, and a rifle grenadier. A squad so reduced in strength as to be ineffective was to be combined with another squad, or its personnel distributed among the other squads.

The squad leader was responsible for maintaining contact with the platoon commander at all times. He could delegate this duty to the assistant squad leader. If the squad was separated from its platoon, the squad leader made every effort to find and join the nearest friendly troops. At the first favourable opportunity, the squad was released and rejoined its platoon.

6 – Security against Air and Mechanized Attacks

For security against air attack, the platoon and the squads made the maximum use of concealment. They opened fire against enemy planes only when their fire was not required on ground targets, and the aircraft actually attacked them.

Ground troops had to learn to recognize friendly planes. A platoon of the attacking echelon would displays its marking panels (panel set AP-50) upon request from an identified friendly plane. The panels had to be displayed on open ground so that they could be read from an aircraft that was not directly overhead. They had to be taken up promptly after the plane flew over.

To protect against a mechanized attack, the platoon leader advanced his platoon, whenever possible, through terrain containing natural tank obstacles, posting the rifle grenadiers on the exposed flanks or likely avenues of approach.

7 – The aid to wounded and the prisoners

The company aid men and the litter bearers followed the attacking platoon of each company, the aid men tagging the wounded and administering first aid. The litter bearers carried the non-walking wounded to the aid station.

Prisoners taken during the attack were sent to the company command post. The walking wounded could be used as guards. The prisoners were disarmed and separated into three groups: officers, non-commissioned officers and privates. The prisoners, in the first instance the officers, were searched to find documents and other papers. The name of the prisoner was noted on the documents removed from him and these were given to the guard conducting the prisoners to the company command post.

8 – The Support Squad

The commander of the support squad advanced with his squad following the orders or signals of the platoon commander or the platoon sergeant. He kept it under cover as far as possible and prevented it from mingling with other squads. The leader of the squad in support constantly observed the action of the squads in the attacking echelon and the situation on the front and the flanks. He was always ready to put his squad in action, continually making tentative plans for so doing.

The support was used frequently by the platoon commander to assist where the attacking echelon made the most progress or where the enemy offered the least resistance. When he was directed to reinforce the attacking echelon, the squad leader of the support squad pointed out the enemy positions and the positions of the attacking squads. His squad was not to intermingle with the attacking echelon. The squad leader was shown the part of the line to be reinforced and prepared the squad for its rush.

If he was ordered to attack an enemy position from a flank, the commander of the support squad chose a starting position and the best covered route thereto. Then he moved the squad, preceded where necessary, by scouts, to the selected position and endeavoured to overwhelm the enemy by opening fire and delivering an assault from an unexpected direction.

The platoon commander aimed to hit the weakest spot in the enemy position by sending his support to attack the point of least resistance, or by manoeuvring the support around a flank to strike the flank or the rear of the enemy with surprise fire.

When fire coming from other enemy positions situated to the flank or the rear made a flanking attack impossible, an assaulting force was built up by infiltration close to the enemy line of resistance. This force was protected by the fire of the remainder of the platoon and of the supporting weapons. One or several automatic rifles, temporarily detached, could be employed to neutralize the fire of the enemy flank or rear. The position was then assaulted.

When a weak resistance opposed it, the platoon drove ahead rapidly to attain the objective of the company, regardless of the lack of progress on its flanks.

If the advance of the platoon was stopped by enemy fire and the platoon commander had employed all means in his power to continue his advance, he notified the company commander. The strengthened platoon held the ground gained and dug foxholes. The platoon commander watched the advance of the adjacent units, in case they forced the enemy to withdraw. He planned for the prompt issuing of orders when the first change in the situation permitted his advance to be resumed.

Depending on the terrain, several intermediate objectives could be captured before the attacking echelon reached the initial objective assigned to the company.

At the time of the capture of the initial objective, the platoon commander made a personal reconnaissance then issued his orders to resume the attack to the next objective. A platoon of the attacking echelon did not delay its action to clean up isolated points of resistance, but left them to be reduced by the following echelons. Every effort was made to continue the attack without a pause.

When, prior to the attack, time was not sufficient to issue detailed orders, or if the situation was obscure, the company commander could control the action closely. He could direct the platoon to seize an objective and be prepared to continue its attack. The company commander had to, after the objective was taken, give the order to resume the attack and assign the next objective.

As the attack progressed and casualties occurred, the platoon commander effected a reorganization of his platoon. The opportunity for reorganization was provided by pauses in firing, protective terrain features, and halts at objectives.

When a squad leader, an automatic rifleman, a scout, or other key personnel were lost during the fighting, another rifleman was designated to take over his duties. The platoon had to continue its attack as a well-balanced team. The men had to be trained to exercise individual initiative and be prepared to take over, without orders, the duties of the leaders or of the specialists who were killed or wounded.

9 – The Assault

The last phase of the firefight was the assault on the enemy position (objective). The assault could take place either as part of the general assault ordered by the company commander or the battalion commander, or on the orders of the platoon commander. It was delivered at the earliest moment that promised success without regard to the progress of the adjacent squads.

Supporting fire would be delivered by friendly supporting weapons: machine guns, mortars, artillery and aircraft. When the attacking echelon had progressed as close to the enemy position as it could advance without masking its supporting fire, these weapons lifted their fire at a specified time or upon a prearranged signal, and the assault was launched.

A general assault was delivered either at an hour fixed by the company commander or the battalion commander, or on a prearranged signal. The supporting weapons covered the assault by directing their fire at those adjacent and rearward enemy elements which were able to fire on the assaulting troops either during the assault or after the position is captured.

The platoon commander initiated the platoon assault. The attacking echelon worked its way as close as possible to the enemy position. The platoon commander gave the signal for lifting the supporting fire and led the assault.

Assault fire was the fire delivered by a unit during its assault on an enemy position. When the supporting fire stopped, the platoon could employ its fire to prevent the enemy from manning his defences. The automatic rifleman and the riflemen with bayonets fixed, taking advantage of existing cover, advanced rapidly toward the enemy. They fired at a rapid rate at areas known, or believed to be, occupied by the enemy.

A hand grenade volley was used just before the final charge against an entrenched enemy. In the heat of the fight, the assault was launched frequently on the initiative of a squad or even of individuals. When the assault was started, it received the immediate cooperation of all individuals and units. In the final stage of the assault, the enemy position was overrun in a single rush with the bayonet (although the bayonet was seldom used in Europe, by the U.S. Army, in WWII).

When the Platoon captured the final objective of the company, the enemy was kept under fire as long as he was within effective small arms range. The company commander gave the orders for the future employment of the rifle platoon. Security detachments were posted at once and the platoon dug in and prepared to meet an enemy counterattack, unless the attack was resumed almost immediately. Guards were posted whenever an objective was taken or the platoon halted or assembled.

The ammunition from the dead and wounded was collected and redistributed. Usually, the ammunition of a rifle platoon in the attacking echelon was replenished only after the capture of a terrain mask or after nightfall.

So that it could continue to be an effective fighting team, the platoon was reorganized. The company commander would be informed about the effective strength of the platoon and the status of ammunition. After issuing his orders for reorganization, the platoon commander made a brief reconnaissance to the front and flanks to observe the area over which his platoon could be ordered to advance.

Pursuit was taken up only on the orders of the company commander. The actions of a rifle platoon during the pursuit were similar to its actions during the approach march and the attack. The formations were changed as necessary to facilitate control, for a rapid advance, and for developing maximum firepower if the enemy resistance strengthened.

The light machine guns and the mortars were attached frequently to the rifle platoons for the pursuit, to assist in overcoming rapidly any enemy detachments attempting to delay the pursuit. Once begun, the pursuit was to be characterized by boldness and rapidity and pushed to the limit of human endurance.

The attack upon new objectives was made similarly to that described for the initial attack. If other troops were used to continue the attack by passing them through the platoon, the elements of the platoon exposed to enemy fire remained in position and supported the new attack by fire until it had progressed far enough to permit them to be assembled without extensive losses.

10 – The Support Platoon

Before starting the attack, the company commander had to keep a support for further use. The support could be used as a manoeuvre element to repel a counterattack, replace a part of the attacking echelon, or to assist in the final attack necessary to capture an objective. The support had to be of a sufficient strength to accomplish its probable missions with an exposed flank. A rifle platoon was usually the minimum.

Since its role required that the support could manoeuvre, advance by fire and movement, and close with the bayonet, it had to contain elements other than those of the weapons platoon.

The company commander could assign an initial concealed emplacement to his support. Because of the limited communication facilities within the company, the support platoon was generally directed to follow by bounds in rear of the part of the attacking echelon nearest to the area of its most probable employment. The support platoon employed an approach march formation until it was committed to action. It was not to be mingled with the attacking echelon. The support platoon was charged with its own protection.

The support platoon was frequently charged with maintaining contact with the adjacent companies. Connecting groups were used to maintain this contact. The connecting groups sent their information directly to the company commander. If the company commander did not prescribe the strength of the connecting groups, the platoon commander made the connecting group which he sent out as small as possible, considering the difficulties of the terrain, the distance over which it was to operate, and the number of required messengers.

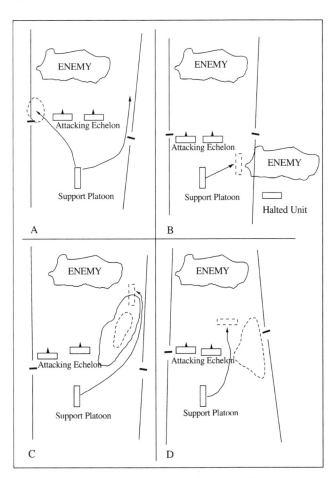

33. The support echelon as manoeuvring force of the company

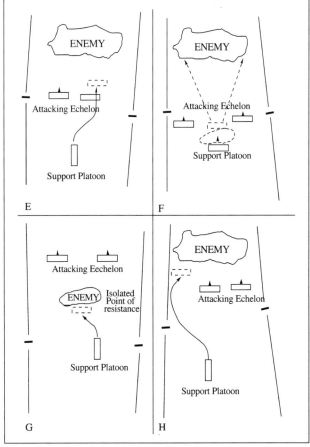

34. Support Platoon

The support echelon was the manoeuvring force of the company. The missions which could be assigned to it included one or more of the following (see charts 33 and 34):
   a) to furnish security to the flanks (connecting groups or flank combat patrols)
   b) to assist in the progression of the adjacent units by fire and manoeuvre
   c) to envelop or attack in the flank points of resistance which were stopping the attacking echelon
   d) to furnish protection against enemy counterattacks during the reorganization of the attacking echelon
   e) to relieve a platoon of the attacking echelon
   f) to support the attacking echelon by fire
   g) to mop up a position overrun and passed by the attacking echelon
   h) to furnish the final blow necessary to seize the objective

During the attack, the commander of the support platoon observed constantly the action of the attacking echelon, the terrain and the situation on the flanks. As the situation changed, he made tentative plans for the employment of the platoon. Whenever a definite employment of the support could be foreseen, the support platoon was directed to be prepared to accomplish this mission. This would enable the platoon commander to conduct a reconnaissance and make plans in advance.

This chapter covering infantry doctrine demonstrates how the infantry units were used. Because of the triangular organization of all units in the infantry division, the rifle platoon and the rifle squad are representative of the use of the infantry. Higher-level units such as the rifle company and the infantry battalion fought on the battlefield in a similar manner. However, the battles were won by the men who made up the platoons and their squads. The infantry division would have been non-existent without the devotion, boldness and deeds of the members of the rifle platoons in seizing enemy ground, and holding it against counterattacks.

CHAPTER 5

DIVISION ARTILLERY, MOTORIZED, INFANTRY DIVISION T/O&E 6-10

The division artillery was, with the three infantry regiments, the most important force of the infantry division. With 2,170 officers and enlisted men (as of 27 September 1944), it was also the largest combat support unit. The division artillery included all artillery units that were permanently a part of the division.[1] For tactical requirements, all artillery units attached to the division and under the command of the division commander were considered as division artillery. Division artillery had the command and control of all artillery units that were permanently or temporarily assigned to the division.

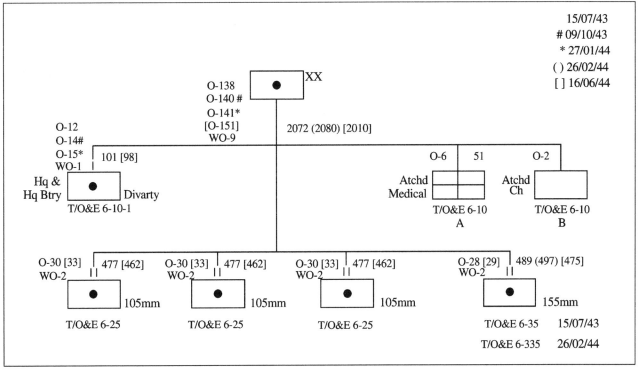

35. Division Artillery, Motorized, Infantry Division

The composition of the division artillery was:
    Headquarters and Headquarters Battery, Motorized, Division Artillery (section 5.2)
    3 Field Artillery Battalions, Motorized, 105mm Howitzer
    1 Field Artillery Battalion, Motorized, 155mm Howitzer (sections 5.3 to 5.6)
Each field artillery battalion, 105mm howitzer, was attached to an infantry regiment when this formed a regimental combat team (RCT). The field artillery battalion, 155mm howitzer, remained under the direct control of the division commander for use as a reinforcement or in a general support role.

---

1. All units which corresponded to this definition, i.e. those which constituted an essential part of the unit to which they belonged are considered organic. The organic parts of a unit are those listed in the Tables of Organization and Equipment. The units permanently assigned were organic or assigned; units temporarily assigned were attached.

A – Medical Detachment, Division Artillery

The medical detachment included:
  Headquarters Detachment (attached to the Headquarters Battery)
  4 Battalion Detachments (each attached to a battalion)
Only the headquarters detachment is examined below. The battalion detachments will be examined with the field artillery battalion.

*1 – HEADQUARTERS DETACHMENT (2 Officers, 7 Enlisted Men)

  1 Major, Medical, General Duty
  1 Captain or 1st Lt, Dental
  1 Technical Sgt, Medical
  1 Sgt, Medical
  1 Pvt, Light truck driver
  1 Techn 5th, Dental technician
  1 Techn 5th, Medical technician
  1 Techn 5th, Surgical technician
  1 Pvt, Basic

Vehicles:
  1 Truck, ¾-ton, WC, with winch
  1 Trailer, ¼-ton

Equipment:
The equipment was similar to that of the battalion detachments, except for the number of items related to personnel. The list of equipment can be found within the organization of the battalion detachment, see section 5.3.
  The headquarters detachment had a dental service, adding the following equipment:
  1 dental kit, officer
  1 dental kit, private
  1 chest, Medical Department, no. 60 (for Dental Officer)

B – Attached Chaplain

  2 Captains or 1st Lts, Chaplain.
  For the vehicles allocated to chaplains and chaplain's assistants, refer to the T/O&E 6-10-1, Headquarters Battery, *2.

Equipment:
  2 gas masks, service, combat, M5-11-7
  2 brassards, Geneva Convention, Red Cross
  2 canvas field bags, olive drab, M1936
  2 pistol belts M1936
  2 canteens, dismounted, M1910
  2 General Purpose (GP) carrying straps (1 per bag M1936)
  2 belt suspenders, M1936 (1 per bag M1936)
  1 water can, 5-gal
  2 shovels, M1943, with carrier
  2 Chaplain outfits (1 per Chaplain)
  1 portable typewriter, with carrying case
  2 flashlights, TL-122-( )

5.1   ARTILLERY DOCTRINE [2]

1 – General Missions of the Field Artillery

The mission of field artillery units was to suppress, to neutralize and to destroy the enemy by means of its organic weapons. The artillery provided close support for the manoeuvre units, and fire to reduce the effectiveness of the manoeuvre firepower of the enemy and disrupt the operations of his command and control elements.

Suppressive fire was aimed at limiting the combat effectiveness of the enemy personnel in the target area. HE[3] projectiles caused apprehension or surprise, and inflicted casualties; smoke projectiles interfered with the observation of the enemy and impeded his operations. The effect was usually limited to the duration of the fire mission. This type of fire was employed against both unknown and suspected enemy positions.

---

  2. This section is based on: *Tactics Overview vol 2* (Combined Arms and Service Staff School, Fort Leavenworth, Kansas, February 1984); correspondence with former WWII officers, Lt Col (U.S. Army Ret.) Richard H. Durst, Brig Gen (U.S. Army, Ret.) William H. Birdsong and Col (U.S. Army Ret.) Chester E. Ball.
  3. HE (high explosive): projectile with a bursting charge of high explosive, used against personnel and material. (AR 320-5, p. 227).

Neutralizing fire was aimed at reducing the combat effectiveness of the enemy in a given area for a determined period of time. Experience indicated that a casualty rate of 10% or more would usually render an enemy unit temporarily ineffective. The unit would become effective again when casualties were replaced and equipment repaired or replaced. The targets for this type mission were usually determined from a map study and observation. The type of unit used for this purpose would vary with the size and nature of the target.

Destructive fire was aimed at inflicting significant damage on a target. Experience indicated that a casualty rate of 30% or more would usually render an enemy unit permanently ineffective. The ability of the enemy to recuperate from such an attack was normally dependent upon the type of unit and the discipline of its personnel. The target would be located and engaged in the same manner as with neutralizing fire. The type of unit used also varied; however, this type of mission required the use of many units. The destruction of armoured or entrenched targets required the expenditure of vast amounts of ammunition.

2 – Tactical Missions of Field Artillery Units

The four basic tactical missions of field artillery units were: direct support (DS), reinforcing (Reinf), general support-reinforcing (GSR), and general support (GS).

a) Direct Support (or Close Support)
An artillery unit with a direct support mission was immediately responsive to requests from the supported unit. It required no other authorization to fire. Each infantry regiment has one field artillery battalion, 105mm, attached to it to provide it direct support. A field artillery battalion could be the direct support of only one infantry regiment and reciprocally an infantry regiment could have only one field artillery battalion in direct support. This mission was the most restrictive but also the most decentralized. A field artillery battalion assigned to a direct support mission would normally implement fire missions in the following order: fire requests from the supported unit, fire requests from its own forward observers, fire requests from division artillery. It developed its own fire support plans.

b) Reinforcing
An artillery unit with a reinforcing mission augmented the fire of another artillery unit. The reinforced unit planned and controlled the fire of the reinforcing unit. An artillery unit with a reinforcing mission reinforced the fires of only one artillery unit. A direct support artillery unit could have more than one unit in a reinforcing mission. A field artillery battalion, 105mm, assigned a reinforcing mission would normally implement fire missions in the following order: fire requests from the reinforced artillery unit, fire requests from its own forward observers, and fire requests from division artillery headquarters. Its zone of fire coincided with that of the reinforced artillery unit. The artillery, as opposed to the infantry, was never held in reserve. If a unit was in the zone of operations, it was assigned a position of fire and a mission would be assigned to it. The field artillery battalion attached to an infantry regiment that was in reserve would normally reinforce the fire of another field artillery battalion. However, the field artillery battalion with a reinforcement mission maintained its position so that it could provide the appropriate infantry unit with direct support in the least possible time.

c) General Support-Reinforcing
An artillery unit with a general support-reinforcing mission (GSR) provided fire support to the entire friendly force and reinforced the fires of other field artillery units. This mission was the most flexible of all tactical missions of the artillery. The field artillery battalion assigned a general support-reinforcing mission would usually implement fire missions in the following order: fire requests from division artillery, fire requests from the reinforced artillery unit, fire requests from its own forward observers. Its zone of fire included the zone of action of the supported unit, including the zone of fire of the reinforced field artillery unit. This type mission was normally assigned to the field artillery battalion, 155mm.

d) General Support
An artillery unit with a general support mission provided fire support for the entire friendly force. Such units were controlled by division artillery headquarters. It could also receive calls for fire from its own observers. This mission was the least restrictive, since it involved the entire infantry division zone. Nevertheless, in terms of control, it was the most centralized. The planning for this type of mission was performed in the division artillery's fire direction center. A GS mission was normally assigned to a field artillery battalion, 155mm. The division commander often employed this type mission to influence his unit's course of action.

3 – The fundamentals of organizing Artillery for Combat

1) maintain the maximum feasible centralized control
2) provide adequate artillery support for committed manoeuvre units
3) give added weight to the support of the main attack during the offensive; give added weight to the support of vulnerable areas during the defence;
4) ensure that a suitable amount of artillery was available for the division commander to influence the action.

Between 1929 and 1941, the Field Artillery School developed means to concentrate all available artillery on an only one target. The first step in this method was the use of radio sets by the forward observers.

The school instructors drew up procedures for observers, and firing charts to provide the battalion headquarters with the means to adjust the fire from the forward observer positions instead of the fire battery position. The firing charts compensated for the differences in the location of the batteries, and one howitzer in each field artillery battery was surveyed in relation to a common point for all artillery units in the area.

The fire direction center (FDC) could provide support to infantry units the size of an entire battalion or more, firing on a target that only one forward observer could see. "Fire direction centers gave the U.S. Army a new and unprecedented degree of infantry-artillery integration."[4]

The organization and the equipment of artillery units assigned to division artillery being relatively similar, we will not detail each individual unit but note, during the study of the units, the differences between these.

Compared to the units of an infantry regiment, division artillery units had a fundamental difference in their organization – they were motorized. They had the capability to move their personnel and equipment from one point to another, simultaneously, without the support of another unit. To move in the same manner an infantry regiment required the support of quartermaster truck companies.

5.2   HEADQUARTERS & HEADQUARTERS BATTERY, MOTORIZED, DIVISION ARTILLERY, INFANTRY DIVISION
T/O&E 6-10-1

The headquarters and headquarters battery included:
    Headquarters, Division Artillery
    Headquarters Battery:
        Battery Headquarters
        Operations Platoon
        Communications Platoon
        Maintenance Section

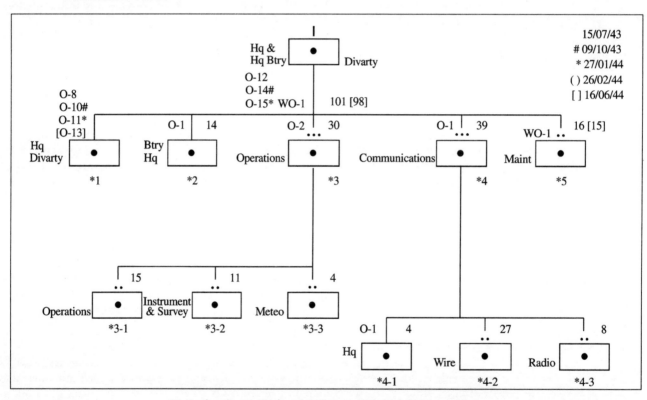

36. Headquarters & Headquarters Battery, Motorized, Division Artillery

The duties of the division artillery headquarters battery were similar to those for other headquarters companies. The battery provided the headquarters, division artillery, with the necessary means to accomplish the mission of command and control of the units assigned or attached to division artillery (see chart 36).

*1 – HEADQUARTERS, DIVISION ARTILLERY (8 Officers, 10 (9 October 1943), 11 (27 January 1944), 13 (27 September 1944)

    1 Brigadier General, Division Artillery Commander-P
    1 Colonel, Executive Officer-P
    1 Lt Col, Operations & Training, S-3-P
    1 Major, Division Artillery Air Officer-P (added 27 January 1944)

4. Capt Jonathan M. House *Toward Combined Arms Warfare: A Survey of 20th Century Tactics, Doctrine and Organisation* (Combat Studies Institute, Research Survey no. 2, U.S. Army Command and General Staff College, August 1982).

1 Major, Intelligence, S-2-P
1 Major, Supply, S-4, also Adjutant & S-1-P
1 1st Lt, Intelligence, S-2 asst, Reconnaissance & Survey Officer-P (became Captain, 27 September 1944)
1 Captain, Liaison Pilot-P (assigned to Hq instead of Op Sec, 27 September 1944)
1 Captain, Orientation, asst S-3-P (added 9 October 1943)
1 1st Lt, Aide-P
1 1st Lt, Athletic & Recreation, Asst S-1-P (added 9 October 1943)
1 1st Lt, Liaison Pilot-P
1 2nd Lt, Aide-P

Equipment:
3 binoculars, M16 or M17, (M17, C1, 20 December 1944)
5 wooden folding chairs
1 bunting flag, Brigadier General, for aircraft and automobile
1 bunting flag, Brigadier General of the line, for boat and field
1 distinguishing plate, automobile, Brig. General of the line, 6 × 9″
1 field safe key lock (C2, 27 January 1944)
4 folding tables, camp
1 tent, Wall, small, complete
1 tent stove, M1941
1 oil burner for tent stove, M1941
13 whistles, thunderer (Off)
13 flashlights, TL-122-( ) (Off)
13 transparent map templates, M2 (Off)
4 canvas dispatch cases (Off)

The lists of equipment given in this section are not exhaustive, they complete or modify those provided in section 5.4 concerning the headquarters & headquarters battery, field artillery battalion, 105mm howitzer. The tables of all units in division artillery were relatively similar, mainly in the field artillery battalions. All equipment for the field artillery battalion, 105mm howitzer, is listed. For other units, only differences are mentioned.

*2 – BATTERY HEADQUARTERS (1 Officer, 16 Enlisted Men, 14 Enlisted Men (16 June 1944)

1 Captain, communication, Battery Commander-P
1 1st Sgt-P
1 Cpl, Battery clerk, classification specialist-C
1 Techn 5th, Athletic Instructor-C (added 16 June 1944)
1 Pvt, Bugler, drove the Artillery Commander's truck-C
2 Techns 5th, Chaplain Assistant, drove the Chaplains' trucks-C
2 Pvts, Orderly-C
1 Techn 5th, Entertainment Director-C (added C4, 16 June 1944, cancelled, 27 September 1944)
1 Techn 5th, Orientation specialist-C (added 27 September 1944)
9 Pvts, Basic-C (5 Basics, 16 June 1944)

Vehicles:
2 Trucks, ¼-ton (for the Chaplains, see B, chapter 5)
2 Trailers, ¼-ton (as above)

Equipment:
4 binoculars, M13 (instead of 2)
1 compass, M1 (instead of 3)
2 grenade launchers, M8 (instead of 4)
4 packboards, plywood (instead of 12)
8 packboard quick-release straps (instead of 24)
4 hand-portable electric lanterns, MX-290/GV (C1, 20 December 1944)
1 canvas dispatch case (Off)
8 whistles, thunderer (Off, 7 for Battery)
2 transparent map templates, M2 (Off, Btry)
3 flashlights, TL-122-( ) (Off, 1st Sgt, Cpl)

*3 – OPERATIONS PLATOON (30 Enlisted Men)

The platoon include three sections:
Operations
Instruments & Survey
Meteorological

*3-1 – Operations Section

1 Capt, Liaison Pilot, Observer-P (assigned Bn Hq, 27 September 1944)
1 1st Lt, Liaison Pilot, Observer-P (assigned Bn Hq, 27 September 1944)
1 Mr Sgt, Operations-P
1 Tech Sgt, Intelligence-P
1 Cpl, Operations-C
1 Techn 4th, Ammunition clerk-C
1 Techn 5th, Headquarters clerk-C
1 Pvt, Headquarters clerk-C
1 Techn 4th, Mail clerk-C
1 Techn 5th, Mail clerk-C
1 Techn 5th, Topographic draftsman-C
2 Pvts or Techns 5th, Light truck driver-C
1 Techn 5th, Observer Intelligence, drove the Operations (S-2) truck-C
1 Techn 4th, Radio operator, drove the Executive Officer's truck-C
1 Techn 5th, Radio operator, drove the Communication Officer's truck-C
1 Techn 4th, Stenographer-C

Weapons:
2 Rocket launcher, AT, 2.36"

Vehicles:
1 Truck, ¼-ton
4 Trucks, ¾-ton, Command (WC, with winch, C4, 16 June 1944)
1 Truck, 2½-ton, cargo
1 Trailer, 1-ton

Aircraft:
2 Airplanes, Liaison (complete with fire extinguisher but without radio (Piper L-4H Grasshopper in Europe or Stinson L-5 Sentinel in the Pacific)

Equipment:
1 drafting equipment, set no. 1, Battalion
1 electric lighting equipment, set no. 3, 3 KVA (C4) (instead of set no. 2)
3 magnifying glasses, self-illuminated (+2)
3 hand-portable electric lamps, CP (1 par tent, CP) (+1)
1 odograph, land, 6 V, M1
1 plastic protractor, fan, range deflection, graduated in mils and in yards, 1/25,000 scale, 26,000 yards range
2 reproduction equipments, set no. 3, gelatin process, 18 × 18" (+1)
5 slide rules, short base triangulation, 20" (replaced by slide rule, military, with case, 10", C1, 20 December 1944)
2 firing tables, M4, 105mm Howitzer
2 firing tables, M12, 155mm Howitzer
5 firing tables, M23, 105mm Howitzer
5 firing tables, M28, 155mm Howitzer (instead of firing tables given in T/O&E 6-26)
1 oil burner for tent stove M1941
2 canvas dispatch cases
1 tent stove M1941
1 stencil outfit, complete with figures and letters, ½ and 1" (C1)
3 tents, Command Post, complete (1 for plane maintenance) (+1)
The following equipments issued in T/O&E 6-26 and 6-36, not issued in T/O&E 6-10-1:
truck mount, pedestal, M31 (¾-ton truck)
truck mount, pedestal, M24A2 (¼-ton truck)
radio set SCR-619-( )
remote control equipment RC-261
Equipment for pilots and planes:
4 drop message bags, type A-1 (2 per airplane)
4 message bags BG-121 (2 per airplane) (C3, 17 March 1944)
2 flyer bags assembly-flyer's clothing, type B-4 (1 per pilot) (3, C2, 27 January 1944)
2 flyer helmets ANH-15 (C4, 16 June 1944) (3 flying helmets, summer, ANH-15, 27 September 1944)
2 flying caps, summer, type B-1 (1 per pilot) (3, C2, 27 January 1944) (cancelled, C4, 16 June 1944)
4 flying sunglasses, comfort, 6¼" (2 per airplane)
2 flying winter jackets, type B-6 (1 per pilot) (3, C2, 27 January 1944) (3 flying winter jackets, heavy type, B-3, C4, 16 June 1944) (3 flying jackets, intermediate, type B-10, 27 September 1944)
2 flying suits, summer, OD, type A-4 (1 per pilot) (3, C2, 27 January 1944)

The following equipment was issued only when the pilots operated in cold climates.

2 flying helmets ANH-16 (C4, 16 June 1944) (3 flying helmets, intermediate, type A-11, 27 September 1944)
2 flying caps, winter, type B-2 (1 per pilot) (3, C2, 27 January 1944) (cancelled, C4, 16 June 1944)
2 flying jackets, winter, heavy, type B-3 (1 per pilot) (3, C2, 27 January 1944)
2 flying shoes, winter, type A-6 (1 per pilot) (3, C2, 27 January 1944)
2 flying trousers, medium, type A-5 (1 per pilot) (3, C2, 27 January 1944)

*3-2 – Instrument & Survey Section

1 S Sgt, Survey & Instruments-P
1 Sgt, Survey & Instruments-C
1 Cpl, Machine Gun-C
1 Pvt, Gunner, MG-C
1 Techn 4th, Survey & Instrument man-C
2 Techns 5th, Survey & Instrument man-C
2 Pvts, Survey & Instrument man, drove the Survey trucks-C
2 Pvts, Survey & Instrument man-C

Weapons:
1 MG, HB, M2, Caliber .50, flexible

Vehicles:
1 Truck, ¼-ton
1 Truck, ¾-ton, WC

Equipment:
1 binocular, M13 (for MG)
For remaining equipment, see section 5.4.

*3-3 – Meteorological Section

1 S Sgt, Observer, Weather chief-P
1 Pvt, Light truck driver-C
2 Techns 5th, Observer, weather-C

Vehicles:
1 Truck, 2½-ton, cargo
1 Trailer, 1-ton

Equipment:
1 galvanized corrugated can, nesting, 24-gal (for SCM-12)
4 water cans, 5-gal
2 psychrometers ML-24 (used for measuring the relative humidity of the atmosphere)
1 meteorological observation set, SCM-12 FA

*4 – COMMUNICATIONS PLATOON (1 Officer, 39 Enlisted Men)

The platoon included:
Platoon Headquarters
Wire Section
Radio Section

*4-1 – Platoon Headquarters

1 1st Lt, Communication, assistant-P
1 Mr Sgt, Communication Chief-P
1 S Sgt, Message Center Chief-P
1 Cpl, Message Center-C
1 Techn 5th, Wireman & Telephone operator, drove the Asst Communication Officer's truck

Vehicle:
1 Truck, ¼-ton

Equipment:
See section 5.4.

*4-2 – Wire Section

1 S Sgt, Wire-P
4 Cpls, Wire-C
2 Techns 5th, Light truck driver & Wireman & Telephone operator-C

2 Pvts, Light truck driver-C
1 Techn 5th, Switchboard operator-C
1 Pvt, Switchboard operator-C
16 Pvts, Wireman & Telephone operator-C

Weapons:
2 MG, HB, M2, caliber .50, flexible
1 Rocket launcher, AT, 2.36"

Vehicles:
2 Trucks, ¾-ton, WC, with winch, Wire trucks
2 Trucks, 2½-ton, cargo, SWB, with winch and Ring mount (Wire trucks)
1 Trailer, 1-ton

Equipment:
2 binoculars, M13 (for MG)
5 compasses M2 (Wire Sgt, Wire Cpl)
14 chest units TD-3, replaced by H-12( )/GT (C1, 20 December 1944) (+2)
2 coils C-161 (1 per BD-72)
24 gloves LC-10 (+2) (C4, 16 June 1944)
14 headsets HS-30 (+2) (1 per 2 EE-8, BD 72)
14 microphones T-45 or T-30 (+2) (1 per 2 EE-8, BD 72)
5 telegraph sets TG-5-( )(+4)
1 telephone central office set TC-4 (outside the U.S.A., if authorized by the Commander of the Theater of Operations, C4 of 16 June 1944))
21 telephones EE-8-( ) (instead of 22 for the T/O&E 6-26 and 17 for the T/O&E 6-36)
28 tool equipments, TE-33 (knife TL-29, pliers TL-13)(1 per radio set) TE-33 (instead of 37)
30 miles of wire W-110-B on reel DR-5
3 miles of wire W-130-A on spool DR-8
2 flashlights, TL-122-( ) (S Sgt, Cpl)

*4-3 – Radio Section

1 S Sgt, Radio-P
2 Techns 4th, Radio operator (740)-C
1 Techn 5th, Radio operator (740)-C
1 Techn 4th, Radio operator (776), drove the Radio truck-C
2 Techns 5th, Radio operator (776)-C [5]
1 Techn 4th, Radio repairman, drove a Radio truck-C

Weapons:
1 Rocket launcher, AT, 2.36"

Vehicle:
1 Truck, ¾-ton, WC, with winch

Equipment:
1 frequency metre set SCR-211
1 maintenance equipment ME-34 (instead of 2) (for radio set SCR-519)
1 radio set SCR-593 (C1, 20 December 1944) (none in the battalions)
2 remote control equipments RC-261 (instead of 9)
1 test set TS-26/TSM
1 test set TS-27/TSM
1 tool equipment TE-41 (instead of 2)

*5 – MAINTENANCE SECTION (1 Warrant Officer, 16 Enlisted Men (15, C4, 16 June 1944)

*5-1 – Mess & Supply

1 S Sgt, Mess-P
1 S Sgt, Supply-P
2 Techns 4th, Cook-C (1 for Officer's Mess)
1 Techn 5th, Cook-C
1 Pvt, Cook's helper-C
2 Techns 5th, Light truck driver-C (1 driver, C4, 16 June 1944)

---

5. On 15 July 1943 all radio operators had 'Military Occupation Specialty' 776 added to their designation; the MOS 740 was added with C2 dated 27 January 1944.

Weapons:

    1 MG, HB, M2, caliber .50, flexible

    2 Rocket launchers, AT, 2.36" (1, C4, 16 June 1944)

Vehicles:

    1 Truck, 2½-ton, cargo

    1 Trailer, 1-ton

*5-2 – Airplane Maintenance

    1 Tech Sgt, Mechanic, airplane & engine-P

    1 Techn 3rd, Mechanic, airplane & engine, drove the Liaison Pilot truck-C

    1 Techn 5th, Mechanic, airplane & engine, drove the Airplane maintenance truck-C (added, C4, 16 June 1944)

    1 Pvt, Gunner, MG-C

    1 Pvt, Ground crew helper-C (cancelled, C4)

Weapons:

    1 MG, HB, M2, caliber .50, flexible (for landing field protection)

Vehicles:

    1 Truck, ¼-ton (for the pilots, added C4)

    1 Truck, 2½-ton, cargo, SWB, with winch (plane maintenance)

    1 Trailer, 1-ton

Equipment:

    2 canvas engine covers (1 per airplane) (cancelled, C1, 9 October 1943)

    2 windshield canvas covers (1 per airplane) (cancelled, C1)

    1 engine, Continental 0-170-3

    1 galvanized iron funnel, round strainer clamp, 2-qt (1 for two airplanes)

    2 airplane mooring kits, type D-1 (1 per airplane) (cancelled, C1)

    1 maintenance parts kit: airplane with container for unit shipment (for type and model of airplane assigned)

    1 maintenance parts kit: engine with container for unit shipment

    1 maintenance supplies kit – 2 parachutes, Pioneer type, P-1-B (1 per airplane) (cancelled C2, 27 January 1944)

    4 parachutes, 24' back, type B-8 (2 per airplane) (added C2)

    1 airplane mechanics' FA tool set

    1 base FA tool set

    1 pilots' FA tool set

    2 radio sets SCR-610 (1 per airplane) replaced, C4, 16 June 1944 by SCR-619-( )

    2 first aid kits, aeronautic (1 per airplane)

    1 galvanized bucket, GP, 14-qt (1 for two airplanes)

    2 paper file, clip, wood back (1 per airplane)

    8 drums, inflammable liquid (gasoline) with carrying handle, 5-gal (4 per airplane)

    8 tubes, flexible nozzle for drum (4 per airplane)

    2 telephones EE-8-( ) (1 per airplane)

    1 headset HS-30-( ) (1 for 2 EE-8)

    1 chest unit TD-3 (1 for 2 EE-8)

    1 tent, Command post (for airplane maintenance) (C4, 16 June 1944)

*5-3 – Motor Maintenance

    1 WO, Motor transport-P

    1 S Sgt, Motor-P-1 Techn 4th, Mechanic, automotive-C

    1 Techn 5th, Mechanic, automotive, drove the Motor maintenance truck-C

    1 Pvt, Repairman utility-C

Vehicle:

    1 Truck, ¾-ton, WC, with winch (automobile maintenance)

    1 Trailer, ¼-ton

Equipment:

    2 binoculars, M13 (for MG)

  For the remainder, see section 5.4.

*6 – ANTI-TANK SECTION

This organization was authorized by Change no. 1 dated 20 December 1944, to the T/O&E dated 27 September 1944. This section was organized only if authorized by the War Department.

    1 Major, Anti-tank-P

1 Sgt, Operations-C
1 Techn 5th, Clerk, typist-C

Equipment:
1 wristwatch, 15 jewels (Off)
1 water can, 5-gal
1 entrenching pick-mattock, M1910 (Section)
2 entrenching shovels, M1943 (1 for Section, 1 for officer)
1 non-portable typewriter, 11″ carriage
2 flashlights, TL-122-( ) (Off, Sgt)

Following the division artillery headquarters battery, we will examine the field artillery battalions that were assigned to division artillery.

The major change to the T/O&E 6-10, Division Artillery, was the replacement, on 26 February 1944, of the T/O&E 6-35 by the 6-335. The infantry division was issued with a field artillery battalion, 155mm howitzer, equipped with M5 tractors instead of 4-ton trucks, SWB, to draw its howitzers. The T/O&E 6-35 (4-ton truck) was replaced by the T/O&E 6-335 (M5 tractor). The headquarters and headquarters battery remained the same for both battalions (T/O&E 6-36).

As the field artillery battalion, 105mm howitzer, showed few differences compared with the field artillery battalion, 155mm, the three tables, 6-25, 6-35, 6-335, will be examined in the same section, describing in detail the T/O&E 6-25 and giving the differences for the others. The same method will be used for the following units included in the battalions:

Headquarters & Headquarters Battery (T/O&Es 6-26, 6-36), section 5.4
Field Artillery Battery (T/O&Es 6-27, 6-37, 6-337), section 5.5
Service Battery (T/O&Es 6-29, 6-39, 6-339), section 5.6

5.3   FIELD ARTILLERY BATTALIONS

FIELD ARTILLERY BATTALION, MOTORIZED, 105mm HOWITZER, TRUCK-DRAWN T/O&E 6-25

FIELD ARTILLERY BATTALION, MOTORIZED, 155mm HOWITZER, TRUCK-DRAWN T/O&E 6-35

FIELD ARTILLERY BATTALION, MOTORIZED, 155mm HOWITZER, TRACTOR-DRAWN T/O&E 6-335

The organization of the field artillery battalions is shown in chart 37.
Each battalion included:
Headquarters & Headquarters Battery
3 Field Artillery Batteries, either 105mm, or 155mm, dependent upon the type of battalion
Service Battery
Medical detachment

A – Medical Detachment, Division Artillery[6]

*2 – BATTALION DETACHMENT

*2-1 – Battalion Aid Station
1 Captain or 1st Lt, Medical general
1 S Sgt, Medical
1 Cpl, Medical
1 Pvt, Medical technician, drove the ¾-ton truck
1 Techn 3rd, Surgical technician
1 Techn 5th, Surgical technician
1 Techn 4th, Surgical technician, drove the ¼-ton truck
1 Pvt, Basic

Vehicles:
1 Truck, ¼-ton

6. The medical detachment, division artillery, included:-
Headquarters Detachment, T/O&E 6-10 (see chapter 5, A*1)
4 Battalion Detachments within the T/O&E of each battalion (see this section). Each battalion detachment (*2) included *2-1 Battalion Aid Station, *2-2 Battery Aid Man.

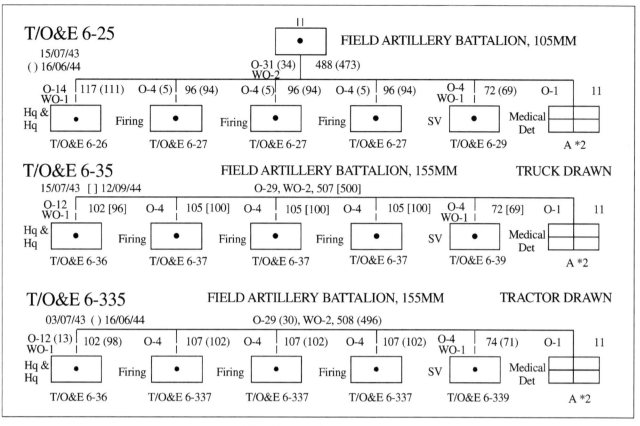

37. Field Artillery Battalions, 105mm, 155mm

1 Truck, ¾-ton, WC, with winch
1 Trailer, ¼-ton

*2-2 – Battery Aid Men
    1 Techn 5th, Surgical technician
    3 Pvts, Surgical technician
(1 Aid Man per Firing Battery, 1 for the Service Battery)
Overseas, a medical detachment was assigned to all field artillery battalions of division artillery. Their organization was always similar and all medical detachments possessed the same equipment.

Battalion Aid Station equipment:
    2 curtains, gas proof, M1 (cancelled, 27 September 1944)
    1 gas alarm, M1
    2 wrist compasses, liquid-filled (Off, Sgt)
    1 electric portable lamp, CP (1 per tent CP)
    1 transparent map template, M2 (Off)
    12 brassards, Geneva Convention, Red Cross
    10 medical kits, NCO (S Sgt, Cpl, Techn Med, Techn Surg), from 12 September 1944; on 15 July 1943, 1 medical kit, NCO
    1 medical kit, Officer – 1 medical kit, Private (for the basic) from 12 September 1944; on 15 July 1943, 9 medical kits, Privates
    1 small blanket set
    1 canvas utility case, empty (C3, 16 June 1944)
    1 chest MD no. 1
    1 chest MD no. 2
    1 chest MD no. 4
    1 lantern set
    1 first aid kit, motor vehicle, 12-unit
    1 suction (snake bite) kit (cancelled 12 September 1944)
    6 straight aluminium litters (steel pole litters, from 15 July 1943 to 12 September 1944)
    2 imprinting machines (27 September 1944)
    1 gas casualty set, M2
    1 sphygmomanometer aneroid (C3 12 September 1944)

1 splint set

2 wristwatches, 7 jewels

1 wristwatch, 15 jewels (C2 6 February 1944)

1 tandem hitch ¼ ton, (only in T/O&E 6-25, FA Bn, 105mm)

2 entrenching axes, M 1910, with carrier

1 water sterilizing canvas bag, porous, complete with cover and hanger

1 delousing bag (1 per 20 individuals in areas where louse-borne typhus was high, when authorized by the WD) (added, 7 October 1944)

2 galvanized buckets, general purpose, heavyweight, without lip, 14-qt

1 oil burner for tent stove M 1941, for tent

2 water cans, 5-gal

1 flag, Geneva Convention, Red Cross

1 sewing kit

1 kerosene lantern, Army

1 cooking outfit, 1 burner (stove M 1942)

3 entrenching pick-mattocks, M 1910, with handle and carrier

7 entrenching shovels, M 1943, with carrier (6 per detachment, 1 Off)

1 tent stove, M 1941

1 tent, Command Post

6 flashlights, TL-122-( ) (Off, S Sgt, Cpl, truck, chest MD no. 2)

1 electric portable lantern

Vehicle equipment:

1 decontaminating apparatus, 1½-qt capacity, M2

1 respirator, dust, M2

1 camouflage net, cotton, shrimp, 22 × 22′ (truck ¼-ton, trailer ¼-ton), or 29 × 29′ (truck ¾-ton)

1 handled axe, chopping, single bit, standard grade, 4-lbs

1 handled mattock, pick, type II, class F, 5-lb (added C2, 7 October 1943)

1 tow rope, 20′ long, 1″ diameter

1 round point shovel, no. 2, D-handled, GP, strap back

1 canvas bucket, water, 18-qt

1 or 2 drums, inflammable-liquid, steel, with carrying handle 5-gal (1 per truck ¼-ton, 2 per truck ¾-ton)

2 goggles, M 1944 (2 per truck), C3, 12 September 1944, (before C3: goggles, M1943 with clear lens)

1 tube, flexible nozzle (for drum)

Individual equipment:

1 gas mask, service, combat, M5-11-7 (replaced gas mask, service, light weight, M3-10-A1-6 or M3-A1-10 A1-6, which replaced, gas mask, service)

For the medical detachment, field artillery battalion, all equipment has been listed. This was for two reasons: first, the detachment was a very specific unit, which did not correspond to a company; second, the reader will better understand the connection between the organic equipment that was assigned to a unit and the general or common equipment of all units, details of which is given in chapter 9. Only individual equipment has been overlooked here because it was common to all medical units, and therefore will be described in chapter 9.

5.4 HEADQUARTERS & HEADQUARTERS BATTERY, MOTORIZED

FIELD ARTILLERY BATTALION, 105mm
T/O&E 6-26

FIELD ARTILLERY BATTALION, 155mm, TRUCK-DRAWN
T/O&E 6-36

FIELD ARTILLERY BATTALION, 155mm, TRACTOR-DRAWN
T/O&E 6-36

The headquarters and headquarters battery, field artillery battalion, was similar to all headquarters companies (battery in the artillery), at least in its general duties. Within the division artillery, it closely resembled the headquarters battery, division artillery that was examined in section 5.2. Chart 38 shows the organization of the headquarters & headquarters battery of the 105mm field artillery battalion, chart 39 shows the equivalent for the 155mm field artillery battalion.

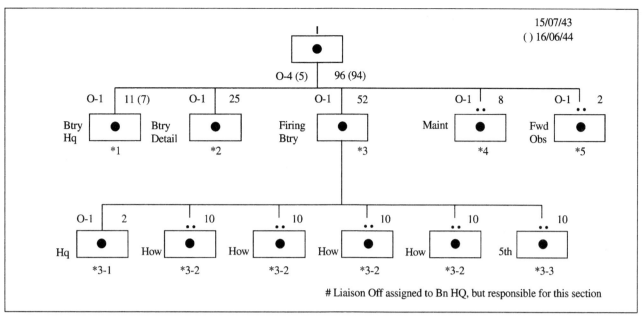

38. Headquarters & Headquarters Battery, Motorized, Field Artillery Battalion, 105mm, T/O&E 6-26

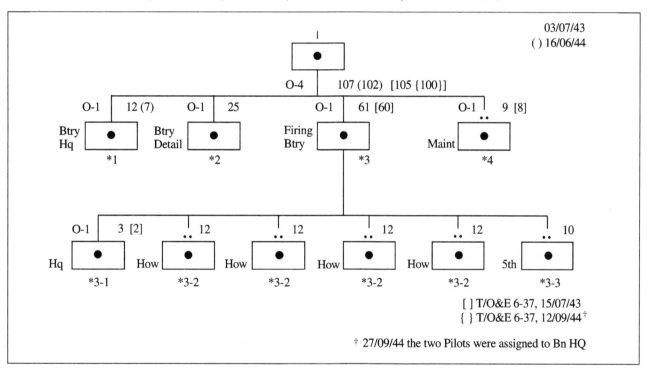

39. Headquarters & Headquarters Battery, Motorized, Field Artillery Battalion, 155mm, T/O&E 6-36

The headquarters battery included:
    Battalion Headquarters
    Battery Headquarters
    Operations Platoon
    Communication Platoon
    Personnel Section
    Maintenance Section
and a section which existed only in battalions assigned to an infantry division:
    Forward Observer Section (T/O&E 6-36); or
    Liaison Sections, (T/O&E 6-26)

*1 – BATTALION HEADQUARTERS (7 Officers, 9 (27 September 1944, T/O&E 6-36), 9 Officers, 7 (27 September 1944, T/O&E 6-26)

1 Lt Colonel, Battalion Commander-P
1 Major, Executive Officer, Adjutant & S-1-P
1 Major, Operations & Training, S-3-P
1 Captain, Intelligence, S-2-P
3 Captains, Liaison-P (1, 27 September 1944)
1 Captain, Operations & Training, Assistant S-3-P
1 1st Lt, Intelligence, Assistant S-2, Reconnaissance & Survey Officer-P
2 1st Lts, Liaison Pilot-P (T/O&E 6-36 from 27 September 1944, in the T/O&E 6-26, the Liaison Pilots are assigned to the Operation & Fire Direction Section (*3-1)

Equipment:

4 binoculars, M 16 or M 17 (6 in the T/O&E 6-26)
7 or 9 flashlights, TL-122-( ) (1 per Off)
7 or 9 whistles, thunderer (Off)
7 or 9 wristwatches, 15 jewels (Off)(6-26, C2, 4 February 1944; 6-36, C4, 6 February 1944)
7 canvas dispatch cases (Off)

The three liaison officers were assigned to the battalion headquarters on 27 September 1944. At this date, the liaison sections were organized independently of the operations platoon, two of the three liaison officers taking command of a section. One of them remained assigned to the battalion headquarters but was responsible for a section.

*2 – BATTERY HEADQUARTERS (1 Officer, 15 Enlisted Men (10, C4, 16 June 1944; 9, 27 September 1944)(6-26) 1 Officer, 14 Enlisted Men (9, C6, 16 June 1944) (6-36)

1 Captain, Communication, Battery Commander-P
1 1st Sgt-P
1 Cpl, Battery clerk, classification specialist-C
2 Pvts, Orderly-C
11 Pvts, Basic-C (6, C4, 16 June 1944, 5 on 27 September 1944) (T/O&E 6-36: 10 basics, 5 on 16 June 1944)

Equipment:

1 transparent map template, M2
2 binoculars, M13
3 compasses, M2
4 grenade launchers, M8
10 wristwatches, 7 jewels
1 wristwatch, 15 jewels (Off) (6-26, C2; 6-36, C4)
1 bunting flag, guidon
1 national flag, standard, silk
1 flag, standard, organisation, silk
1 crosscut saw, 2-man, length 6′
1 qualification card selector
2 slings, color, web, OD, (1 per Standard)
1 detector set, SCR-625
1 panel set, AP-30-C
1 panel set, AP-30-D
3 panel sets, AP-50-A
5 hand-portable electric lanterns
3 flashlights, TL-122-( ) (Off, 1st Sgt, Cpl)
12 packboards, plywood (T/O&E 6-26 only)
1 rubber stamp, official (T/O&E 6-26 only)
24 packboard quick-release straps (2 per packboard) (T/O&E 6-26 only)
24 packboard attachments, cargo (2 per packboard) (T/O&E 6-26 only)
8 whistles, thunderer (Off, 7 per battery)

*3 – OPERATIONS PLATOON (T/O&E 6-36 2 Officers, 28 Enlisted Men (27 September 1944, the two officers were transferred to the Bn Hq) T/O&E 6-26 2 Officers, 27 Enlisted Men)

The operations platoon included:
Operation & Fire direction Section (*3-1)
Instrument & Survey Section (*3-2)
3 Liaison Sections (from 15 July 1943 to 27 September 1944, see *7A)

*3-1 – Operation & Fire Direction Section

2 1st Lts, Liaison Pilot-P (T/O&E 6-26, 6-36 to 27 September 1944)
1 Mr Sgt, Sergeant Major-P
1 Tech Sgt, Operations-P
1 S Sgt, Computer, Fire direction-P
1 Cpl, Agent, drove the Agent's truck-C
1 Cpl, Machine Gun-C
1 Pvt, Bugler, drove the Battalion Commander's truck-C
1 Techn 5th, Headquarters clerk-C
2 Techns 4th, Computer, Fire direction-C
3 Techns 5th, Light truck driver-C
2 Pvts, Light truck driver-C (T/O&E 6-36); 1 Pvt (T/O&E 6-26)
2 Pvts, Machine Gunner-C
1 Techn 4th, Operator, Horizontal control-C
2 Techns 4th, Radio operator-C
1 Techn 5th, Radio operator-C
1 Techn 4th, Operator, Vertical control-C

Aircraft:
2 Airplanes, Liaison

Weapons:
2 MG, HB, M2, caliber .50, flexible
2 Rocket launchers, AT, 2.36″

Vehicles:
3 Trucks, ¼-ton (1 Liaison Officers' truck)
3 Trucks, ¾-ton, WC
1 Truck, 2½-ton, cargo, with Ring Mount
1 Trailer, 1-ton

Equipment:
2 altimeters, surveying, 6,000′ and 10′ divisions (23 October 1943)
1 Command Post and Fire Direction Center Equipment, set no. 1
4 wrist compasses, liquid-filled
1 electric lighting equipment, set no. 2, 1½ KW
1 magnifying glass, self-illuminated, 2″ diameter, 5 power
2 electric portable lamps, CP (1 per tent CP)
1 map measurer
9 mine probes, M1
1 polarimeter, British, M1
4 plastic protractors, fan, range deflection, graduated in mils and yards: 1/25,000 scale, 26,000 yards range (T/O&E 6-36 only)
1 plastic protractor, fan, range deflection, graduated in mils and yards: 1/50,000 scale, 35,000 yards range
1 reproduction equipment, set no. 3, gelatin process, 18 × 18
1 slide rule, short base triangulation, 20″
1 magnifying stereoscope, mirror, with binocular and case, pocket
2 magnifying stereoscopes pocket
1 surveying equipment, set no. 1, FA Bn
2 tubes, tin or fibre substitute, map storage, 4 × 39″
2 binoculars, M13 (1 per MG)
2 aiming circles, M1
1 range finder, M7, with FA equipment
2 aiming post lights, M14
2 truck mounts, pedestal, M24A2 (for ¾-ton truck)
1 truck mount, pedestal, M31 (for ¼-ton truck)
4 slides, M1 (2 in T/O&E 6-26)
2 graphical firing tables, M12 (155mm M1, T/O&E 6-36)
8 graphical firing tables, M28 (155mm M1, T/O&E 6-36)
2 graphical firing tables, M4 (105mm M2 A1, T/O&E 6-26)
8 graphical firing tables, M23 (105mm M2 A1, T/O&E 6-26)
1 telescope, Battery Commander, M65
1 telescope, observation, M48 or M49
1 pocket watch, 15 jewels

2 wristwatches, 15 jewels (Off, C2, 6-26 or C4, 6-36)

1 stop watch, type B, class 15

2 oil burners for tent stove M1941

2 empty field desks, headquarters

2 lanterns, kerosene, Army

1 duplicating machine, spirit process, military field kit

1 latrine screen

2 tent stoves, M1941, complete (1 per tent CP)

2 tents, Command Post, complete

2 non-portable typewriters, 11-in carriage

2 portable typewriters, with carrying case

14 flashlights, TL-122-( ) (Off, Mr Sgt, T Sgt, S Sgt, Cpl, radio set, trucks) (T/O&E 6-36); 16 flashlights (T/O&E 6-26) – 3 radio sets SCR-610 (SCR-619, 16 June 1944) (Fire direction Center)

2 whistles, thunderer (Off)

For aircraft and pilot's equipment, see section 5.2.

*3-2 – Instrument & Survey

1 S Sgt, Survey & Instrument-P

1 Techn 4th, Survey & Instrumentman-C

1 Techn 5th, Survey & Instrumentman-C

2 Pvts, Survey & Instrumentman-C

2 Pvts, Survey & Instrumentman, drove the Survey trucks-C

Vehicles:

1 Truck, ¼-ton

1 Truck, ¾-ton, WC

Equipment:

2 handled axes, single bit, standard grade, weight 4-lbs

4 machetes 18″ blade, M 1942

4 machete sheaths, M 1942

4 sharpening stones, pocket (1 per machete)

*4 – COMMUNICATION PLATOON (1 Officer, 42 Enlisted Men)

The communication platoon included:

Platoon Headquarters (*4-1)

Wire Section (*4-2)

Radio Section (*4-3)

*4-1 – Platoon Headquarters

1 1st or 2nd Lt, Communication, assistant-P

1 Tech Sgt, Communication chief-P

1 Sgt, Message Center-C

1 Cpl, Message Center-C

Equipment:

1 compass, M2 (Com chief)

2 converters M-209 (message center)

6 flag kits, M-113

4 flashlights, TL-122-( ) (Off, T Sgt, Sgt, Cpl)

1 whistle, thunderer (Off)

1 wristwatch, 15 jewels (Off, C2 6-26, C4 6-36)

*4-2 – Wire Section

1 S Sgt, Wire-P

1 Cpl, Wire-C

1 Pvt, Light truck driver-C

3 Techns 5th, Light truck driver, Wireman & telephone operator-C

1 Techn 5th, Switchboard operator-C

1 Pvt, Switchboard operator-C

13 Pvts or Techns 5th, Wireman & telephone operator-C

1 Pvt, Wireman & telephone operator, drove the Assistant Communication Officer's truck-C

Weapons:
  1 Rocket launcher, AT, 2.36″

Vehicles:
  1 Truck, ¼-ton (Assistant Communication Officer)
  3 Trucks, ¾-ton, WC, with winch (Wire trucks)
  1 Truck, 2½-ton, cargo, SWB, with winch (Wire truck)

Equipment:
  14 respirators, dust, M2 (1 per Wireman & telephone operator)
  5 compasses M2 (Wire Sgt, Wire Cpl)
  4 compasses M6 (1 per Wire truck)
  29 goggles, M 1944 (Cpl Wire, Wireman & telephone operator, 2 per truck)
  4 handled mattocks, pick, type II, Class F, 5-lbs (1 per Wire truck)
  4 round point shovels, D-handled, strap back, GP, no. 2 (1 per Wire truck)
  9 flashlights, TL-122-( ) (Sgt, Cpl, truck)
  1 alignment equipment ME-73-( )
  3 axles RL-27-( ) (1 per ¾-ton Wire truck)
  4 belts LC-23-( ) (1 per Wire truck)
  7 cable assemblies, CC-345, 100-ft. long
  14 cable stubs, CC-344
  2 chests BC-5
  12 chest sets TD-3 (1 for 2 EE-8, 1 per switchboard)
  4 climbers LC-6-( ) (1 with each LC-3)
  2 emergency switchboards, SB-18/GT (27 September 1944)
  22 gloves, LC-10 (1 per Wire Sgt, Wire Cpl, Wireman & telephone operator) (C6, 16 June 1944)
  12 headsets, HS-30 (1 for 2 EE-8, Switchboard)
  5 holders, M-167
  10 lance poles PO-2
  12 microphones T-45-( ) or T-30-( ) (1 for 2 EE-8, Sb)
  2 reels RL-39 (includes: 1 DR-8, 1 connector M-221, 3 straps (ST-33, ST-34, ST-35), 1 handset TS-10) (2 per 2½-ton Wire truck)
  1 reel unit RL-26, for 2 reels DR-5 (1 per 2½-ton Wire truck)
  3 reel units RL-31
  1 switchboard BD-71
  2 switchboards BD-72
  1 telegraph set TG-5-( )
  17 telephones EE-8-( ) (22 telephones T/O&E 6-26)
  6 terminal strips TM-184
  26 tool equipments, TE-33 (1 par Wire Sgt, Wire Cpl, Rcn Sgt, Wireman & telephone operator, switchboard operator)
  3 miles of wire W-110-B on reel DR-4
  9 miles of wire W-110-B on reel DR-5
  3 miles of wire W-130-A on spool DR-8
  4 wire pikes MC-123 (1 per Wire truck)

*4-3 – Radio Section

  1 S Sgt, Radio (740)-P
  1 Cpl, Machine Gun-C
  1 Cpl, Radio (740)-C
  1 Pvt, Machine gunner-C
  2 Techns 4th, Radio operator (740)-C (T/O&E 6-36; 3 in T/O&E 6-26)
  2 Techns 5th, Radio operator (740)-C
  3 Techns 4th or 5th, Radio operator (776)-C (T/O&E 6-36; 2 in T/O&E 6-26)
  1 Techn 5th, Radio operator (776), drove a Radio truck-C
  1 Techn 4th, Radio repairman-C
  1 Techn 5th, Radio repairman & Radio operator, drove a Radio truck-C

Weapons:
  1 MG, HB, M2, caliber .50, flexible
  1 Rocket launcher, AT, 2.36″

Vehicles:
  2 Trucks, ¾-ton, WC, with winch

Equipment:

    1 truck mount, pedestal, M24A2 (¾-ton truck)

    1 binocular, M13 (for MG)

    13 flashlights, TL-122-( ) (S Sgt, Cpl, radio set, trucks)

    1 radio set SCR-193 (added 17 March 1944, C3 6-26, C5 6-36)

    2 radio sets SCR-608

    2 radio sets SCR-284 (SCR-694, 16 June 1944)

    4 radio sets SCR-610 (SCR-619, 16 June 1944) (1 for S-2, 2 in replacement)

    2 converters M-209 (1 per SCR-694)

    1 maintenance equipment ME-13-( )

    2 maintenance equipments ME-34

    4 power units PE-210-( ) (27 September 1944)

    6 remote control equipments RC-290 (RC-261, 16 June 1944) (1 per radio set SCR-608, SCR-619, not mounted in plane)

    2 remote control equipments RC-289 [RC-290] (1 per radio set SCR-694)

    1 test set I-56-( ) (C5, 17 March 1944, C3 in 6-26)

    2 tool equipments TE-41 (1 per Radio repairman)

    1 vibrator pack PP-68-( )/U (C5, 17 March 1944, C3 in 6-26)

    1 voltammeter I-50

*5 – PERSONNEL SECTION

    1 WO, Military Personnel-P

    1 Tech Sgt, Personnel-P

    1 Techn 4th, Classification specialist-C

    1 Pvt, Headquarters clerk-C

    1 Pvt, Clerk, Typist-C

Equipment:

    2 flashlights, TL-122-( ) (WO, T Sgt)

    1 fibre chest, record

    1 empty field desk, Company

    1 portable typewriter, with carrying case

    1 wristwatch, 15 jewels (WO, C2 6-26, 4 February 1944; C4 6-36, 6 February 1944)

*6 – MAINTENANCE SECTION

    1 1st or 2nd Lt, Motor transport-P

    1 S Sgt, Mess-P

    1 S Sgt, Motor-P

    1 S Sgt, Supply-P

    2 Techns 4th, Cook-C (1 for Officer's Mess)

    1 Techn 5th, Cook-C

    1 Pvt, Ground crew helper-C (cancelled C4, 16 June 1944, 6-26; C6, 6-36)

    1 Pvt, Cook's helper-C

    2 Pvts, Light truck driver-C (1 driver on 16 June 1944)

    1 Pvt, Machine gunner-C

    1 Techn 3rd, Mechanic, Airplane & Engine (747), drove the Liaison Pilot's truck-C

    1 Techn 5th, Mechanic, Airplane & Engine (747), drove the Airplane maintenance truck-C (added 6-26; C6, 16 June 1944)

    1 Techn 4th, Mechanic, Automotive (014)-C

    1 Techn 5th, Mechanic, Automotive (014), drove the Battery motor maintenance truck-C

Weapons:

    2 MG, HB, M2, caliber .50, flexible (1 for landing field protection)

    2 Rocket launchers, AT, 2.36″

Vehicles:

    1 Truck, ¼-ton

    2 Trucks, ¾-ton, WC, with winch (1 for Airplane maintenance)

    1 Truck, 2½-ton, cargo, with Ring mount

    2 Trailers, ¼-ton (1 for Airplane maintenance)

    1 Trailer, 1-ton

Equipment:

    2 binoculars, M13 (1 per MG)

2 truck mounts, pedestal, M24A2 (¾-ton truck)
2 motor vehicles mechanics' tool sets (1 per Mechanic)
1 unit equipment tool set, 2nd echelon, set no. 1 (minor repair & preventive maintenance)
1 unit equipment tool set, 2nd echelon, set no. 4 (block & tackle set)
1 tool set, carpenters', no. 2
12 flashlights, TL-122-( ) (Off, S Sgt, Mechanic, truck)
1 tool set, Airplane mechanics', FA
1 lock pad, brass (1 per tool set, Airplane mechanics')
1 whistle, thunderer (Off)

*7 – FORWARD OBSERVER SECTION

(T/O&E 6-36, only in Battalion assigned to Division Artillery, Infantry Division, added C6, 16 June 1944)
1 1st Lt, Forward Observer-P
1 Sgt, Reconnaissance-C
1 Techn 4th or 5th, Radio operator, drove the Forward Observer truck-C

Vehicles:
1 Truck, ¼-ton
1 Trailer, ¼-ton

Equipment:
2 binoculars, M13
4 flashlights, TL-122-( )
1 radio set SCR-610 (SCR-619, 16 June 1944)
2 respirators, dust, M2 [M1]
1 telescope, observation, M 48 or M 49
1 whistle, thunderer (Off)
1 wristwatch, 15 jewels (Off)

*7A – Liaison Section (× 3) (T/O&E 6-26 only)

1 Captain, Liaison-P (in two Sections only, the third Liaison Officer was assigned to Battalion Headquarters (*1),
   before 27 September 1944, the three Captains were assigned to Bn Hq)
1 Sgt, Liaison-C
1 Cpl, Liaison-C
1 Pvt, Liaison, drove the Liaison truck-C
1 Techn 5th, Radio operator-C
1 Techn 5th, Wireman & telephone operator, drove the Wire truck-C
1 Pvt, Basic-C (added in one Section only, 27 September 1944)

Vehicles:
1 Truck, ¼-ton, Liaison (in two Sections only, for the third Liaison Officer the ¼-ton truck was assigned to
   Operation & Fire direction Section (*3-1)
1 Truck, ¼-ton, Wire truck
1 Trailer, ¼-ton (Wire)

Equipment:
For the three Liaison Sections:
13 goggles, M 1944 (2 per truck)
2 grenade launchers, M8
3 wire pikes MC-123 (1 per Wire truck)
5 miles of W-130-A wire on spool DR-8
5 tool equipments, TE-33
2 telephones EE-8-( )
2 remote control equipments RC-290 (RC-261, 16 June 1944) (1 per SCR-610 or 619)
3 reel units RL-31 (1 per Wire truck)
2 radio sets SCR-610 (SCR-619, 16 June 1944) (1 per Liaison Officer)
1 microphone T-45 or T-30-( ) (1 for two EE-8)
1 headset HS-30 (1 for two EE-8)
3 gloves LC-10 (1 per Wireman)
15 flashlights, TL-122-( ) (Off, Sgt, Cpl, radio set, truck)
3 climbers LC-6-( ) (1 per belt LC-23)
3 belts LC-23-( ) (1 par Wire truck)
1 whistle, thunderer (Off)
1 wristwatch, 15 jewels (C2, 4 February 1944)

We have already noted that the differences between the headquarters batteries of the field artillery battalions, 105mm and 155mm, were not numerous. The most important concerned the liaison unit. On 15 July 1943, there was no forward observer unit in the field artillery battalion, 155mm, (T/O&E 6-35). This section was assigned with change no. 4 dated 16 June 1944. For those field artillery battalions, 105mm, (T/O&E 6-25), in direct support of infantry regiments, the liaison sections provided, at battalion level (1 section per battalion), the link between the artillery and the infantry. The 105mm battalions possessed forward observers assigned to each battery (T/O&E 6-27), who would be in contact with each rifle company.

The models of radio sets changed frequently in the U.S. Army during this period. The various models used in artillery units are noted below:

SCR-171, replaced on 15 July 1943 by SCR-608 (The SCR-171 could not communicate with SCR-608 or 610; only changed to SCR-608 if all battalion units were equipped with it)

SCR-194, replaced on 15 July 1943 by SCR-610 (The SCR-194 could not communicate with SCR-608; only changed to SCR-610 if all battalion units were equipped with it)

SCR-245, replaced on 15 July 1943 by SCR-284 (replaced by SCR-284 pending availability)

3 antenna equipments RC-63 and 7 equipments RC-67 were issued for the SCR-194

3 remote control equipments RC-66 were issued for the SCR-194

2 tuning units TU-25-A were issued for the SCR-245

With changes no. 4 (6-26) and no. 6 (6-36) dated 16 June 1944, the following models replaced the older models of 15 July 1943:

SCR-619 replaced the SCR-610 issued until exhausted

SCR-694-( ) replaced the SCR-284, which was a substitution pending the availability of the SCR-694.

Each field artillery battalion was issued with two planes. In the field, the ten planes of the division artillery were gathered on a single landing field, which was under the control of division artillery headquarters. However, each battalion kept the control of its planes and could receive help from other planes from division artillery. The maintenance capability of all units was combined. The divisional headquarters was located near the landing field. In combat, the liaison planes, in addition to their primary mission of conducting artillery fire, conducted reconnaissance, undertook location of lost vehicles, conducted mortar and machine gun fire and even co-ordinated the capture of enemy troops.[7]

5.5 FIELD ARTILLERY BATTERY, MOTORIZED

FIELD ARTILLERY BATTERY, T/O&E 6-27, FIELD ARITLLERY BATTALION, 105mm

FIELD ARTILLERY BATTERY, T/O&E 6-37, FIELD ARTILLERY BATTALION, 155mm, TRUCK-DRAWN

FIELD ARTILLERY BATTERY, T/O&E 6-337, FIELD ARTILLERY BATTALION, 155mm, TRACTOR-DRAWN

The field artillery battery was the unit that provided artillery support to the infantry regiments, by the means of its howitzers. Like other units in division artillery, the differences between the batteries of each battalion were not numerous, so all batteries will be examined in the same section. The principal difference was the assignment on 16 June 1944, in the 105mm batteries, of forward observers. These observers did not exist in the 155mm batteries because these did not have the same mission. The 155mm battalion was reorganized under the T/O&E 6-335 on 26 February 1944.

The field artillery battery included:

Battery Headquarters (*1)
Battery Detail (*2)
Firing Battery (*3)
Headquarters (*3-1)
4 Howitzer Sections (*3-2)
5th Section (*3-3)
Maintenance Section (*4)

and a section which existed only in the field artillery battery, 105mm howitzer:

Forward Observer Section (*5).

*1 – BATTERY HEADQUARTERS (1 Officer, 11 Enlisted Men (6-27, 15 July 1943) 1 Officer, 12 Enlisted Men (6-337, 3 July 1943, 6-37, 15 July 1943) 1 Officer, 7 Enlisted Men (C4, 16 June 1944, 6-27, 6-337)

1 Captain, Battery Commander-P
1 1st Sgt-P

---

7. Letter of 29 November 1996 from Col. (Ret.) Jean W. Christy.

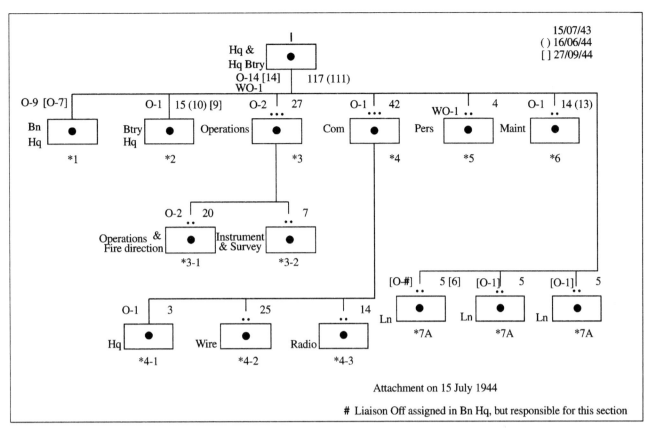

40. Field Artillery Battery, Field Artillery Battalion, 105mm

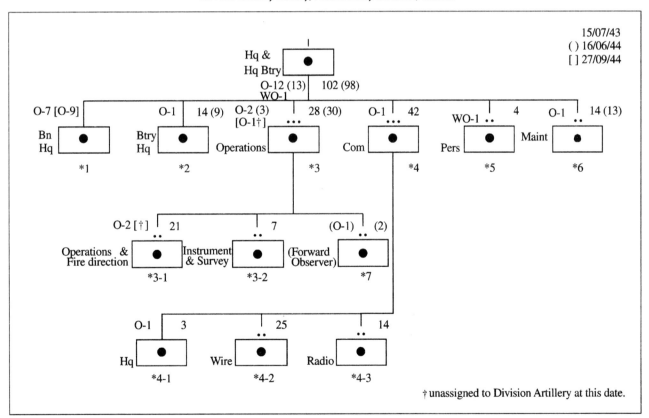

41. Field Artillery Battery, Field Artillery Battalion, 155mm

1 Cpl, Battery clerk, classification specialist-C
9 Pvts, Basic-C (6-27, 5 Basics, C4, 16 June 1944
10 Pvts, Basic-C (6-37, 6-337, 5 Basics, C4)

Weapons:
- 1 Submachine Gun, caliber .45, M3

Equipment:
- 1 polarimeter, British, M1 (27 September 1944) (only T/O&E 6-37 and 6-337)
- 2 fan protractors, range deflection – graduated in mils and yards, 1/25,000 scale, 26,000 yards range (only T/O&E 6-37 and 6-337)
- 1 fan protractor, range deflection – graduated in mils and yards, 1/50,000 scale, 35,000 yards range
- 1 magnifying stereoscope, pocket
- 1 surveying equipment, set no. 4, FA, Topog. (B)
- 2 transparent map templates, M2 (Off, battery)
- 1 tube, tin or fire substitute, map storage, 4 × 39"
- 1 binocular, M 13 (Off)
- 4 binoculars, M 16 or M 17(C3, 4 February 1944, 6-27)
- 2 aiming circles, M1
- 2 compasses, M2
- 1 grenade launcher, M8 (2 grenade launchers, C4, 16 June 1944)
- 2 telescopes, Battery Commander, M 65
- 1 telescope, observer, M 48 or M 49
- 1 thermometer, powder, M1
- 1 pocket watch, 15 jewels
- 4 wristwatches, 7 jewels
- 2 wristwatches, 15 jewels (Off) (C4, 4 February 1944)
- 8 packboard attachments, cargo (C4, 16 June 1944)
- 4 canvas dispatch cases
- 1 chest, record, fibre
- 1 crosscut saw, 2-man, length 6'
- 8 packboard quick-release straps (added, C4, 16 June 1944)
- 4 packboards, plywood (added, C4)
- 4 portable electric lanterns (added, C4)
- 3 panel sets, AP-50A
- 8 whistles, thunderer (1 for Off, 7 for the battery)

*2 – BATTERY DETAIL (1 Officer, 25 Enlisted Men)

- 1 1st or 2nd Lt, Reconnaissance-P
- 1 S Sgt, Chief of Detail-P
- 1 Cpl, Agent-C
- 1 Cpl, Instrument, drove the Rcn Officer's truck-C
- 2 Cpls, Scout-C
- 1 Cpl, Machine Gun-C
- 1 Cpl, Wire-C
- 1 Pvt, Bugler, drove the Battery Commander truck-C
- 1 Techn 5th, Light truck driver, Wireman & telephone operator-C
- 1 Pvt, Light truck driver, Wireman & telephone operator, Switchboard operator-C
- 2 Pvts, Gunner, Machine Gun-C
- 1 Techn 5th, Radio operator-C (became Techn 4th, 16 June 1944)
- 2 Pvts, Radio operator-C (became Techns 5th, 16 June 1944)
- 1 Techn 5th, Switchboard operator-C
- 1 Techn 4th, Repairman radio, Radio operator-C
- 1 Techn 5th, Wireman & telephone operator-C
- 1 Techn 5th, Wireman & telephone operator, drove the ¼-ton, Wire truck-C
- 6 Pvts, Wireman & telephone operator-C

Weapons:
- 2 MG, HB, M2, caliber .50, flexible
- 2 Rocket launchers, AT, 2.36"

Vehicles:
- 1 Truck, ¼-ton, Reconnaissance Officer's truck
- 1 Truck, ¼-ton, Wire truck
- 1 Truck, ¾-ton, WC, Battery Commander's truck
- 1 Truck, ¾-ton, WC
- 1 Truck, ¾-ton, WC, Wire truck
- 2 Trailers, ¼-ton (T/O&E 6-27, only 1 trailer before 21 October 1944)

Equipment:
    4 wrist compasses, liquid-filled
    3 transparent map templates, M2 (Off, Cpl Scout)
    3 binoculars, M13 (Off, MG)
    2 compasses M2 (Wire Cpl)
    2 truck mounts, pedestal, M24A2 (¾-ton, except Wire truck)
    1 wristwatch, 15 jewels (Off) (added, C3 4 February 1944)
    1 whistle, thunderer (Off)
    10 goggles, M 1944 (wireman, Wire Cpl) [8]
    1 handled pick, railroad, 6 to 7-lbs
    1 mattock, pick, with handle, weight 5-lbs
    1 alignment equipment ME-73-( ) (added 16 June 1944)
    1 axle RL-27-( ) (1 per ¾-ton, wire truck)
    2 belts, LC-23-( ) (1 per wire truck)
    1 chest, BC-5
    7 chest sets, TD-3 (1 for 2 EE-8, switchboard)
    2 climbers, LC-6-( ) (1 per belt LC-23)
    1 emergency switchboard SB-18/GT (27 September 1944)
    4 flag kits, M-113
    52 flashlights, TL-122-( ) (Off, 1st Sgt, Sgt, Cpl, Mech, Truck, radio)
    10 gloves, LC-10 (1 per Wire Cpl, wireman) (16 June 1944)
    7 headsets, HS-30 (1 for 2 EE-8, switchboard)
    2 holders, M-167
    4 asbestos mittens, MG (2 per MG)
    4 rocket-carrying bags, M6 (2 per rocket launcher)
    1 intercommunication set PA-8-( ) (outside the U.S.A., if authorized by the Commander of the Theater of
      Operations, 27 September 1944) [9]
    1 maintenance equipment ME-34 (added 4 February 1944)
    7 microphones TE-45 or TE-30-( ) (1 per 2 EE-8, switchboard)
    4 radio sets SCR-610 (SCR-619 16 June 1944)
    1 reel RL-39 (¼-ton, wire truck) (2 reels, 16 June 1944)
    1 reel unit RL-31 (2 reels, 16 June 1944) (wire trucks)
    1 reel cart (for ¼-ton wire truck) (cancelled 16 June 1944)
    4 remote control equipments RM-29 (4 February 1944 for SCR-610), RC-261 (16 June 1944 for SCR-619,
      pending availability the RC-290 could be issued)
    2 switchboards BD-71
    9 telephones EE-8-( ) (for the Battery)
    1 tests unit I-176 (16 June 1944)
    1 voltommeter I-166 (16 June 1944)
    15 tool equipments, TE-33 (1 per Wire Cpl, wireman; 2 per Switchboard, remote control equipment)
    1 tool equipment TE-41 (Radio repairman)
    2 miles of wire W-130-A on spool DR-8
    2½ miles of wire W-110-B on reel DR-4
    4 miles of wire W-110-B on reel DR-5
    2 wire pikes MC-123 (1 per wire truck)
Before 21 October 1944 the T/O&E 6-27 authorized:
    8 miles of wire W-130-A on reel DR-4
    2 miles of wire W-130-A on spool DR-8
From 21 October 1944, it was similar to the T/O&E 6-337.

*3 – FIRING BATTERY (1 Officer, 61 Enlisted Men (52 EM for the T/O&E 6-27)

The firing battery was the unit in the field artillery battery, which operated the howitzers. The firing battery was primarily composed of four howitzer sections, which each included a 105mm, or a 155mm howitzer, according to the type of the battery (T/O&E 6-27, 105mm; or T/O&E 6-337 [6-37], 155mm).

---

8. Only goggles M 1944 are listed; however, they were only issued by the T/O&Es dated 27 September 1944. Before this date goggles M 1943 were issued in the following variants – goggles with clear lens per driver; goggles with red lens per MG; goggles with green lens per other individuals.
9. If the PA-18 was not authorised or available, the following were issued: 5 TD-3, 5 HS-30, 5 T-45 and 5 EE-8; 1 set per battery executive and per chief of howitzer section.

*3-1 – Headquarters, Firing Battery

1 1st Lt, Executive Officer-P
1 Pvt, Light truck driver-C (only in T/O&E 6-337)
1 Techn 4th, Mechanic, Artillery, drove the Executive Officer truck-C
1 Pvt, Instrument operator-C

Vehicles:
1 Truck, ¼-ton, Executive Officer truck
The T/O&E 6-337 and the T/O&E 6-37, on 15 July 1943, added the following vehicles:
1 Truck, 2½-ton, cargo
1 Trailer, ammunition, M10.

Equipment:
1 transparent map template, M2 (Off)
1 binoculars, M13 (Off)
1 ammunition frame, M 17, 18 rounds (1 per 2½-ton truck, T/O&E 6-37, 6-337)
3 ammunition frames, M 21, 6 rounds (1 per trailer M 10, T/O&E 6-37, 6-337)
1 graphical firing table M28 (155mm, M1) (T/O&E 6-37, 6-337)
1 wristwatch, 15 jewels (Off) (4 February 1944)
1 whistle, thunderer (Off)

*3-2 – Howitzer Section (× 4) (12 Enlisted Men (T/O&E 6-37,6-337), 10 EM (T/O&E 6-27))

1 S Sgt, Chief of Section-P (1st Section only), or:
1 Sgt, Chief of Section-C (2nd, 3rd, 4th Section)
1 Cpl, Ammunition-C (T/O&E 6-37, 6-337, only)
1 Cpl, Gunner-C
8 Pvts, Cannoneer-C (T/O&E 6-37, 6-337), or:
7 Pvts, Cannoneer-C (T/O&E 6-27)
1 Techn 5th, Tractor driver-C (T/O&E 6-337), or:
1 Techn 5th or Pvt, Light truck driver-C (T/O&E 6-27 and T/O&E 6-37)

Weapons:
1 Rocket launcher, AT, 2.36″
1 Howitzer 155mm, M1, with carriage M1A1 (T/O&E 6-37, 6-337)
1 Howitzer 105mm, M2A1, with carriage M2A2 (T/O&E 6-27)

Vehicles:
1 Truck, 2½-ton, Short Wheel Base, with winch (T/O&E 6-27)
1 Truck, 4-ton, cargo (T/O&E 6-37, 15 July 1943)
1 Tractor, High speed, 13-ton, M5 (T/O&E 6-337)

Equipment:
1 lighting equipment chest M21
1 vehicular compass, hull, GP (1 per tractor M5, 6-337, cancelled 16 June 1944)

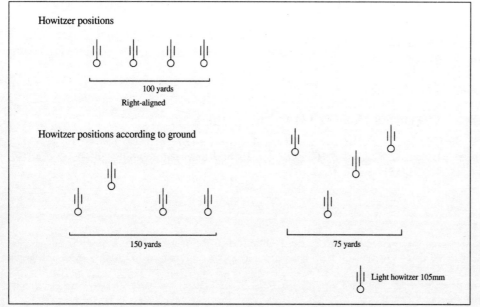

42. Position of 105mm Howitzers

1 graphical firing table M28 (155mm, M1) (T/O&E 6-37, 6-337)
2 handled axes, single bit, chopping, weight 4-lbs
12 goggles M1944 (1 per individual)
1 hatchet, claw, 4-in cutting edge
2 handled picks, railroad, 6 to 7-lbs
2 round point shovels, D-handled, strap back, General Purpose, no. 2
2 round point shovels, long handled, strap back, no. 2
2 mattocks, pick, with handle, weight 5-lbs
2 rocket-carrying bags, M6 (2 per Rocket launcher)
1 reel RL-39
2 small canvas paulins

*3-3 – 5th Section

1 Sgt, Chief of Section-C
1 Cpl, Machine Gun-C
2 Techns 5th, Tractor driver-C (T/O&E 6-337), or:
2 Techns 5th or Pvt, Light truck driver-C, (T/O&E 6-27, 6-37)
2 Pvts, Machine Gun-C
4 Pvts, Ammunition handler-C

Weapons:
1 Rocket launcher, AT, 2.36"
2 MG, HB, M2, caliber .50, flexible

Vehicles:
T/O&E 6-27:
2 Trucks, 2½-ton, cargo, Short Wheel Base, with winch and ring mount
2 Trailers, M10
T/O&E 6-37:
1 Truck, 2½-ton, cargo
1 Truck, 2½-ton, SWB
2 Trailers, M10
T/O&E 6-337:
2 Tractors, High speed, 13-ton, M5
2 Trailers, M21, ammunition

Equipment:
2 binoculars, M13 (Machine Gun)
1 hatchet, claw, 4-in cutting edge
2 handled picks, railroad, weight 6 to 7-lbs
2 round point shovels, D handled, Strap back, GP, N$2
2 mattocks, pick, with handled, weight 5-lbs
2 rocket-carrying bags, M6 (2 per Rocket launcher)

*4 – MAINTENANCE SECTION (1 Officer, 9 Enlisted Men (T/O&E 6-337), 1 Officer, 8 Enlisted Men (T/O&E 6-27, 6-37)

1 1st or 2nd Lt, Assistant Ex-Officer, Motor Officer-P
1 S Sgt, Mess-P
1 S Sgt, Motor-P (Sgt in T/O&E 6-27)
1 S Sgt, Supply-P
1 Techn 4th, Cook-C
1 Techn 5th, Cook-C
1 Pvt, Cook's helper-C
1 Pvt or Techn 5th, Light truck driver-C
1 Techn 4th, Mechanic, automotive, drove the Motor maintenance truck-C (Techn 5th, T/O&E 6-337)
1 Techn 4th, Mechanic, tractor-C (only on T/O&E 6-337)

Weapons:
1 Rocket launcher, AT, 2.36"

Vehicles:
1 Truck, ¾-ton, WC
1 Truck, 2½-ton, cargo
1 Trailer, ¼-ton
1 Trailer, 1-ton

Equipment:
  1 cleaning material and small stores chest
  1 miscellaneous spare parts chest
  2 motor vehicles mechanics' tool sets (1 only in T/O&E 6-27)
  1 unit equipment tool set, 2nd echelon, set no. 1 (minor repair and preventive maintenance)
  1 unit equipment tool set, 2nd echelon, set no. 4
  1 tool set, carpenter's no. 2
  1 whistle, thunderer (Off)
  1 small canvas paulin (tarpaulin)
  2 rocket-carrying bags, M6 (2 per Rocket launcher)

*5 – FORWARD OBSERVER SECTION (T/O&E 6-27 only from C4, 16 June 1944)

  1 1st Lt, Forward Observer-P
  1 Sgt, Reconnaissance-C
  1 Techn 5th, Radio operator, drove the Forward Observer truck-C

Vehicles:
  1 Truck, ¼-ton
  1 Trailer, ¼-ton

Equipment:
  1 transparent map template, M2 (Off)
  2 binoculars, M13
  1 wristwatch, 15 jewels (Off)
  2 goggles, M1944
  1 whistle, thunderer (Off)
  1 entrenching shovel, M1943
  1 cooking outfit, 1-burner (Coleman stove M1942)
  1 chest unit TD-3
  4 flashlights, TL-122-( )
  1 headset HS-30
  1 microphone T-45 or T-30-( )
  1 reel RL-39
  1 radio set SCR-610 (SCR-619, 16 June 1944)
  1 remote control equipment RC-261 (or RC-290 if RC-261 was not available)
  2 telephones EE-8-( )
  2 tool equipments TE-33
  2 miles of wire W-130-A on spool DR-8

"The forward observers operate with frontline troops. They are trained to adjust ground or naval gunfire and air bombardment, and pass back (field artillery battery), battlefield information." [10]

"The liaison officer sent to a frontline infantry battalion by an artillery battalion in direct support is the personal representative of his artillery commander and remains under his command. Whenever practicable, the liaison officer makes early contact with the infantry battalion commander, accompanies him in reconnaissance, and after that remains with him. The liaison officer secures detailed information as to the specific fire missions needed. He is assisted by an artillery liaison section." (see section 5.4)

"The primary mission of the artillery liaison officer was to keep his artillery commander informed of the plans and operations of the supported infantry battalion and to assist the infantry battalion commander in obtaining the desired supporting fires." "As a secondary mission the artillery liaison officer may be called upon to adjust the fire of his unit, but he will not be used normally as a forward observer of artillery fire."

"In order to secure timely information as to the location of targets and enable the artillery to place accurate observed fire on those targets which cannot be engaged by infantry weapons, each artillery battery sends out a forward observer. He is provided with a detail of assistants and suitable means of communication. The forward observer (FO) makes contact with the leading rifle company commander and observers for 81mm mortars and renders assistance by calls for fire direct to his battery. He is not attached to any rifle unit and does not permit his contact with a supported unit to interfere with his primary mission." [11]

Only one forward observer observing the target could coordinate the fire of all batteries of the field artillery battalion in direct support, and those of a field artillery battalion in a reinforcement role.

10. AR 320-5, p. 203.
11. Field Manual, FM 7-20, *Rifle Battalion*, September 1942, War Department, p. 11-12.

5.6 SERVICE BATTERY, MOTORIZED

SERVICE BATTERY, T/O&E 6-29, FIELD ARTILLERY BATTALION, 105mm

SERVICE BATTERY, T/O&E 6-39, FIELD ARTILLERY BATTALION, 155mm, TRUCK-DRAWN

SERVICE BATTERY, T/O&E 6-339, FIELD ARTILLERY BATTALION, 155mm, TRACTOR-DRAWN

The service battery, field artillery battalion, included all services that the battalion needed to operate in combat, e.g. maintenance, supplies and ammunition supply.

The service battery included the following units:
- Battery Headquarters
- Service Platoon
  - Battalion Supply Section
  - Battalion Motor Maintenance Section
- Ammunition Train
  - Train Headquarters
  - 3 Ammunition Sections
- Battery Maintenance Section

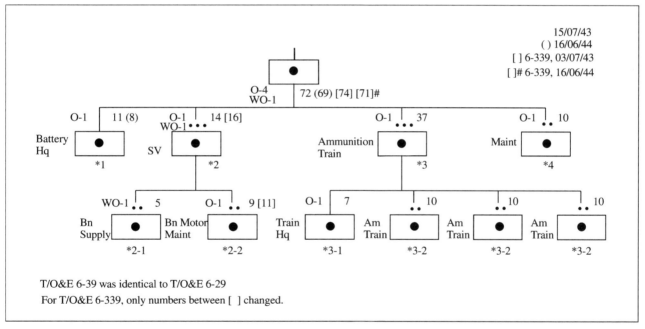

43. Service Battery, Motorized, Field Artillery Battalion

The service platoon had two sections, one responsible for the supply and the other responsible for the second echelon maintenance for the vehicles of the entire battalion. The ammunition train had three ammunition sections that were responsible for the ammunition supply of the field artillery batteries. The battery maintenance section undertook the first echelon maintenance for the vehicles of the service battery.

*1 – BATTERY HEADQUARTERS (1 Officer, 11 Enlisted Men (8 EM, 16 June 1944)

1 Captain, Battery Commander, Battalion S-4 and Munition Officer-P
1 1st Sgt-P
1 Cpl, Battery clerk, Classification specialist-C
1 Pvt, Bugler, drove the Battery Commander truck-C
1 Techn 5th, Radio operator-C
7 Pvts, Basic-C (4 Basics, 16 June 1944)

Vehicle:
1 Truck, ¾-ton, WC (before 12 September 1944, ¾-ton, Command)

Equipment:
    1 wrist compass, liquid-filled, compass (Off)
    1 transparent map template, M2 (Off, Battery)
    3 compasses M2
    1 pocket watch, 15 jewels
    4 wristwatches, 7 jewels
    1 wristwatch, 15 jewels (Off) (C2, 4 February 1944)
    5 canvas dispatch cases
    1 chest, record, fibre
    4 small canvas paulins (tarpaulins)
    1 large canvas paulin (tarpaulins)
    1 commissary roll, complete (to break down rations)
    1 crosscut saw, type L, 2-man, 6′
    7 hand-portable electric lanterns (C2, 7 April 1944, 6-339; C3, 16 June 1944, 6-29)
    3 panel sets, AP-50A
    1 radio set SCR-610 (SCR-619, 16 June 1944)
    1 remote control equipment RM-29 (4 February 1944 for SCR-610), RC-261 (16 June 1944 for SCR-619) or RC-290 in replacement
    50 flashlights, TL-122-( ) (Off, WO, Mr Sgt, 1st Sgt, T Sgt, S Sgt, Sgt, Cpl, mech, radio set, repairman utility, truck)
    8 whistles, thunderer (Off, 7 for the battery)

*2 – SERVICE PLATOON (1 Officer, 1 Warrant Officer, 14 Enlisted Men (16 EM, T/O&E 6-339)

*2-1 – Battalion Supply Section

    1 WO, Supply general-P
    1 Tech Sgt, Supply-P
    1 S Sgt, Supply, assistant-P
    1 Techn 5th, Supply clerk-C
    1 Pvt, Supply clerk-C
    1 Techn 5th, Light truck driver-C

Weapons:
    1 Rocket launcher, AT, 2.36″

Vehicles:
    1 Truck, 2½-ton, cargo
    1 Trailer, 1-ton

Equipment:
    1 transparent map template, M2 (WO)
    1 wristwatches, 15 jewels (WO)
    1 oil burner for tent stove M1941
    1 empty field desk, headquarters
    1 small canvas paulin (tarpaulin)
    1 tent stove M1941
    1 tent, Squad, M1942
    1 portable typewriter, with carrying case
    1 whistle, thunderer (WO)

*2-2 – Battalion Motor Maintenance Section (1 Officer, 9 Enlisted Men (11 EM, T/O&E 6-339)

    1 1st Lt, Motor transport, Battalion Motor Officer-P (Captain, T/O&E 6-339)
    1 Mr Sgt, Motor-P
    1 Cpl, Machine Gun-C
    1 Cpl, Supply parts, Automotive-C
    1 Pvt, Machine Gunner-C
    1 Techn 4th, Welder-C
T/O&E 6-339:
    1 Techn 4th, Mechanic, Automotive-C
    1 Techn 5th, Mechanic, Automotive, drove the Battalion Motor Officer truck-C
    1 Techn 5th, Mechanic, Automotive, drove a Battalion Motor Maintenance truck-C
    1 Techn 4th, Mechanic, Tractor-C
    2 Techns 5th, Mechanic, Tractor, drove the Battalion Motor Maintenance trucks-C
T/O&E 6-29, 6-39:
    1 Techn 4th, Mechanic, Automotive-C

1 Techn 5th, Mechanic, Automotive, drove the Battalion Motor Officer truck-C
2 Techns 5th, Mechanic, Automotive, drove the Battalion Motor Maintenance truck-C [12]

Weapons:
 1 MG, HB, M2, caliber .50, flexible
 1 Rocket launcher, AT, 2.36″

Vehicles:
 1 Truck, ¼-ton
 1 Truck, 2½-ton, cargo, SWB, with Ring Mount
 1 Truck, 2½-ton, cargo, SWB
 1 Truck, 4-ton, Wrecker (T/O&E 6-39, 6-339)

Equipment:
 1 wrist compass, liquid-filled (Off)
 1 transparent map template, M2 (Off)
 1 binocular, M13 (for MG)
 1 chest, cleaning material and small stores
 1 tool set, Armorer's FA Bn
 1 wristwatch, 15 jewels (Off)(C2, 4 February 1944)
 3 cabinets, spare parts, type 1, M1940
 6 motor vehicles mechanics' tool sets (1 per Mechanic) (4 tool sets only in the T/O&E 6-29)
 1 tool set, tractor, high speed, 13-ton, M5, Regimental Maintenance Platoon Set (T/O&E 6-339, only)
 1 unit equipment tool set, 2nd echelon, set no. 1, minor repair and preventive maintenance
 1 unit equipment tool set, 2nd echelon, set no. 2, repair set, 2nd echelon shop
 1 unit equipment tool set, 2nd echelon, set no. 5, welding equipment (T/O&E 6-29 only)
 1 unit equipment tool set, 2nd echelon, set no. 7, wrecking set
 1 unit equipment tool set, 2nd echelon, set no. 9, ground anchor set
 1 pair asbestos mittens (welder)
 1 tool set, Welders' (T/O&E 6-29 only)
 3 small canvas paulins (tarpaulins)
 1 whistle, thunderer (Off)

Equipment of the 4-ton, Wrecker:
 1 crow bar, pinch point diameter stock 1¼″, length 72″
 1 towing bar, universal type
 1 tow chain, motor vehicle, 16′ × 7⁄16″
 1 tow chain, motor vehicle, 20′ × 5⁄8″
 1 chuck-gauge, tire pressure, 20-130-lb
 1 air compressor, portable, 3-cu. ft. capacity
 1 air hose, ¼″ inside diameter, 25′ length, with connections
 1 unit equipment tool set, 2nd echelon, set no. 4
 1 unit equipment tool set, 2nd echelon, set no. 5
 1 unit equipment tool set, 2nd echelon, set no. 9
 1 tool set, Welders

*3 – AMMUNITION TRAIN (1 Officer, 37 Enlisted Men)

 The ammunition train included:
 Train Headquarters
 3 Ammunition Sections

*3-1 – Train Headquarters

 1 1st or 2nd Lt, Train Commander-P (T/O&E 6-39, 1st Lt only to C3, 12 August 1944, then 1st or 2nd Lt)
 1 S Sgt, Ammunition-P
 1 Cpl, Agent, drove the Agent's truck-C
 1 Cpl, Machine Gun-C
 1 Pvt, Light truck driver-C
 2 Pvts, Machine Gunner-C
 1 Techn 4th, Radio operator-C

Weapons:
 2 MG, HB, M2, caliber .50, flexible

---

12. From 27 September 1944 the term 'Automotive' replaced 'Automobile'; both terms are used in this book. Both refer to the same duties, and both had the 'Specification Serial Number' (SSN or MOS) no. 014.

Vehicles:
  1 Truck, ¼-ton
  1 Truck, ¾-ton, WC (¾-ton, Command, on 15 July 1943, replaced by ¾-ton, WC, C4, 12 September 1944)

Equipment:
  1 wrist compass, liquid-filled (Off)
  1 transparent map template, M2 (Off)
  2 binoculars, M13 (for MG)
  1 wristwatch, 15 jewels (Off)(C2, 4 February 1944)
  1 radio set SCR-610 (SCR-619, 16 June 1944)
  1 remote control equipment RM-29 (4 February 1944 for SCR-610), RC-261 (16 June 1944 for SCR-619) or
    RC-290 in replacement
  1 whistle, thunderer (Off)
  2 asbestos mittens (2 per MG)

*3-2 – Ammunition Section (× 3)

  1 Sgt, Chief of Section-C
  3 Techns 5th or Pvts, Light truck driver-C
  6 Pvts, Ammunition handler-C

Weapons:
  2 Rocket launchers, AT, 2.36″

Vehicles:
  2 Trucks, 2½-ton, cargo
  1 Truck, 2½-ton, cargo, with winch (2 with Ring mount in the 3 Sections)
  3 Trailers, Ammunition, M10

Equipment:
  6 ammunition frames, M17, 18 rounds (2 per Truck, 2½-ton, T/O&E 6-339, 6-39 from C2, 6 February 1944)
  9 ammunition frames, M21, 6 rounds (3 per Trailer, M10, T/O&E 6-339, 6-39 from C2, 6 February 1944)
(T/O&E 6-39, 9 frames M17 before C2, if the unit was equipped with 1-ton trailers instead of M10 trailers)
  1 claw hatchet, 4″ cutting edge

*4 – BATTERY MAINTENANCE SECTION

  1 1st or 2nd Lt, Motor transport, Battery Motor Officer-P (T/O&E 6-39, 15 July 1943, 2nd Lt, to C3, 12 August 1944)
  1 S Sgt, Mess-P
  1 S Sgt, Supply-P
  1 Sgt, Motor-C
  1 Techn 4th, Cook-C
  1 Techn 5th, Cook-C
  1 Pvt, Cook's helper-C
  1 Pvt, Light truck driver-C
  1 Pvt, Machine Gunner-C
  1 Techn 4th or Techn 5th, Mechanic, Automotive, drove the Battery Motor Maintenance Truck-C
  1 Pvt, Repairman utility-C

Weapons:
  1 MG, HB, M2, caliber. 50, flexible
  2 Rocket launchers, AT, 2.36″

Vehicles:
  1 Truck, ¾-ton, WC
  1 Truck, 2½-ton, cargo, with Ring mount
  1 Trailer, ¼-ton
  1 Trailer, 1-ton

Equipment:
  1 wrist compass, liquid-filled (Off)
  1 transparent map template, M2 (Off)
  1 binocular, M13 (for MG)
  1 wristwatch, 15 jewels (Off) (C2, 4 February 1944)
  1 motor vehicles mechanics' tool set (per Mechanic)
  2 small canvas paulins (tarpaulins)
  1 tool set Carpenters' no. 1
  1 whistle, thunderer (Off)

CHAPTER 6

ENGINEER COMBAT BATTALION T/O&E 5-15

In a Theater of Operations, the engineers participated actively as a support to combat. The engineer units, either organic or attached to a unit, played an important role in every type of operation, offensive or defensive. The casualties of an engineer unit were often similar to the casualties of the infantry units.

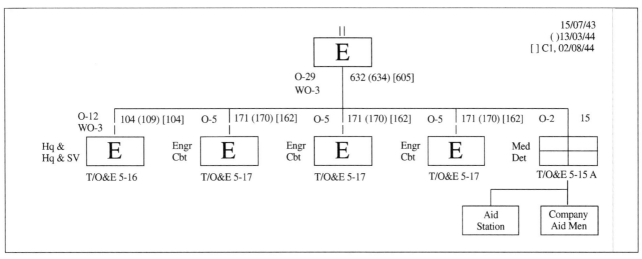

44. Engineer Combat Battalion

An engineer unit was not only a support unit, but also a combat unit. It could be ordered to undertake a tactical mission or a technical mission. There was no precise line between the tactical and the technical missions. All activities of the engineers, except fighting as infantry in an emergency, were in a sense technical, since they involved specialized techniques, equipment and supplies. However, the greater part of engineer operations were carried out under enemy fire.

During the offensive, the engineer troops supported the advance, the attack and the pursuit. They were assigned important roles such as the passage of obstacles, the assault of fortified positions, and river crossings in the presence of the enemy.

In defence, engineer units participated in the organisation of defensive positions, in the establishment of obstacles and roadblocks, in the laying of mine fields, and in all sorts of retrograde movements. In every situation, engineer units were responsible for their own security.

The engineer combat battalion operated as an organic unit of an infantry division for all engineer combat duties, during the offensive and during the defensive. It was trained and equipped to increase the combat effectiveness of the division by general engineering work, and provide specifically the following missions:

it planned and supervised the engineer operations in the division, including the operations of the attached units.

it conducted technical reconnaissance

it built, repaired, maintained and marked roads, trails, fords, bridges, and culverts, including the installation of standard bridging equipment, organic and other

it constructed landing strips and undertook simple type of construction

it undertook demolitions

it established and operated the divisional water supply points, and provided engineer supply service to the division

it provided technical assistance and services to other troops in the different phases of the defensive combat and retrograde movements, including the construction and supervision of specialized defensive installations, the installation of roadblocks and if necessary their defence and, under certain conditions, the laying of mine fields

it provided technical assistance and services to other troops during the different phases of the offensive combat, including the advance, the attack and the pursuit, the passage or the destruction of obstacles, the breaching and clearing of mine fields under certain conditions, and the assault of fortified positions

The engineer combat battalion included the following units:
    Battalion Headquarters (T/O&E 5-16)
    Headquarters and Headquarters and Service Company (T/O&E 5-16, section 6.2):
        Company Headquarters Section
        Bridge Platoon
        Equipment Platoon
    3 Engineer Combat Companies (T/O&E 5-17, section 6.3):
        Company Headquarters
        3 Engineer Combat Platoons
    Medical detachment (T/O&E 5-15)

A – Medical Detachment (T/O&E 5-15)

1 – BATTALION AID STATION (2 Officers, 9 Enlisted Men)

    1 Capt or 1st Lt, Dental
    1 Capt or 1st Lt, Medical
    1 S Sgt, Medical
    1 Cpl, Medical
    1 Pvt, Light truck driver
    1 Techn 5th, Dental technician
    1 Techn 5th, Medical technician
    1 Pvt, Medical technician
    1 Techn 3rd, Surgical technician
    1 Techn 5th, Surgical technician
    1 Pvt, Basic

2 – COMPANY AID MEN (6 men)

    2 Techns 4th, Surgical technician
    2 Techns 5th, Surgical technician
    2 Pvts, Surgical technician
Two aid men, also called medics, operated in each engineer combat company.

Vehicles:
(Detachment)
    1 Truck, 1½-ton, cargo
    1 Trailer, 1-ton, cargo

Equipment:
    The equipment being identical, see the equipment lists of the Field Artillery Battalions (chapter 5, section 5.3).

6.1 ENGINEER DOCTRINE [1]

In the regimental combat team (RCT), an engineer combat company was attached to the infantry regiment.

1 – THE ADVANCE

Each marching column was to have an engineer support, and there was also to be a reserve under the immediate control of the engineer battalion commander. When a RCT was heading a column, an engineer combat company was attached to it; another company, or a part of it could be attached to the covering force.
    When the engineer company was attached to a column the typical disposition was:
        a platoon with the advance guard, of which:
            a squad with the advance party
            the remainder with the support or reserve
            the company, less the platoon, near the head of the main body
    A reconnaissance party from the engineer battalion could accompany the leading element. Engineer companies, platoons and squads had to have with them whichever tools, equipment and supplies they would need for emergency work.
    The engineer unit with an advance guard could temporarily leave one or more work parties at critical points when it was foreseen that engineering assistance would be needed. If this resulted in excessive weakening of the advance guard, the battalion commander could relieve it with another similar unit.
    The engineer combat battalion, less the detachments, was so placed in one of the advancing columns. It could reinforce

---

1. Field Manual, FM 5-6, *Operations of Engineer Troop Units*, War Department, 23 April 1943 (hereafter referred to as FM 5-6), and C4, 16 December 1944. See chapter 4 for further details concerning these operations and an explanation of the terms used.

any engineer detachment needing assistance, or could perform any task ordered by the division headquarters.

The engineer duties in the advance were: reconnaissance, the improvement of roads, the water supply, map supply, etc.

a) The reconnaissance

An initial reconnaissance had to be performed prior to the advance, usually by reconnaissance teams provided by the battalion headquarters. It was completed, if necessary, by aerial reconnaissance and map study, photographs, and other data. The reconnaissance parties examined carefully the proposed routes of advance for the condition of roads; the condition, load capacity, and clearance of bridges; alternative roads; materials and resources; enemy mines; potential water points, etc. Plans and work estimates were prepared for the improvement and maintenance of roads. Traffic circulation plans were made in cooperation with other agencies, particularly the military police platoon.

b) The improvement of roads

The improvement of roads and bridges had to be completed before the movement of the division started. However, supplementary works were often necessary during the advance because of accidents, enemy bombing, unexpected weakness of bridge structures and heavy rains or floods. The primary duty of the engineers with the advancing column was to keep the roads open and the troops moving.

c) Water Supply, Road Maps, Etc

Water supply could be handled by battalion headquarters, or detachments from its supply section. These could be attached to the engineer companies with the various columns. Maps were distributed before the advance began. The construction of forward landing strips (liaison planes of division artillery), the removal of mine fields and the destruction of obstacles could be necessary during the advance.

2 – THE ATTACK

Engineer duties in the period of development and during the attack were similar. When the RCT formation ended, engineer components of the RCT reverted automatically to battalion command.

Assistance to the attacking troops, especially the infantry, was the characteristic feature of the offensive mission of the engineer combat battalion. This assistance required that the engineers should be in such close contact with the attacking troops as to know and anticipate their needs, and so that the maximum engineer support would be available to meet them.

Normally, these needs were satisfied by placing an engineer combat company in direct support of each infantry regiment in attack. The remainder of the battalion was kept in general support. The regiment could count on this minimum support at all times, and the engineer combat battalion could provide an effective assistance to the supporting company in case of emergency.

The supporting company commander was responsible for maintaining liaison with the regimental headquarters. He was to attend the planning phases of the attack.

The same engineer combat company was always placed in support of the same infantry regiment. The engineers also assisted other divisional units in direct or general support roles.

a) Engineer duties

These resembled, in part, the duties of the engineers in the advance. However, the attack developed new demands for engineer assistance. Reconnaissance was required both before and during the attack, especially of the main supply route (MSR), and other routes of advance, and of enemy obstacles. The routes of advance and the bridges were established and maintained for the combat troops and for forward supply movements. Advanced landing strips for liaison airplanes were often constructed, and the water supply was maintained. Specialized assistance could be required from engineers for the passage, the breaching, or removal of obstacles, the assault of fortified positions and the organization of captured territory against counter-attack.

The commander of an engineer unit operating in direct support retained full control of his unit, but had to adapt its actions to the needs of the supported unit. The engineer combat battalion commander had full command responsibility for his unit at all times, and remained responsible for technical supervision. He maintained contact with advance elements and staff and exercised command supervision by frequent visits to the regimental headquarters and to supporting engineer units.

b) Liaison

Liaison between the supporting units and the supported units was the responsibility of the former. Liaison between adjacent units in line was the responsibility of the left-hand unit. Liaison between the engineer battalion and the divisional headquarters was the responsibility of the assistant division engineer.

c) Assistance provided to the Engineer Combat Battalion, Divisional

In a major attack, the engineer battalion, divisional, required and received assistance from a corps engineer combat group (T/O&E 5-192). This assistance could take several forms, including the following:

the group, at the beginning of the attack, could take over certain of the responsibilities of the divisional battalion in the divisional rear area

as the attack progressed, the group would progressively extend its boundary forward to relieve the divisional battalion

if the division was launching a main assault, the group could designate one or more of its combat battalions as direct support, operating with the division and often in the same areas as elements of the divisional battalion. The other units, such as the bridge companies, could be similarly assigned. All units remained under group control.

the attachment of corps engineer units to the division or to the divisional battalion was exceptional since the number of engineer troops in a division was limited, the infantry and other troops in an attack had to do a part of their own pioneer work. The infantry could have to clear passages through wire and provide bridges over narrow streams by the most expedient means. The infantry pioneer and ammunition platoon had much the same training and equipment as the combat engineer squad. The infantry and other troops had equipment and responsibilities with respect to removing enemy mines.

3 – THE PURSUIT

The goal of the pursuit was to capture or to destroy a defeated enemy. The pursuing force had to maintain the continuity of the attack, exert constant pressure, and seek to place troops across the line of retreat of the enemy. It had to be highly mobile.

An engineer element was often attached to the pursuing force to ensure adequate coordination if the force was separated from the remainder of the division. This element was to be well forward of the pursuing column, with the primary mission of opening routes of movement, providing for stream crossings and clearing obstacles in the path of the troops. Engineer operations in the pursuit were fundamentally the same as in the attack. The assistance provided by the corps engineer units was, generally, the same as in the attack. The pursuing force sometimes needed the help of certain units of an engineer combat group, such as a bridge company.

4 – THE DEFENCE

The U.S. Army's defensive doctrine was based on the principle that a battle position was to be held at all costs. Supplemented by covering forces, the mission of the battle position was to delay, disorganize, and deceive the enemy before he reached the battle position. These forces would be assisted by reserves to counter-attack the enemy and eject him if he reached and penetrated the position.

The engineers had to reinforce a defensive position by erecting field fortifications and installations. This began as soon as the position was occupied then continued progressively. Typical installations were: entrenchments, emplacements, shelters, and obstacles including minefields. A shelter was designed primarily to protect the personnel from enemy fire. An emplacement was designed to protect a weapon, while allowing it to fire from the emplacement, and to protect the crew and their equipment.

The types of shelters were: shell craters hastily improved with entrenching tools, a skirmisher's trench, a prone shelter, foxholes (1-man, 2-man, or 3-man, Y-type or V-type), a cave hole, or more deliberate structures (utilizing heavy timber, steel, concrete, deep earth cover, deep excavation, or a combination of these), trenches, command posts and observation posts, which could vary from simple and improvised structures to very elaborate ones.

The emplacements depended upon the weapon requiring protection: infantry weapons (machine guns, mortars), field artillery, anti-aircraft artillery, searchlights and accessories.

a) Disposition of the engineers in defence

The covering force of a defensive position normally operated some distance in front, dependent upon the conditions, thus permitting quick decisions and close coordination.

On the outpost's line of resistance, the engineer troops were employed as dictated by the situation. Generally, the engineer supporting units were attached to the infantry units to achieve a local unity of command.

In the battle position, the normal RCT association was maintained. The engineer support needed for the combat outpost line was to be provided from the engineer element supporting the troops that manned the line.

The remainder of the engineer combat battalion operated in general support.

b) The engineers' duties in defence:

reconnaissance
maintenance of routes of communication
co-operation in the preparation of traffic control plans
engineer supply
map supply
installation and operation of general engineer service facilities
combat as infantry in an emergency

c) Organization of the ground

The combat troops were generally responsible for organization of the ground and the construction of defensive works in their assigned areas. The responsibilities of the divisional engineers were advice and assistance, engineer work, and engineer supply. The engineers provided plans, supervision, supplies and assistance as needed for command posts, emplacements, camouflage, and special problems encountered in drainage, clearing, excavation, and construction. The engineer troops undertook specialized construction work.

When a division organized its own defensive positions, it needed the entire engineer combat battalion. This received assistance from the corps. This assistance could be extended in the same form as in the attack. The tasks that could be realized by the engineer combat group (army corps) were the following: road work and water supply in the rear areas; emergency installation of standard equipment bridges; replacement of bridges in the divisional area destroyed by enemy fire or bombing; earthmoving, using light equipment and dump truck companies. Other tasks, such as special camouflage tasks, used engineer camouflage troops, if available; the preparation of obstacles for flank or blocking positions was also performed also by corps units. Engineer from corps or army could assist divisional engineers via the loan of technical specialists. A position could be prepared before the arrival of the occupying troops when the need could be foreseen and conditions permitted. Such work was normally a corps or army responsibility. Civilian labour was used to the maximum practicable extent.

Engineer Combat Group (T/O&E 5-192)

The engineer group was composed according to its mission. Generally, it included four battalions or equivalent, on the following basis.

Engineer Combat Group, Corps:
>Engineer Combat Battalion (T/O&E 5-15)
>Light Pontoon Company (T/O&E 5-87)
>Light Equipment Company (T/O&E 5-367)
>Topographic Company, Corps (T/O&E 5-167)
>Water Supply Company (T/O&E 5-67)
>Maintenance Company (T/O&E 5-157)
>Depot Company (T/O&E 5-47)
>Treadway Bridge Company (T/O&E 5-627)
>Dump Truck company (T/O&E 5-88)

Engineer Combat Group, Army:
>Engineer Combat Battalion (T/O&E 5-15)
>Heavy Pontoon Battalion (T/O&E 5-275)
>Light Equipment Company (T/O&E 5-367)
>Topographic Battalion, Army (T/O&E 5-55) or,
>Topographic Company, Army (T/O&E 5-57)
>Camouflage Battalion, Army (T/O&E 5-95) or,
>Camouflage Company, Army (T/O&E 5-97)
>Water Supply Company (T/O&E 5-67)
>Maintenance Company (T/O&E 5-157)
>Depot Company (T/O&E 5-47)
>Treadway Bridge Company (T/O&E 5-627)
>Dump Truck company (T/O&E 5-88)

Camps and Bivouacs

Engineer work at camps and bivouacs intended for or occupied by troops of other arms normally included the items listed below:
>water supply, including development of sources, purification, storage, the organization of water points and water distribution as far as that could be directed by higher authority
>construction of roads, walkways, hard surfaces, and installation of traffic signs
>utilities (electric, etc.) as far as they could be provided
>general construction as directed; the erection of tents other than individual shelter tents, provision of tent floors if authorized
>erection and the supervision of any installations which needed special skills or special equipment
>maintenance and repair of items, and operation of utilities, for which engineers were responsible, during the period of occupation of the camp or bivouac.

6.2 HEADQUARTERS AND HEADQUARTERS AND SERVICE COMPANY, ENGINEER COMBAT BATTALION T/O&E 5-16

The headquarters and headquarters & service company included, like all headquarters companies, the administrative and staff assistance sections, as well as mess and supply. The many and various vehicles in the engineer combat battalion caused service sections to be added to the headquarters company. In all independent battalions issued with many vehicles, the headquarters company become the headquarters and service company.

The headquarters and headquarters & service company included:
>Battalion Headquarters
>Company Headquarters
>Division Engineer Section (in Division staff)
>Administrative Section
>Intelligence Section
>Operation Section
>Reconnaissance Section

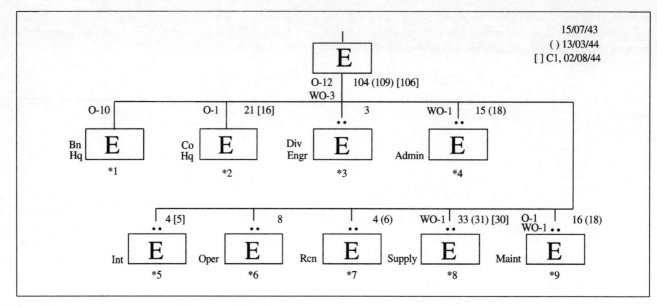

45. Headquarters and Headquarters & Service Company, Engineer Combat Battalion

Supply Section
Maintenance Section

*1 – BATTALION HEADQUARTERS (10 Officers)

1 Lt Colonel, Battalion Commander, Division Engineer-P
1 Major, Executive-P
1 Major, Operations and Training, S-3, Chemical Officer-P
1 Capt, Intelligence, S-2, Camouflage Officer-C
1 Capt, Liaison, Asst Division Engineer-C
1 Capt, Supply, S-4-C
1 1st Lt, Adjutant and S-1-C
1 2nd Lt, Intelligence, S-2 assistant-C (Photo interpreter, C1, 2 August 1944 to the table dated 13 March 1944)
1 2nd Lt, Operations and Training, S-3 assistant-C
1 2nd Lt, Reconnaissance-C

Equipment:
2 gas proof curtains, M1
1 interpreter photographic kit, type F-2 (C1, 2 August 1944 to the table dated 13 March 1944)
10 luminous dial compasses (Off)
1 reading glass, 4½″, with case
2 hand-portable electric lamps, CP (1 per tent CP, C1, 2 August 1944)
1 magnifying stereoscope, mirror, with binocular and case
10 binoculars, M13 (Off)
10 wristwatches, 15 jewels (Off)
10 canvas dispatch cases
1 empty field desk, headquarters
1 oil burner for tent stove M1941
1 tent stove M1941
1 tent Command Post, complete
1 screen, latrine, complete
1 duplicating machine, spirit process, military field kit
1 non-portable typewriter, 11″ carriage
1 portable typewriter, with carrying case
3 panel sets, AP-50-A
1 photographic equipment, PH-383
10 whistles, thunderer (Off)

*2 – COMPANY HEADQUARTERS (1 Officer, 13 Enlisted Men (21 EM 2 August 1944)

1 Capt, Company Commander-C
1 1st Sgt-C

1 S Sgt, Mess-C
1 S Sgt, Company Supply-C
1 Cpl, Company clerk, Classification specialist-R
1 Pvt, Bugler, drove the ¾-ton truck-C
2 Techns 4th, Cook-R (1 for officers' Mess)
1 Techn 5th, Cook-R
1 Pvt, Cook's helper-R
1 Techn 5th or Pvt, Light truck driver-R
1 Pvt, Painter, general-R
10 Pvts, Basic-R (5 Basics, C1, 2 August 1944)

Weapons:
2 Rocket launchers, AT, 2.36″

Vehicles:
1 Truck, ¾-ton, WC
1 Truck, 2½-ton, cargo, kitchen and water
1 Trailer, 1-ton

Equipment:
1 luminous dial compass (Off)
5 wrist compasses, liquid-filled (1st Sgt, S Sgt, Cpl, bugler)
119 pocket knives, Engineer (1 per individual in the company)
1 hand-portable electric lamp, CP (1 per tent CP, C1, 2 August 1944)
96 luminous markers, radioactive, Type 1
9 mine probes, M1 (13 March 1944)
1 odograph, land, 6V, M1 (C1, 2 August 1944)
2 compasses, M6
28 grenade launchers, M7 (1 for 3 M1 rifle in the company)
11 grenade launchers, M8 (2 per Bn Hq, Co Hq, 1 per Section)
1 pocket watch, 15 jewels (1st Sgt)
1 wristwatch, 15 jewels (Off)
2 wristwatches, 7 (or 15) jewels (S Sgt Mess, bugler)
119 rubber boots, Hip or rubber boots, Knee M1937 Heavy or Light (1 per individual in the company when
   authorized by the Company Commander)
24 gauntlets, barbed-wire (for the company)
8 waders, over-the-shoe
1 sign painting equipment, set no. 1
1 sign reproduction kit, no. 1
20 packboard attachments, cargo (2 per packboard)
2 canvas dispatch cases (Off, 1st Sgt)
1 oil burner for tent stove M1941
1 tent stove M1941
1 tent, Command Post
10 packboards, plywood
20 packboard quick-release straps
1 portable typewriter, with carrying case
6 panel sets AP-50-A (1 for 4 vehicles)
24 goggles, M1943, clear lens (1 per driver, for the entire company, cancelled C1, 2 August 1944)
97 goggles, M1943, green lens (1 per individual not otherwise issued goggles, for the entire company, cancelled C1)
9 goggles, M1943, red lens (1 per MG caliber .50, for the entire company, cancelled C1)
48 goggles, M1944 (2 per vehicle, added C1)
1 commissary roll, complete
2 whistles, thunderer (Off, 1st Sgt)

*3 – DIVISION ENGINEER SECTION (3 Enlisted Men)

1 Sgt, Construction Foreman-R
1 Techn 4th, Draftsman, drove the ¼-ton truck-S
1 Techn 5th or Pvt, Light truck drover-R

Vehicles:
1 Truck, ¼-ton
1 Truck, ¾-ton, WC

Equipment:

    2 gas proof curtains, M1
    1 wrist compass, liquid-filled (Sgt)
    1 drafting equipment, set no. 2, Co
    1 drafting equipment, set no. 3, Regt
    1 library, reference set, no. 5, Regt
    1 lettering pen, Leroy, with guide
    1 reproduction equipment, gelatin process, set no. 3, 18 × 18"
    1 reproduction equipment, gelatin process, set no. 4, 22 × 33" (13 March 1944)
    1 steel rule, tape, pull-push, 72" (Sgt, Foreman)
    1 empty field desk, headquarters
    1 oil burner for tent stove M1941
    1 tent stove M1941
    1 tent, Command Post
    1 stencil outfit, complete, with figures and letters, ½" and 1"

The division engineer section was relatively weak, containing only three specialists. A large part of the division staff work was done by personnel from battalion headquarters. These personnel were not from division staff, but were members of the division engineer section of the engineer battalion headquarters. However, like all personnel of the division staff, they were located at division headquarters (chapter 1, section 1.2) and worked in close cooperation with the personnel of the division staff. [2]

*4 – ADMINISTRATIVE SECTION (1 Warrant Officer, 15 Enlisted Men (18 EM 13 March 1944)

    1 WO, Military personnel-C
    1 Mr Sgt, Sgt Major-C
    1 Tech Sgt, Communication chief & Message Center chief-C
    1 Tech Sgt, Personnel-C
    1 Techn 5th, Record clerk-R (cancelled 13 March 1944)
    1 Techn 4th, Classification specialist-R (added 13 March 1944)
    1 Pvt, Clerk, general-R
    1 Techn 4th, Record clerk-R (Techn 3rd, 13 March 1944)
    2 Techns 5th or Pvts, Light truck driver-R
    1 Techn 4th, Radio operator-R (776) (cancelled 13 March 1944)
    2 Pvts or Techns 5th, Radio operator-R (776) (cancelled 13 March 1944)
    3 Techns 4th, Radio operator-R (740) (added 13 March 1944)
    3 Techns 5th, Radio operator-R (740) (added 13 March 1944)
    1 Pvt, Orderly, drove the ¼-ton truck-S
    1 Pvt, Orderly-R
    1 Techn 4th, Radio repairman-R
    1 Techn 5th, Stenographer-R

Vehicles:

    1 Truck, ¼-ton
    1 Truck, ¾-ton, WC
    1 Truck, 2½-ton, cargo
    1 Trailer, 1-ton

Equipment:

    4 wrist compasses, liquid-filled (WO, Mr Sgt, Tech Sgt)
    1 wristwatch, 7 jewels (Tech Sgt, Com)
    1 canvas dispatch case (WO)
    1 chest BC-5
    5 chest sets TD-3 (1 per EE-8, Sb BD-71)
    6 converters M-209
    6 detector sets, SCR-625-( )
    62 flashlights, TL-122-( ) (1 per Off, WO, NCO, mech auto, vehicles in the company)
    1 frequency metre SCR-211-( )
    5 headset HS-30 (1 for 2 EE-8, 1 per Sb BD-71)
    5 hand-portable electric lamps
    5 microphones T-45 or T-30-( ) (1 for 2 EE-8, 1 per Sb BD-71)
    2 radio sets SCR-284 (SCR-694, 13 March 1944)
    9 radio sets SCR-511 (cancelled 13 March 1944)

2. FM 5-6, with changes, Engineer Maintenance.

27 radio sets SCR-593 (cancelled 13 March 1944)
1 reel cart RL-16 (RL-35, 13 March 1944) (for 3 DR-4 or 1 DR-5)
2 reel RL-39
1 reel unit RL-31
1 soldering equipment TE-26
2 straps ST-34 (1 per reel RL-39)
2 straps ST-35 (1 per reel RL-39)
2 switchboards, BD-71
5 telephones EE-8-( )
2 telephones TP-3
1 test set I-56-( )
3 tool equipments, TE-31-( )
1 tool equipment, TE-41 (Radio repairman)
2 miles of wire W-110-B on reel DR-4
1 mile of wire W-130-A on spool DR-8 (13 March 1944)

*5 – INTELLIGENCE SECTION (4 Enlisted Men (5, C1, 2 August 1944)

1 Tech Sgt, Intelligence-C
1 S Sgt, Camouflage-C
1 Techn 5th, Draftsman-R
1 Techn 5th or Pvt, Light truck driver-R
1 Techn 5th, Photographer-R (C1, 2 August 1944)

Vehicle:
1 Truck, ¾-ton, WC, Bn Commander's Car

Equipment:
2 wrist compasses, liquid-filled (Tech Sgt, S Sgt)
2 steel rules, tape, pull-push, 72″ (Sgt camouflage, Techn 5th Draftsman)
1 drafting equipment, set no. 1
2 magnifying stereoscopes, pocket
1 topographic equipment, set no. 6, GP
1 wristwatch, 7 or 15 jewels (Tech Sgt, Intelligence)

*6 – OPERATIONS SECTION (8 Enlisted Men)

1 Mr Sgt, Construction Foreman-C
1 Tech Sgt, Foreman, Mechanic-C
1 Sgt, Chemical-R
1 Techn 5th, Carpenter, general-R
1 Pvt, Carpenter, general-R
1 Techn 4th, Demolition man-R
1 Techn 5th or Pvt, Light truck driver-R
1 Techn 5th, Electrician-R

Vehicle:
1 Truck, ¾-ton, WC

Equipment:
3 wrist compasses, liquid-filled (Mr Sgt, Tech Sgt, Sgt)
2 steel rules, tape, pull-push, 72″ (Mr Sgt Foreman, Techn 5th Carpenter)
2 steel tapes, measuring, metric and U.S., 100′ (C1, 2 August 1944)
2 wristwatches, 7 jewels (or 15 jewels) (Mr Sgt, Tech Sgt Foreman)
1 tool set, Carpenters', no. 2

*7 – RECONNAISSANCE SECTION (4 Enlisted Men (6 EM 13 March 1944)

2 S Sgts, Construction Foreman-C
1 Techn 4th, Radio operator-R (776)
1 Techn 5th, Radio operator-S (776) (2 Techns 5th, 13 March 1944, drove the ¼-ton trucks)
1 Techn 5th, Radio operator-R (776) (13 March 1944)

Vehicles:
2 Trucks, ¼-ton

Equipment:
2 luminous dial compasses

2 wrist compasses, liquid-filled (S Sgt)
2 steel rules, tape, pull-push, 72″ (S Sgt)
2 radio sets SCR-284 (SCR-694, 13 March 1944) mounted on ¼-ton trucks

*8 – SUPPLY SECTION (1 Warrant Officer, 33 Enlisted Men) (31 EM, 13 March 1944; 30 EM, 2 August 1944)

1 WO, Supply general, S-4 assistant-C
1 Tech Sgt, Foreman, Water supply-C
1 Tech Sgt, Supply, Battalion-C
1 S Sgt, Supply, Battalion, assistant-C
1 Pvt, Clerk, general-R
8 Techns 5th or Pvts, Light truck driver-R
3 Pvts, Mechanic, Water supply-R
1 Techn 5th, Air compressor operator-R
3 Techns 5th, Motor boat operator-R (2 Techns 5th, 13 March 1944; 1 Techn 5th, C1, 2 August 1944)
3 Pvts, Motor boat operator-R (2 Pvts, 13 March 1944)
1 Pvt, Storekeeper-R
1 Techn 5th, Toolroom keeper-R
2 Techns 4th, Water supply-R
3 Techns 5th, Water supply-R
4 Pvts, Water supply-R

Weapons:
2 MG, HB, M2, caliber .50, flexible

Vehicles:
1 Air compressor, 105cfm, on 2½-ton Truck
1 Shop equipment, motorized, GP on 2½-ton Truck
1 Truck, ¾-ton, WC (13 March 1944)
2 Trucks, 2½-ton, cargo, Anti-tank mine & Explosives
4 Trucks, 2½-ton, cargo, Water supply (2 with Ring Mount)
1 Truck, 2½-ton, Assault boats
1 Trailer, Utility, Pole type, 2½-ton, Type 1 (for Assault boats)
6 Trailers, 1-ton, cargo

Equipment:
6 reconnaissance boats, complete, with 4 paddles (reconnaissance boats, pneumatic, 2-man, 13 March 1944)
14 assault boats, M2, with paddles and canvas bag
1 manifold, inflation and deflation, pneumatic float (13 March 1944) (cancelled, C1, 2 August 1944)
1 pneumatic tamper, backfill (13 March 1944)
4 wrist compasses, liquid-filled (WO, Tech Sgt, S Sgt)
2 camouflage nets, twine, fabric garnished, 15 × 15″ (MG)
1 pipefitting equipment, set no. 1
1 pump, sump, pneumatic, 3″ discharge, 175 GPM at 25′ head
4 water supply equipments, set no. 1, Engineer
1 canvas dispatch case (WO)
6 gasoline drums, 5-gal (1 per water supply equipment, 2 for Shop equipment)
4 oil burners for tent stove M1941
4 tent stoves M1941
2 tents Squad, M1942, complete
24 flamethrowers, M1A1 (to be held in depot available for issue, cancelled 13 March 1944)
1 fuel filling kit, for portable flamethrower (cancelled 13 March 1944)
1 fuel mixing kit, for portable flamethrower (cancelled 13 March 1944)
1 service kit, for portable flamethrower (cancelled 13 March 1944)

The division engineer was responsible for the engineer supply of the division. As engineer battalion commander, he was also responsible for the supply of the divisional engineer battalion. His activities included the establishment and operations of engineer divisional supply installations. He normally delegated details of these tasks to the S-4 of the divisional engineer battalion. The S-4 was assisted in supply operations by the supply section of the battalion headquarters. He could obtain more personnel from other sections of the headquarters & service company. The combat companies could assist the supply section in its supply tasks. For example, personnel from companies could perform road work at supply points, or provide details to load and unload trucks and handle supplies.

At least one engineer supply point was always operated for each division. During a rapid advance or in defence, or when the division operated on a broad front, or when the road net was poor or congested, a second supply point, with limited stocks, could be needed. The main supply point was to be beyond the range of enemy medium artillery. When the division was in bivouac, the point was usually located near the bivouac of the headquarters & headquarters & service company. The principal supply point was operated by at least an NCO and several privates. The units using it sent their own transportation to the supply point, unless the engineer supply officer could spare enough transportation to make deliveries. [3]

*9 – MAINTENANCE SECTION (1 Officer, 1 Warrant Officer, 16 Enlisted Men) (18, 13 March 1944)

    1 1st Lt, Motor transport, Battalion Motor Officer-C
    1 WO, Motor transport, Company Motor Officer and Bn Motor Officer Assistant-C
    1 Mr Sgt, Motor Battalion-C
    1 S Sgt, Motor Company-C
    1 Cpl, Supply, Automobile parts-R
    1 Techn 5th, Armorer-R (added, C1, 2 August 1944)
    1 Techn 5th, Blacksmith-R
    1 Techn 5th, Electrician-R
    1 Techn 4th, Machinist-R (added 13 March 1944)
    4 Techns 4th, Mechanic, Automobile-R
    3 Techns 5th, Mechanic, Automobile, drove the Trucks-R
    1 Techn 4th, Mechanic, Tractor-R
    1 Pvt, Repairman utility-R (cancelled, C1)
    1 Techn 4th, Sheet metal worker-R
    1 Techn 4th, Welder-R
    1 Techn 5th, Welder-R (added 13 March 1944)

Weapons:
    1 MG, HB, M2, caliber .50, flexible

Vehicles:
    1 Truck, ¾-ton, WC
    1 Truck, 2½-ton, cargo, Motor repair and spare parts
    1 Truck, 4-ton, Wrecker
    1 Trailer, 1-ton, cargo
    1 Trailer, Welding equipment, set no. 1, Electric arc 300 A

Equipment:
    1 gas mask repair kit, universal, M8
    1 blacksmith's equipment, set no. 1, Engineers
    1 canvas worker equipment, set no. 1
    1 luminous dial compass
    4 wrist compasses, liquid-filled (WO, Mr Sgt, S Sgt, Cpl)
    1 pneumatic drill, piston type, portable, non-reversible
    1 pneumatic grinder, rotary type, 5 × 1″ vitrified, 8 × 1″ organic wheel (13 March 1944)
    1 repair equipment, set no. 3 (plywood boat, 13 March 1944) (set no. 6, C1)
    2 repair equipment, set no. 3 (pneumatic float, general, 13 March 1944, cancelled, C1)
    1 steel rule, tape, pull-push, 72″ (Techn 4th, Sheet metal worker)
    1 sharpener, chain saw, pneumatic operated
    1 paint sprayer, pneumatic, portable, without compressor, complete (13 March 1944)
    1 supplementary equipment, set no. 4, Combat Battalion
    1 tinsmith equipment, set no. 1
    1 wristwatch, 15 jewels (Off)
    1 wristwatch, 7 jewels (or 15 jewels) (S Sgt, Motor)
    1 lubricating gun, high pressure, manually operated, 25-lb capacity
    7 motor vehicles mechanics' tool sets (1 per Mechanic, Automobile)
    1 unit equipment tool set, second echelon, set no. 2
    1 canvas dispatch case (Off, WO)
    4 gasoline drums, 5-gal (compressor)
    1 whistle, thunderer (Off)

The maintenance section, under the supervision of the battalion motor officer, was responsible for second echelon maintenance of all vehicles in the engineer battalion. It operated the battalion shop for the second echelon maintenance. The section inspected, supervised, and assisted company maintenance.

Any individual using engineer equipment had to perform preventive maintenance (first echelon). Each engineer unit had personnel trained to perform second echelon maintenance. A combat company had a maintenance section which had the necessary equipment to perform the following maintenance:

    minor adjustments of the type which were needed periodically and could be made with first and second echelon tools

---

3. FM 5-6, with changes, Divisional Supply.

replacement of minor assemblies and subassemblies
replacement of such parts as those having a high wear factor and were easily replaced
minor reconditioning of parts, assemblies, and subassemblies.

6.3   ENGINEER COMBAT COMPANY
T/O&E 5-17

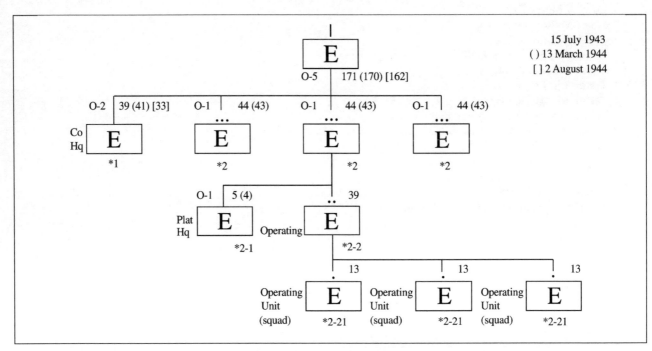

46. Engineer Combat Company, Engineer Combat Battalion

The engineer combat company is shown in chart 46. It included the following units:
Company Headquarters
3 Engineer Platoons
Platoon Headquarters
Operating Section
3 Operating Units.

To accomplish their mission, engineer units often had to engage in, or be prepared for, small-scale combat, to provide security on the march, in bivouac or at work. In addition, combat and other engineer units could on occasion be relieved of most of their normal functions by higher authority, and be assigned specific infantry combat missions.

The situations in which a divisional engineer battalion would fight as infantry were the following:
if the divisional defensive front was overextended
if the enemy suddenly penetrated the position, or engaged in a flanking movement
if the divisional rear area saw an enemy airdrop or an outbreak of organized guerrilla activity
if the relief of infantry units for some decisive combat role was necessary

Before giving his engineers an infantry mission, a commander would weigh carefully the effect of the resultant reduction of engineer support available to the rest of his command. Certain normal engineer missions, such as water supply, must in any case be carried on in all but the most critical emergencies.

Though it could be assigned an infantry combat mission, the engineer combat battalion was inferior for combat purpose in three major respects:
it lacked the vital supporting weapons of the infantry battalion
the men had normally received less combat training
its internal organization was not designed primarily for infantry combat missions

These deficiencies could be compensated for by certain measures:
the engineer combat company was usually attached to an infantry regiment, which was then responsible for providing supporting fire
it would, preferably, be placed in reserve or given a defensive assignment

Nevertheless, engineer companies could be used for the most aggressive types of infantry mission, and had to be prepared to undertake them as needed. As a preliminary to undertaking an infantry mission, the company would be reorganized.[4]

4. FM 5-6, with changes, Combat as Infantry.

*1 – COMPANY HEADQUARTERS (2 Officers, 39 Enlisted Men (15 July 1943), 41(13 March 1944), 33 (2 August 1944)

*1-1 – Command Group

    1 Capt, Company Commander-C
    1 1st Sgt-C
    1 Sgt, Foreman, Mechanic-R
    1 Cpl, Company clerk, Classification specialist-R
    1 Pvt, Bugler, drove the ¼-ton truck-S
    1 Techn 4th or 5th, Carpenter, general-R
    1 Techn 4th, Mechanic, Automobile-R
    1 Techn 5th, Mechanic, Automobile-R
    1 Techn 5th, Air compressor operator-R
    1 Techn 4th, Radio operator (740)-R (added 13 March 1944)
    1 Techn 4th, Radio operator (776)-R (added 13 March 1944)
    1 Techn 5th, Radio operator (776)-R (added 13 March 1944)
    16 Pvts, Basic-R (8 Basics, C1, 2 August 1944)

*1-2 – Administration Group

    1 2nd Lt, Mess, Supply, Transportation-C
    1 S Sgt, Mess-C
    1 S Sgt, Supply-C
    1 S Sgt, Motor-C
    1 Pvt, Clerk, stock-R
    2 Techns 4th, Cook-R
    2 Techns 5th, Cook-R
    2 Pvts, Cooks' helper, 1 drove the 2½-ton truck-R (1 cooks' helper cancelled on 13 March 1944)
    1 Techn 5th, Tractor driver-R
    1 Techn 5th, Heavy Truck driver-R
    3 Pvts or Techns 5th, Light truck driver-R

Vehicles:
    1 Air compressor, truck mounted, 105cfm
    1 Semi-trailer, Low bed, 8-ton (15 July 1943), replaced by Semi-trailer, Low bed, 20-ton (13 March 1944)
    1 Tractor, Gasoline engine driven, Crawler type, 35 DBHP, with Bulldozer (15 July 1943), Angledozer could be substituted until it was exhausted, replaced by: Tractor, Diesel engine driven, Crawler type, 55 to 65 DBHP, with Angledozer or Bulldozer (13 March 1944)
    1 Truck, ¼-ton, Reconnaissance
    1 Truck, ¾-ton, Command (15 July 1943) replaced by: Truck, ¾-ton, WC, Company Commander (13 March 1944)
    1 Truck, ¾-ton, WC, Company tools and Maintenance
    1 Truck, 2½-ton, cargo, Kitchen and water
    1 Truck, 4-ton, cargo, Prime mover replaced by: Truck, 6-ton, Prime mover, with winch, for Semi-trailer and Tractor (13 March 1944)
    1 Trailer, 1-ton, kitchen and water

Equipment:
    3 reconnaissance boats, with paddles (15 July 1943), replaced by: reconnaissance boats, pneumatic, canvas, 2-man, or reconnaissance boats, pneumatic, complete, with 4 paddles (13 March 1944)
    2 luminous dial compasses (Off)
    7 wrist compasses, liquid-filled (NCO, bugler)
    175 pocket knives, Engineer (1 per individual in the company)
    1 library, reference, set no. 2, Company
    1 manifold, inflation and deflation, pneumatic float, complete (added, 13 March 1944)
    48 luminous markers, radioactive, type 1
    1 repair kit, pneumatic float and boat (cancelled 13 March 1944, replaced by set no. 3)
    1 pioneer equipment, repair equipment, set no. 3, pneumatic float, general (added 13 March 1944)
    3 binoculars, M13
    2 compasses M6 (added 13 March 1944)
    3 grenade launchers, M8
    4 ammunition-carrying bags (1 per grenade launcher, SMG)
    1 pocket watch, 15 jewels (1st Sgt)
    3 wristwatches, 7 jewels (S Sgt Mess, S Sgt Motor, bugler)

3 transparent map templates, M2 (Off, 1st Sgt)

2 motor vehicles mechanics' tool sets (1 per mech auto)

1 unit equipment tool set, 2nd echelon, set no. 1

1 unit equipment tool set, 2nd echelon, set no. 6

175 rubber boots, hip or rubber boots, knee M1937, Heavy or Light (1 per individual in the company)

6 brassards, arm, gas

16 gauntlets, barbed-wire

3 canvas dispatch cases (officer, 1st Sgt)

36 flashlights, TL-122-( ) (Off, NCO, mech, trucks)

3 converters M-209

6 panel sets, AP-50-A

1 radio set SCR-694-( ) (added 13 March 1944, if non available SCR-284 is issued)

2 reels RL-39 (13 March 1944)

2 straps ST-34 (1 per RL-39) (13 March 1944)

2 straps ST-35 (1 per RL-39) (13 March 1944)

2 telephones TP-3 (13 March 1944)

1 mile of wire W-130-A on spool DR-8 (13 March 1944)

3 whistles, thunderer (Off, 1st Sgt)

175 goggles, M1943, (40, M1944, 2 August 1944, identical to chapter 6-2)

*2 – ENGINEER PLATOON (× 3) (1 Officer, 44 Enlisted Men (43 EM 13 March 1944)

*2-1 – Platoon Headquarters

1 1st Lt, Platoon Commander-C

1 S Sgt, Platoon-C

1 Sgt, Weapons-R (cancelled, 13 March 1944)

1 Techn 5th, Light truck driver, drove the ¼-ton truck-S

1 Pvt, Light truck driver, drove the 2½-ton truck-R

1 Techn 5th, Toolroom keeper-R

Weapons:

1 MG, HB, M2, caliber .50, flexible

2 MG, Heavy, caliber .30, M1917A1

Vehicles:

1 Truck, ¼-ton, Reconnaissance

1 Truck, 2½-ton, cargo, with Ring Mount, Platoon tools

1 Trailer, ¼-ton

1 Trailer, 1-ton

1 Trailer, 2 wheel utility, pole type, 2½-ton, type 1, for bridging equipment

Equipment:

1 carpenter equipment, set no. 3, Engineer Combat Platoon

2 luminous dial compasses (Off, Platoon Sgt)

1 wrist compass, liquid-filled (S Sgt)

1 demolition equipment, set no. 2, Engineer Platoon

1 pioneer equipment, set no. 3, Engineer Combat Platoon

1 binoculars, M13

1 grenade launcher, M8

2 ammunition-carrying bags (1 per grenade launcher, SMG)

1 wristwatch, 7 jewels (S Sgt)

1 canvas dispatch case (Off)

1 transparent map template, M2 (Off)

1 whistle, thunderer (Off)

1 detector set, SCR-625-( )

1 hand-portable electric lantern

*2-2 – Engineer Section (39 Enlisted Men)

It included 3 operating units of 13 enlisted men each.

*2-21 – Operating Unit (× 3)

1 Sgt, Unit foreman-R

1 Cpl, Unit foreman assistant-R

1 Techn 4th or 5th, Carpenter, Bridge-R

2 Techns 4th or 5th, Carpenter, General-R
1 Pvt, Demolition man-R
1 Techn 5th or Pvt, Light truck driver-R
1 Techn 5th or Pvt, Electrician-R (1 Pvt and 2 T/5 in the 3 Units)
1 Pvt, Jackhammer operator-R
2 Pvts, Repairman utility-R
2 Pvts, Rigger, general-R

Weapons:
1 Rocket launcher, AT, 2.36" M1 (15 July 1943) M9 (13 March 1944)

Vehicle:
1 Truck, 2½-ton, dump (tools and personnel)

Equipment:
1 carpenter equipment, set no. 1, Engineer Squad
2 wrist compasses, liquid-filled (Sgt, Cpl)
1 demolition equipment, set no. 1, Engineer Squad
1 mine probe, M1 (added 13 March 1944)
1 pioneer equipment, set no. 1, Engineer Squad
1 grenade launcher, M7
1 ammunition-carrying bag (for grenade launcher)
2 rocket carrying bag, M6 (for rocket launcher)

Reorganization for combat as Infantry

When an engineer unit was about to enter combat, it was divided into a forward echelon and a rear echelon.

The forward echelon was composed of the elements which actually engaged in combat, and the necessary command, communications and supply elements. Normally, light vehicles were included for security needs, communication, ammunition supply and the manoeuvre of crew served weapons.

The rear echelon included those personnel and equipment which were not necessary for combat. Its organization varied following the situation and the size of the unit. The equipment usually included kitchen trucks, trucks carrying supplies, and equipment not needed with the forward echelon, and the special vehicles (compressors, tractors, graders). The personnel in this echelon were the minimum needed to protect it, render it mobile and to carry on essential administration. The echelon was commanded by the senior officer present.

In the case of small isolated units, the rear echelon would stay close the forward echelon. When an engineer battalion was in defence, the rear echelon would be well to the rear.

When it was reorganized for combat, the engineer battalion had to improve and supplement its communication system. How this was done depended on the situation:

if the battalion needed lateral radio communications, radios could be taken from the battalion net and netted with the units on the right and the left

a radio set of the battalion communication section could join the regimental net

the infantry regiment could lay a wire from its switchboard to the engineer battalion switchboard. The field artillery could lay a wire to the battalion switchboard and continue its wire lines down to each frontline engineer company.

the engineer battalion communication system could lay wires to each of the engineer companies, lay a lateral line to the battalion on the right, and receive a lateral line from the battalion on the left.

For more information concerning communication nets inside the division, see the chapter 7, section 7.4, regarding the signal company.

When it was reorganized as infantry, the engineer battalion follows the same doctrine as that for the infantry – see chapter 4, Infantry Doctrine.

CHAPTER 7

SPECIAL TROOPS, INFANTRY DIVISION

All units assigned to special troops will be examined in this chapter. The headquarters, special troops, attached medical special troops and attached chaplains were, for mess and administration purposes, attached to the headquarters company, infantry division. The headquarters, special troops was in charge of all service support units that were assigned to it, including division, headquarters company, T/O&E 7-2 (chapter 1, section 1.3).

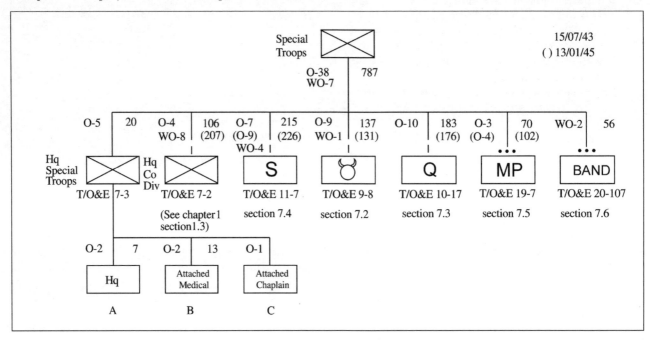

47. Special Troops, Infantry Division

An infantry division was composed of three types of units:
    Combat units:
        3 Infantry Regiments with 3 Infantry Battalions
        1 Cavalry Reconnaissance Troop, under the direct control of the Division Commander
    Combat Support units:
        4 Field Artillery Battalions, under the control of Division Artillery
        1 Engineer Battalion, under the control of the Division Commander
    Service Support units:
        1 Medical Battalion, under the direct control of the Division Commander
        1 Ordnance Company, under the control of Special Troops
        1 Quartermaster Company, under the control of Special Troops
        1 Signal Company, under the control of Special Troops
        1 Military Police Platoon, under the control of Special Troops
        1 Divisional Band, under the control of Special Troops
The headquarters, special troops commanded the following service support units:
    Ordnance Light Maintenance Company, Infantry Division (T/O&E 9-8)
    Quartermaster Company, Infantry Division (T/O&E 10-17)
    Signal Company, Infantry Division (T/O&E 11-7)
    Military Police Platoon, Infantry Division (T/O&E 19-7)
    Band, Infantry Division (T/O&E 20-107)

7.1 HEADQUARTERS, SPECIAL TROOPS
T/O&E 7-3

A – HEADQUARTERS (2 Officers, 7 Enlisted Men)

1 Lt Col, Commanding Officer Special Troops and Headquarters Commandant-P
1 Captain, Executive-C
1 Tech Sgt, Chief clerk-C
1 S Sgt, Operations-C
1 Sgt, Duty-C
1 Techn 5th, Chaplain asst, from 13 January 1945 he drove the ¼-ton truck for the Chaplain-C
1 Techn 5th, Light truck driver-C
1 Pvt, Light truck driver-C
1 Pvt, Orderly-C

Vehicles:
1 Truck, ¼-ton
1 Trailer, ¼-ton
1 Truck, ¾-ton, Command
1 Truck, ¼-ton for the Chaplain (added 13 January 1945)
1 Trailer, ¼-ton (added 13 January 1945)

Equipment:
2 canvas dispatch cases (Off)
5 whistles, thunderer (Off, T Sgt, S Sgt, Sgt)
5 flashlights, TL-122-( ) (Off, drivers)

The organization of the headquarters, special troops, did not change between 15 July 1943 and 5 November 1945, except for the addition of a vehicle for the chaplain.

B – ATTACHED MEDICAL, SPECIAL TROOPS (2 Officers, 13 Enlisted Men)

1 Major
1 Capt or 1st Lt, Dental
1 Tech Sgt, Medical
1 Sgt, Medical
1 Techn 5th, Dental technician
1 Techn 5th, Medical technician, drove the ¾-ton truck
1 Pvt, Medical technician
1 Techn 3rd, Surgical technician
1 Techn 4th, Surgical technician
3 Techns 5th, Surgical technician
2 Pvts, Surgical technician
1 Pvt, Basic

Vehicles:
1 Truck, ¾-ton, Weapons Carrier
1 Trailer, 1-ton

Of the six surgical technicians, four served as company aid men (one with the signal company (T/O&E 11-7), and one with each reconnaissance platoon of the reconnaissance troop (T/O&E 2-27). Their duties were as those described in chapter 2, section 2.6, concerning the medical detachment of the infantry regiment.

Medical Detachment Equipment:
1 dental kit, Officer
1 dental kit, Private, for the Dental technician
2 medical kits, NCO, 1 for the Tech Sgt, 1 for the Sgt
1 medical kit, Officer
11 medical kits, Privates
2 canvas dispatch cases (Off)
2 small blanket sets
1 tent pins chest
2 chests, MD no. 1
1 chest, MD no. 2
1 chest, MD no. 4
1 chest, MD no. 60, for the dental officer
1 sphygmomanometer aneroid (added 13 January 1945)

1 chest, gas casualties
2 suction kits
12 steel pole litters (replaced on 13 January 1945 by aluminium litters)
12 splint litter bars
2 splint sets
2 imprinting machines
27 brassards, Geneva Convention (Red Cross)
1 canvas bag, water sterilizing, complete, with hanger and cover
1 galvanized bucket, general purpose, heavyweight, without lip, 14-qt
1 gasoline lantern, two-mantle, commercial (replaced by hand-portable electric lantern, C5, 15 June 1944)
1 oil burner for tent stove M1941
1 tent stove M1941, complete
1 tent (wall, small)
1 panel set, AP-50-A (¾-ton truck)
3 flashlights, TL-122-( ) (Off, driver)

C – ATTACHED CHAPLAIN

1 1st Lt, Chaplain (Captain or 1st Lt from 13 January 1945)

7.2 ORDNANCE LIGHT MAINTENANCE COMPANY, INFANTRY DIVISION
T/O&E 9-8

The ordnance light maintenance company was proposed by Army Ground Forces in its 'Revised Tables' of 1 March 1943. It became organic to the infantry division on 15 July 1943, when automobile maintenance responsibility was transferred from the Quartermaster Corps to the Ordnance Department. This latter was in charge of the following military equipment: all kinds of combat weapons as well as ammunition and equipment for their use, vehicles, machines and specialised repair tools. It was composed of technically trained troops, attached or assigned to a tactical unit to provide it with maintenance, supply and technical service. The ordnance company attached to the infantry division was designed to effect 60% of the third echelon maintenance of the division in quiet periods and 30% during combat.

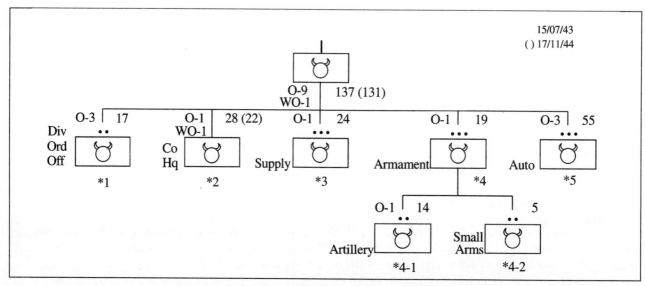

48. Ordnance Light Maintenance Company, Infantry Division

Maintenance

Maintenance included all actions taken to retain materiel in serviceable condition or to restore it to serviceability. It also included all supply or repair actions necessary to keep a force in condition to carry out its assignment. Maintenance operations were classified into three maintenance categories:

1. Organizational maintenance
Each organization using equipment had to perform maintenance of its own equipment. It was authorized and was responsible for that maintenance. It normally took the form of inspecting, preserving, lubricating, and cleaning the materiel. It also consisted of replacing minor parts when highly technical skills were not required.

First echelon: The degree of maintenance performed by the user or operator of the equipment and prescribed by pertinent technical publications and tool and parts lists.

Second echelon: The degree of maintenance performed by specially trained personnel within the organization, but beyond the capabilities and facilities of the first echelon (company maintenance).

2. Field Maintenance

Maintenance authorized and performed by designated maintenance activities in support of using organizations. Normally it was limited to the replacement of unserviceable parts, subassemblies or assemblies.

Third echelon: The degree of maintenance performed by specially trained units in direct support of using organizations as prescribed by appropriate technical publications. This included the ordnance company, which will be examined in this chapter.

Fourth echelon: The degree of maintenance performed by units organized as semi-fixed or permanent shops to serve lower echelon maintenance, usually for return to supply channels.

3. Depot Maintenance

Maintenance required for the repair of materiel, which involved a major overhaul or complete rebuild of parts, subassemblies, assemblies, and the end item as required.

Fifth echelon: The degree of maintenance authorised for rebuilding major items, assemblies, parts, accessories, tools, and test equipment. [1]

The ordnance light maintenance company, shown in chart 48, included:

Division Ordnance Officer Section
Company Headquarters
Supply Platoon
Armament Platoon
Artillery Section
Small arms Section
Automotive Platoon

*1 – DIVISION ORDNANCE OFFICER SECTION (3 Officers, 11 Enlisted Men)

1 Lt Col, Division Ordnance-P
1 Major, Maintenance & supply-P
1 Capt, Ammunition-C
1 Mr Sgt, Chief clerk-C
1 Tech Sgt, Ammunition-C
1 Techn 4th, Ammunition clerk-C
1 Techn 5th, Clerk, general-R
1 Pvt, Clerk, general-R
1 Techn 3rd, Clerk, statistical-C
1 Techn 5th, Clerk, typist-C
1 Pvt, Clerk, typist-C
1 Techn 5th, Light truck driver, orderly-R
2 Pvts, Light truck driver, orderly-S

Weapons:
1 Rocket launcher, AT, 2.36"

Vehicles:
1 Truck, ¼-ton
1 Truck, ¾-ton, WC
1 Truck, 2½-ton, cargo
1 Trailer, 1-ton

Equipment:
2 luminous markers, radioactive, type 1 (Mr Sgt, Tech Sgt)
3 luminous markers, radioactive, type 2 (1 per truck)
3 transparent map templates, M2 (Off)
5 files, visible record, book type, with 50 pockets, bound canvas, 1¾" back, 22 × 12" (for ammunition records)
4 files, visible record, book type, with 96 pockets, visibility, ¼", complete (for ordnance general supply records)
2 wristwatches, 15 jewels (Lt Col, Capt)
1 oil burner for tent stove M1941
2 canvas dispatch cases (Lt Col, Capt)
4 folding chairs
1 empty field desk, headquarters
5 files, paper, clip, wood back
2 rocket-carrying bags, M6 (2 per rocket launcher)

1. AR 320-5, Maintenance.

1 ammunition-carrying bag (1 per SMG)
2 face masks for rocket launcher (2 per rocket launcher) (17 November 1944)
1 tent stove M1941
3 folding tables, camp
1 tent, Command Post
1 computing machine, listing, portable, hand-operated
2 non-portable typewriters, 11″ carriage
1 portable typewriter, with carrying case (1 per desk)
8 flashlights, TL-122-( ) (Off, Mr Sgt, Tech Sgt, truck)

*2 – COMPANY HEADQUARTERS (1 Officer, 1 Warrant Officer, 28 Enlisted Men (15 July 1943) 22 EM (17 November 1944)

1 Capt, Company Commander-C
1 WO, Administrative-C
1 1st Sgt-C
1 S Sgt, Mess-C
1 S Sgt, Motor-C
1 S Sgt, Supply, Unit-C
1 Cpl, Company clerk, Classification specialist-C
1 Techn 5th, Carpenter, general-C
1 Techn 5th, Clerk, general-C
1 Techn 5th, Clerk, Work order-C
2 Techns 4th, Cook-C
1 Techn 5th, Cook-C
1 Pvt, Cooks' helper-C
1 Techn 5th, Light truck driver-R
1 Pvt, Light truck driver-S
1 Techn 5th, Painter-C
4 Pvts, Basic-C (2 Basics 17 November 1944)
7 Pvts, Basic-R (5 Basics 17 November 1944)

Weapons:
1 MG, HB, M2 caliber .50, flexible
1 Rocket launcher, AT, 2.36″

Vehicles:
1 Truck, ¼-ton
1 Truck, 2½-ton, cargo, with winch and Ring Mount
1 Trailer, 1-ton

Equipment:
4 luminous dial compasses
9 wrist compasses, liquid-filled
4 luminous markers, radioactive, type 1 (1 Sgt, S Sgt)
2 luminous markers, radioactive, type 2 (1 truck)
6 grenade launchers, M7 (1 per 5 rifles)
7 ammunition-carrying bags (1 per grenade launcher, SMG)
2 rocket-carrying bags, M6 (2 per rocket launcher)
2 face masks for rocket launcher (2 per rocket launcher) (17 November 1944)
2 wristwatches, 7 jewels (1st Sgt, Mess Sgt)
1 wristwatch, 15 jewels (Company Commander)
2 asbestos mittens M1942 (per MG, caliber .50)
10 gasoline drums, 5-gallon (for technical use)
1 gasoline lantern, two-mantle, commercial
1 stencil outfit, complete, with figures and letters
1 tin pot, marking
1 canvas paulin, large (tarpaulin)
1 tool set, Carpenters, no. 2 (per carpenter)
60 goggles, M 1944 (2 per truck, for the entire company)
1 portable typewriter, with carrying case
4 hand-portable electric lanterns (15 July 1943 replaced by:
4 electric lanterns, MX-290/GV (17 November 1944)
1 panel set, AP-50-A
8 flashlights, TL-122-( ) (Off, WO, 1st Sgt, S Sgt, truck)

2 whistles, thunderer (Capt, 1st Sgt)

*3 – SUPPLY PLATOON (1 Officer, 24 Enlisted Men)

1 1st Lt, Supply-C
1 Tech Sgt, Supply-C
1 S Sgt, Supply-C
1 Sgt, Clerk, parts, armament-C
1 Sgt, Clerk, parts, automotive-C
1 Techn 4th, Clerk, parts, armament-C
1 Techn 5th, Clerk, parts, armament-C
2 Pvts, Clerk, parts, armament-C
1 Techn 4th, Clerk, parts, automotive-C
1 Techn 5th, Clerk, parts, automotive-C
2 Pvts, Clerk, parts, automotive-C
1 Techn 4th, Clerk, stock-C
1 Techn 5th, Clerk, stock-C
1 Techn 5th, Clerk, typist-C
1 Pvt, Clerk, typist-C
3 Techns 5th, Light truck driver, clerk, parts-R
3 Pvts, Light truck driver, clerk, parts-R
2 Pvts, Light truck driver, clerk, parts-S

Weapons:
2 MG, HB, M2, caliber .50, flexible
1 Rocket launcher, AT, 2.36″

Vehicles:
2 Trucks, ¾-ton, WC, with winch
4 Trucks, 2½-ton, cargo
2 Trucks, 2½-ton, cargo, with winch and Ring Mount
6 Trailers, 1-ton

Equipment:
2 luminous markers, radioactive, type 1 (Tech Sgt, S Sgt)
8 luminous markers, radioactive, type 2 (1 per Truck)
24 cabinets, spare parts, type 1, M1940 (6 per 2½-ton truck)
4 asbestos mittens, M1942 (2 per MG, caliber .50)
2 rocket-carrying bags, M6 (2 per rocket launcher)
2 face masks for rocket launcher (2 per rocket launcher) (17 November 1944)
2 ammunition-carrying bags (1 per SMG)
2 oil burners for tent stove M1941
2 tent stoves M1941
1 tent Squad, M1942
11 flashlights, TL-122-( ) (Off, Tech Sgt, S Sgt, truck)

*4 – ARMAMENT PLATOON (1 Officer, 19 Enlisted Men)

*4-1 – Artillery Section

1 1st Lt, Armament-C-1 Tech Sgt, Mechanic, artillery chief-C
1 S Sgt, Mechanic, artillery-C
1 Techn 4th, Machinist-R
2 Techns 3rd, Mechanic, artillery-C
2 Techns 4th, Mechanic, artillery-C
2 Techns 5th, Mechanic, artillery, drove the ¼ and ¾-ton trucks-S
1 Techn 5th, Mechanic, artillery, drove 2½-ton truck-R
1 Techn 5th, Mechanic, artillery-C
1 Techn 3rd, Instrument repairman-C
1 Techn 5th, Instrument repairman-C
1 Techn 5th, Watch repairman-C

Weapons:
1 Rocket launcher, AT, 2.36″

Vehicles:
1 Truck, ¼-ton

1 Truck, ¾-ton
1 Truck, 2½-ton, cargo
1 Trailer, 1-ton

Equipment:

2 luminous markers, radioactive, type 1 (T Sgt, S Sgt)
3 luminous markers, radioactive, type 2 (1 per truck)
1 maintenance equipment, Ordnance set "B" (¾-ton truck)
1 tool set, Battery experts
1 pocket watch, railroad grade (1 per watch repairman)
1 tool set, machinists (1 per machinist)
2 rocket-carrying bags, M6 (2 per rocket launcher)
2 face masks for rocket launcher (2 per rocket launcher) (17 November 1944)
2 ammunition-carrying bags (1 per SMG)
1 oil burner for tent stove M1941
1 tent stove M 1941
1 tent, wall, large
14 flashlights, TL-122-( ) (Off, T Sgt, S Sgt, truck, Artillery mechanic)

*4-2 – Small Arms Section

1 S Sgt, Small arms repairman-C
1 Techn 4th, Small arms repairman-C
1 Techn 4th, Small arms repairman, drove ¼-ton truck-S
1 Techn 5th, Small arms repairman-C
1 Techn 5th, Small arms repairman, drove the 2½-ton truck, small arms repair-R

Vehicles:

1 Truck, ¼-ton
1 Truck, 2½-ton, small arms repair, M7A2

Equipment:

1 luminous marker, radioactive, type 1 (S Sgt)
2 luminous markers, radioactive, type 2 (1 per truck)
5 asbestos mittens, M1942 (1 per repairman)
1 ammunition-carrying bag (1 per SMG)
3 flashlights, TL-122-( ) (S Sgt, truck)

*5 – AUTOMOTIVE PLATOON (3 Officers, 55 Enlisted Men)

1 1st Lt, Automotive-C
1 2nd Lt, Automotive-C
1 2nd Lt, Evacuation-C
1 Tech Sgt, Mechanic, automotive chief-C
1 S Sgt, Crew chief, wrecking-C
1 S Sgt, Mechanic, automotive, assistant chief-C
3 Sgts, Crewman, wrecker-C
1 Techn 5th, Blacksmith-C
1 Techn 5th, Blacksmith-R
1 Techn 4th, Electrician, automotive-C
1 Techn 5th, Electrician, automotive-C
1 Pvt, Electrician, automotive-R
2 Techns 3rd, Inspector, motor-C
1 Techn 3rd, Machinist-C
5 Techns 3rd, Mechanic, automotive-C
5 Techns 4th, Mechanic, automotive-C
4 Techns 5th, Mechanic, automotive, drove trucks-R
4 Techns 5th, Mechanic, automotive, drove trucks-S
2 Techns 5th, Mechanic, automotive-C
1 Techn 4th, Mechanic, carburettor-C
1 Techn 5th, Mechanic, carburettor-C
1 Pvt 4th, Mechanic, carburettor-C
1 Techn 3rd, Mechanic, chassis, track vehicle-C
1 Techn 4th, Mechanic, chassis, track vehicle-C
1 Techn 5th, Mechanic, chassis, track vehicle-R
1 Techn 3rd, Mechanic, engine, track vehicle-C

1 Techn 4th, Mechanic, engine, track vehicle-C
3 Techns 5th, Wrecker operator-R
1 Techn 4th, Repairman, automobile body-C
1 Techn 5th, Repairman, automobile body-C
1 Techn 4th, Repairman, radiator-C
1 Techn 5th, Repairman, radiator-C
2 Techns 3rd, Welder, general-C
1 Techn 4th, Welder, general-C
1 Techn 4th, Welder, general-R
1 Techn 5th, Welder, general-C
1 Techn 5th, Welder, general, drove ¼-ton truck, welder-C

Weapons:
2 MG, HB, M2, caliber .50, flexible
1 Rocket launcher, AT, 2.36″

Vehicles:
3 Trucks, ¼-ton
1 Truck, ¼-ton, carries the tool set, arc welder
1 Truck, ¾-ton, WC
1 Truck, 2½-ton, cargo, with winch and Ring Mount
2 Trucks, 2½-ton, cargo, with winch, carried tool sets
1 Truck, 2½-ton, cargo, carried a tool set
2 Trucks, 4-ton, Wrecker
1 Truck, Heavy wrecking, M1A1, with Ring Mount
3 Trailers, 1-ton, carried tool sets

Equipment:
3 luminous markers, radioactive, type 1 (Tech Sgt, S Sgt)
12 luminous marker, radioactive, type 2 (1 per truck)
1 Ordnance maintenance set "B" (¾-ton truck, emergency vehicle)
2 tool sets, Blacksmiths, no. 2
29 motor vehicles mechanics' tool sets, (1 per Mechanic)
3 tool sets, Ignition Mechanics, (1 per Electrician)
1 tool set, Machinist (for Machinist)
1 tool set, painter (for Painter)
3 tool sets, sheet metal and radiator mechanics (1 per Repairman, radiator and Repairman, automobile body)
1 tool set, Trimmers
1 unit equipment tool set, 3rd echelon, set no. 1
1 tool set, vulcanizers
6 tool sets, welders (1 per Welder)
1 tool set, Mobile Arc Welder (mounted on ¼-ton truck)
4 asbestos mittens, M1942 (2 per MG, caliber .50)
2 rocket-carrying bags, M6 (2 per rocket launcher)
2 face masks for rocket launcher (2 per rocket launcher) (17 November 1944)
4 ammunition-carrying bags (1 per SMG)
4 wrecking bars, gooseneck, 24″ length, diameter of stock ¾″
1 gasoline heater, tent (1 per tent, maintenance)
1 tent, maintenance, shelter, with frame
1 tool set, Carpenters no. 1 (1 per 2 Repairman, automobile body)
49 flashlights, TL-122-( ) (Off, Tech Sgt, S Sgt, Mechns, trucks, Electricians)

As a maintenance unit in direct support (DS), the company was to be dispersed laterally and in depth to allow close maintenance to the supported units. The maintenance was to be done as far forward as the tactical situation, the complexity of the equipment, the availability of the spare parts and repair tools, and the skills of the mechanics permitted.

The ordnance company had to provide technical assistance to users, including:
training in maintenance operations, use of the equipment, supporting maintenance
assistance in maintenance planning
liaison
introduction to new equipment and spare parts to supported units.

7.3 QUARTERMASTER COMPANY, INFANTRY DIVISION
T/O&E 10-17

On 1 August 1942 the quartermaster company numbered 344 personnel. With the transfer of automobile maintenance to the Ordnance Corps, the company lost half its personnel. In addition, the responsibility for food and gasoline supply was decentralized to regimental level, or battalion level for an independent battalion.

In the tables of March 1943, Army Ground Forces anticipated reducing the company to 152 personnel and removing the service platoon. However, in the definitive table of 15 July 1943, the company retained its service platoon, albeit with limited responsibilities. Transportation was transferred to user units, for example the service company, infantry regiment. The trucks of the quartermaster company were principally a reserve. They had to secure water supplies, and carry the reserve supply, a ration for a day for the entire division.

All trucks had an organic freight, except five that were kept as replacements. These were to be unloaded when a unit asked for them to carry troops or act as a reserve transportation. The quartermaster company was capable of the tactical transport of one infantry battalion. [2]

The Quartermaster Corps was responsible for staff and technical supervision concerning the supply of subsistence, clothing and textiles, petroleum, and general supply equipment. It operated commissaries, laundries and dry cleaning plants. [3]

By the attachment of six quartermaster truck companies, the infantry division could become entirely motorized. Six companies were sufficient since only the three infantry regiments required supplementary transportation. The quartermaster truck company, T/O&E 10-57, was assigned at army-level. It contained 48 2½-ton trucks on 8 August 1943. Therefore 288 trucks were necessary to entirely motorize a division.

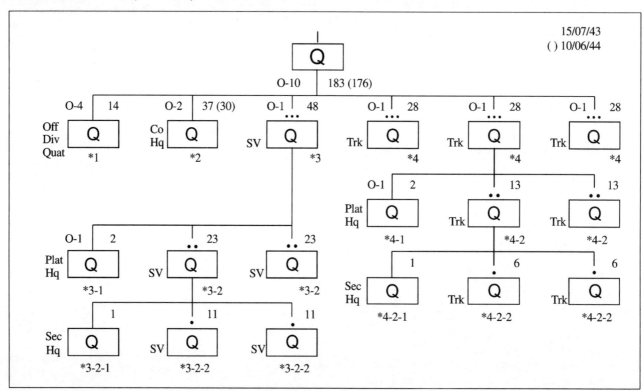

49. Quartermaster Company, Infantry Division

The quartermaster company, infantry division (see chart 49), included:
  Office of the Division Quartermaster
  Company Headquarters
  Service Platoon
      Platoon Headquarters
      2 Service Sections
  3 Truck Platoons
      Platoon Headquarters
      2 Truck Sections

2. Greenfield, Palmer, Wiley, op. cit., p. 311 and 317.
3. AR 320-5, Quartermaster.

*1 – OFFICE OF THE DIVISION QUARTERMASTER (4 Officers, 14 Enlisted Men)

1 Lt Col, Division Quartermaster, Unit Commander-P
1 Major, Assistant Division Quartermaster-P (Executive Officer, Operation and Training S-3)
1 Capt, Division Quartermaster Supply-C
1 Capt, Purchasing and contracting, Transportation-C
1 Mr Sgt, Chief clerk-C
1 Tech Sgt, Supply-C
1 Tech Sgt, Transportation-C
1 Sgt, Supply class I-C
1 Sgt, Supply class II and III-C
1 Sgt, Purchasing and contracting-C
1 Techn 5th, General clerk-C
1 Techn 4th, Headquarters clerk-C
2 Pvts, Headquarters clerk-C
2 Techns 5th, Light truck driver-R
1 Pvt, Light truck driver-R
1 Techn 4th, Stenographer-C

Vehicles:
1 Truck, ¼-ton
1 Truck, ¾-ton, WC
1 Truck, 2½-ton, cargo
1 Trailer, 1-ton

Equipment:
10 wrist compasses, liquid-filled (Off, Mr Sgt, Tech Sgt, Sgt)
2 hand-portable electric lanterns (added 19 February 1944)
4 transparent map templates, M2 (Off)
1 binoculars, M13
1 oil burner for tent stove M1941
4 canvas dispatch cases (Off)
3 folding chairs, wooden
1 record chest, fibre (desk)
1 empty field desk, headquarters
1 paper file, arch, board, without index and covers
1 file, clip, wood back, 9″ × 15½″
1 rubber stamp, official
1 combination lock
2 gasoline lanterns, two-mantle, commercial
1 computing machine, non-listing
1 duplicating machine, stencil surface, hand-operated, 8 × 13″
4 paper fastening machines, lever-or-plunger-type, wire staple, light-duty
1 tent stove M1941
3 folding tables, camp
1 tent, Command Post
3 non-portable typewriters, 11-in carriage
1 portable typewriter, with carrying case
11 flashlights, TL-122-( ) (Off, Mr Sgt, Tech Sgt, S Sgt, trk)
4 whistles, thunderer (Off)

*2 – COMPANY HEADQUARTERS (2 Officers, 37 Enlisted Men (30 EM, 10 June 1944)

1 Capt, Administrative, Supply-C
1 1st Lt, Company motor maintenance-C
1 1st Sgt, and Truckmaster-C
1 S Sgt, Chief mechanic-C
1 S Sgt, Mess-C
1 S Sgt, Supply-C
1 Cpl, Company clerk, classification specialist-C
1 Cpl, Dispatcher-C
1 Techn 5th, Armorer-C (added, 19 February 1944)
1 Pvt, Bugler and messenger, drove the ¼-ton truck-C
2 Techns 4th, Cook-C
2 Techns 5th, Cook-C

1 Pvt, Cooks' helper-C
1 Pvt, Cooks' helper, drove the 2½-ton truck-C (cancelled, 19 February 1944)
1 Pvt, Light truck driver-R (added, 19 February 1944)
3 Techns 4th, Mechanic, automobile-C
2 Techns 5th, Mechanic, automobile-C
1 Techn 5th, Mechanic, automobile, drove the 2½-ton truck-C
1 Pvt, Orderly, drove the ¼-ton truck-C
7 Pvts, Basics-R (5 Pvts, C1, 10 June 1944 to the table of 19 February 1944)
10 Pvts, Basics-C (9 Pvts, 19 February 1944 ; 4 Pvts, C1)

Weapons:
1 MG, HB, M2, caliber .50, flexible
5 Rocket launchers, AT, 2.36"

Vehicles:
2 Trucks, ¼-ton
1 Truck, 2½-ton, cargo, with Ring Mount, (Kitchen, supply and equipment)
1 Truck, 2½-ton, cargo, with winch, 2nd echelon equipment and spare parts
1 Trailer, 1-ton

Equipment:
6 wrist compasses, liquid-filled (Off, 1st Sgt, S Sgt)
4 fire extinguishers, carbon-tetrachloride, 4-qt, pressure type
2 transparent map templates, M2
1 folding litter
7 motor vehicles mechanics' tool sets (1 per Mechanic)
1 tool set, body mechanics (1 per 2 set no. 2)
1 unit equipment tool set, 2nd echelon, set no. 2
1 unit equipment tool set, 2nd echelon, set no. 5
1 unit equipment tool set, 2nd echelon, set no. 7
1 tool set, welders
2 oil burners for tent stove M1941
3 canvas dispatch cases (Off, 1st Sgt)
3 gasoline lanterns, two-mantle, commercial
6 canvas paulins, large (tarpaulin)
2 gasoline pumps, dispending, portable
1 stencil outfit, with figures and letters, ½" and 1"
2 tent stoves M1941
1 tent, Squad, M1942
1 tool set, carpenters', no. 2
3 panel sets, AP-50-A (1 per 4 trucks)
16 flashlights, TL-122-( ) (Off, 1st Sgt, S Sgt, Mech, trk)
3 whistles, thunderer (Off, 1st Sgt)

The following items were issued for the company:
43 grenade launchers, M1 (replaced by M7, C2, 10 January 1944) (1 per rifle M1903 for the model M1 and rifle M1 for M7 model)
15 grenade launchers, M8 (1 per 10 carbines) (from C1, 10 June 1944, 48 M8, 1 per 3 carbines)
58 ammunition-carrying bags (1 per grenade launcher)
800 gasoline drums, 5-gallon, with carrying handle
59 goggles, M1943, clear lens (1 per driver, replace the model M1942) (cancelled 1 June 1945)
13 goggles, M1943, red lens (1 per MG, caliber .50) (cancelled 1 June 1945)
121 goggles, M1943, green lens (1 per individual not otherwise issued) (114 goggles, C1) (cancelled 1 June 1945)
118 goggles, M1944 (added 1 June 1945, 2 per truck)
10 face masks for rocket launcher (added 1 June 1945, 2 per rocket launcher)
15 cooking outfits, 1-burner (stove M1942) (1 per 4 vehicles) (stove cooking, gasoline, M1941, was issued in lieu of cooking outfit until the latter was available; this was cancelled with C1)

*3 – SERVICE PLATOON (1 Officer, 48 Enlisted Men)

*3-1 – Platoon Headquarters

1 2nd Lt, Platoon Commander-C
1 S Sgt Platoon-C
1 Pvt, Light truck driver-R

Vehicle:
   1 Truck, ¾-ton, WC

Equipment:
   2 wrist, liquid-filled, compasses
   1 transparent map template, M2
   1 canvas dispatch case
   3 flashlights, TL-122-( ) (Off, S Sgt, truck)

*3-2 – Service Section (× 2)

*3-2-1 – Section Headquarters
   1 Sgt, Section Leader-C

Equipment:
   1 wrist compass, liquid-filled (Sect Leader)
   1 whistle, thunderer (Sect Leader)

*3-2-2 – Service Squad (× 2)
   1 Cpl, Squad Leader-C
   2 Pvts, Laborer-R (3 in the second Squad)
   7 Pvts, Laborer-C
   1 Techn 5th, Butcher-C (not in the 2nd Squad)

Equipment:
   1 commissary chest, complete with equipment (Butcher)

*4 – TRUCK PLATOON (× 3) (1 Officer, 28 Enlisted Men)
*4-1 – Platoon Headquarters
   1 1st or 2nd Lt, Platoon Commander-C
   1 S Sgt, Platoon-C
   1 techn 5th, Light truck driver-R

Vehicle:
   1 Truck, ¼-ton

Equipment:
   2 wrist compasses, liquid-filled (Off, S Sgt)
   1 transparent map template, M2 (Off)
   1 canvas dispatch case
   3 flashlights, TL-122-( ) (Off, S Sgt, truck)

*4-2 – Truck Section (× 2)

*4-2-1 – Section Headquarters
   1 Sgt, Section Leader-C

Equipment:
   1 wrist compass, liquid-filled (Sect Leader)
   1 whistle, thunderer (Sect Leader)

*4-2-2 – Truck Squad (× 2)
   1 Cpl, Squad Leader, assistant truck driver-C
   3 Techns 5th or Pvts, Light truck driver-C (2 armed with rifle in the 2nd squad)
   1 Techn 5th or Pvt, Light truck driver-R (2 armed with carbine in the 2nd squad)
   1 Techn 5th or Pvt, Light truck driver assistant-C

Weapons:
   1 MG, HB, M2, caliber .50, flexible

Vehicles:
   1 Truck, 2½-ton, cargo, with Ring Mount
   2 Trucks, 2½-ton, cargo
   1 Truck, 2½-ton, cargo, with winch
   4 Trailers, 1-ton

Equipment:
   1 panel set, AP-50-A (1 per 4 trucks)
   4 flashlights, TL-122-( ) (trucks)

The Quartermaster Corps was responsible for supplies of classes I and III, except for solid fuels which were the responsibility of the Corps of Engineers. It was the provider for a part of class II, particularly clothing. The classes of supplies were:

Class I: Supplies such as rations, forage, and Post Exchange (PX) supplies, that were consumed at an approximately uniform daily rate under all conditions.

Class II: Clothing, organizational equipment, and vehicles, including spare parts for which allowances for initial issue to individuals and organizations were fixed by Tables of Allowances and Tables of Organization and Equipment, or appropriate lists or tables, and which were not included in Classes II (A), IV or IV (A).

Class II (A): Aviation supplies and equipment for which allowances for initial issue to organizations were prescribed in appropriate Tables of Allowances lists.

Class III: Fuels and lubricants for all purposes except for operating aircraft or for use as ammunition in weapons such as flamethrowers.

Class III (A): Aviation fuels and lubricants.

Class IV: Items not otherwise classified and for which initial issue allowances were not prescribed by approved issue tables.

Class IV (A): Aviation supplies and equipments for which allowances for initial issue to organizations were not prescribed by appropriate tables of allowances lists, or which required special measures of control.

Class V: Ammunition of all types (including chemical), explosives, anti-tank and antipersonnel mines, fuses, detonators and pyrotechnics.

Class V (A): Aviation ammunition, bombs, rockets, pyrotechnics and similar expendable accessories. [4]

7.4   SIGNAL COMPANY, INFANTRY DIVISION
T/O&E 11-7

The signal company, infantry division, was the Signal Corps organization assigned to each infantry division. It performed all signal communication and signal supply functions of the Signal Corps within the division.

In the triangular division, the company was assigned to special troops. The signal company commander was responsible, under the special troops commander, for the administration and discipline of the company.

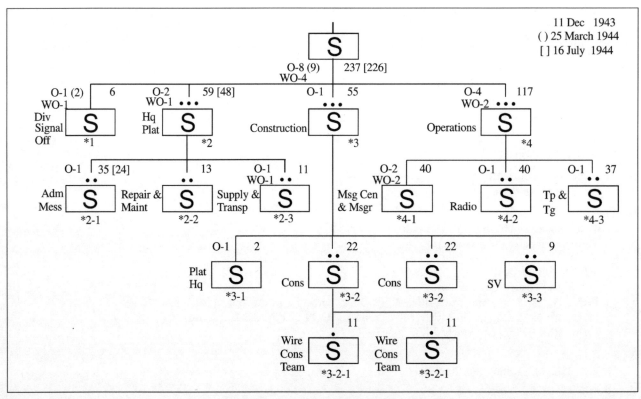

50. Signal Company, Infantry Division

The division signal officer (a lieutenant-colonel) commanded the signal company for training and operations only. The signal company commander (a captain) administered the company and conducted the training and operations in accordance with the orders of the division signal officer. He was also his assistant until an assistant division signal officer was added, on

4. AR 320-5, p. 479.

25 March 1944. Successful conduct of signal operations required that the division signal officer and his assistant work well as a team; each was to be capable of acting for the other and must not hesitate to do what the situation required, informing the other of the action taken as soon as possible. However, the division signal officer could not delegate the responsibility for the conduct of signal operations.

The duties of the Signal Company

The duties of the signal company were:

installation, operation and maintenance of signal communications at division headquarters, including all echelons, from division headquarters to each major subordinate unit, and to other subordinate or attached units or to adjacent units when required, including liaison officers

supply and minor repair of signal equipment for all units of the division, organic or attached

collection, charging and distribution of storage batteries issued by the Signal Corps to units of the division which were not equipped with charging sets

surveillance of all signal communication channels within the division as prescribed by the division commander to ensure that signal security measures were being taken in conformity with his orders.

The signal company, shown in chart 50, included:

Division Signal Officer Section
Headquarters Platoon
Administrative & Mess Section
Repair & Maintenance Section
Supply & Transportation Section
Construction Platoon
Platoon Headquarters
2 Construction Sections
Service Section
Operations Section
Message Center & Messengers Section
Radio Section
Telephone & Telegraph Section

*1 – DIVISION SIGNAL OFFICER SECTION (1 Officer (2, C1, 25 March 1944), 1 Warrant Officer, 6 Enlisted Men)

1 Lt Col, Division Signal Officer-P
1 Major, Assistant Division Signal Officer-P (added C1)
1 WO, Supply-C
1 Tech Sgt, Chief clerk-C
1 Techn 5th, Clerk, general-C
1 Pvt, Clerk, general, drove the ¼-ton truck-S
1 Techn 4th, Clerk, stock records-C
1 Techn 5th, Draftsman, electrical-C
1 Techn 5th, Light truck driver-R

Vehicles:
1 Truck, ¼-ton
1 Truck, 1½-ton, cargo
1 Trailer, 1-ton

Equipment:
1 gas proof curtain, M1
3 luminous dial compasses (Off, WO)
1 wrist compass, liquid-filled (Tech Sgt)
1 drafting equipment, set no. 2, Company
1 drawing instruments, office set
4 transparent map templates, M2
1 triangle, plastic, transparent, 45 degree, 12"
1 triangle, plastic, transparent, 30-60 degree, 14"
1 T-square, maple, plastic lined, fixed head, 60"
1 binocular, M13 (Lt Col)
1 pocket watch, 15 jewels
1 lamp, electric, portable, CP (1 per tent, Command Post)
1 oil burner for tent stove M1941
3 canvas dispatch cases (Off, WO)
1 ammunition-carrying bag (SMG)

3 folding chairs, wooden
2 empty field desks, headquarters
4 files, paper, clip, wood back
2 gasoline lanterns, two-mantle, commercial
1 duplicating machine, stencil, surface, hand operated, 8 × 13″
1 combination lock, safe, field
1 tent stove, M1941 (for tent, CP)
1 tent, Command Post
3 folding tables, camp
1 non-portable typewriter, 11″ carriage
2 portable typewriters, with carrying case
1 classified cryptographic equipment (C1, 25 March 1944, as issued by Chief Signal Officer
6 flashlights, TL-122-( ) (Off, WO, Tech Sgt, trucks)
1 hand-portable electric lantern (C1, 25 March 1944)
3 whistles, thunderer (Off, WO)

*2 – HEADQUARTERS PLATOON (2 Officers, 1 Warrant Officer, 59 Enlisted Men (48 EM, C2, 16 July 1944)

*2-1 – Administrative & Mess Section

1 Capt, Signal Officer, general, Company Commander-C
1 1st Sgt-C
1 S Sgt, Mess-C
1 Cpl, Company clerk-C
1 Techn 5th, Clerk, general, drove the ¼-ton truck-S
3 Techns 4th, Cook-C
2 Techns 5th, Cook-C
2 Pvts, Cooks' helper-C
1 Techn 5th, Light truck driver-R
1 Pvt, Light truck driver-R
12 Pvts, Basic-R (6 Basics, C2, 16 July 1944)
10 Pvts, Basic-C (5 Basics, C2)

Weapons:
1 Rocket launcher, AT, 2.36″

Vehicles:
1 Truck, ¼-ton
2 Trucks, 2½-ton, cargo
2 Trailers, 1-ton

Equipment:
1 luminous dial compass (Off)
2 wrist compasses, liquid-filled (1st Sgt, S Sgt)
48 luminous markers, radioactive, type I
9 mine probes M1 (C1, 25 March 1944)
1 navigation equipment, set no. 2, dead reckoning
3 transparent map templates, M2
1 binocular, M13 (Capt)
1 pocket watch, 15 jewels (Capt)
2 wristwatches, 7 jewels (1st Sgt, S Sgt)
4 galvanized buckets, GP, without lip, heavyweight, 14-qt,
1 canvas dispatch case (Off)
2 gasoline lanterns, leaded fuel
2 lanterns, kerosene, Army
1 combination lock, safe, field
1 ammunition-carrying bag (SMG)
1 rocket-carrying bag, M6 (rocket-launcher)
6 flashlights, TL-122-( ) (Off, 1st Sgt, S Sgt, trucks)
3 hand-portable electric lanterns (C1, 25 March 1944)
1 whistle, thunderer (Off)

For the entire company:
55 grenade launchers, M7 (1 per rifle M1) (49 bags, C2, 16 July 1944)
3 grenade launchers, M8 (51 bags, C2, 1 per 3 carbines)

58 ammunition-carrying bags (1 per grenade launcher, 90 bags, C2)
40 panel sets, AP-50-A (1 per truck except ¼-ton)

*2-2 – Repair & Maintenance Section

1 Tech Sgt, Radio repairman-C
1 Tech Sgt, Telephone & Telegraph repairman-C
1 Techn 5th, Armorer-C
1 Techn 4th, Mechanic, teletypewriter-C
2 Techns 3rd, Radio repairman-C
1 Techn 4th, Radio repairman-C
1 Techn 5th, Radio repairman-C
1 Techn 5th, Radio repairman, drove the 1½-ton truck-R (2½-ton truck, C2, 16 July 1944)
1 Techn 5th, Radio repairman, drove a 2½-ton truck-R
1 Techn 4th, Tp &Tg repairman-C
1 Techn 5th, Tp &Tg repairman, drove a 2½-ton truck-C
1 Pvt, Tp &Tg repairman-C

Vehicles:

1 Truck, 1½-ton, cargo (replaced by 2½-ton, C2, 16 July 1944)
2 Trucks, 2½-ton, small arms repair, M7A1, Signal Corps (replaced by Signal Corps Repair, M30, C2, 16 July 1944)
2 Trailers, 1-ton (3 trailers, C2)

Equipment:

2 wrist compasses, liquid-filled (Tech Sgt)
2 transparent map templates, M2
2 handle axes, camp
1 stencil outfit, with figures and letters, ½″ and 1″
1 tool set, Carpenters', no. 1
1 tent, Squad M1942
2 oil burners for tent stoves, M1941
2 tent stoves, M1941 (2 per tent squad)
1 alignment equipment ME-73 (for radio repair truck)
23 chests BC-5
2 chests CH-112 (1 per Power Unit PE-95, used with Signal Corps Repair Truck, C1, 25 March 1944)
1 converter M-209 (to cipher and decipher)
2 cords, CO-313 (1 per PE-95, C1)
2 cords, CO-316 (1 per PE-95, C1)
1 crystal kit (2700 crystals) MC-535, for SR-694 (C2, 16 July 1944)
5 flashlights, TL-122-( ) (Tech Sgt, truck)
4 hydrometers HY-2 (2 per radio repair truck, wire repair truck, C1, 25 March 1944)
2 maintenance equipments ME-34 (spare parts for SCR-609, 610 (C1)
2 maintenance equipments ME-40
2 maintenance equipments ME-36-( ) (C1)
7 multimeters I-239-( ) (1 per tool equipment TE-113, C1)
2 power units PE-95-( ) (1 per radio repair truck, wire repair truck)
1 radio kit MX-49/MRM (kit of spare parts to modify the small arms repair truck in radio repair truck)
1 radio set SCR-193
6 radio sets SCR-300-( )
1 radio set SCR-506 (12V)
1 radio set SCR-508-( ) (12V)
1 radio set SCR-510-( ) – 10 radio sets SCR-536 (25 SCR-536, when authorized by the Commander of the Theater of Operations, C2, 16 July 1944)
1 radio set SCR-543
2 radio sets SCR-593
2 radio sets SCR-608
10 radio sets SCR-610-( ) (SCR-619, C2)
1 radio set SCR-694 (pending availability, 1 SCR-284 could be issued) (with C4, 3 December 1945, the SCR-694 was replaced by the AN/GRC9)
1 power unit PP-34-( )/MRM for PE-95 (for radio repair truck to charge the batteries, pending availability, RA-91-( ) or RA-36-( ) could be issued)
1 rectifier RA-83-( ) (pending availability RA-91-( ) or RA-36-( ) could be issued
2 reel units, RL-31

1 remote control equipment RM-29-( ) (RC-290, C2, 16 July 1944)

1 test equipment IE-9-( )[5] (For radio repair truck, radio repair devices: signal generators HF and LF, power unit PA-48, frequency-metre SCR-211, etc.)

1 test equipment IE-17-( ) (for radio repair truck, for SCR-536)

1 signal generator, HF, I-72-( ) (for radio repair truck, not issued when IE-9-C was issued)

2 tools TL-202, (wrench for antenna mount MP-14-( ), 37, 47-( ), 48-( ), 57)

1 tool equipment TE-50 (TE-50-A, C2, 16 July 1944, tool chest for teletypewriter repair)

7 tool equipments TE-113 (1 per Radio repairman)

1 tool equipment TE-114 (1 per radio repair truck)

1 tool set TE-16

1 vulcanizing equipment TE-55 (to vulcanize under rubber the cable connectors, TE-54 could be issued until exhausted)

1 test equipment IE-29 (1 test chest BE-70, 1 test set I-49, 1 test set I-61, 1 test set WE Co no9-A, 1 tester Supreme no. 592, 1 thermometer, 1 hydrometer HY-2) (Wire repair truck, pending availability the IE-10 could be issued)

1 tool equipment TE-111 (Wire repair truck, pending availability the TE-47 could be issued)

*2-3 – Supply & Transportation Section

1 1st Lt, Supply Officer-C

1 WO, Motor-C

1 Tech Sgt, Motor-C

1 S Sgt, Supply-C

1 Techn 5th, Supply clerk-C

3 Techns 4th, Mechanic, automobile-C

1 Techn 4th, Mechanic, automobile-R

1 Techn 5th, Mechanic, automobile-C

2 Techns 5th, Mechanic, automobile, drove the 2½-ton trucks-R

1 Techn 5th, Storekeeper, drove the ¼-ton truck-S

Vehicles:

1 Truck, ¼-ton

2 Trucks, 2½-ton, cargo

2 Trailers, 1-ton

Equipment:

2 luminous dial compasses (Off, WO)

2 wrist compasses, liquid-filled (Tech Sgt, S Sgt)

4 transparent map templates, M2

1 wristwatch, 7 jewels (Tech Sgt, Motor)

1 cabinet, spare parts, type 1, M1940

7 motor vehicles mechanics' tool sets (1 per Mechanic)

1 unit equipment tool set, 2nd echelon, set no. 2

1 unit equipment tool set, 2nd echelon, set no. 5

1 unit equipment tool set, 2nd echelon, set no. 7

1 tool set, welders

1 wrecking bar, gooseneck, diameter of stock ¾", length 24"

2 canvas dispatch cases (Off, WO)

1 ammunition-carrying bag (SMG)

7 flashlights, TL-122-( ) (Off, WO, T Sgt, S Sgt, truck)

1 ladder, LC-15

3 whistles, thunderer (Off, Tech Sgt motor)

*3 – CONSTRUCTION PLATOON (1 Officer, 55 Enlisted Men)

*3-1 – Platoon Headquarters

1 1st Lt, Field Line Construction Officer-C

1 Mr Sgt, Chief field lineman-C

1 Techn 5th, Field lineman, drove the ¼-ton truck-S

Vehicles:

1 Truck, ¼-ton

---

5. The parenthesis after the Signal Corps references signifies that any model of the equipment could be issued. For example, IE-9-( ) could signify IE-9-A, IE-9-B or IE-9-C.

Equipment:
- 1 luminous dial compass (Off)
- 1 wrist compass, liquid-filled (Mr Sgt)
- 2 transparent map templates, M2
- 1 binocular, M13 (Off)
- 1 canvas dispatch case (Off)
- 1 ammunition-carrying bag (SMG)
- 4 flashlights, TL-122-( ) (Off, Mr Sgt, lineman, truck)
- 3 respirators, dust, M2 (Lineman, truck, M1 model could be issued until exhausted)
- 2 whistles, thunderer (Off, Mr Sgt)

*3-2 – Construction Section (× 2)

*3-2-1 Wire Construction Team (× 2)
- 1 S Sgt, Assistant Chief Lineman-C
- 1 Sgt, Assistant Chief Lineman-R
- 1 Techn 5th, Field lineman, drove the 2½-ton truck-R
- 1 Pvt, Field lineman, Machine-gunner-C
- 1 Techn 5th, Field lineman, drove the ¾-ton truck-S
- 2 Pvts, Field lineman-R
- 4 Pvts, Field lineman-C

Weapons:
- 1 MG, HB, M2, caliber .50, flexible

Vehicles:
- 1 Truck, ¾-ton, WC, with winch
- 1 Truck, 2½-ton, cargo, with Ring Mount
- 1 Trailer, 1-ton

Equipment:
- 14 respirators, dust, M2 (Lineman, truck, M1 model could be issued until exhausted)
- 1 wrist compass, liquid-filled (S Sgt)
- 1 transparent map template, M2
- 1 ammunition-carrying bag (SMG)
- 1 handled axe, camp
- 2 machetes, 18″ blade
- 1 crosscut saw, type N, hand, 24″, 8-point (1 for both Wire Teams)
- 2 sharpening stones, pocket (1 per machete)
- 2 axles RL-27-( )
- 1 chest BC-5
- 3 chest sets TD-3 (1 for 2 EE-8) (1 per Sb BD-72, C2, 16 July 1944)
- 1 chest CH-203 (1 per 2 ½-ton wire truck, C2, 16 July 1944)
- 1 climbers, tree (1 per 10 linemen equipped with TE-21, C2)
- 20 coils C-114 (for wire W-110-B)
- 13 flashlights, TL-122-( ) (S Sgt, lineman ,truck)
- 1 Gauge TL-144 (for the Section, to verify the climbers, tree)
- 11 gloves LC-10 (1 per lineman)
- 1 gloves LC-29 (for the Section, electrician gloves)
- 3 headsets HS-30 (1 for 2 EE-8) (1 per Sb BD-72, C2, 16 July 1944)
- 16 lance poles, PO-2
- 1 hand-portable electric lanterns (for the Section) (C1, 25 March 1944)
- 11 lineman equipments TE-21 (1 belt LC-23, 1 climbers LC-5, 1 hatchet LC-1, 1 pliers TL-107, 1 pliers LC-24, 1 screw driver TL-106, 1 wrench LC-25, 1 hammer HM-1)
- 3 microphones T-45 (1 for 2 EE-8, T-30-( ) before the availability of the T-45) (1 per Sb BD-72, C2, 16 July 1944)
- 1 reel frame, FM-81 (to mount on 2½-ton truck, for 8 reels DR-5) (C2)
- 1 reel unit, RL-26-( )
- 1 reel unit, RL-31
- 1 switchboard, BD-72
- 1 tailgate step, MX-134/MT (1 per 2½-ton wire truck, C2)
- 3 telephones, EE-8-( )
- 20 terminal strips, TM-184
- 1 test equipment, TS-26/TSM (voltommeter to test the wires, pending the availability, EE-65-( ) could be issued)
- 11 tool equipments, TE-33 (knife TL-29, pliers TL-13) (1 per lineman)

1 mile of wire W-110-B on reel DR-4
15 miles of wire W-110-B on reel DR-5
2 wire pikes, MC-123
2 whistles, thunderer (S Sgt, Sgt)

*3-3 – Service Section

1 Tech Sgt, Assistant chief field lineman-C
2 Sgts, Assistant chief field lineman-C
2 Techns 5th or Pvts, Light truck driver-R
2 Pvts, Field lineman, drove the ¾-ton trucks-S
1 Pvt, Field lineman-R
1 Pvt, Field lineman-C

Vehicles:
2 Trucks, ¾-ton, WC, with winch
2 Trucks, 2½-ton, cargo, with winch

Equipment:
1 wrist compass, liquid-filled (Tech Sgt)
1 transparent map template, M2
1 climbers, tree (C1, 25 March 1944)
2 ammunition-carrying bags (1 per SMG)
11 flashlights, TL-122-( ) (Tech Sgt, Lineman, truck)
8 gloves, LC-10 (C2, 16 July 1944)
2 reel units, RL-26
2 reel units, RL-31
4 tool equipments, TE-33 (lineman)
50 miles of wire W-110-B on reel DR-5
2 wire pikes, MC-123
3 whistles, thunderer (Tech Sgt, Sgts)

*4 – OPERATION PLATOON (4 Officers, 2 Warrant Officers, 117 Enlisted Men)
*4-1 – Message Center & Messenger Section

1 1st Lt, Message Center Officer-C
1 2nd Lt, Message Center Officer-C
2 WO, Message Center-C
1 Tech Sgt, Message Center chief-C
1 S Sgt, Assistant Message Center chief-C
1 Sgt, Assistant Message Center chief-C
1 Cpl, Messenger dispatcher-C
2 Techns 5th, Message Center clerk-C
1 Techn 5th, Message Center clerk, drove a 1½-ton truck-R
1 Pvt, Message Center clerk-C
1 Pvt, Message Center clerk-R
1 Pvt, Message Center clerk, drove the ¾-ton truck-S
6 Pvts, Messengers, dismounted-C
4 Techns 5th, Messenger, motor, drove ¼-ton trucks-C
10 Pvts, Messenger, motor, drove ¼-ton trucks-S
1 Pvt, Messenger, motor, drove a ¼-ton truck-C
3 Techns 3rd, Cryptographic technician-C
2 Techns 4th, Cryptographic technician-C
1 Techn 5th, Cryptographic technician-C
2 Techns 5th, Cryptographic technician, teletypewriter operator-C
1 Techn 5th, Cryptographic technician, drove a 1½-ton truck-R

Weapons:
1 MG, HB, M2, caliber .50, flexible

Vehicles:
10 Trucks, ¼-ton
1 Truck, ¾-ton, WC
2 Trucks, 1½-ton, cargo (1 with Ring Mount)
1 trailer, 1-ton

Equipment:
  For two Message Centers
      2 gas proof curtains, M1
      4 luminous dial compasses (Off, WO)
      2 wrist compasses, liquid-filled (T Sgt, S Sgt)
      21 transparent map templates, M2 (messengers)
      11 ammunition-carrying bags (1 per SMG)
      3 clocks, Message Center, M1
      21 wristwatches, 7 jewels (messengers)
      10 canvas mailbags
      5 oil burners for tent stove, M1941
      4 canvas dispatch cases (Off, WO)
      3 folding chairs, wooden
      2 gasoline lanterns, two-mantle, commercial
      4 combination lock, safe, field
      5 tent stoves, M1941
      5 tents, Command Post
      3 folding tables, camp
      4 converters M-209 (2 per Message Center)
      19 flashlights, TL-122-( ) (Off, WO, T Sgt, S Sgt, trucks)
      17 holders M-167 (to hold documents) (T Sgt, S Sgt, motorized messengers)
      2 hand-portable electric lanterns (C1, 25 March 1944)
      4 power units, PE-75-( ) (2 per Message Center)
      3 stamps, MC-181-( ) (for time stamping, for Message Center)
      2 telephones TP-3-( )
      10 telephones with amplifier TP-9-( ) (C2, 16 July 1944)
      4 typewriters, MC-88 (for telegraphist) (2 per Message Center)
      4 whistles, thunderer (Off, WO)

*4-2 – Radio Section

      1 1st Lt, Radio Officer-C
      1 Mr Sgt, Chief radio operator-C
      1 Tech Sgt, Chief radio operator-C
      2 S Sgts, Assistant chief radio operator-C
      2 Techns 3rd, Radio operator (766)-C
      2 Techns 4th, Radio operator (766)-C
      2 Techns 5th, Radio operator (766)-C
      2 Techns 5th, Radio operator (766)-R
      12 Techns 4th, Radio operator (740)-C
      2 Techns 4th, Radio operator (740)-R
      1 Techn 5th, Radio operator (740)-C
      2 Techns 5th, Radio operator (740), drove the 2½-ton trucks-R
      1 Techn 5th, Radio operator (740), drove the ¼-ton truck-S
      10 Techns 5th, Radio operator (740), drove the ¾-ton trucks-S

Weapons:
      1 MG, HB, M2, caliber .50, flexible
      1 Rocket launcher, AT, 2.36″

Vehicles:
      1 Truck, ¼-ton
      8 Trucks, ¾-ton, Command (replaced by Weapons Carrier, C1, 25 March 1944)
      2 Trucks, ¾-ton, WC
      1 Truck, 2½-ton, cargo, with Ring Mount
      1 Truck, 2½-ton, cargo
      1 Trailer, 1-ton
      1 Trailer, K-52

Equipment:
      24 respirators, dust, M2 (Radio operator, respirator M1 is issued until exhausted)
      1 luminous dial compass (Off)
      4 wrist compasses, liquid-filled (Mr Sgt, Tech Sgt, S Sgt)
      5 transparent map templates, M2
      40 wristwatches, 7 jewels (Radio operator, Chief rad opr, C2, 16 July 1944, before 1 watch per radio set)

1 canvas dispatch case (Off)
11 ammunition-carrying bags (1 per SMG)
2 rocket-carrying bags, M6 (2 per rocket launcher)
11 converters M-209 (1 per radio set)
17 flashlights, TL-122-( ) (Off, Mr Sgt, T Sgt, S Sgt, truck)
1 frequency meter set, SCR-211-( )
25 holders M-167 (1 per radio set, Mr Sgt, T Sgt, S Sgt, to hold documents)
1 key J-36 (1 per radio set, SCR-399)
2 hand-portable electric lanterns (C1)
3 panel sets, AP-30-C
3 panel sets, AP-30-D
8 radio sets, SCR-193-( ) (mounted on ¾-ton truck)
1 radio set, SCR-399-( ) (pending availability the SCR-299 could be issued)
9 telephones, TP-3
36 tool equipments, TE-33 (Radio operator)
1 whistle, thunderer (Off)

*4-3 – Telephone & Telegraph Section

1 1st Lt, Signal Officer, general-C
1 Mr Sgt, Field wire chief-C
1 Tech Sgt, Chief teletypewriter operator-C
1 S Sgt, Assistant field wire chief-C
1 S Sgt, Chief telegraph operator-C
1 Sgt, Assistant chief teletypewriter operator-C
1 Sgt, Chief switchboard operator-C-1 Sgt, foreman, installer-repairman tp & tg-C
2 Techns 4th, Installer-repairman, telephone & telegraph-C
2 Techns 5th, Installer-repairman, telephone & telegraph-C
1 Techn 5th, Installer-repairman, telephone & telegraph, drove the ¼-ton truck-C
2 Pvts, Installer-repairman, telephone & telegraph-C
2 Pvts, Installer-repairman, telephone & telegraph, drove the ¾-ton trucks-C
1 Techn 4th, Switchboard operator-C
2 Techns 5th, Switchboard operator-C
1 Techn 5th, Switchboard operator, drove the 2½-ton truck-R
4 Pvts, Switchboard operator-C
2 Pvts, Switchboard operator-R
1 Techn 3rd, Telegraph operator-C
1 Techn 4th, Telegraph operator-C
1 Techn 5th, Telegraph operator-R
3 Techns 5th, Teletypewriter operator-C
1 Techn 5th, Teletypewriter operator, drove a 2½-ton truck-R
2 Pvts, Teletypewriter operator-C
1 Pvt, Teletypewriter operator, drove the 1½-ton truck-R
1 Techn 4th, Cable repairman-C

Vehicles:
1 Truck, ¼-ton
2 Trucks, ¾-ton, WC
1 Truck, 1½-ton, cargo
2 Trucks, 2½-ton, cargo
2 Trailers, 1-ton

Equipment:
1 gas proof curtain, M1
1 luminous dial compass (Off)
5 transparent map templates, M2
24 wristwatches (Sb Opr, TT Opr, Chiefs)
1 canvas dispatch case (Off)
2 oil burners for tent stove, M1941
2 tent stoves, M1941 (for tent, CP)
2 tents, Command Post (for Central Office Set TC-4)
6 axles RL-27
16 cable assemblies, CC-345, 5 pairs wire, isolated with rubber and with waterproof connectors at each end, for reel DR-7, 100-ft long, (11 December 1943, cancelled C2)

6 cable assemblies CC-345, 1000-ft long, on reel DR-15 (11 December 1943, cancelled C2)

12 cable assemblies CC-345, 500-ft long , (C2, 16 July 1944)

16 cable assemblies CC-355, 10 pairs wire, 100-ft long (C2)

40 cable stubs, CC-344, (1 end with connector)

2 chests BC-5

32 chest sets TD-3 (1 for 2 EE-8, 1 per Sb BD-71, BD-72)

1 climbers, tree (1 per 10 equipments TE-21)

12 coils C-161-1 facsimile equipment, RC-120

22 flashlights, TL-122-( ) (Off, Mr Sgt, T Sgt, S Sgt, Sb Opr, truck)

10 gloves, LC-10 (1 per Installer-repairman)

32 headsets, HS-30 (1 for 2 EE-8, 1 per Sb BD, BD-72)

30 lance poles, PO-2

2 hand-portable electric lanterns (C1, 25 March 1944)

10 lineman equipments, TE-21 (lineman)

1 maintenance equipment, ME-11 (maintenance of switchboards BD-96 and TC-4)

32 microphones T-45 (1 for 2 EE-8, 1 per Sb BD-71, BD-72, pending availability T-30-( ) could be issued)

2 pliers TL-103 (cutting pliers)

3 pliers TL-126 (flat pliers

24 protectors AR-6 (8 per TC-4, C2, 16 July 1944) (fuse and lightning conductors for switchboard)

1 switchboard, BD-71

3 switchboards, BD-72

4 Telegraph printer sets, EE-97 (the Telegraph printer set EE-97 becomes with C4, 03/12/45, Teletypewriter set EE-97-( )

6 telegraph sets, TG-5-( )

60 telephones, EE-8-( )

3 central office sets, TC-4 (Command Post switchboard)

10 telephone repeaters, EE-89 (amplifier for wire W-110-B)

12 terminal strips, TM-184 (28 terminals)

3 test sets, TS-26/TSM (voltommeter for line test)

3 test sets, TS-27/TSM (Wheatstone bridge for line test)

9 tool equipments, TE-33 (1 per Installer-repairman)

6 tool equipments, TE-49 (tool chest for line repairman)

6 miles of wire W-110-B on reel DR-4

3 wire pikes, MC-123

2 wrenches, TL-108 (for telephone, 3/8-in)

1 whistle, thunderer (Off)

The company was usually subdivided into a command post group and a rear echelon group. The composition of each group was determined by the signal means required by each echelon of the headquarters. The section was the working unit.

The command post group was divided into a first and a second echelon to provide continuous service when the command post was advancing by bounds. Teams of radio, message center and wire sections were assigned to each group. When a team was required to operate day and night, it was divided into reliefs.

Organization for Combat

To provide communications during the march, the movement of the division command post (forward echelon and rear echelon) and during other combat situations, the signal company was organized into a command post group and a rear echelon group.

First Echelon of the Command Group

The command post group consisted of a first and second echelon, which included teams from operations and construction platoons. The size of the first echelon was the minimum required to ensure the initial requirements of signal agencies at the new command post location. This echelon usually included:

the division signal officer section, including clerks from the signal company if necessary

the company commander

one or more reliefs from the command post team, message center section, with a complement of messengers

teams from the radio section to operate radio stations required on the march and for initial operations at the new command post

one or more reliefs from command post teams, a telephone and telegraph section to install, operate and maintain the initial telephone and telegraph communications for the new command post

constructions teams from the construction platoon to install and maintain the initial wire circuits for the division

Second Echelon of the Command Group

The second echelon consisted of the remaining operation and construction teams, less those assigned to the rear echelon group.

Rear Echelon Group

This was constituted with the minimum number of operation teams and with the required construction teams to provide signal communication for the rear echelon of the division headquarters, when it is not located with the forward echelon. When the rear echelon was with the division commander, this group joined the second echelon of the command post group. [6]

7.5 SIGNAL DOCTRINE, SIGNAL COMPANY, INFANTRY DIVISION

1 – Signal communication during the march

During the march, communication channels were provided from the division command post to:
  reconnaissance and security elements operating under division control
  command posts of column commanders
  advance message centers
  control points
  rear echelon, when established

   When a security force, division reconnaissance, or special column was organized, a detachment from the signal company, including the necessary personnel and equipment, would be attached.

A) MESSAGE CENTER

Message centers were established at division command post, division rear echelon, and at each control point or advance command post foreseen in the march plan. When the division commander accompanied the division on the march, the operations of the message center were conducted in a vehicle moving with the march command post. A message center team with two reliefs was provided to each control group to permit an advance by bounds. When an advance message center was used, the assignment of a team including at least one relief was deemed sufficient.

B) MESSENGERS

The number of messengers and the type of service provided to each message center varied with the size of the echelon served. When the march command post was motorized, a messenger would be detached to ride behind the vehicle of the division commander, the others being assigned to ride in the rear of certain vehicles of the staff, the message center and in the rear of radio station vehicles that were operational.

C) COMMUNICATIONS RADIO

Command Net

The command net included the radio stations at the division command post, the march command post or separate columns, the control points and at the advance message center. Vehicular radio station teams from the signal company could be attached to each marching column. The operations of the command net could be stopped after the installation of the wire net in the new divisional bivouac area.

Reconnaissance Net

The division reconnaissance net included the radio stations at the division command post, with the reconnaissance troop and the reconnaissance and security detachments under division control and in division observation planes. The operations of the reconnaissance net were continuous and the stations silent only when absolute security was essential. Vehicular stations of the signal company could be attached to reconnaissance and security detachments.

Warning Net

The division commander could order the operation of a warning net. The frequency of the warning net was selected to permit as many units as possible to listen. The warning signals were prearranged and published in signal operating instructions. The transmission on the warning frequency of messages other than the warning signals was prohibited.

D) VISUAL COMMUNICATIONS

The principal means of visual communications were pyrotechnics and panels.

Panels

The panels were used to mark message center positions in the marching columns, to identify units on call from friendly aviation and to effect the transmission of messages. They could be operated by either the message center section or the radio section.

Pyrotechnics

Special pyrotechnic codes could be prescribed for use during the march.

---

6. Signal Corps Field Manual FM 11-10, *Organization and Operations in the Infantry Division*, War Department, October 6 1941, with changes (hereafter referred to as FM 11-10).

E) WIRE COMMUNICATIONS

Wire Lines

In the zone of advance, all existing wire facilities were used. When the control points or the advance message centers were installed near commercial wires circuits, all effort was made to use these circuits. When the commercial circuits led into territory occupied by the enemy, arrangements were made to interrupt the wire circuits at the point beyond which they are being used in order to prevent the enemy from intercepting transmissions over them. The interruption point was determined by the extent these lines could be employed by the division or other friendly forces. It was not usual to lay field wire circuits for march communications. Wire had to be conserved for combat.

Wire Teams

Teams from the telephone & telegraph section accompanied the division march command post, the control groups, and the advance message centers. A team could be provided to reconnaissance and security detachments from the division when they used wire communications. When the division advanced through unfamiliar territory, this team reconnoitred the existing wire facilities in the area. Wire construction teams from the construction platoon were frequently attached to columns of combat teams, to begin wire line construction immediately after completion of the march.

2 – Deployment from the march

During the deployment of the division, the columns were split into smaller groups moving on assigned march objectives, or into assembly positions preliminary to deployment for attack or defence. The artillery was moved directly into action to support units in contact and to protect the deployment. The signal company had to be prepared to meet signal requirements created by the changing tactical situation.

A) DIVISION COMMAND POST

The signal officer sought early information on the action contemplated and would be prepared to recommend a location for the command posts, temporary or battle, of the division and major subordinate units. He issued timely warning orders to the signal company.

The first echelon of the command post group of the signal company moved directly to the location selected for the division command post and began to install the division communication system.

The second echelon, if operating in the old bivouac area, was usually ordered to close the old location of the command post at the hour the command post changed, and to move to the new location by a defined route to arrive at a specified time.

The rear echelon could be moved or remain where it was already established. It had to conform to the plans announced for the rear echelon of headquarters.

B) SUBORDINATE UNITS

The command posts of the principal subordinate units were usually located in their respective assembly areas, if these positions were to be occupied for an appreciable time, otherwise they would be in the initial battle location. Usually, a command post was located well forward, where it would gain the greatest protection against enemy ground attack, including mechanized attack, and where the routes to its subordinate units would facilitate signal communication and control and, as far as practicable, be accessible from the division command post.

C) MESSAGE CENTERS

The message center of the march command post continued its operations. If no march command post was employed in the march, a message center would be rapidly established by a team from the first echelon of the command post group at the division command post. If a temporary command post was designated, the establishment of an advance message center by the second echelon, at the probable battle command post location, could be necessary.

D) MESSENGERS

The changing location of subordinate units in the transition from the march to the assembly areas and the movement of many small columns on all routes made the duties of messengers extremely difficult during deployment. The messengers were to be instructed as to routes and locations of the units.

E) RADIO COMMUNICATION

Command Net

The operation of the division command net was usually initiated at this time. The operation of the secondary stations could be limited to combat teams in contact with the enemy. A radio channel could be established between the division command post and the covering forces under division control. A vehicular radio station from the signal company could be attached to the covering force, if it did not have suitable radio equipment. Transmissions were forbidden from the radio station of a unit whose location in the area was concealed from the enemy.

Reconnaissance and Warning Nets

The curtailing of radio operations in the reconnaissance or warning nets during deployment was uncommon. The division commander had to receive information regularly concerning the enemy. The warning net had to continue to warn of enemy air or mechanized attacks.

F) WIRE COMMUNICATION

All efforts were made to initiate the wire system required for combat. Those lines which could not be used during combat were held to a minimum, even when the division and the subordinate units had to remain in their assembly areas for an extended period of time. If the wire circuits from the division battle command post to the battle command posts of the major subordinate units could be conveniently routed via the assembly areas command post locations of the subordinates units, such routing was prescribed, so that the wire communication for the deployment could use the system to be installed for the next tactical operation.

3 – The Attack

In order that signal installations could be initiated without delay, the division signal officer had to constantly plan ahead. He maintained a close liaison with the staff, to obtain early news of the division commander's plans. He issued orders to the signal company as soon as was possible. A careful study was made of the ground and of possible results of various actions as they affected the command post locations, axes of signal communication and protected routes for wire lines and messengers. The division signal officer and the signal company were particularly concerned by the location of the main attack of the division. It was this attack which would probably require the greater proportion of the efforts of the signal company in maintaining adequate signal channels.

Command Posts

As the attack progressed, the signal officer could be called to recommend the probable successive locations of the command posts. The depth of the advance planned by the division commander would determine the number of probable displacements required. In recommending the location for the initial command post for an attack, the signal officer selected a location as far forward as possible, considering the following factors:

    manoeuver plan
    line of departure
    road net and the existing wire facilities
    distance between the command posts of the division and of subordinate units
    security from hostile observation and fire
    shelters for personnel and installations

A) MESSAGE CENTERS

Rear Echelon

The message center at the rear echelon of the division headquarters, even when well to the rear, required protective shelter, particularly if enemy aviation was active.

Command Post

The operations of the message center of the division command post could include its movement from its establishment in a temporary location for the deployment, to a later location for the battle position. This operation was effected by leapfrogging reliefs of the command post team. The message center would always be prepared for a forward movement.

Advance Message Center

When reconnaissance and security forces were operating on a flank or when an attack force was moving to an assembly area on a flank, an advance message center could be established on this flank. The personnel needed to operate the advance message center came from the command post group.

B) MESSENGERS

After the attack was launched, only special messengers were employed forward of the division command post.

C) RADIO COMMUNICATION

When surprise was important, the operations of the radio stations within the division were initially limited to units in contact with the enemy. The radio stations in the assembly areas could continue their operations. In attack positions, the silent stations copied all messages transmitted on the net. If the division moved to a stabilized area for participating in the attack, it maintained strict radio silence until the attack was launched. If the division was already occupying an area, it could, prior to launching the attack, continue radio operations as previously conducted. When the attack was launched, all restrictions on radio operations were removed.

D) WIRE COMMUNICATION

Attack in encounter engagements

For an attack in an encounter engagement with enemy forces, the initial wire system included only essential circuits to units and establishments.

Attack after a period of preparation

When the attack was made against an organized position, after a period of preparation, the wire system installed was adapted to meet the initial requirements for the attack. It could include multiple wire lines, each via a different route, from the division command post to each of the major subordinate units and to some the auxiliary units and establishments.

Use of existing wire lines

In any attack, the existing facilities were always used to the maximum, from the division command post to the rear echelon. Commercial circuits leading into the territory occupied by the enemy were interrupted if they crossed the division front. Commercial circuits on the flank could be interrupted or supervised depending upon their routes, services for which they were being used, and the sympathies of the civilian population.

Local installations

1) Telephones

In an encounter engagement, the installation of local telephones at the division command post had to be held to the minimum, particularly when the attack was launched without delay. Without standing instructions, the division signal officer would recommend installing the telephones to the G-3.

During an attack on an organized position, for which detailed preparations had been made, the number of telephones with the staff would be more important. The switchboards and associated equipment could be installed in dugouts or other prepared shelters.

2) Telegraph

One telegraph circuit, at least, would be established between the rear echelon and the division command post, although the station in the rear echelon could be operated as a way station on a circuit from a higher headquarters (corps headquarters). At least one circuit would be established between the division command post and each of the major subordinate units of the division. In addition, a telegraphic communication could be established from the rear echelon to supply and evacuation establishments in the rear service area.

E) WIRE LINES CONSTRUCTION

In the infantry division, the wire system for the attack consisted of two circuits to each subordinate unit of infantry and field artillery. There had to be a minimum of one circuit to the division reserve, to the division observation post, to the advance message center and to the advance landing field of the observation planes. Two or more circuits could be constructed to the rear echelon. In some situations, a temporary shortage of wire could limit to one the initial number of circuits to subordinate units of infantry and artillery. Additional circuits were constructed at the earliest practicable time.

The circuits to the observation post, to the advance message center and to the division reserve were connected into the nearest switchboard.

F) INTELLIGENCE

During deployment, spare radio sets could be installed to intercept enemy radio transmissions, to obtain information of the movements, the dispositions and the plans of battle of the enemy. Wire circuits leading into territory occupied by the enemy could be tapped and transmissions intercepted. When the division operated as a part of a larger force, detachments of Army Signal Service units could be sent to the division area for signal intelligence purposes.

4 – Defence

A defensive position comprised a zone of resistance consisting of several mutually supporting defensive areas, irregular in width and in depth, each organized for all-around defence. The line joining the forward edge of the most advanced defence areas was the main line of resistance.

A) COMMAND POSTS

The signal officer had to anticipate that the enemy would try to disrupt command and communication installations by using combat aviation, mechanized forces, artillery fires and parachute troops. When he recommended the command post locations, the signal officer would consider concealment, cover and protective shelter for signal agencies at command posts, and would also consider whether to establish signal facilities at alternate command post locations. The division command post was to be located well forward in defence to ease control of subordinate units, and to gain protection against air, tank and parachute attack afforded by the combat troops. In this manner, the risk of the command post being cut off from the troops it controlled would be reduced. The same considerations applied to the selection and location of regimental command posts.

The communication system of the division had to provide for signal channels to the major subordinate infantry and field artillery units, covering forces and outposts under division control, the division reserve, division anti-tank units, division observation posts and advance message centers, advance landing fields, attached troops, supply and evacuation establishments, and all echelons of the division headquarters

B) MESSAGE CENTERS

Since an early movement of the command post was not anticipated, the message center teams did not need to be held in readiness for movement, unless alternate command post locations were available. When advance message centers were established, they would be operated by personnel from the command post message center team. When their operation was to extend over a considerable period, the operating personnel were organized into reliefs. The advance message centers on flanks were held in readiness for movement.

C) MESSENGERS

When a defensive position was first occupied, a special messenger service would usually be required from the division command post to all units and establishments. After the troops were established in their positions and before an enemy attack, the special messenger service would be reduced. However, during an enemy attack, the other means could be interrupted and a greater than usual number of special messengers might be required. A schedule messenger service was employed throughout the division, after the troops were established in their locations and prior to an enemy attack. The schedule service could be organized between the command post and the rear echelon, and within the rear service area throughout the conduct of the defence.

D) RADIO COMMUNICATION

Command Net

The operations of the radio nets prior to the enemy attack would furnish information on the defensive organization to an alert enemy. The radio sets could indicate the location of the command posts and enable the enemy to employ his artillery or air support to attack these emplacements at the most critical time for the defenders. When wire and messenger services were available and could satisfactorily handle the traffic, the command radio net would not be operational. One of the division radio stations was used to monitor the nets throughout the division to verify radio silence. When a detachment was employed at some distance from a flank against an enemy envelopment or flanking movement, vehicular radio equipment from the signal company could be attached to this force.

Reconnaissance Net

In certain situations, it was necessary to have the radio reconnaissance net operating before the enemy attack. The net could include stations at the division command post, in aircraft observing for the division and with ground forces operating under division control. The division radio station was not to be close to the command post. A wire circuit connecting this station to the division command post could be necessary.

Warning net

The expansion of the division warning net to include as many listening stations as possible ensured rapid receipt of urgent warnings of air, mechanized or gas attack.

E) PANELS

Panels were employed by frontline troops to mark their position on request from friendly observation or combat aircraft. A panel station would be established to serve the division command post. The station was located near the reconnaissance net radio station.

F) WIRE COMMUNICATIONS

Wire Line Construction

Usually, the initial installations would require the use of field wire. When time was short, this initial installation would generally be made along roads. However, as soon as possible, additional lines would be installed across country so routed as to avoid crossroads, buildings, villages, and high-profile terrain features. These lines had to be sunk below ground for additional protection against enemy bombing, tanks and artillery fire. Requests could be submitted to higher authorities for additional labour and equipment for the construction and protection of the more important wire circuits.

The minimum number of wire circuits for a division on the defensive was:

> 2 or more from the division command post to the command posts of the infantry regiments and division artillery, and to the rear echelon
> 1 from the division command post to the following units: division reserve, observation posts, division clearing station (medical battalion), advance message center, advanced landing field, engineer battalion, ammunition control point and attached such as anti-aircraft artillery and chemical troops.

In addition, lateral circuits had to be installed between the subordinate infantry units and parallel circuits made to the major subordinate headquarters. The necessary installations were to be made so as to permit immediate communication from the alternate division command post if the initial command post had to be abandoned.

Local installations

1) Telephone

The local installations had to be completed at the alternate command post, if time and equipment were available.

2) Telegraph

At least one circuit on the wire line to each major subordinate unit or establishment was used for telegraphy. A telegraph printer channel was generally installed between the higher headquarters (corps headquarters) and the division. The rear echelon could be connected to the telegraph printer channel.

G) SIGNAL SECURITY AND SIGNAL INTELLIGENCE

Precautions in signal operations and installations were taken to avoid disclosing the location of reserves. The wire lines leading into territory occupied by the enemy were interrupted where they crossed the defensive positions. Other actions were identical to those taken during the attack.

5 – Organization for Combat, Standing Operating Procedure[7]

5-1 AGENCIES OF SIGNAL COMMUNICATION

A) Message Centers

In the field, message center operations were continuous at each command post, in each rear echelon when it was separated from the command post, and at each other echelon of the headquarters while it was functioning.

Each vehicular radio station team had to be capable of rendering into cipher and deciphering messages during movement. Personnel from the message center could be attached to the radio teams.

B) Radio Communication

The establishment of the following radio nets was routine:

> Division command net. It comprised the stations at: division command post, division advance message center, combat team 1, combat team 2, combat team 3, (division artillery when so directed)
> Division reconnaissance net. It comprised the stations at: division command post, division advance message center, reconnaissance troop, and observation planes.

C) Wire Communication

Routinely this consisted of the installation of telephone centrals (switchboards) at: division command post, division advance message center, division rear echelon.

The order of priority for the installation of local telephones at division headquarters was the following: chief of staff, G-3, G-2, G-4, signal officer, division commander, message center, wire chief, adjutant general*, division surgeon, ordnance officer, quartermaster officer*, public telephone. (*installed at division rear echelon).

The telegraph stations were located in message centers at all echelons of the division headquarters.

D) Signal Supplies

The unit reserve of Signal Corps supplies of the signal company had to be kept mobile at the signal distributing point. The distributing point was located at the signal company bivouac.

At each bivouac or assembly area, the locations of the division signal installations were assigned by the headquarters commandant (see headquarters company, infantry division). The division signal officer was always at division command post, except during the march when he was with the division march command post.

5-2 ORGANIZATION DURING THE MARCH

A) Combat Team Detachments

The combat team detachments of the signal company accompanied each RCT (regimental combat team) during the march, to provide the necessary means of communication.

> Combat Team 1 Detachment (CT1 Det.), commanded by the senior NCO, it comprised:
>> Vehicular Radio Team 1: Team Chief, 2 Radio operators, 1 driver, ¾-ton truck, SCR-193.
>> Wire Construction Team 1: Team Chief (Sgt), Basic Pvt, 6 Linemen of whom one drove the 2½-ton, cargo, carrying the Reel unit RL-26, chest BC-5, 10 miles of wire W-110-B (2 miles on reel RL-26)
> Combat Team 2 Detachment: (identical to 1)
>> Vehicular Radio Team 2
>> Wire Construction Team 2
> Combat Team 3 Detachment: (identical to 1)
>> Vehicular Radio Team 3
>> Wire Construction Team 3

---

7. Standing Operating Procedure: A set of instructions having the force of orders. This SOP was the example SOP in FM 11-10 with Change no. 1, January 23, 1942. Data has been modified according to the 1943 organization. Except for organization and equipment, which were taken from the Tables of Organization and Equipment, FM 11-10 was the primary reference book used in the preparation of this section.

B) 1st Echelon Signal Company

The first echelon was located with the division advance command post at the head of the main body of the designated marching group.

Division Signal Officer Section:

Lt Col, Division Signal Officer, Pvt Clerk who drove the ¼-ton truck.

Truck 1 – Division Signal Officer Section (less the Pvt Clerk) with the Major in a 1½-ton, cargo truck.

Detachment from the Message Center & Messenger Section consisting of:

Truck 3 – 1st Lt, Section Commander, 3 Clerks of whom one drove the 1½-ton truck.

Truck 4 -Tech Sgt, Message Center Chief, Basic Pvt, Clerk Pvt (from the Div Signal Officer Sect), 1 Techn 5th Cryptographic technician who drove the 1½-ton truck.

(Trucks 3 and 4 together carried the equipment of the message center, the panel sets and ammunition).

Truck 2 -Motorized Messenger in a ¼-ton truck.

Messenger truck 1 – 1 motorized messenger and 1 messenger (dismounted), ¼-ton truck.

Messenger truck 2 – 1 motorized messenger and 1 messenger (dismounted), ¼-ton truck.

Detachment from the Radio Section consisting of:

Truck 5 – Vehicular Radio Team 4: Team Chief, 2 Radio operators of whom one drove the ¾-ton Radio truck, SCR-193, (Division Command Net Station).

Truck 6 -Vehicular Radio Team 5: 1st Lt, Section Commander, Team Chief, 1 Radio operator who drove the ¾-ton Radio truck, SCR-193, (Division Reconnaissance Net Station).

Detachment from the Telephone & Telegraph Section consisting of:

Telephone Center Team

Truck 7: 1st Lt, Section Commander, Cable repairman, 3 Installer-repairmen of whom one drove the ¾-ton truck, T/5 Switchboard operator.

Truck 8: Wire Chief (Mr Sgt), Chief Switchboard operator (Sgt), 2 Switchboard operators, T/5 Teletypewriter operator driving the 2 ½-ton truck, cargo.

Trucks 7 and 8 together carried the switchboard and the equipment to operate the division advance message center with 15 local telephones and a telegraph set TG-5.

Telegraph Station Team

Truck 9: Chief teletypewriter operator (Tech Sgt), installer-repairman, Teletypewriter operator driving the truck 1½-ton, cargo, carrying the equipment to install and operate 3 Telegraph Stations.

Detachment from the Construction Platoon consisting in:

Platoon Commander's party:

Truck 10: 1st Lt, Platoon Commander and Construction Officer, Chief field lineman (Mr Sgt), Field lineman driving the ¼-ton truck carrying the cable repairman equipment.

Construction Section chief party:

Truck 11: Section Chief (S Sgt), 3 Linemen of whom one drove the ¾-ton truck carrying the cable repairman equipment.

Construction Section Team 4:

Truck 12: Team Chief (Sgt), 6 linemen of whom one drove the 2½-ton truck, cargo, Basic Pvt. The equipment was identical to Team 1 (Combat Team Detachment).

The order of march in the column of the vehicles was: trucks 1 to 5, messenger trucks 1 and 2, trucks 7 to 12.

C) Second Echelon Signal Company

During the march, the second echelon would be at the division command post. It was made up of the remainder of the signal company less the 1st echelon and the rear echelon, without those detachments that went with the combat teams.

D) Rear Echelon Signal Company

Detachment Message Center and Messenger Section:

Truck ¼: – Assistant Message Center chief (S Sgt), Messenger Motor (Pvt) driving a ¼-ton truck.

Truck ¾: – Assistant Message Center chief (Sgt), 5 Clerks of whom one drove the ¾-ton truck, Messenger (dismounted), Basic Pvt.

Truck ¼: – Messenger, motor and Basic Private in ¼-ton truck.

Detachment Telephone and Telegraph Section:

Truck ¾: – Assistant field wire chief (S Sgt), 2 Installer-repairmen of whom one drove the ¾-ton truck.

Telephone Center Team: 2 Switchboard operators, 3 Installer-repairmen of whom one drove the ¾-ton truck, Basic Pvt.

Telegraph Station Team: Assistant chief teletypewriter operator (Sgt), 2 Teletypewriter operators of whom one drove the 2½-ton truck, cargo.

These carried the switchboard and its equipment, with 15 local telephones TC-4 and the line repair equipment to install and operate the division rear echelon station.

5-3 ORGANIZATION FOR OFFENSIVE COMBAT

A) Division Command Post

Initially the 1st echelon would be at the division command post. It had the same organization as it had for the march. The detachments of each section established the initial installations operated by their respective sections. After installation, those personnel not required for operations were relieved for rest or directed to other duties. A relief of each team, message center, messengers, division command net station, division reconnaissance net station, telephone center, telegraph printer station, switching center, telegraph printer switching center, was operated as soon as the initial installation was complete.

When a radio station of a combat team was ready to operate on the division command net, the communication officer concerned (infantry regiment) directed that this team took over operation of the station in the division command net. The team chief of the vehicular radio station team of the signal company (which was with the combat team) relayed reports by radio to the net control station for instructions, these either remaining with the combat team or returning to the signal company bivouac.

Upon the arrival of the 2nd echelon at the new division command post, the operating teams relieved the 1st echelon reliefs and exchanged equipment. The SCR-284 (or 694) was installed and replaced the SCR-193 as net control station of the division command net. A radio set SCR-399 (or 299) was installed to operate in the corps command net, and if it was not required, took over the net control station (NCS) of the division reconnaissance net. The remainder of the signal company, less the detachments and the construction platoon, established a bivouac and a signal supply distribution point.

The construction platoon followed the procedure below:

The platoon commander's party moved when required. The section chief's party from the 2nd construction section proceeded to wirehead[8] test, took control over team 4, operated the wirehead test station and was responsible for the maintenance of the circuits 201-207, 121-122, 301-307. The section chief's party from the 1st construction section moved out to supervise its two teams, team 1 and 2, and team 3. The service section proceeded to wirehead test and re-supplied with wire construction teams 1, 2, 3 and 4. It then joined the bivouac of the signal company to await orders. Construction teams 1, 2 and 3, when re-supplied, returned to the command posts of the combat teams and prepared to extend the circuits forward. The constructions teams were attached to the combats teams for ration purposes.

B) Division Rear Echelon

The organization of the rear echelon was identical to its organization on the march. It continued to operate without change.

5-4 ORGANIZATION FOR DEFENSIVE COMBAT, FOLLOWING THE MARCH

A) Division Command Post

Initially the 1st echelon was at the division command post. It was organized in the same manner as for the march. The detachments from each section established the initial installations to be operated by their respective sections. After installation, the personnel not required for operations were relieved for rest or directed to other duties. A relief for each team, message center, messengers, division command net station, division reconnaissance net station, telephone center, telegraph printer station, switching center, and telegraph printer switching center was operated as soon as the initial installation was complete. When the radio station of a combat team was ready to operate on the division command net, the communication officer concerned (infantry regiment) directed that this team take over operation of station in the division command net. The team chief of the vehicular radio station team of the signal company (which was with the combat team) relayed reports by radio to the net control station for instructions, either remaining with the combat team or returning to the signal company bivouac.

Upon the arrival of the 2nd echelon at the new command post, the teams relieved the reliefs from the 1st echelon and exchanged equipment. The vehicular radio station team 6 opened its station as NCS of the division anti-tank/anti-aircraft warning net. A SCR-284 (or 694) would be installed and relieve the SCR-193 as NCS of the division command net. A radio set SCR-399 (or 299) would be installed to operate in the corps command net, and if not required, would take over the NCS of the division reconnaissance net. The remainder of the signal company, less the detachments and the construction platoon, established a bivouac and a signal supply distribution point.

The construction platoon followed the procedure below:

The platoon commander's party moved when required. The 1st construction section reassembled at the bivouac to await new orders. The section chief's party from the 2nd construction section proceeded to wirehead test, took over from team 4, operated the wirehead test station and was responsible for the maintenance of the circuits 201-207, 210 and 307. The section chief's party from the 1st construction section moved to supervise its two teams (1 and 2), and team 3. The service section proceeded to wirehead test and re-supply with wire construction teams 1, 2, 3 and 4. It joined the bivouac of the signal company and awaited orders. Construction teams 1, 2 and 3 then returned to the command posts of the combat teams. Team 1 installed the circuit 311, team 2 the circuit 312, and team 3 the circuit 313. Each Team was responsible for maintaining its own circuits and the circuits 301-302, 303-304, 305-306, respectively. Then they awaited orders and are prepared to extend the circuits forward. For ration purposes, the constructions teams were attached to the combat teams.

B) Division Rear Echelon

The organization of the rear echelon was identical to its organization on the march. It continued to operate without any changes.

---

8. Wirehead: forward limit of telephone or telegraphic communications in a command (AR 320-5, p. 539).

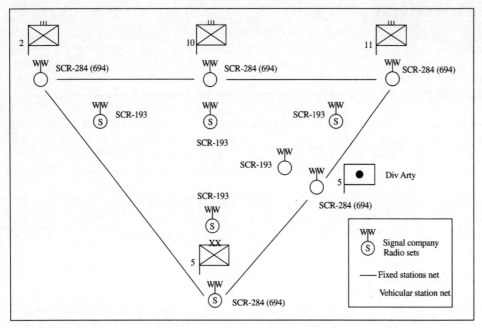

51. Division Command Net

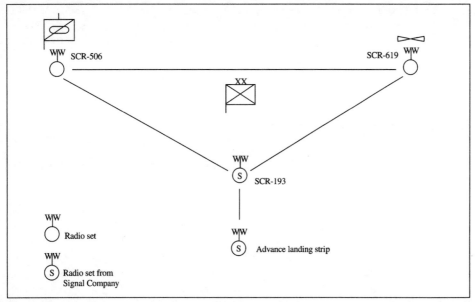

52. Division Reconnaissance Net

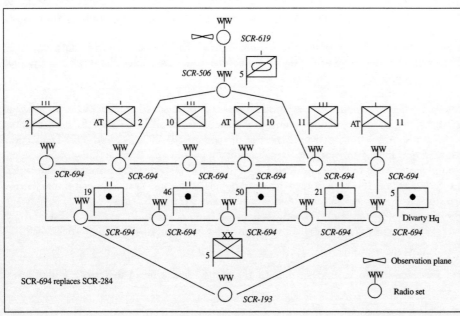

53. Division Warning Net

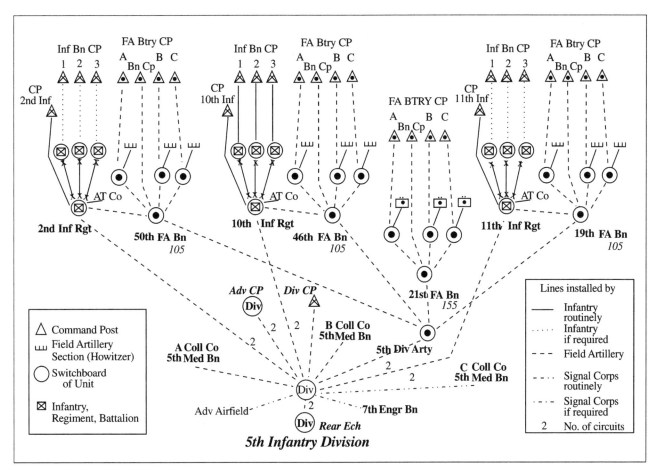

54. Wire Net, Infantry Division

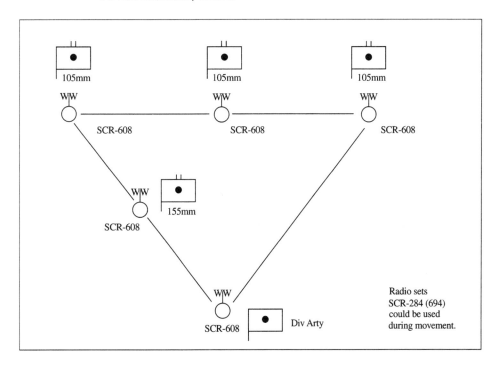

55. Division Artillery Net

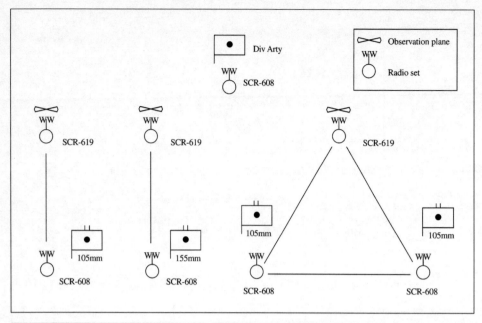

56. Division Artillery Air-Ground Channels

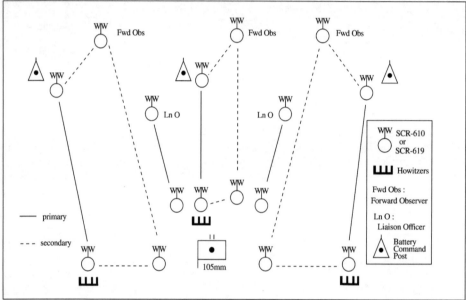

57. Field Artillery Battalion Radio Net

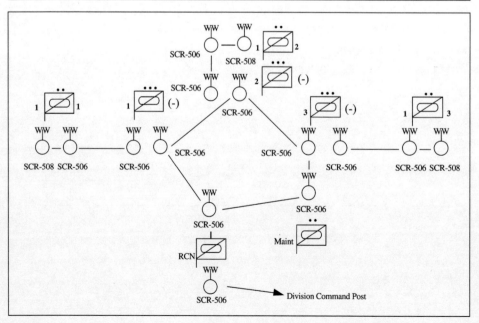

58. Cavalry Reconnaissance Troop Radio Net

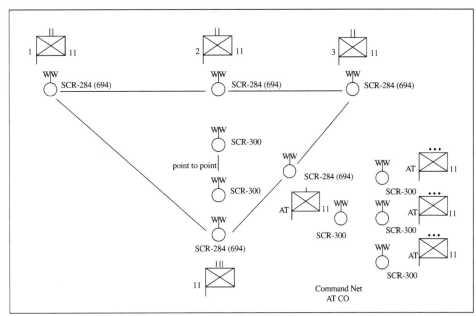

59. Infantry Regiment Radio Net

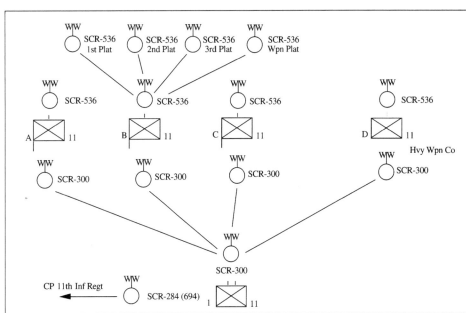

60. Infantry Battalion Radio Net

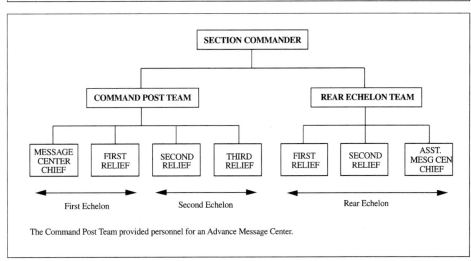

61. Message Center Section, Team Organization

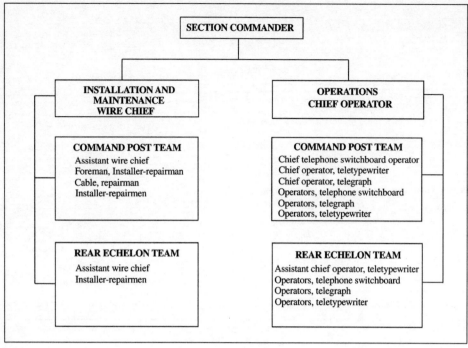

62. Telephone and Telegraph Section, Team Organization

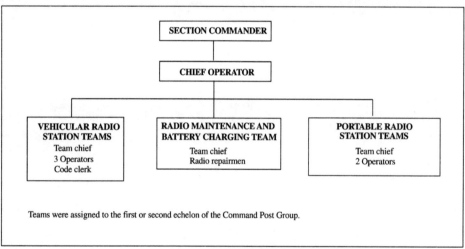

63. Radio Section, Team Organization

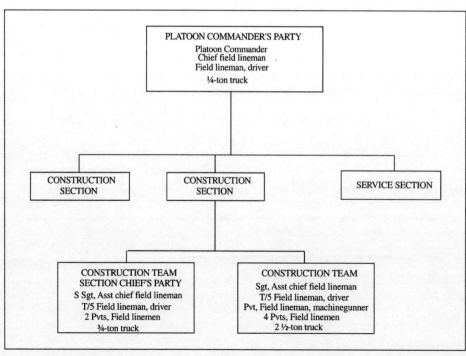

64. Construction Platoon, Team Organization

7.6 MILITARY POLICE PLATOON, INFANTRY DIVISION
Doctrine

The military police platoon had two major duties:
  to perform police missions within the division
  to plan and supervise traffic control operations

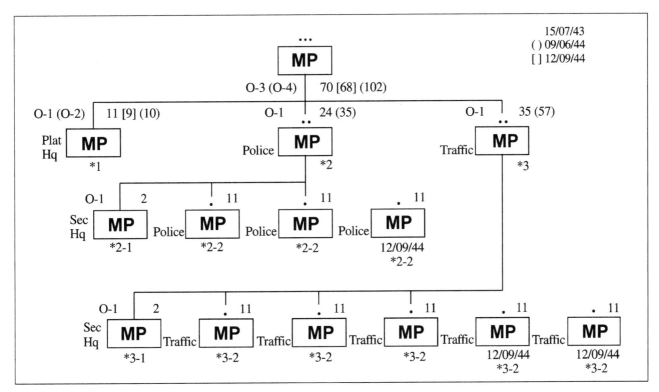

65. Military Police Platoon, Infantry Division

A – POLICE MISSIONS

Police missions consisted of:
    keeping order
    enforcing military regulations and civil laws
    controlling civilian movement
    supervising the camps and keeping of prisoners of war
  Infantry units were authorized to perform police missions, but as this would divert them their own mission, the War Department decided to add a military police platoon to the infantry division. Military policing missions were very similar to those of the civil police, and will therefore not be examined; however traffic control operations are studied below.

B – TRAFFIC CONTROL

1) Responsibilities
The responsibilities for traffic regulation and control in the area occupied by troops under the jurisdiction of any headquarters lay with the following agencies:
    the commander: he was the senior officer in the area in question. In a division area, he would be the division commander. He exercised this function chiefly by delegation.
    G-4 was responsible for staff coordination and supervision of traffic regulation plans. He worked closely with G-3.
    the traffic headquarters of a unit could be either an element of the transportation section of the special staff or an element of G-4. Under the supervision of G-4, and with the information it received, it would be responsible for formulating traffic plans. It received, correlated and distributed traffic information, submitted traffic reports to the commander, and supervised the activities of other agencies which had traffic responsibilities.
    the division engineer was responsible for traffic regulations on roads and bridges, dependent upon their condition. He prepared and distributed road maps and approved traffic circulation maps. The engineer battalion provided and installed road signs and route markers, except those for temporary and emergency traffic control. These were provided by the military police platoon. The division engineer worked closely with the provost marshal over traffic matters.

the provost marshal was responsible for traffic control reconnaissance and planning, and traffic control itself, including emergency control measures. He provided traffic information and directions to persons or units moving on the roads. He submitted reports on traffic obstructions, accidents and damage.

the signal officer was responsible for providing the means of communication necessary for traffic control.

the commanders of the units that moved by highway or operated highway transport were responsible for the organization of such movement. This included adhering to traffic regulations and schedules and the enforcement of march discipline. The unit commander also had to set the speed and spacing of the vehicles. He provided traffic control personnel at points of doubt or congestion, and supplied guides.

2) Traffic Control

Traffic control was one of the responsibilities of the Corps of Military Police, but also sometimes of the Corps of Engineers. Traffic control could be organizational or by area. Which one depended upon the road system, traffic conditions and tactical considerations.

a) Organizational control

This was the control exercised, usually in the form of an escort, by the commander of a unit on the march. The escort regulated the traffic only along the route travelled by the column and only to the extent needed to ensure that the column moved according to its priority and schedule, and with minimum interruption from other traffic with a lower priority. This organizational control was primarily used in the movement of individual units when the only difficulty anticipated would be interruptions or congestion caused by civilian or less important military traffic.

b) Area control

In area control, the traffic control headquarters assigned personnel to regulate all traffic according to the traffic circulation plan. Area control was used when traffic was heavy and unified control was necessary.

3) Control Techniques

a) Point-control technique

This technique used traffic control posts at road intersections, bridges, roadblocks and defiles. Each post enforced compliance with general traffic regulations and special traffic orders in effect at that point. It helped units to maintain march discipline.

b) Escort

Regulation by an escort would be effected by a motorized traffic control group, which preceded each column. The escort ordered any control posts to block all traffic until the column had passed. At key points, such as intersections and supply points, if there was no traffic control post, the escort itself performed this duty. When the head of the column reached a post thus established, the escort proceeded to the next point, clearing the road as it advanced. The escort system was most appropriate when the moving column had first priority on the road.

c) Patrols

Regulation by patrols consisted of using vehicles, singly or in groups of two or more, to constantly patrol sections of road between traffic control posts. They were charged with the same missions as a traffic control posts and were provided with the same type of information.

The combination of control points and patrols was usually required in area control. The escort method was often used in organizational control.

4) Traffic control by engineers

Engineers could be given traffic control responsibilities at points where engineer works or engineer interests were important or where engineer assistance could be necessary. These were, in particular, at fixed or floating bridges, defiles and engineer supply points. When traffic was heavy and traffic control complex, a military police control point could be added. The military policemen and engineer personnel worked together.

5) Priorities

a) The establishment of priorities

The establishment of priorities on a road was a command decision, often delegated by the commander, to G-3 and G-4 for coordination within prescribed policies. The system of priorities in an average situation would be the following:

1 engineer and ordnance equipment proceeding to a traffic block
2 tactical troop movements
3 wire patrols and construction teams from the signal company
4 ambulances
5 staff and messengers' vehicles
6 supply vehicles: supply class V, class III, class I, and others

b) Conditions of the emergency

However, actual priorities depended upon conditions. Situations could arise in which highest priority would be assigned to:

the movement of ammunition
the evacuation of wounded
the retrograde movements of key equipment

Organization

The military police platoon comprised:
    Platoon headquarters
    Police Section:
        Section Headquarters
        2 Police Squads (3 Police Squads, T/O&E 19-7, dated 12 September 1944)
    Traffic Section:
        Section Headquarters
        3 Traffic Squads (5 Traffic Squads, T/O&E 19-7, dated 12 September 1944).

The personnel were trained to perform police missions and traffic missions, as the situation demanded. The military police platoon was attached to the headquarters company, infantry division, for mess and administration purposes.

*1 – PLATOON HEADQUARTERS (1 Officer, 11 Enlisted Men (9 EM, C1, 9 June 1944) 2 Officers, 10 Enlisted men (T/O&E dated 12 September 1944)

1 Maj, Field Provost Marshal, Division Provost Marshal-P
1 1st Lt, MP-C (12 September 1944)
1 S Sgt, MP-C
1 Sgt, Motor & Supply-C (S Sgt, 12 September 1944)
1 Cpl, Co clerk, Classification specialist-C
1 Techn 4th, Mechanic, automobile-C
1 Techn 5th, Mechanic, automobile, drove the ¾-ton truck-C (12 September 1944)
1 Pvt, MP, drove the ¼-ton truck-R
6 Pvts, Basic-C (4 Basics, C1, 9 June 1944)

Vehicles:
1 Truck, ¼-ton
1 Truck, ¾-ton, WC, Automobile maintenance.

Equipment:
1 luminous dial compass
2 wrist compasses, liquid-filled (Off, Motor & Supply Sgt), 3 wrist compasses, liquid-filled (12 September 1944)
1 electric lamp, warning, red, vehicle, MP letters, 6 V
1 electric siren, 6 V, for vehicle
1 drafting equipment, set no. 1
1 transparent map template, M2 (Off), 2 transparent map templates (12 September 1944)
1 binocular M13 (Off), 2 binoculars (12 September 1944), M17 (C1, 15 March 1945 to the table dated 12 September 1944)
1 grenade launcher, M7 (1 per rifle M1)
1 grenade launcher, M8 (1 for 10 carbines M1), 3 grenade launchers, M8 (1 for 3 carbines, C1)
2 ammunition-carrying bags (4 bags, 9 June 1944, 1 per grenade launcher)
2 wristwatches, 7 jewels (S Sgt, 12 September 1944)
2 wristwatches, 15 jewels (Off, 12 September 1944)
1 motor vehicles mechanics' tool set (1 per Mechanic), 2 tool sets (12 September 1944)
4 flashlights, TL-122-( ) (Off, Motor & Supply Sgt, Pvt MP) 6 flashlights (+ trucks, 12 September 1944)
1 unit equipment tool set, 2nd echelon, set no. 1 (C1, 15 March 1945)
2 canvas dispatch cases (Off, C1, 15 March 1945)
4 whistles, thunderer (Off, S Sgt MP, Pvt MP)

*2 – POLICE SECTION (1 Officer, 24 Enlisted Men (35 EM, T/O&E dated 12 September 1944)

*2-1 – Section Headquarters

1 2nd Lt, MP-C
1 Sgt, Section Leader-C
1 Pvt, MP, drove the ¼-ton truck-R

Vehicle:
1 Truck, ¼-ton

Equipment:
2 wrist compasses, liquid-filled (Off, Sec Ldr)
1 transparent map template, M2
1 binocular, M13 (Off), M17 (C1, 15 March 1945)
1 grenade launcher, M7 (M1 rifle)

1 ammunition-carrying bag (grenade launcher)
1 wristwatch, 15 jewels (Off) (12 September 1944)
1 wristwatch, 7 jewels (Sec Ldr)
1 canvas dispatch case (C1, 15 March 1945)
2 flashlights, TL-122-( ) (MP except driver) (3 flashlights, MP+ truck, 12 September 1944)
2 whistles, thunderer (Off, Pvt MP)

*2-2 – Police Squad (× 2, then × 3)

A third squad was added by the T/O&E dated 12 September 1944.

1 Sgt, MP-C
1 Cpl, MP-C
8 Pvts, MP-C
1 Pvt, MP, drove the ¾-ton truck-R

Vehicle:

1 Truck, ¾-ton, WC

Equipment:

1 grenade launcher, M7 (M1 rifle)
1 grenade launcher, M8 (1 for 10 carbines), 4 grenade launchers (1 for 3 carbines, 12 September 1944, two squads with 4, 1 squad with 3)
2 ammunition-carrying bags (5 bags 9 June 1944, 1 per grenade launcher)
2 wristwatches, 7 jewels (Sgt, Cpl) (12 September 1944)
10 flashlights, TL-122-( ) (MP except driver) (11 flashlight, + truck, 12 September 1944)
11 whistles, thunderer (MP)

*3 – TRAFFIC SECTION (1 Officer, 35 Enlisted Men (57 EM, 12 September 1944)

*3-1 – Section Headquarters

1 1st Lt, MP-C
1 Sgt, Section Leader-C
1 Pvt, MP, drove the ¼-ton truck-R

Vehicle:

1 Truck, ¼-ton

Equipment:

2 reflector batons, type 1 (1 per EM)
2 wrist compasses, liquid-filled (Off, Sec Ldr)
20 electric lamps, flasher
1500 reflectors, road delineation (for the entire Section)
1500 mounting skates, reflector, delineation (for the entire Section)
1 stapler, wire-stitcher (cancelled, 12 September 1944)
1 hammer, stapling, automatic staple feed (added, C1, 9 June 1944)
1 plier, stapling, heavy duty, grip type (12 September 1944)
1 transparent map template, M2 (Off)
1 binocular, M13 (Off) (M17, C1, 15 March 1945)
1 grenade launcher, M7 (1 per rifle M1)
2 grenade launchers, M8 (1 for 3 carbines, 9 June 1944)
3 ammunition-carrying bags (1 per grenade launcher)
1 wristwatch, 7 jewels (Sec Ldr)
1 wristwatch, 15 jewels (Off, 12 September 1944)
2 flashlights, TL-122-( ) (Off, Sec Ldr), 3 flashlights (+truck, 12 September 1944)
1 canvas dispatch case (Off, C1, 15 March 1945)
2 whistles, thunderer (Off, Pvt MP)

*3-2 – Traffic Squad (× 3 then × 5)

Two squads were added by the T/O&E dated 12 September 1944.

1 Sgt, MP-C
1 Cpl, MP-C
5 Pvts, MP-C
4 Pvts, MP, drove the ¼-ton trucks-R

Vehicles:

4 Trucks, ¼-ton

Equipment:
- 11 reflector batons, type 1 (1 per EM)
- 11 electric lamps, flasher
- 1 hammer, stapling, automatic staple feed (added, C1, 9 June 1944)
- 1 plier, stapling, heavy duty, grip type (12 September 1944)
- 1 stapler, wire-stitcher (cancelled, 12 September 1944)
- 4 grenade launchers, M7 (1 per rifle M1)
- 1 grenade launcher, M8 (1 for 10 carbines), 2 grenade launchers (1 for 3 carbines, 9 June 1944)
- 5 ammunition-carrying bags (6 bags, 9 June 1944, 1 per grenade launcher)
- 2 wristwatches, 7 jewels (Sgt, Cpl, 12 September 1944)
- 7 flashlights, TL-122-( ) (except drivers), 11 flashlights (+ truck, 12 September 1944)
- 11 whistles, thunderer (MP)

For the entire Platoon:
- 18 goggles M1943, clear lens (1 per driver) (cancelled, 12 September 1944)
- 55 goggles M1943, green lens (for others) (cancelled, 12 September 1944)
- 90 goggles M1944 (2 per truck, added 12 September 1944)

On 1 June 1945, change no. 2 renamed the table: T/O&E 19-7-OS. At this date, a new T/O&E was issued under the same number 19-7.

7.7 BAND, INFANTRY DIVISION
T/O&E 20-107

Military bands were involved in the reorganization of 1943. Each infantry regiment had a band. However, with the new T/O&E 7 dated 15 July 1943, the regimental bands in the infantry division were replaced by a unique division band of 56 musicians. The band would be designated after the name and the number of the division to which it was assigned. Thus, the band of the 1st Infantry Division was designated '1st Infantry Division Band'. The 5th Infantry Division Band played at Angers, on 11 August 1944, during an award ceremony after the liberation of the city.

Division Band (2 Warrant Officers, 56 Enlisted Men)

- 1 Chief Warrant Officer-C
- 1 Warrant Officer, Junior Grade-C
- 1 Bandsman, Oboe-C
- 1 Bandsman, Bassoon-C
- 15 Bandsmen, Clarinet, B or E flat-C
- 10 Bandsmen, Cornet or Trumpet-C (6 cornets and 4 trumpets)
- 1 Bandsman, Drum, bass-C -1 Bandsman, Drum, snare-C
- 2 Bandsmen, Euphonium or Baritone-C
- 3 Bandsmen, Flute or piccolo-C
- 4 Bandsmen, French horn-C
- 7 Bandsmen, Saxophone-C
- 6 Bandsmen, Trombone-C
- 5 Bandsmen, Tuba-C

The Table of Organization 20-107 dated 8 March 1944, authorized the following ranks for the Bandsmen:
- 2 Tech Sgts
- 2 S Sgts
- 14 Techns 4th
- 16 Techns 5th
- 22 Pvts

Equipment:
- 58 gas masks, lightweight, M3-10A1-6
- 2 First Aid kits, gas casualty (1 per 25 individuals)
- 3 brassards, arm, gas (1 per gas sentry)
- 1 protective glove, impermeable (1 per 40 EM)
- 1 protective suit, impermeable (1 per 40 EM)
- 58 canvas field bags, M1936
- 58 pistol belts, M1936- 58 canteen covers, dismounted, M1910
- 58 muzzle covers, rifle or carbine
- 116 magazine pockets for carbine M1 Cal. .30
- 6 entrenching axes, M1910 (1 per 10 EM)
- 2 to 3 delousing bags, (1 per 20 individuals when chances of louse-born typhus was high, 1 per 35 individuals

otherwise, if authorized by the War Department)

2 oil burners for tent stove, M1941 (1 if the Tent, Wall, Large is issued)

12 water cans, 5-gallon (1 per 5 individuals)

6 entrenching axe carriers M1910 (1 per axe)

11 entrenching pick-mattock M1910, with handle (2 per 10 EM)

11 pick-mattock carriers M1910 (1 per pick-mattock)

39 entrenching shovels M1943 (7 per 10 EM)

39 entrenching shovel carriers M1943 (1 per shovel M1943)

2 canvas dispatch cases (1 per Tech Sgt)

1 hair clipper (1 per 10 individuals)

1 empty field desk, Company

58 goggles M1943, green lens (when authorized by the Commander of the Theater of Operations, except artic)

5 sewing kits (1 per 12 EM)

2 tent stoves, M1941 (1, if the Tent, Wall, Large is issued)

1 tent, Squad, M1942 (1 per Band) (the Tent, Wall, Large may be issued if the Tent, Squad, M1942 is not available)

2 tool kits, brass instruments repair

2 tool kits, pocket wallet type, woodwind

1 portable typewriter, with carrying case

6 whistles, thunderer (WO, Tech Sgt, S Sgt).

Musical instruments remained on issue when in the combat zone.

During combat, the band was attached to the military police platoon or to the medical battalion. The bandsmen were trained to perform the duties of these units. Bandsmen would often serve in these units as drivers. They were also useful when the need for labour was important, such as when establishing the collecting companies and aid stations.

CHAPTER 8

MEDICAL BATTALION, INFANTRY DIVISION T/O&E 8-15

The objective of the Army Medical Corps in the field was to conserve the fighting strength of the combat units. It performed preventive medicine, the evacuation of wounded, hospitalization, dental support and the supply of medical equipment and materiel to supported units.

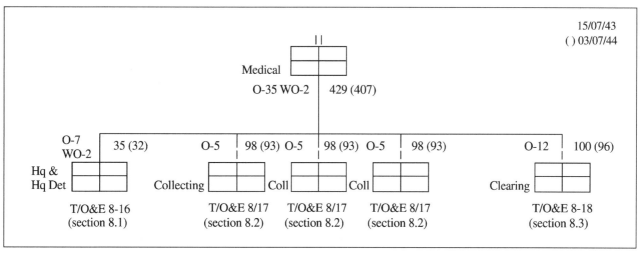

66. Medical Battalion, Infantry Division

1 – GENERAL PRINCIPLES

The principles of field medical support were the following:

a) Continuity

Medical service must be continuous. Interruptions would cause an increase in the death rate among patients. The locations of medical facilities were to be chosen to reduce unnecessary movements.

b) Control

Demands in health care and evacuation could rapidly exceed the resources of the medical battalion. The division surgeon was to observe available resources and request urgent requirements.

c) Proximity

A wounded soldier had a better chance of recovery if he could be quickly evacuated to a hospital. Since the evacuation time was largely dependent on the distance to be travelled by ambulance, the medical services had to be located as close as possible, according to tactical considerations, to the combat zone.

d) Flexibility

Medical services had to be responsive to the many changes that occurred on a battlefield.

e) Mobility

The medical unit had to be as mobile as the unit that it supported. However, medical units were largely dependent on the number of patients being cared for, when it came to their own movements.

f) Conformity with the tactical plan

Medical support plan had to conform to the tactical plan. After conducting an analysis of the operation plan the division surgeon had to determine medical requirements and plan the commitment of medical support to meet them. When resources were stretched, medical support had to be provided to the main effort as determined by the division commander.

181

2 – ORGANIZATION AND DOCTRINE

We have already seen the role and activities of the medical service when examining the medical detachments, particularly with regard to the medical detachment, infantry regiment (chapter 2, section 2.6). This chapter will study the duties of the medical battalion within the medical system.

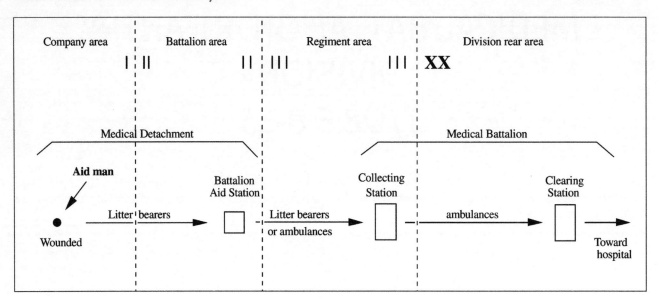

67. Evacuation of the wounded

Medical support was provided to the infantry division by the medical battalion. It undertook the evacuation of the wounded from the aid stations of the combat units, provided and distributed division-level medical treatment, and gave medical support to units without an organic medical detachment. The medical battalion also provided emergency dental service and optometry services. It undertook a consultation service for patients referred from unit level, and other division-level activities. It provided the medical supply support for the units of the division and maintained the medical equipment.

The organization of the medical battalion was as follows:

Headquarters & Headquarters Detachment (T/O&E 8-16, section 8.1)
3 Collecting Companies: A, B, C (T/O&E 8-17, section 8.2)
1 Clearing Company: D (T/O&E 8-18, section 8.3)

Whereas the medical detachments provided the first aid, the medical battalion furnished division-level medical support. It provided medical assistance to the division staff and unit-level medical support to all division units, assigned or attached. Each company's activities will be examined.

8.1   HEADQUARTERS & HEADQUARTERS DETACHMENT, MEDICAL BATTALION, INFANTRY DIVISION T/O&E 8-16

The headquarters and headquarters detachment, medical battalion was the administrative unit of the battalion. It was located in the division rear area and provided medical support to the units stationed in this area. It was responsible for medical maintenance and medical supply for the entire division. The headquarters section, which was the divisional surgeon's staff section, would be with the division staff, at the rear command post (see chapter 1, section 1.2, Special Staff).

The headquarters and headquarters detachment, medical battalion included:

Headquarters Section
Personnel Section
General & Medical Supply Section
Motor Maintenance Section
Detachment Headquarters Section
Attached Chaplain

*1 – HEADQUARTERS SECTION

1 Lt Col, Bn Comdr
1 Maj, Ex-O
1 Capt, S-2, Medical Administration Corps (MAC)
1 Capt or 1st Lt, S-3 (MAC, C4, 3 July 1944)

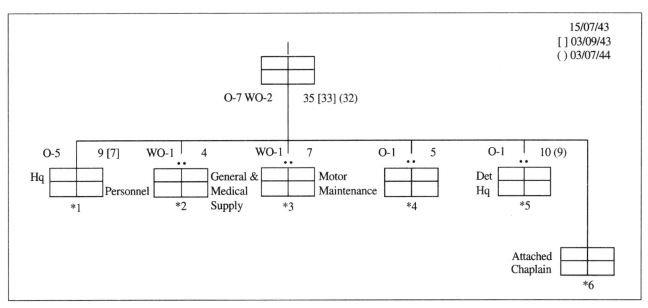

15/07/43
[ ] 03/09/43
( ) 03/07/44

O-7 WO-2   35 [33] (32)

O-5   9 [7]   WO-1   4   WO-1   7   O-1   5   O-1   10 (9)

Hq   Personnel   General &   Motor   Det
          Medical   Maintenance   Hq
          Supply
*1   *2   *3   *4   *5

Attached
Chaplain
*6

68. Headquarters & Headquarters Detachment, Medical Battalion

1 1st Lt, S-1 and Adjutant, MAC
1 Mr Sgt, Sgt Major
1 Tech Sgt, Communication
1 Techn 5th, Chaplain assistant
1 Pvt, Clerk, typist
1 Pvt, Light truck driver
1 Techn 5th, Radio operator (cancelled, C1, 3 September 1943)
1 Pvt, Orderly, drove the ¾-ton truck, command (¾-ton, WC, 3 July 1944)
1 Techn 4th, Radio repairman (cancelled by C1, 3 September 1943)
1 techn 5th, stenographer

Vehicles:
1 Truck, ¾-ton, command (cancelled, C4, 3 July 1944)
1 Truck, ¾-ton, WC (2 trucks ¾-ton, WC, C4)

Equipment:
3 luminous dial compasses (Bn Comdr, Ex-O, S-3)
5 transparent map templates, M2 (Off, Sgt Major)
44 brassards, Geneva Convention (Red Cross) (42 brassards, C4, 3 July 1944)
1 binocular, M13 (Bn Comdr)
1 wristwatch, 7 jewels (Tech Sgt, Com Chief)
1 protective glove, impermeable
1 protective suit, one-piece, impermeable
4 canvas dispatch cases (Bn Comdr, Ex-O, S-3, S-4)
1 empty field desk, headquarters
1 national flag, Standard, silk
1 organization flag, Standard, silk
1 duplicating machine, spirit process, military field kit
2 web slings, color
1 tent, Command Post
1 tent stove, M1941
1 oil burner for tent stove M1941
1 non-portable typewriter, 14-in carriage
1 portable typewriter, with carrying case
31 flashlights, TL-122-( ) (Off, Chaplain, WO, Mr Sgt, Tech Sgt, S Sgt, Cpl, Mechanic auto, trucks)
3 electric lighting equipments, set no. 2, 1½ KW (C3, 15 June 1944)
1 electric lighting equipment, set no. 3, 3 KVA (C3)
3 whistles, thunderer (Bn Comdr, Ex-O, S-3)
The following items listed in the T/O&E dated 15 July 1943, were cancelled by the C1 dated 3 September 1943:
1 maintenance equipment ME-40
1 radio set SCR-284 (mounted in ¾-ton, Command)

1 test equipment I-56
1 tool equipment TE-41 (Radio repairman).
The following items listed in the T/O&E dated 15 July 1943, were cancelled by the C4 dated 3 July 1944:

5 protective drawers, cotton
5 protective gloves, cotton
5 protective hoods, wool, OD
5 canvas leggings, M1938, dismounted, protective
5 flannel shirts, OD, coat style, protective
5 wool socks, protective
5 wool trousers, OD light shade, protective
5 protective undershirts, cotton

*2 – PERSONNEL SECTION

1 WO, Clerical, general
1 Tech Sgt, Personnel
1 Pvt, Clerk, general
1 Techn 4th, Personnel clerk
1 Techn 5th, Record clerk

Equipment:

1 classification card selector

*3 – GENERAL AND MEDICAL SUPPLY SECTION

1 WO, Supply, Medical department
1 Tech Sgt, Supply, Medical
1 S Sgt, Supply, General
1 Techn 4th, clerk, Receiving and shipping
1 Pvt, Clerk, Supply
2 Techn 5th, Light truck driver
1 Pvt, Light truck driver

Vehicles:

3 Trucks, 2½-ton, cargo
2 trailers, 1-ton

Equipment:

2 wrist compasses, liquid-filled (Tech Sgt, S Sgt)
1 transparent map template, M2 (S Sgt, Supply)
3 large blanket sets
1 drugs chest, complete
1 plain field chest
1 miscellaneous supplies chest
2 plasma chests
1 chest, surgical supplies "A"
1 chest, surgical supplies "B"
1 colorimeter chlorine and toxic gases
4 oxygen cylinders, 750 gal
24 steel pole litters (aluminium litters, C4, 3 July 1944)
48 litter bar splints (6 per splint sets, cancelled, 3 September 1943)
8 splint sets (cancelled, 3 September 1943)
48 Thomas splint, arm, hinged (cancelled, 3 September 1943)
6 boxes of surgical dressings
2 trays no. 6, plain
2 small canvas paulins (tarpaulins)
1 roll commissary, complete, stock no. 64-R-552
2 keylock, safe, field
1 stencil outfit with figure and letters ½ and 1"
2 tents, Squad , M1942
2 tent stoves, M1941
2 oil burners for tent stove M1941
1 non-portable typewriter, 14-in carriage
7 medical manuals (anaesthesia, dermatology, surgical anatomy, etc.)

*4 – MOTOR MAINTENANCE SECTION

    1 1st Lt, MAC
    1 Tech Sgt, Motor
    2 Techns 4th, Mechanic auto, one drove the ¼-ton truck
    2 Techns 5th, Mechanic auto, drove the 2 ½-ton trucks)

Vehicles:

    1 Truck, ¼-ton
    2 Trucks, 2½-ton, cargo, with winch

Equipment:

    1 luminous dial compass (Motor Officer)
    1 wrist compass, liquid-filled (Sgt, Motor)
    2 transparent map templates, M2 (Off, Tech Sgt)
    1 wristwatch, 7 jewels (Tech Sgt)
    3 cabinets, spare parts, type 1, M1940
    1 motor vehicles mechanics' tool set, body
    4 motor vehicles mechanics' tool sets, engine
    1 unit equipment tool set, 2nd echelon, set no. 2
    1 unit equipment tool set, 2nd echelon, set no. 5
    1 unit equipment tool set, 2nd echelon, set no. 7
    1 tool set, welders
    2 whistles, thunderer (1st Lt, Tech Sgt)

*5 – DETACHMENT HEADQUARTERS SECTION

    1 Capt, S-4, MAC
    1 S Sgt, Supply, General
    1 Cpl, Clerk, detachment
    1 Pvt, Bugler, drove the ¼-ton truck
    1 Pvt, Clerk, typist
    1 Techn 4th, Cook (for Officers' Mess)
    1 Techn 5th, Cook
    1 Pvt, Cook's helper
    3 Pvts, Basic (2 Basics, C4, 3 July 1944)
The cooks and the cook's helper were attached to the company with which the detachment took its meal.

Vehicle:

    1 Truck, ¼-ton

Equipment:

    1 chest, records
    1 empty field desk, company
    1 flag, guidon, bunting
    1 portable typewriter, with carrying case
    1 whistle, thunderer (S-4)

*6 – ATTACHED CHAPLAIN

    1 Chaplain

Equipment:

    1 Chaplain's outfit, stock no. 36-O-800, Christian; no. 36-O-810, Jewish
    The Chaplain's outfit included:
        1 steel chest, container, Hymnal, Music-Edition
        1 empty field desk, headquarters (replaced when exhausted by the field desk, M1945)
        1 flag, chaplain, Christian-Faith, Jewish-Faith
        1 Music book set, Hymnal, 'Song and Service' (150 books)
        1 portable typewriter, with carrying case.

For the entire Company:

    9 goggles, M1943, clear lens (drivers)
    36 goggles, M1943, green lens (other than drivers) 33 goggles (3 July 1944); replaced by:
    18 goggles, M1944 (2 per truck, 14 February 1945).
  On 1 June 1945, the T/O&E was renamed 8-16-OS. At this date a new table was issued under the number 8-16.

8.2 COLLECTING COMPANY, MEDICAL BATTALION, INFANTRY DIVISION
T/O&E 8-17

The collecting companies provided the supported units with the personnel and the means necessary for evacuating the wounded. These were picked up on the battlefield by the aid men and litter bearers from the medical detachments, then collected at the aid station to be conducted to the collecting company. The wounded recovering from wounds were sent back to their units. The others were carried by the ambulance sections toward the clearing company. A collecting company was attached to each infantry regiment and worked with the medical detachment from this regiment. The collecting companies were located in the rear areas of the infantry regiments.

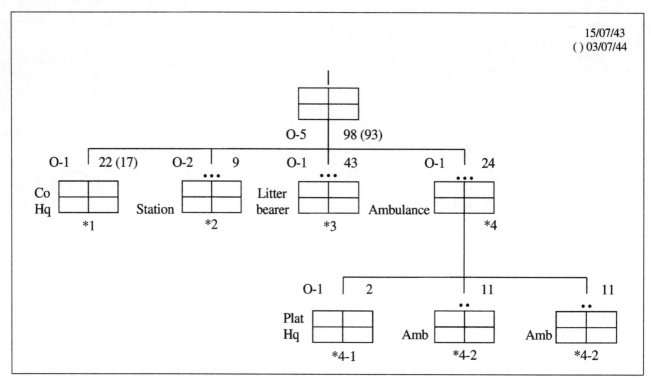

69. Collecting Company, Medical Battalion

The collecting company, medical battalion included:
    Company Headquarters
    Station Platoon
    Litter bearers Platoon
    Ambulance Platoon
        Platoon Headquarters
        2 Ambulance Sections

*1 – COMPANY HEADQUARTERS

    1 Capt, Co Comdr
    1 1st Sgt
    1 S Sgt, Mess
    1 S Sgt, Supply, general
    1 Sgt, Communication and liaison
    1 Sgt, Motor
    1 Cpl, Co clerk, Classification specialist
    1 Pvt, Bugler, drove the ¼-ton truck
    1 Techn 4th, Cook
    1 Techn 5th, Cook
    1 Pvt, Cooks' helper
    1 Techn 5th, Light truck driver
    1 Techn 5th, Mechanic, automotive, drove the ¾-ton truck (became Techn 4th, 14 February 1945)
    1 Techn 5th, Radio operator (cancelled, C1, 3 September 1943)
    9 Pvts, Basic (5 Basics, C3, 3 July 1944)

Vehicles:
    1 Truck, ¼-ton
    1 Truck, ¾-ton, WC
    1 Truck, 2½-ton, cargo
    1 Trailer, 1-ton, water tank, 250 gal

Equipment:
    2 luminous dial compasses (Co Comdr, Sgt Liaison)
    1 wrist compass, liquid-filled (1st Sgt)
    4 transparent map templates, M2 (Off, 1st Sgt, S Sgt Mess, Sgt Motor)
    98 brassards, Geneva Convention (1 per individual)
    1 medical kit, Officer
    9 medical kits, Private (1 per Basic, 5 kits, C3, 3 July 1944)
    1 binocular, M13 (Co Comdr) (M17, 13 February 1945)
    1 wristwatch, 7 jewels (1st Sgt)
    1 wristwatch, 15 jewels (Off)
    1 motor vehicles mechanics' tool set (1 per Mechanic)
    1 unit equipment tool set, 2nd echelon, set no. 1
    2 canvas dispatch cases (Co Comdr, Sgt Liaison)
    1 gasoline lantern, leaded fuel
    6 lanterns, kerosene, army
    4 sledges, blacksmith, double face, 6-8 lbs
    1 tool set, carpenters', no. 2
    11 flashlights, TL-122-( ) (Off, NCO, Mechanics, trucks)
    2 panel sets, AP-50-( ) (1 per 4 vehicles)
    1 radio set SCR-284 (cancelled, C1, 3 September 1943)
    1 radio set SCR-300 (cancelled, C1)
    3 whistles, thunderer (Co Comdr, 1st Sgt, Sgt Motor)

*2 – STATION PLATOON

    1 Capt or 1st Lt, General duty
    1 S Sgt, Platoon
    1 Sgt, Section Leader
    1 Cpl, Sec Leader assistant
    1 Techn 4th, Podiatrist
    1 Techn 4th, Medical technician, drove a ¾-ton truck
    2 Techns 3rd, Surgical technician
    2 Pvts, Medical technician, drove the ¾-ton trucks (from 15 July 1943 to 13 February 1945, one of them was
      Techn 5th)

Vehicles:
    3 Trucks, ¾-ton, WC
    2 Trailers, ¼-ton

Equipment:
    4 wrist compasses, liquid-filled (Plat Comdr, Platoon Sgt, Sgt Sec Leader, Cpl)
    1 portable electric lamp, CP
    2 transparent map templates, M2 (Off, Plat Sgt)
    8 medical kits, NCO, complete (S Sgt, Sgt, Cpl, Med Techn, Surg Techn)
    1 medical kit, Officer
    1 medical kit, Private (Podiatrist)
    3 large blanket sets
    1 bucket set, hospital (set of 3)
    3 chests MD, no. 1, complete
    2 chests MD, no. 2, complete
    1 chest MD, no. 4, complete
    1 chest, plasma, complete
    2 gas casualty sets
    20 litters, steel pole (litter, straight, aluminium, C3, 3 July 1944)
    2 imprinting machines
    1 sphygmomanometer aneroid (14 February 1945)
    18 splints, litter bar (6 per splint set, cancelled, C1, 3 September 1943)
    3 splint sets (cancelled, C1)
    3 sets, surgical dressings

2 wristwatches, 15 jewels (Off)
6 oil burners for tent stove, M1941
1 canvas dispatch case (Platoon Comdr)
6 gasoline drums, inflammable liquid, with carrying handle, 5-gal (1 per burner)
2 flags, Geneva Convention (Red Cross, for ambulance)
2 gasoline lanterns, leaded fuel
6 tent stoves, M1941 (2 per tent squad)
3 tents, Squad, M1942 (if non available, 3 tents, wall, large)
1 fly, tent, Wall, large (cancelled, 14 February 1945)
10 flashlights, TL-122-( ) (Off, NCO, trucks, chests MD N$2)
2 whistles, thunderer (Off, S Sgt)

*3 – LITTER BEARER PLATOON

1 2nd Lt, Platoon Comdr, MAC
1 S Sgt, Platoon
1 Sgt, Section Leader
1 Cpl, Section Leader assistant
31 Pvts, Litter bearer
2 Techns 4th, Surgical technician, Litter bearer
4 Techns 5th, Surgical technician, Litter bearer (3 T/5, 13 February 1945)
3 Pvts, Surgical technician, Litter bearer (4 Pvts, 13 February 1945)

Equipment:
12 wrist compasses, liquid-filled (Plat Comdr, Plat Sgt, Sgt, Cpl, 1 per 4 litter bearers)
2 transparent map templates, M2 (Plat Sgt, Off)
12 medical kits, NCO, complete (S Sgt, Sgt, Cpl, Surg Techn)
1 medical kit, Officer
31 medical kits, Private (1 per litter bearer)
1 large blanket set
10 litters, steel pole (litter, straight, aluminium, C3, 3 July 1944)
1 splint set
1 wristwatch, 15 jewels (Off)
1 canvas dispatch case (Plat Comdr)
12 flashlights, TL-122-( ) (Off, NCO, 1 per 4 litter bearers)
2 whistles, thunderer (Off, S Sgt)

*4 – AMBULANCE PLATOON (1 Officer, 24 Enlisted Men)

*4-1 – Platoon Headquarters

1 1st Lt, Platoon Commander, MAC
1 S Sgt, Platoon-1 Pvt, Light truck driver

Vehicle:
1 Truck, ¼-ton

Equipment:
2 wrist compasses, liquid-filled (Off, Plat Sgt)
2 transparent map templates, M2 (Off, Plat Sgt)
1 medical kit, NCO, complete (S Sgt)
1 wristwatch, 15 jewels (Off)
1 canvas dispatch case (Plat Comdr)
3 flashlights, TL-122-( ) (Off, NCO)
3 large blanket sets (for the platoon)
2 whistles, thunderer (Off, S Sgt)

*4-2 – Ambulance Section (× 2)

1 Sgt, Section Leader
5 Pvts or Techns 5th, Ambulance driver (in both Sections, of the 10 drivers, 3 were T/5 and 7 Pvts)
5 Pvts, Orderly, Ambulance

Vehicles:
5 Trucks, ¾-ton, Ambulance KD.

Equipment:
6 wrist compasses, liquid-filled (Sgt, ambulances)

1 medical kit, NCO, complete (Sgt)
5 medical kits, Private (Orderly)
5 bed pans (1 per ambulance, 14 February 1945)
20 litters, steel pole (litter, straight, aluminium, C3, 3 July 1944)
1 splint set
5 urinals, enamelware (1 per ambulance, 14 February 1945)
20 sleeping bags, casualty evacuation (4 per ambulance in Arctic or outside the U.S.A., if authorized by the Commander of the Theater of Operations, 14 February 1945)
6 flashlights, TL-122-( ) (NCO, trucks)
5 flags, Geneva Convention, Red Cross, ambulance (1 per ambulance)
5 panel sets, AP-50-( ) (1 per ambulance)

For the entire Company:
17 goggles, M1943, clear lens (drivers)
86 goggles, M1943, green lens (other than drivers) 81 goggles (3 July 1944); replaced by:
34 goggles, M1944 (2 per truck).
On 1 June 1945, the table was renamed T/O&E 8-17-OS.

8.3 CLEARING COMPANY, MEDICAL BATTALION, INFANTRY DIVISION T/O&E 8-18

The clearing company was located in the division rear area. The wounded arrived via the collecting companies. They were prioritised by degree of the severity of their wound(s) and received emergency treatment to keep them alive before their evacuation to a field hospital. The clearing company also provided treatment for illnesses or injuries which did not require hospitalization, the patients then returning to their units.

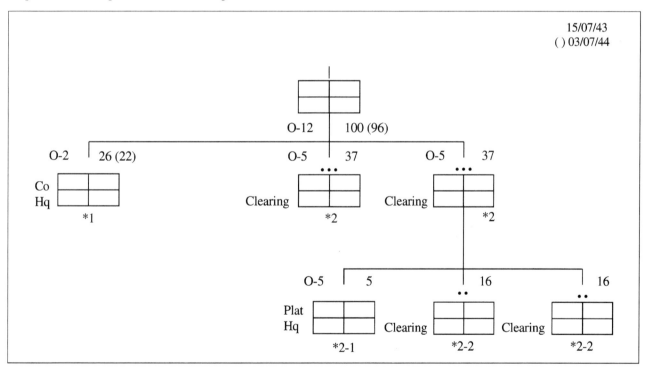

70. Clearing Company, Medical Battalion

The clearing company, medical battalion included:
Company Headquarters
2 Clearing Platoons
2 Clearing Sections

*1 – COMPANY HEADQUARTERS

1 Major, Co Comdr
1 1st Lt, Mess, Supply, Transportation, MAC
1 1st Sgt
1 S Sgt, Mess

1 S Sgt, Supply
1 Sgt, Motor
1 Cpl, Co clerk, Classification specialist
1 Pvt, Bugler, drove the ¼-ton truck
3 Techns 4th, Cook
3 Techns 5th, Cook
2 Pvts, Cooks' helper
2 Techns 5th or Pvt, Light truck driver
1 Techn 4th, Mechanic, automobile, drove the ¾-ton truck
9 Pvts Basic (5 Basics, C2, 3 July 1944)

Vehicles:

1 Truck, ¼-ton
1 Truck, ¾-ton, WC
2 Trucks, 1½-ton, cargo
2 Trailers, 1-ton

Equipment:

1 sign box, interior illuminated, electric, 4 × 15", messages (14 February 1945)
1 luminous dial compass
1 wrist compass, liquid-filled (1st Sgt)
1 electric lighting equipment, set no. 3, 3 KVA (C1, 17 January 1945) (replaced electric power unit)
1 fire extinguisher, water, 4-gal, pump type (14 February 1945)
1 generator, portable, engine driven, skid mounted, 1½ kW, 115 V, 60 Hz, 1 phase, C1, 17 January 1945)
2 transparent map templates, M2 (Co Comdr, 1st Sgt)
28 brassards, Geneva Convention, Red Cross (1 per individual in the platoon; 24 brassards, 3 July 1944)
1 medical kit, Officer – 9 medical kits, Private (1 per Basic) (5 kits, 3 July 1944)
1 chest, laboratory field (C1, 17 January 1945)
3 wristwatches, 7 jewels (1st Sgt, S Sgt Mess, Sgt Motor)
1 wristwatch, 15 jewels (Major)
1 motor vehicles mechanics' tool set (1 per Mechanic)
1 unit equipment tool set, 2nd echelon, set no. 1
250 sleeping bags, casualty evacuation (in Arctic or outside the U.S.A., if authorized by the Commander of the Theater of Operations)
2 canvas dispatch cases (CO, 1st Sgt)
1 flag, field hospital
2 gasoline lanterns, leaded fuel
2 lanterns, kerosene, army
1 tool set, carpenters', no. 2
17 panel sets, AP-50-( ) (1 per 4 vehicles and 16 for the Company)
12 flashlights, TL-122-( ) (Off, NCO, Mech, trucks)
3 whistles, thunderer (Co Comdr, 1st Sgt, Sgt Motor)

*2 – CLEARING PLATOON (× 2) (5 Officers, 37 Enlisted Men)

*2-1 – Platoon Headquarters

1 Capt or 1st Lt, Dental
4 Capts or 1st Lt, General duty
1 S Sgt, Platoon
1 Cpl, Admission clerk
1 Techn 5th, Light truck driver
1 Techn 4th, Pharmacist
1 Techn 5th, Dental technician

Vehicles:

1 Truck, 2½-ton, cargo
1 Trailer, 1-ton, Water tank, 250 gal

Equipment:

1 gas alarm, M1
2 gas proof curtains, M1
2 wrist compasses, liquid-filled (Plat Comdr, S Sgt)
1 fire extinguisher, carbon dioxide, 15-lb (14 February 1945)
3 fire extinguishers, carbon tetrachloride, 1-qt
1 fire extinguisher, water, 4-gal, pump type (1 per 6 tents, 14 February 1945)

2 transparent map templates, M2 (Plat Comdr, S Sgt)

42 brassards, Geneva Convention, Red Cross, (1 per individual)

1 dental kit, Officer

4 medical kits, Officer

1 medical kit, NCO (S Sgt)

1 chest, drugs

1 chest MD, no. 4

1 chest MD, no. 5 (cancelled, C1, 17 January 1945)

1 chest MD, no. 60 (for Dental Officer)

1 chest, miscellaneous, supply

1 chest, sterilization, complete

1 chest, surgical supply "A"

1 chest, tableware

25 cots, folding, canvas (for the entire platoon)

25 cups, enamelware (for the entire platoon)

1 curette, ear

1 elevator, periosteal, sharp

1 forceps, bone, 10¼ (C1, 17 January 1945)

2 gas casualty sets (replaced, C1, 17 January 1945, by: 1 gas casualty case, aprons and gloves)

1 knife, amputating, 6" blade

1 lamp, operating, field, generator (cancelled, C1, 17 January 1945)

1 gas casualty treatment kit (added C1, 17 January 1945, cancelled, 14 February 1945)

1 otoscope ophthalmoscope, combined, electric (14 February 1945)

1 oxygen-therapy apparatus, close circuit

3 pitchers, 4 qt (enamelware, 5 qt, C1, 17 January 1945)

1 resuscitator, portable, bellows type (14 February 1945)

1 retractor, muscle

1 saw, amputating

1 saw, metacarpal

1 sheet set

1 sphygmomanometer aneroid

1 sterilizer, instrument, 20"

1 suction apparatus, portable, 110 v, 60 Hz (C1, 17 January 1945)

3 sets, surgical dressings

1 towel set, hand

1 tourniquet, kirk (cancelled, C2, 3 July 1944)

1 large tube, breathing

1 tube, trachea, size 5

1 wristwatch, 7 jewels (S Sgt Plat)

5 wristwatches, 15 jewels (Off)

1 canvas bag, water sterilizing, complete with cover and hanger

25 bars, insect, field (14 February 1945)

25 frames, mosquito bar, wood (14 February 1945)

1 canvas dispatch case (Plat Comdr)

1 hair clipper

1 tent, Squad, M1942

1 fly, tent, Squad, M1942

2 gasoline drums, inflammable liquid, 5-gal (1 per burner)

2 oil burners for tent stove M1941- 2 tent stoves, M1941 (2 per tent Squad)

1 canvas marker, Red Cross (1 per tent Squad)

1 large canvas paulin (tarpaulin)

1 gasoline lantern, leaded fuel

1 heater, water, immersion type, gasoline operated, type 1 (1 per trailer, water tank, 250 gal)

1 panel set, AP-50-( ) (1 per 4 vehicles in the platoon)

8 flashlights, TL-122-( ) (Off, NCO, truck, chest MD no. 2)

2 whistles, thunderer (Plat Comdr, S Sgt)

*2-2 – Clearing Section (× 2)

1 Sgt, Sec Leader

1 Pvt, Light truck driver

3 Techns 4th or 5th or Pvts, Medical technician (within the Company: 2 T/4, 3 T/5, 7 Pvts)

1 Techn 5th or Pvt, sanitary technician (within the Company: 1 T/5, 3 Pvts, all become T/5, on 14 February 1945)

4 Techns 3rd or 4th or 5th or Pvts, Surgical technician (within the Company: 3 T/3, 2 T/4, 6 T/5, 5 Pvts)

6 Pvts, Ward attendant

Vehicles:

1 Truck, 2½-ton, cargo

1 Trailer, 1-ton

Equipment:

1 sign box, interior illuminated, electric, 4 × 15″, messages (14 February 1945)

8 medical kits, NCO (Sgt, Med Techn, Surg Techn)

1 field autoclave, portable (C1, 17 January 1945)

1 basic instrument set, complete, M1942 model

3 basins, pus

3 basins, sponge

9 large blanket sets

1 empty case, for large blankets

1 bucket set, hospital (3 in set)

1 field chest, plain

1 chest MD, no. 1

1 chest MD, no. 2

1 chest, plasma

1 chest, surgical supply "B", complete

1 oxygen cylinder, 750 gal, filled

3 operating gowns, large

6 operating gowns, medium

3 operating gowns, small

1 irrigator

1 operating lamp, field

50 litters, steel pole (litters, straight, aluminium, C1, 17 January 1945)

1 imprinting machine

3 splint sets

18 splint, litter bar (cancelled, C1)

1 gasoline stove, 2-burner (added, C2, 3 July 1944)

1 towel set, bath

1 tray, no. 6

1 galvanized bucket, GP, 14-qt

1 flag, Geneva Convention (Red Cross, ambulance)

4 flies for tent, Squad M1942

4 tents, Squad, M1942

8 gasoline drums, inflammable liquid, 5 gal (1 per burner)

8 oil burners for tent stove M1941

8 tent stoves, M1941 (2 per tent Squad)

4 canvas markers, Red Cross (1 per tent Squad)

1 small canvas paulin (tarpaulin)

1 screen, latrine, complete

3 sledges, blacksmith, double-face, 6-8 lbs

3 lanterns, kerosene, army

1 gasoline lantern, leaded fuel

3 flashlights, TL-122-( ) (Off, NCO, truck, chest MD N$2)

For the entire Company:

10 goggles, M1943, clear lens (drivers, cancelled 14 February 1945)

10 goggles, M1943, green lens (other than drivers, cancelled 14 February 1945)

20 goggles, M1944 (2 per truck, added 14 February 1945)

CHAPTER 9

EQUIPMENT

Throughout this book equipment lists have been given. These, provided for each unit of every company within the division, included only the equipment specific to a unit. However, all companies possessed certain identical equipment, not included in the equipment lists for each unit. These were:

standard equipments of a company (section 9.1)
equipment provided with vehicles and heavy weapons (section 9.2)
individual equipment (section 9.3)
clothing and soldier's minor items of equipment (section 9.4)

The lists appear theoretical and demand some explanation. Did units really possess what appeared in the tables of organization and equipment? Information from unit histories and correspondence with veterans indicates that the tables corresponded to what existed in units, the only problem being the delay between the date of the table and the date of issue in units. Of course, some individuals managed to obtain or retain material that was not authorized, but was not representative of their type of unit. Modifications or adaptations which occurred to certain vehicles and equipment were not included in the tables of organization and equipment. Based on conversations with some American veterans the following information came to light.

The issue of personnel and equipment to a unit was governed by:

A Rules
B Logistical problems, foreseen and unforeseen
C Decisions of the Commanders of the Theaters of Operations or of the Armies

A – Rules

The Tables of Organization and Equipment (T/O&E), the Tables of Organization (T/O) and the Tables of Equipment (T/E) were authorizations for the units described therein to requisition the personnel and the equipment listed. Every unit had to be equipped and issued with personnel according to its T/O&E, and could not have more than the table called for. Only in exceptional circumstances would a unit be authorized to be over strength. Divisions were rarely under their theoretical strength. With the replacement system developed by Army Ground Forces, the units were maintained nearly always at 90% of their strength (80% for the rifle platoons and 110% for the headquarters), except during and after combat, before replacements arrived.

The T/O&E was an order for equipment requisition against services responsible for its issue. New materials were exchanged for old. Others were changed only when they had been used up, others were expendable.

The date of issue of new equipment in units varied with regard to the date of the T/O&E. The table was verified before being issued, and arrived at the units only in the month following its date of publication. The units were classified by an order of priority for the issue of equipment. All divisions would not therefore be re-equipped at the same date. To ensure this, it was necessary that the equipment was in the chain of supply.

When a new table modified the ranks of personnel, for example, when on 26 February 1944 (date of publication), the squad leader became staff sergeant, the modification would become effective only upon an order from the higher headquarters, in this instance the infantry regiment.

Unit reorganization according to a new table was also variable. For example, on 6 June 1944 the headquarters, 5th Infantry Division issued a classified order giving the organization of the division at this date, with the number of the T/O&E for each unit (see Appendix V). The engineer combat battalion, T/O&E 5-15, was organized according to the T/O&E dated 15 July 1943 whereas a new table had been issued on 13 March 1944. However, the infantry regiments were well-organized according to the latest tables issued, those of 26 February 1944. It is only an example, but gives an idea of the elapsed time between the date of the table and the date of the reorganization.

Another example is the General Order No. 6 dated 28 March 1944, issued by the headquarters, 5th Infantry Division, concerning the reorganization of the signal company. It read: "Pursuant to authority contained in teletype message, Hq XV Corps, 27 March 1944, the reorganization of the 5th Signal Company, 5th Infantry Division under tables of organization and equipment 11-7, dated 11 December 1943, is announced effective 0001 hours, 28 March 1944 …. Additional and new equipment will be requisitioned from the proper supply agencies without delay. Equipment rendered surplus will be retained until receipt of new equipment."

The examples mentioned, from official sources, show an elapsed time of four months between the date of the table and the reorganization becoming effective.

B – Logistical Problems

The equipment had to be in the chain of supply to be distributed to units. When a new table authorized a unit to be issued with an existing equipment, this would be in the chain of supply and the unit would be rapidly issued with it, especially if it had an order of priority. This was the case with the signal company mentioned above. When equipment was new and was not yet in the chain of supply, the unit authorized to be issued with this equipment would have to wait several months before being issued with it, especially if it did not have an order of priority. Certain highly-valued equipment was often out of stock and not available for units demanding it.

In the European Theater, the rapidity of the advance during August changed the plans of the Quartermaster Corps, which was unable to supply the units. Only rations and POL (Petrol Oil Lubricants) were delivered to the units. The other equipment had to be repaired and salvaged in the quartermaster units of the divisions. These were not issued with new equipment before October 1944. Certain equipment replaced in the T/O&E had to be provided until exhausted. For example, at the end of the war in Europe, SCR-284 radio sets were still in service in certain infantry regiments[1], whereas they had been replaced in the table dated 26 February 1944.

C – Decisions of the Commanders

Some equipment listed in the tables of equipment would not be authorized by certain higher unit commanders. This was the case with the 'beanie', the woollen knitted cap, which George S. Patton, Jr. did not wish to see in the 3rd Army. Fortunately it was replaced by the cotton field cap, which was a part of the combat outfit M1943. Nevertheless, it was exactly this outfit, which not being appreciated by some commanders of the European Theater, was refused by them when it became available. Parts of this outfit, particularly the field jacket, were authorized in the European Theater from October 1944. However, with the problems of supply, it was initially issued only in small numbers. It was only at the end of October when it started to equip units in larger numbers. Another element of the M1943 combat outfit issued from October 1944, in Europe, was the Field Pack, Combat and Cargo.

Although one would like to give the date of issue in units for some important equipment, the explanations given above show why this is impossible. Although information was requested from many veterans, it was without result. They well remember a great deal about the T/O&Es, organization, rules – especially the officers. However, nobody remembered the dates of issue in the units for that equipment. It is reasonable to assume it took three to four months, more sometimes, before all the units were reorganized under the T/O&E issued at a determined date.

9.1 COMPANY STANDARD EQUIPMENT

The equipment described in this section is listed in all T/O&Es that have been detailed in this book. This equipment was for all the company, and was usually present with the headquarters company platoon. Equipments specific to certain companies are mentioned.

1 gas alarm, M1
6 decontaminating apparatus, 3-gal, M1 (cancelled, July 1944)
1 kit, chemical agent detector, M9
4 first aid kits, gas casualty (1 per 25 individuals)
first aid kits, motor vehicle, 12 units (1 per 4 vehicles)
1 brassard, arm, gas
3 protective gloves, impermeable (1 per 40 EM)
3 protective suits, one-piece, impermeable (1 per 40 EM)
1 canvas bag, water sterilizing, with cover and hanger (1 per 100 individuals)
3 or 5 delousing bags (1 per 20 individuals in areas contaminated by typhus, 1 per 35 individuals in areas where risk of typhus was low)
2 galvanized buckets, GP, heavy weight, without lip, 14-qt
1 corrugated can, galvanized, nesting, with cover, 10-gal (stock no. 42-C-1720)
1 corrugated can, galvanized, nesting, with cover, 16-gal (42-C-1730)
1 corrugated can, galvanized, nesting, with cover, 24-gal (42-C-1740)
1 corrugated can, galvanized, nesting, with cover, 32-gal (42-C-1750)
3 heaters, immersion type, for corrugated cans (65-J-1911-70)
20 water cans, 5-gal (1 per 5 individuals) (stock no. 64-C-281)
1 chest, record, fibre (company clerk) (26-C-2834)
4 round containers, insulated, M1941, with 3 inserts (1 per 25 individuals) (64-C-1105)
1 hair clipper (1 per 24 individuals)
1 empty field desk, company (26-D-135)
1 flag, guidon, bunting
1 barber kit, with case (barber kit, M1944, 29-K-82)
8 sewing kits (1 per 12 EM) (27-K-300)

1. 11th Infantry Regiment, *History of the Eleventh Infantry in WWII* (Baton Rouge, La.: Army and Navy Publishing Company, 1946).

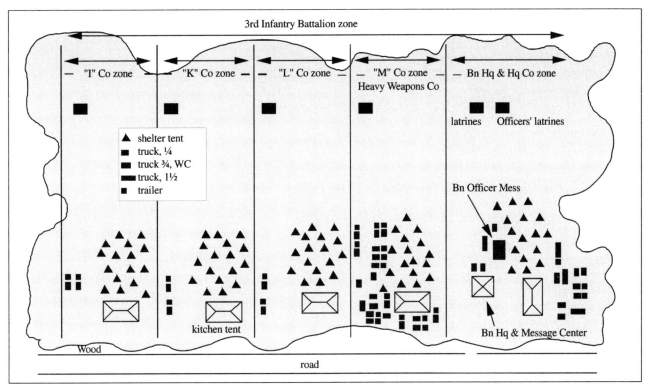

71. Bivouac of an infantry battalion in a combat area

1 fly, tent, wall, large, 24-F-140, replaced July 1944 by: 1 tent, kitchen, fly proof, from July 1944)
3 hand-portable electric lanterns
2 gasoline lanterns, two-mantle commercial (replaced by: gasoline lantern, leaded fuel)
1 cooking outfit, two-burner, M1942, per 20 EM (Engr Co, only) (64-O-300)
8 cooking outfits, one-burner, M1942 (64-O-202) (1 per 12 individuals in Infantry, Field Artillery) (none in the Medical Battalion)
40 cooking outfits, one-burner, M1942 (64-O-202) (1 per vehicle in Cavalry)
1 field range, M1937, 3-unit (65-J-2227)
1 screen, latrine, complete with pins and poles
1 trumpet, G, with slide to F, plastic (bugler) (36-T-648)
1 portable typewriter, with carrying case (54-T-16000)
10 to 40 whistles, thunderer (1 per officer, 1st Sgt, and other NCOs, see unit chapters) (74-W-80).

9.2   EQUIPMENT ISSUED WITH VEHICLES AND WEAPONS

This section details equipment provided with each type of vehicle. This equipment was only listed in all T/O&Es from 1944. However, some T/O&Es list it before this date. The Ordnance Corps issued this equipment with the vehicles and they were listed on the Standard Nomenclature Lists (SNL). That they appeared in the T/O&Es did not change the real status of this equipment. Combat vehicle equipment remained listed in the SNLs and never appeared in the T/O&Es.

A – Equipment per vehicle

1 – TRUCK, ¼-ton

1 decontaminating apparatus, 1½ qt, M2
2 respirators, dust, M2 (replaced model M1)
1 defroster and de-icer, windshield, electric
1 canvas bucket, water, 18-qt
1 gasoline drum, inflammable liquid, with carrying handle, 5-gal
1 tube, flexible nozzle
1 camouflage net, twine, with fabric, 22 × 22'
1 tow rope, 20' long, 1" diameter
1 round point shovel, GP, D handled, no. 2
1 handled axe, chopping, single bit, standard grade, 4-lb

2 – TRUCK, ¾-ton, WC

1 decontaminating apparatus, 1½ qt, M2
2 respirators, dust, M2
1 defroster and de-icer, windshield, electric
1 canvas bucket, water, 18-qt
2 gasoline drums, inflammable liquid, with carrying handle, 5-gal
1 tube, flexible nozzle
1 camouflage net, twine, with fabric, shrimp, 29 × 29'
1 tow rope, 20" long, 1" diameter
1 round point shovel, GP, D handled, no. 2
1 handled mattock with pick, type II, class F, 5-lb
1 handled axe, chopping, single bit, standard grade, 4-lb

3 – TRUCK, 1½-ton, CARGO

1 decontaminating apparatus, 1½ qt, M2
2 respirators, dust, M2
1 defroster and de-icer, windshield, electric
1 canvas bucket, water, 18-qt
2 gasoline drums, inflammable liquid, with carrying handle, 5-gal
1 tube, flexible nozzle
1 camouflage net, twine, with fabric, shrimp, 36 × 44'
1 tow rope, 20' long, 1" diameter
1 round point shovel, GP, D handled, no. 2
1 handled axe, chopping, single bit, standard grade, 4-lb

4 – TRUCK, 2½-ton, CARGO / TRUCK, 4-ton

1 decontaminating apparatus, 1½ qt, M2
2 respirators, dust, M2
1 defroster and de-icer, windshield, electric
1 canvas bucket, water, 18-qt
2 gasoline drums, inflammable liquid, with carrying handle, 5-gal
1 tube, flexible nozzle
1 camouflage net, twine, with fabric, shrimp, 36 × 44'
1 tow rope, 20' long, 1" diameter
1 round point shovel, GP, D handled, no. 2
1 handled mattock with pick, type II, class F, 5-lb
1 handled axe, chopping, single bit, standard grade, 4-lb
1 tow chain, motor vehicle, 16' long, 7⁄16" diameter (16' × 5⁄8" for the 4-ton)

5 – TRUCK, 4-ton, WRECKER

1 decontaminating apparatus, 1½ qt, M2
2 respirators, dust, M2
1 defroster and de-icer, windshield, electric
1 canvas bucket, water, 18-qt
2 gasoline drums, inflammable liquid, with carrying handle, 5-gal
1 tube, flexible nozzle
1 camouflage net, twine, with fabric, shrimp, 36 × 44'
1 tow rope, 20' long, 1" diameter
1 round point shovel, GP, D handled, no. 2
1 handled mattock with pick, type II, class F, 5-lb
1 handled axe, chopping, single bit, standard grade, 4-lb
1 crow bar, pinch point diameter stock 1¼", length 72"
1 towing bar, universal type
1 tow chain, motor vehicle, 16' long, 7⁄16" diameter
1 tow chain, motor vehicle, 20' × 5⁄8"
1 chuck-gauge, tire pressure, 20-130-lb
1 air compressor, portable, engine driven, 3-cu. ft. Capacity
1 air hose, ¼" inside diameter, 25-ft length, with connections
1 unit equipment tool set, 2nd echelon, set no. 4
1 unit equipment tool set, 2nd echelon, set no. 5
1 unit equipment tool set, 2nd echelon, set no. 9

1 tool set, welders

6 – TRACTOR, HIGH SPEED, 13-ton, M5

1 decontaminating apparatus, 1½ qt, M2
respirators, dust, M2 (as many as individuals were carried by the tractor)
1 canvas bucket, water, 18-qt
2 gasoline drums, inflammable liquid, with carrying handle, 5-gal
1 tube, flexible nozzle
1 camouflage net, twine, with fabric, shrimp, 36 × 44′
1 round point shovel, GP, D handled, no. 2
1 handled mattock with pick, type II, class F, 5-lb
1 handled axe, chopping, single bit, standard grade, 4-lb
1 tow chain, motor vehicle, 16′ long, ⅝″ diameter

7 – CAR, HALF-TRACK, M3A1

a) carried outside the half-track:
2 gasoline drums, inflammable liquid, with carrying handle, 5-gal
1 crosscut saw, 1 man, 4½′
1 canvas cover, 5′, crosscut saw
1 camouflage net, twine, with fabric, shrimp, 36 × 44′
1 round point shovel, GP, D handled, no. 2
1 mattock, pick, M1
1 handled axe, chopping, single bit, standard grade, 4-lb
1 top, assembly, complete with bows and bag

b) carried inside the half-track:
1 decontaminating apparatus, 1½ qt, M2
2 respirators, dust, M2
1 defroster and de-icer, windshield, electric
1 canvas bucket, water, 18-qt
2 gasoline drums, inflammable liquid, with carrying handle, 5-gal
1 antenna, complete with cover
3 flashlights, TL-122-( )
2 asbestos mittens, M1942
1 first aid kit, motor vehicle, 24 units
1 radio set (see chapter 1-4)
1 tube, flexible nozzle
1 towing cable, S, 15′ long, ⅝″ diameter
1 fire extinguisher, carbon dioxide, 2-lb
13 bedding rolls

c) ammunition storage:
7,750 rounds for Machine Gun, M1919A4, caliber .30
700 rounds for Machine Gun, M2, HB , caliber .50
540 rounds for Submachine gun, caliber .45, M1928A1, M1, M1A1, then M3
22 hand grenades
24 mines, AT, M1

8 – TRAILERS

a) M1, M10, Ammunition
1 camouflage net, twine, with fabric, shrimp, 29 × 29′
b) trailer, ¼-ton
1 camouflage net, twine, with fabric, shrimp, 22 × 22′

B – Equipment issued with weapons

Some equipment has already been listed in the relevant section for each unit (for example, ammunition bags)

1 – MACHINE GUN, M2, HB, caliber .50

1 camouflage net, twine, with fabric, 15 × 15′ (per MG, used on ground)
2 asbestos mittens, M1942
1 goggles, M1943 (red lens) (cancelled January 1944)
1 mount, tripod, M3

1 mount, AA, M63 (used in anti-aircraft role)

2 – MACHINE GUN, M1917 A1, caliber .30
1 camouflage net, twine, with fabric, 15 × 15′ (per MG, used on ground)
1 mount, tripod for MG, caliber .30, M1917A1 replaced by
1 mount, tripod, M2 (Dec. 1944)

3 – ROCKET LAUNCHER, AT, 2.36″
2 rocket-carrying bags, M6 (3 in the units of an infantry battalion and in the infantry cannon company)

4 – MORTAR M2, 60 mm &SMG M3, caliber .45
1 ammunition-carrying bag

5 – GRENADE LAUNCHER M7 & M8
2 ammunition-carrying bags

6 – GUN 57mm, ANTI-TANK
1 camouflage net, twine, with fabric, shrimp, 29 × 29′
2 asbestos mittens, M1942
2 goggles, M1943, red lens

7 – HOWITZER 105mm, M3 (Infantry Cannon Company)
1 camouflage net, twine, with fabric, 29 × 29′
1 handled axe, chopping, single bit, standard grade, 4-lb
1 mattock, handled, railroad, 6 to 7 lbs
1 round point shovel, GP, D handled, no. 2

9.3 INDIVIDUAL EQUIPMENT

The tables of organization and equipment also allocated individual equipment. Rather than give a list by unit, all are listed in this section. The reader will find below the equipment classified by arm-of-service (infantry, artillery, etc.), by rank (enlisted man, officer and warrant officer), and by weapon (pistol, carbine, rifle) issued to them.

1 – INFANTRY

a) Enlisted man (armed with a M1 Rifle)
gas mask M3-10A1-6 (then M3A1-10A1-6) replaced by M5-11-7 (from 12 September 1944)
cartridge belt, caliber .30, dismounted, M1923
haversack, M1928 (except Alaska)
pack carrier, M1928 (except Alaska)
canteen cover, dismounted, M1910
canteen, dismounted, M1910
canvas muzzle cover, rifle or carbine
bayonet M1 with scabbard M7 (30 January 1945) [2]

b) Enlisted man (armed with a M1 carbine)
gas mask M3-10A1-6 (then M3A1-10A1-6) replaced by M5-11-7 (from 12 September 1944)
pistol belt, M1936
2 magazine pockets for carbine, caliber .30, M1
haversack, M1928 (except Alaska)
pack carrier, M1928 (except Alaska)
canteen cover, dismounted, M1910
canteen, dismounted, M1910
canvas muzzle cover, rifle or carbine
trench knife M3 with scabbard M8, replaced by
bayonet M4 with scabbard M8A1 (30 June 1944)

c) Enlisted man (armed with a pistol)
gas mask M3-10A1-6 (then M3A1-10A1-6) replaced by M5-11-7 (from 12 September 1944)
pistol belt, M1936

2. Before this date the bayonet was not listed in the tables, it was issued with the rifle.

magazine pocket, double web, EM, M1923
haversack, M1928 (except Alaska)
pack carrier, M1928 (except Alaska)
canteen cover, dismounted, M1910
canteen, dismounted, M1910
trench knife M3 with scabbard M8, replaced by
bayonet M4 with scabbard M8A1 (30 June 1944)

d) Enlisted man (armed with the Automatic Rifle BAR, M1918A2)
gas mask M3-10A1-6 (then M3A1-10A1-6) replaced by M5-11-7 (from 12 September 1944)
magazine belt, M1937, BAR (provided to the assistant automatic rifleman and to the ammunition bearer until June 1944)
haversack, M1928 (except Alaska)
pack carrier, M1928 (except Alaska)
canteen cover, dismounted, M1910
canteen, dismounted, M1910
trench knife M3 with scabbard M8, replaced by
bayonet M4 with scabbard M8A1 (30 June 1944)

e) Enlisted man (with any of the above weapons)
entrenching axe, M1910, with handle (1 per 10 EM)
entrenching pick mattock, M1910, with handle (2 per 10 EM)
entrenching shovel, M 1910 then M1943 (7 per 10 EM) the shovel M1943 began to replace the shovel M1910 in March 1944)
wire cutter, M1938 (2 per 10 EM)

f) Warrant Officer (armed with a carbine)
gas mask M3-10A1-6 (then M3A1-10A1-6) replaced by M5-11-7 (from 12 September 1944)
canvas field bag, olive drab, M1936
pistol belt, M1936
2 magazine pockets for carbine, caliber .30, M1
canteen cover, dismounted, M1910
canteen, dismounted, M1910
carrying strap, GP (replaced carrying strap, canvas field bag, M1936)
belt suspenders, M1936
trench knife M3 with scabbard M8, replaced by
bayonet M4 with scabbard M8A1 (30 June 1944)

g) Officer (armed with a pistol)
gas mask M3-10A1-6 (then M3A1-10A1-6) replaced by M5-11-7 (from 12 September 1944)
canvas field bag, olive drab, M1936)
pistol belt, M1936
canteen cover, dismounted, M1910
canteen, dismounted, M1910
magazine pocket, double web, EM, M1923
carrying strap, GP (replaced carrying strap, canvas field bag, M1936)
belt suspenders, M1936
trench knife M3 with scabbard M8, replaced by
bayonet M4 with scabbard M8A1 (30 June 1944)

h) Officer (armed with a carbine)
gas mask M3-10A1-6 (then M3A1-10A1-6) replaced by M5-11-7 (from 12 September 1944)
canvas field bag, olive drab, M1936
pistol belt, M1936
2 magazine pockets for carbine, caliber .30, M1
canteen cover, dismounted, M1910
canteen, dismounted, M1910
carrying strap, GP (replaced carrying strap, canvas field bag, M1936)
belt suspenders, M1936
entrenching shovel, M 1910 then M1943) (Officer in Infantry Rifle Company, Heavy Weapons Company)
trench knife M3 with scabbard M8, replaced by
bayonet M4 with scabbard M8A1 (30 June 1944)

2 – CAVALRY (Cavalry Reconnaissance Troop)

a) Enlisted man (armed with a M1 Rifle)

gas mask M3-10A1-6 (then M3A1-10A1-6) replaced by M5-11-7 (from 12 September 1944)
cartridge belt, caliber .30, dismounted, M1923
canvas field bag, olive drab, M1936
carrying strap, GP (replaced carrying strap, canvas field bag, M1936)
belt suspenders, M1936
canteen cover, mounted, M1941
canteen, dismounted, M1941
canvas muzzle cover, rifle or carbine
bayonet M1 with scabbard M7

b) Enlisted man (armed with a carbine)

gas mask M3-10A1-6 (then M3A1-10A1-6) replaced by M5-11-7 (from 12 September 1944)
pistol belt, M1936
5 magazine pockets for carbine, caliber .30, M1
canvas field bag, olive drab, M1936
carrying strap, GP (replaced carrying strap, canvas field bag, M1936)
belt suspenders, M1936
canteen cover, mounted, M1941
canteen, mounted, M1941
canvas muzzle cover, rifle or carbine
bayonet M4 with scabbard M8A1 (6 July 1944)

c) Enlisted man (armed with a submachine gun)

gas mask M3-10A1-6 (then M3A1-10A1-6) replaced by M5-11-7 (from 12 September 1944)
pistol belt, M1936
canvas field bag, olive drab, M1936
carrying strap, GP (replaced carrying strap, canvas field bag, M1936)
belt suspenders, M1936
canteen cover, mounted, M1941
canteen, mounted, M1941
ammunition-carrying bag
bayonet M4 with scabbard M8A1 (6 July 1944)

d) Enlisted man (with any of the above weapons)

entrenching axe, M1910, with handle (1 per 10 EM)
entrenching pick mattock, M1910, with handle (2 per 10 EM)
entrenching shovel, M 1910 then M1943 (7 per 10 EM)
wire cutter, M1938 (1 per motor vehicle)

e) Officer (armed with a carbine)

gas mask M3-10A1-6 (then M3A1-10A1-6) replaced by M5-11-7 (from 12 September 1944)
pistol belt, M1936
5 magazine pockets for carbine, caliber .30, M1
canvas field bag, olive drab, M1936
carrying strap, GP (replaced carrying strap, canvas field bag, M1936)
belt suspenders, M1936
canteen cover, mounted, M1941
canteen, mounted, M1941
bayonet M4 with scabbard M8A1 (6 July 1944)

3 – ARTILLERY

a) Enlisted man (armed with a carbine)

gas mask M3-10A1-6 (then M3A1-10A1-6) replaced by M5-11-7 (from 12 September 1944)
canvas field bag, olive drab, M1936- pistol belt, M1936
2 magazine pockets for carbine, caliber .30, M1
canteen cover, dismounted, M1910
canteen, dismounted, M1910
carrying strap, GP (replaced carrying strap, canvas field bag, M1936)
belt suspenders, M1936
canvas muzzle cover, rifle or carbine

b) Enlisted man (armed with a pistol)
gas mask M3-10A1-6 (then M3A1-10A1-6) replaced by M5-11-7 (from 12 September 1944)
canvas field bag, olive drab, M1936
pistol belt, M1936
magazine pocket, double web, EM, M1923
canteen cover, dismounted, M1910
canteen, dismounted, M1910
carrying strap, GP (replaced carrying strap, canvas field bag, M1936)
belt suspenders, M1936

c) Enlisted man (with any of the above weapons)
entrenching axe, M1910, with handle (1 per 10 EM)
entrenching pick mattock, M1910, with handle (3 per 10 EM)
entrenching shovel, M 1910 then M1943 (6 per 10 EM)

d) Officer (armed with a pistol)
gas mask M3-10A1-6 (then M3A1-10A1-6) replaced by M5-11-7 (from 12 September 1944)
canvas field bag, olive drab, M1936
pistol belt, M1936
magazine pocket, double web, EM, M1923
carrying strap, GP (replaced carrying strap, canvas field bag, M1936)
belt suspenders, M1936
canteen cover, dismounted, M1910
canteen, dismounted, M1910
entrenching shovel, M 1910 then M1943

4 – MEDICAL CORPS, MEDICAL BATTALION AND MEDICAL DETACHMENTS

a) Enlisted man
gas mask M3-10A1-6 (then M3A1-10A1-6) replaced by M5-11-7 (from 12 September 1944)
pistol belt, M1936
haversack, M1928 (except Alaska)
pack carrier, M1928 (except Alaska)
canteen cover, dismounted, M1910
canteen, dismounted, M1910
entrenching axe, M1910, with handle (1 per 10 EM)
entrenching pick mattock, M1910, with handle (2 per 10 EM)
entrenching shovel, M 1910 then M1943 (7 per 10 EM)
wire cutter, M1938 (2 per 2 EM, only in the Medical Detachment, Infantry Regiment)

b) Officer
gas mask M3-10A1-6 (then M3A1-10A1-6) replaced by M5-11-7 (from 12 September 1944)
canvas field bag, olive drab, M1936
pistol belt, M1936
carrying strap, GP (replaced carrying strap, canvas field bag, M1936)
belt suspenders, M1936
canteen cover, dismounted, M1910
canteen, dismounted, M1910

5 – CORPS OF ENGINEERS

a) Enlisted man (armed with a M1 Rifle)
gas mask M3-10A1-6 (then M3A1-10A1-6) replaced by M5-11-7 (from 12 September 1944)
cartridge belt, caliber .30, dismounted, M1923
haversack, M1928 (except Alaska)
pack carrier, M1928 (except Alaska)
canteen cover, dismounted, M1910
canteen, dismounted, M1910
canvas muzzle cover, rifle or carbine
bayonet M1 with scabbard M7

b) Enlisted man (armed with a carbine)
gas mask M3-10A1-6 (then M3A1-10A1-6) replaced by M5-11-7 (from 12 September 1944)
pistol belt, M1936
2 magazine pockets for carbine, caliber .30, M1

canvas muzzle cover, rifle or carbine
haversack, M1928 (except Alaska)
pack carrier, M1928 (except Alaska)
canteen cover, dismounted, M1910
canteen, dismounted, M1910
canvas muzzle cover, rifle or carbine
trench knife M3 with scabbard M8, replaced by
bayonet M4 with scabbard M8A1 (30 June 1944)

c) Enlisted man (with any of the above weapons)
entrenching axe, M1910, with handle (1 per 10 EM)
entrenching pick mattock, M1910, with handle (2 per 10 EM)
entrenching shovel, M 1910 then M1943 (7 per 10 EM)
wire cutter, M1938 (10 for a company)

d) Warrant officer (armed with a carbine)
gas mask M3-10A1-6 (then M3A1-10A1-6) replaced by M5-11-7 (from 12 September 1944)
canvas field bag, olive drab, M1936
pistol belt, M1936
2 magazine pockets for carbine, caliber .30, M1
canvas muzzle cover, rifle or carbine
canteen cover, dismounted, M1910
canteen, dismounted, M1910
carrying strap, GP (replaced carrying strap, canvas field bag, M1936)
belt suspenders, M1936
trench knife M3 with scabbard M8, replaced by
bayonet M4 with scabbard M8A1 (30 June 1944)

e) Officer (armed with a pistol)
gas mask M3-10A1-6 (then M3A1-10A1-6) replaced by M5-11-7 (from 12 September 1944)
canvas field bag, olive drab, M1936
pistol belt, M1936
canteen cover, dismounted, M1910
canteen, dismounted, M1910
magazine pocket, double web, EM, M1923
carrying strap, GP (replaced carrying strap, canvas field bag, M1936)
belt suspenders, M1936
trench knife M3 with scabbard M8, replaced by
bayonet M4 with scabbard M8A1 (30 June 1944)

f) Officer (armed with a carbine)
gas mask M3-10A1-6 (then M3A1-10A1-6) replaced by M5-11-7 (from 12 September 1944)
canvas field bag, olive drab, M1936
pistol belt, M1936
2 magazine pockets for carbine, caliber .30, M1
canvas muzzle cover, rifle or carbine
canteen cover, dismounted, M1910
canteen, dismounted, M1910
carrying strap, GP (replaced carrying strap, canvas field bag, M1936)
belt suspenders, M1936
entrenching shovel, M 1910 then M1943) (Officer in Engineer Combat Company)
trench knife M3 with scabbard M8, replaced by
bayonet M4 with scabbard M8A1 (30 June 1944)

6 – CORPS OF MILITARY POLICE

a) Enlisted man (armed with a M1 Rifle)
gas mask M3-10A1-6 (then M3A1-10A1-6) replaced by M5-11-7 (from 12 September 1944)
cartridge belt, caliber .30, dismounted, M1923
haversack, M1928 (except Alaska)
pack carrier, M1928 (except Alaska)
canteen cover, dismounted, M1910
canteen, dismounted, M1910
canvas muzzle cover, rifle or carbine
bayonet M1 with scabbard M7

b) Enlisted man (armed with a carbine)
gas mask M3-10A1-6 (then M3A1-10A1-6) replaced by M5-11-7 (from 12 September 1944)
pistol belt, M1936
2 magazine pockets for carbine, caliber .30, M1
haversack, M1928 (except Alaska)
pack carrier, M1928 (except Alaska)
canteen cover, dismounted, M1910
canteen, dismounted, M1910
canvas muzzle cover, rifle or carbine
bayonet M4 with scabbard M8A1 (15 March 1945)

c) Enlisted man (with any of the above weapons)
entrenching axe, M1910, with handle (1 per 10 EM)
entrenching pick mattock, M1910, with handle (2 per 10 EM)
entrenching shovel, M 1910 then M1943 (7 per 10 EM)

d) Officer (armed with a pistol)
gas mask M3-10A1-6 (then M3A1-10A1-6) replaced by M5-11-7 (from 12 September 1944)
canvas field bag, olive drab, M1936
pistol belt, M1936
canteen cover, dismounted, M1910
canteen, dismounted, M1910
magazine pocket, double web, EM, M1923
carrying strap, GP (replaced carrying strap, canvas field bag, M1936)
belt suspenders, M1936
bayonet M4 with scabbard M8A1 (15 March 1945)

e) Officer (armed with a carbine)
gas mask M3-10A1-6 (then M3A1-10A1-6) replaced by M5-11-7 (from 12 September 1944)
canvas field bag, olive drab, M1936
pistol belt, M1936
2 magazine pockets for carbine, caliber .30, M1
canvas muzzle cover, rifle or carbine
canteen cover, dismounted, M1910
canteen, dismounted, M1910
carrying strap, GP (replaced carrying strap, canvas field bag, M1936)
belt suspenders, M1936
bayonet M4 with scabbard M8A1 (15 March 1945)

7 – SIGNAL CORPS

a) Enlisted man (armed with a M1 Rifle)
gas mask M3-10A1-6 (then M3A1-10A1-6) replaced by M5-11-7 (from 12 September 1944)
canvas field bag, olive drab, M1936
cartridge belt, caliber .30, dismounted, M1923
canteen cover, dismounted, M1910
canteen, dismounted, M1910
carrying strap, GP (replaced carrying strap, canvas field bag, M1936)
belt suspenders, M1936
canvas muzzle cover, rifle or carbine
bayonet M1 with scabbard M7

b) Enlisted man (armed with a carbine)
gas mask M3-10A1-6 (then M3A1-10A1-6) replaced by M5-11-7 (from 12 September 1944)
canvas field bag, olive drab, M1936
pistol belt, M1936
2 magazine pockets for carbine, caliber .30, M1
canteen cover, dismounted, M1910
canteen, dismounted, M1910
bayonet M4 with scabbard M8A1 (3 December 1945)
carrying strap, GP (replaced carrying strap, canvas field bag, M1936)
belt suspenders, M1936
canvas muzzle cover, rifle or carbine

c) Enlisted man (with any of the above weapons)
entrenching axe, M1910, with handle (1 per 10 EM)
entrenching pick mattock, M1910, with handle (2 per 10 EM)
entrenching shovel, M 1910 then M1943 (7 per 10 EM)

d) Warrant Officer (armed with a carbine)
gas mask M3-10A1-6 (then M3A1-10A1-6) replaced by M5-11-7 (from 12 September 1944)
canvas field bag, olive drab, M1936
pistol belt, M1936
2 magazine pockets for carbine, caliber .30, M1
canteen cover, dismounted, M1910
canteen, dismounted, M1910
carrying strap, GP (replaced carrying strap, canvas field bag, M1936)
belt suspenders, M1936
bayonet M4 with scabbard M8A1 (3 December 1945)

e) Officer (armed with a carbine)
gas mask M3-10A1-6 (then M3A1-10A1-6) replaced by M5-11-7 (from 12 September 1944)
canvas field bag, olive drab, M1936
pistol belt, M1936
2 magazine pockets for carbine, caliber .30, M1
canteen cover, dismounted, M1910
canteen, dismounted, M1910
carrying strap, GP (replaced carrying strap, canvas field bag, M1936)
belt suspenders, M1936
bayonet M4 with scabbard M8A1 (3 December 1945)

f) Officer (armed with a pistol)
gas mask M3-10A1-6 (then M3A1-10A1-6) replaced by M5-11-7 (from 12 September 1944)
canvas field bag, olive drab, M1936
pistol belt, M1936
magazine pocket, double web, EM, M1923
carrying strap, GP (replaced carrying strap, canvas field bag, M1936)
belt suspenders, M1936
canteen cover, dismounted, M1910
canteen, dismounted, M1910
bayonet M4 with scabbard M8A1 (3 December 1945)

8 – ORDNANCE CORPS

a) Enlisted man (armed with a M1 Rifle)
gas mask M3-10A1-6 (then M3A1-10A1-6) replaced by M5-11-7 (from 12 September 1944)
cartridge belt, caliber .30, dismounted, M1923
haversack, M1928 (except Alaska)
pack carrier, M1928 (except Alaska)
canteen cover, dismounted, M1910
canteen, dismounted, M1910
canvas muzzle cover, rifle or carbine

b) Enlisted man (armed with a carbine)
gas mask M3-10A1-6 (then M3A1-10A1-6) replaced by M5-11-7 (from 12 September 1944)
pistol belt, M1936
1 magazine pocket for carbine, caliber .30, M1
haversack, M1928 (except Alaska)
pack carrier, M1928 (except Alaska)
canteen cover, dismounted, M1910
canteen, dismounted, M1910
canvas muzzle cover, rifle or carbine
bayonet M4 with scabbard M8A1 (17 November 1944)

c) Enlisted man (with any of the above weapons)
entrenching axe, M1910, with handle (1 per 10 EM)
entrenching pick mattock, M1910, with handle (2 per 10 EM)
entrenching shovel, M 1910 then M1943 (7 per 10 EM)

d) Warrant Officer (armed with a carbine)

gas mask M3-10A1-6 (then M3A1-10A1-6) replaced by M5-11-7 (from 12 September 1944)
canvas field bag, olive drab, M1936
pistol belt, M1936
2 magazine pockets for carbine, caliber .30, M1
canteen cover, dismounted, M1910
canteen, dismounted, M1910
carrying strap, GP (replaced carrying strap, canvas field bag, M1936)
belt suspenders, M1936
canvas muzzle cover, rifle or carbine
entrenching shovel, M1910 then M1943 (when authorized by the Commander of the Theater of Operations)
bayonet M4 with scabbard M8A1 (17 November 1944)

e) Officer (armed with a pistol)

gas mask M3-10A1-6 (then M3A1-10A1-6) replaced by M5-11-7 (from 12 September 1944)
canvas field bag, olive drab, M1936
pistol belt, M1936
canteen cover, dismounted, M1910
canteen, dismounted, M1910
magazine pocket, double web, EM, M1923
carrying strap, GP (replaced carrying strap, canvas field bag, M1936)
belt suspenders, M1936
entrenching shovel, M 1910 then M1943 (when authorized by the Commander of the Theater of Operations)
bayonet M4 with scabbard M8A1 (17 November 1944)

f) Officer (armed with a carbine)

gas mask M3-10A1-6 (then M3A1-10A1-6) replaced by M5-11-7 (from 12 September 1944)
canvas field bag, olive drab, M1936
pistol belt, M1936
2 magazine pockets for carbine, caliber .30, M1
canteen cover, dismounted, M1910
canteen, dismounted, M1910
carrying strap, GP (replaced carrying strap, canvas field bag, M1936)
belt suspenders, M1936
canvas muzzle cover, rifle or carbine
entrenching shovel, M1910 then M1943 (when authorized by the Commander of the Theater of Operations)
bayonet M4 with scabbard M8A1 (17 November 1944)

9 – QUARTERMASTER CORPS

a) Enlisted man (armed with a M1 Rifle)

gas mask M3-10A1-6 (then M3A1-10A1-6) replaced by M5-11-7 (from 12 September 1944)
canvas field bag, olive drab, M1936
cartridge belt, caliber .30, dismounted, M1923
canteen cover, dismounted, M1910
canteen, dismounted, M1910
carrying strap, GP (replaced carrying strap, canvas field bag, M1936)
belt suspenders, M1936
canvas muzzle cover, rifle or carbine

b) Enlisted man (armed with a carbine)

gas mask M3-10A1-6 (then M3A1-10A1-6) replaced by M5-11-7 (from 12 September 1944)
canvas field bag, olive drab, M1936
pistol belt, M1936
1 magazine pocket for carbine, caliber .30, M1
canteen cover, dismounted, M1910
canteen, dismounted, M1910
carrying strap, GP (replaced carrying strap, canvas field bag, M1936)
belt suspenders, M1936
canvas muzzle cover, rifle or carbine
bayonet M4 with scabbard M8A1 (1 June 1945)

c) Enlisted man (with any of the above weapons)

entrenching axe, M1910, with handle (1 per 10 EM)
entrenching pick mattock, M1910, with handle (2 per 10 EM)
entrenching shovel, M 1910 then M1943 (7 per 10 EM)

d) Officer (armed with a carbine)

gas mask M3-10A1-6 (then M3A1-10A1-6) replaced by M5-11-7 (from 12 September 1944)
canvas field bag, olive drab, M1936
pistol belt, M1936
1 magazine pocket for carbine, caliber .30, M1
canteen cover, dismounted, M1910
canteen, dismounted, M1910
carrying strap, GP (replaced carrying strap, canvas field bag, M1936)
belt suspenders, M1936
bayonet M4 with scabbard M8A1 (1 June 1945)

e) Officer (armed with a pistol)

gas mask M3-10A1-6 (then M3A1-10A1-6) replaced by M5-11-7 (from 12 September 1944)
canvas field bag, olive drab, M1936
pistol belt, M1936
1 magazine pocket, double web, EM, M1923
carrying strap, GP (replaced carrying strap, canvas field bag, M1936)
belt suspenders, M1936
canteen cover, dismounted, M1910
canteen, dismounted, M1910
bayonet M4 with scabbard M8A1 (1 June 1945)

10 – BAND

a) Enlisted man (armed with a carbine)

gas mask M3-10A1-6 (then M3A1-10A1-6) replaced by M5-11-7 (from 12 September 1944)
canvas field bag, olive drab, M1936
pistol belt, M1936
2 magazine pockets for carbine, caliber .30, M1
canteen cover, dismounted, M1910
canteen, dismounted, M1910
carrying strap, GP (replaced carrying strap, canvas field bag, M1936)
belt suspenders, M1936
canvas muzzle cover, rifle or carbine
entrenching axe, M1910, with handle (1 per 10 EM)
entrenching pick mattock, M1910, with handle (2 per 10 EM)
entrenching shovel, M 1910 then M1943 (7 per 10 EM)

b) Warrant Officer (armed with a carbine)

gas mask M3-10A1-6 (then M3A1-10A1-6) replaced by M5-11-7 (from 12 September 1944)
canvas field bag, olive drab, M1936
pistol belt, M1936
2 magazine pockets for carbine, caliber .30, M1
canteen cover, dismounted, M1910
canteen, dismounted, M1910
carrying strap, GP (replaced carrying strap, canvas field bag, M1936)
belt suspenders, M1936.

Changes in Equipment

The haversack M1928 and the pack carrier M1928 were replaced progressively from September 1944 by:
field pack, combat
field pack, cargo
field pack suspenders, cargo and combat. In the military police platoon (T/O&E 19-7, C1 dated 15 March 1945), the field packs, cargo and combat replaced not only the haversack M1928, but also the canvas field bag M1936 for officers.

The magazine pocket, carbine, caliber .30, M1 was replaced from December 1944 by:
cartridge pocket, caliber .30, M1, carbine or rifle.

The T/O&Es that gave these changes were:
>   5-16, Headquarters & Headquarters & Service Company, Engineer Combat Battalion, C2 dated 2 August 1944 to the T/O&E 5-16 dated 13 March 1944
>   7-2, Headquarters Company, Infantry Division, 13 January 1945
>   7-16, Headquarters & Headquarters Company, Infantry Battalion, C2 dated 19 February 1945 to the T/O&E 7-16 dated 26 February 1944
>   7-17, Infantry Rifle Company, C2 dated 30 January 1945 to the T/O&E 7-17 dated 26 February 1944
>   7-19, Infantry Antitank Company, 29 January 1945
>   8-17, Collecting Company, Medical Battalion, 14 February 1945
>   8-18, Clearing Company, Medical Battalion, 14 February 1945
>   9-8, Ordnance Light Maintenance Company, 17 November 1944
>   19-7, Military Police Platoon, Infantry Division, C1 dated 15 March 1945 to the T/O&E 19-7 dated 12 September 1944.

After June 1945, the officers, like the soldiers, were issued with the following equipment:
>   field pack, combat, M1945
>   field pack, cargo, M1945
>   field pack suspenders, cargo and combat
>   carrying strap, GP
>   cartridge pocket, caliber .30, M1, carbine or rifle (individual armed with a rifle or a carbine)
>   1 magazine pocket, double web, EM, M1923 (individual armed with a pistol)
>   canteen cover, dismounted, M1910 (including the Cavalry and the Armored Forces)
>   pistol belt, M1936 (per individual armed with a carbine)
>   cartridge belt, caliber .30, dismounted, M1923 (per individual armed with a rifle)

The T/O&Es that gave these changes were:
>   7-2, Headquarters Company, Infantry Division, C2 dated 6 June 1945 to the T/O&E 7-2 dated 13 January 1945
>   2-27, Cavalry Reconnaissance Troop, Mechanized, 16 June 1945
>   11-7-OS, Signal Company, Infantry Division, C4 dated 3 December 1945 to the T/O&E 11-7 dated 11 December 1943.

On the other hand, the T/O&E 10-17, Quartermaster Company, Infantry Division, dated 1 June 1945 gave the same equipment as above but with the Field Pack, Cargo and Combat, M1944.

The T/O&Es dated 1 June 1945 concerned the reorganization of the infantry divisions for redeployment against Japan. The units were authorized by the War Department to be reorganized under these tables only in October 1945. On the other hand, the new equipment listed in the changes dated June 1945, to the T/O&Es published before those of 1 June 1945, were sometimes issued to units before the end of the war against Japan.

When the tables gave as individual equipment the Field Pack, Cargo and Combat, the following remark appeared:
>   "the Haversack M1928 and the Pack Carrier M1928 will be issued in replacement, until exhausted" (T/O&E 5-16, C1 dated 2 August 1944; T/O&E 8-18, 14 February 1945; T/O&E 7-2 dated 13 January 1945).

When the equipment was the Field Pack, Cargo and Combat M1945, it was specified:
>   "the Field Pack, Cargo and Combat will be issued in replacement, until exhausted; then in pending the availability the Field Bag, Canvas M1936, with Suspenders, or the Haversack M1928 and the Pack Carrier M1928 will be issued." (T/O&E 2-27, 16 June 1945; T/O&E 7-2 dated 13 January 1945, C2 dated 6 June 1945).

The T/O&Es are given in this chapter as examples and are not an exhaustive list.

Equipment was issued following a priority order. The units with highest priority were issued with equipment before those units with a lower priority, even if they were both organized under the same T/O&E. A unit from an infantry division could receive the equipment as soon as it was available (for new equipment); the same type of unit in another division could be issued with it some weeks later.

9.4 CLOTHING AND SMALL EQUIPMENT

This section lists clothing and small items of individual equipment. The changes that occurred during the war to the lists of equipment, including those authorized by the Theater of Operations, were numerous and not all are mentioned in this study. Instead, it has been decided to provide a list corresponding to those for the European Theater of Operations (ETO) on 1 January 1945.

The numbers in parenthesis indicate the part of the equipment that was to be carried in the duffel bag. The stock numbers are mentioned for information, they could vary according to the quartermaster catalogue, particularly that dated 1 May 1946.

A – ENLISTED MAN

a) Items issued for overseas duty in temperate zones:
>   1 helmet, steel, M1, complete:
>   Band, head, liner, helmet, M1 (stock no. 74-B-59)
>   Band, neck, liner, helmet, M1 (74-B-61-64-B-53)
>   Helmet, steel, M1 (74-H-120)

Liner, helmet, M1 (74-L-72-30)
1 Release, chinstrap, T-1 (74-R-40)
1 belt, web, waist (73-B-5117 – 73-B-5140)
1 cap, field, cotton, olive drab (73-C-16010 – 73-C-16035), replaces cap, wool, knit
1 Gloves, wool, leather palm, replace wool gloves (73-G-43860 – 73-G-43875)
3 (1) Undershirts, wool, 2 may be replaced by cotton undershirts) (55-U-7766 – 55-U-7790)
3 (1) drawers, wool, 2 may be replaced by cotton drawers) (55-D-526 – 55-D-535)
3 (1) Socks, wool, cushion sole (73-S-31824 – 73-S-31840)
2 (2) Socks, wool, light (73-S-33221 – 73-S-33229)
4 handkerchiefs, cotton (73-H-3880)
2 (1) Shirts, flannel, OD, coat-style (55-S-5500-2 – 55-S-5517-4)
2 (1) Neckties, cotton, mohair, khaki (73-N-120) replaced the cotton khaki necktie which was issued until exhausted
2 (1) Trousers, wool, OD (55-T-82005 – 55-T-82267-30)
1 Jacket, field, M1943 (55-J-190 – 55-J-192-98) replaced the Field jacket, OD, (M1941) (55-J-210 – 55-J-300) which was issued until exhausted
1 Hood, jacket, field, M1943, issued only with the Field jacket M1943 (73-H-66815, large; 73-H-66817, medium; 73-H-66819, small)
1 (1) Raincoat, rubberized, M1938, dismounted (72-R-3435 – 72-R-3450)
1 Poncho, lightweight, OD (issued to replace the raincoat when authorized by the War Department) (72-P-9780)
1 Sweater, high neck (55-S-64237, large; 55-S-64241, medium; 55-S-64245, small; 55-S-64249, X-large)
1 (1) Overcoat, wool, melton, OD (55-O-8900 – 55-O-9115)
2 boots, service, combat (72-B-2740-20 – 72-B-2746-41) replaced 2 shoes, service, combat (72-S-2225-35 – 72-S-2248-65) and 1 leggings M1938, dismounted, OD (72-L-61920 – 72-L-61929)
1 (1) jacket, Herringbone twill (HBT)(55-J-420 – 55-J-494) (if authorized by the Commander of the Theater of Operations)
1 Bag, duffel (replaces the bag, barrack, for overseas) (74-B-54-55)
1 Bag, sleeping, wool (27-B-317) (2 wool blankets, M1934 could be issued when the sleeping bag is not available) (27-B-678)
1 Case, water repellent, bag, sleeping (27-C-123)
1 Can, meat (aluminium, 74-C-62; stainless steel, 74-C-66)
1 Canteen, M 1910 (aluminium, 74-C-80; stainless steel, 74-C-87)
1 Cup, canteen (aluminium, 74-C-314; stainless steel, 74-C-317-25) listed only from 1 September 1945, and only for the combat units.
1 Fork, M1926 (74-F-63)
1 Knife, M1926 (74-K-60)
1 Necklace, identification tag, with extension (74-N-300)
5 Pins, tent, shelter, wood (74-P-125)
3 Poles, tent, single section (tent pole in three sections, the pole in a single section was to be issued until exhausted) (74-P-230)
1 Pouch, first-aid packet (74-P-260)
1 Spoon, M1926 (74-S-312)
2 Tag, identification (74-T-60)
1 Tent, shelter, half (74-T-100, model with one triangular end, limited standard in May 1946; 74-T-102, model with two triangular ends.

The following items were issued only upon enlistment, they were not replaced unless if lost or destroyed without fault of their owner:
1 Brush, shaving
1 Brush, tooth
1 Comb, rubber or plastic
1 Razor, safety, with 5 blades
2 (1) Towel, bath (27-T-28590)

b) Items issued by decision of the Commander of the Theater of Operations, temperate zone
1 Bag, barrack, OD (replaced by the duffel bag for overseas duty; if the bag, barrack was issued with the duffel bag it was for use as a dirty clothing bag)
2 Blankets, wool, OD, M1934 (27-B-678)
1 Cap, winter, OD (73-C-64286 – 73-C-64302, limited standard on 1 August 1943, issued until exhausted)
1 Gloves, leather, heavy (73-G-30500, large; 73-G-30508, medium)
2 Drawers, cotton, short (55-D-400 – 55-D-412)
2 Undershirts, cotton (55-U-3782 – 55-U-3800)
2 Socks, wool, heavy (73-S-32176 – 73-S-32192)
1 Overshoes, artic, cloth-top (72-O-450 – 72-O-472, replaced in March 1945, by overshoes M1945, 72-O-625 – 72-O-635)

1 Cap, garrison, OD (73-C-18170 – 73-C-18194)

1 Insignia, collar, EM

1 Insignia, collar, "US", EM

1 Jacket, field, wool, OD ("Ike" jacket) (55-J-384-510 – 55-J-384-940). The Coat, wool, serge, OD, (55-C-69299 – 55-C-69510) was to be issued until exhausted excepting another decision from the War Department. When the wool field jacket was issued the wool coat had to be returned.

1 (1) Trousers, Herringbone Twill (if authorised by the Commander of the Theater of Operations) (55-T-38001-78 – 55-T-38108-10)

1 Cap, Herringbone Twill (if authorised by the Commander of the Theater of Operations) (73-C-25605 – 73-C-25639)

c) Equipment by specialty:

The personnel listed below were issued, in addition to the equipment from the 'a' list, with:

Cooks:

    2 Towels, bath

Enlisted men in the Signal Corps, except mechanics:

    1 Coat, mackinaw, OD (55-C-33090-55-C-33190)

Mechanics:

    1 Coat, mackinaw, OD

    1 Gloves, inserts, wool (73-G-55005, large; 73-G-55010, medium; 73-G-55015, small)

    1 Gloves-shells, leather (73-G-55755, large; 73-G-55760, medium; 73-G-55765, small)

Drivers, except mechanics:

    1 Gloves, inserts, wool

    1 Gloves-shells, leather

Military Police:

    2 Gloves, cotton, white (73-G-12338 – 73-G-12559)

    1 Jacket, Herringbone twill (except MP mechanics who were issued with two)

    1 Trousers, Herringbone twill (2 per MP mechanics)

    1 Brassard, arm, MP

    1 Club, policeman, M1944 (41-C-2453, replaced the club, policeman 41-C-2450)

The following items were issued, in addition to those on list 'a', when authorized by the War Department, to the EM who performed guard or sentry duty, or who were regularly assigned as truck drivers of vehicles not equipped with enclosed cabs or equivalent.

1 Cap, field, pile, OD 73-C-16350 – 73-C-16375)

1 Mittens, insert, trigger-finger (if others were not authorized) (73-M-2705, large; 73-M-2710, medium; 73-M-2715, small; 73-M-2720, X-large)

1 Mittens, shell, trigger-finger (if others were not authorized) (73-M-3610)

1 Muffler, wool, OD (73-M-9010).

B – OFFICERS AND WARRANT OFFICERS

The officers and warrant officers were issued only a small part of their equipment by the War Department. They had to buy the greater proportion of it. This equipment is given in T/E 21, in two lists, allowances (mandatory and discretionary), and purchases (mandatory and optional). The second list, purchase, was for information only. It implied no obligation for the War Department to provide or to make available for purchase the items listed. A large part of the clothing of the officers and warrant officers was therefore purchased privately. The clothing for an officer was expensive and so, a second lieutenant or a warrant officer, junior grade, normally procured only the equipment strictly necessary for his service. Equipment normally was identical for both officers and warrant officers; where equipment differed, it is mentioned to whom it was intended.

a) Mandatory allowances for Officers and Warrant Officers

1 Cap, field, cotton, OD, with visor

1 helmet, steel, M1, complete:

Band, head, liner, helmet, M1

Band, neck, liner, helmet, M1

Helmet, steel, M1

Liner, helmet, M1

1 Release, chinstrap, T-1

1 Bag, duffel

1 Bag, sleeping, wool (2 wool blankets, M1934 could be issued when the sleeping bag was unavailable)

1 Case, water repellent, bag, sleeping

1 Can, meat

1 Canteen, M 1910

1 Cup, canteen

1 Fork, M1926

1 Knife, M1926

1 Necklace, identification tag, with extension
5 Pins, tent, shelter, wood
3 Poles, tent, single section
1 Pouch, first-aid packet
1 Roll, bedding, water-proofed, M1935
1 Spoon, M1926
2 Tag, identification
1 Tent, shelter, half

b) Discretionary allowances, if authorized by the Commander of the Theater of Operations, temperate zones:
2 Blankets, wool, M1934
1 Cap, winter, OD (until exhausted)
1 Overshoes, artic, cloth-top
1 Brassard, MP (Military Police units only)

c) Mandatory purchase (required)
1 belt, web, waist
2 boots, service, combat (replaced 2 shoes, service, combat and 1 leggings M1938, dismounted, OD)
1 Brush, clothes
1 Brush, hair
1 Brush, shaving
1 Brush, shoes
1 Brush, tooth
1 Cap, garrison, OD, Officer's
1 Coat, wool, service
1 Insignia, cap, Officer's
1 Insignia, cap, Warrant Officer's
1 Insignia, collar, US, Officer's
1 Insignia, collar, Officer's, Arm, Service
1 Insignia, collar, Warrant Officer's
1 Insignia, Officer's grade, metal
1 Insignia, shoulder sleeve
1 Jacket, field (Field jacket M1943 at this date)
1 laces, shoes, extra
1 Comb
1 Necktie, cotton, mohair, khaki
1 Razor, safety, with 5 blades
2 Towels, bath
2 Towels, face
2 Drawers, cotton, shorts
2 Drawers, wool
2 Undershirts, cotton
2 Undershirts, wool
2 Socks, wool, light or heavy
3 Socks, wool, cushion sole
2 Trousers, wool, service
2 Shirts, wool, OD
1 Book, memorandum, pocket, with pencil
1 Shoes, low quarter, tan
1 Shoes, service
1 Uniform, white (only as required outside continental U.S. for formal occasions)

d) Optional purchase
1 Cap, service, tropical worsted, khaki
1 Cap, service, wool, OD, dark, Officer's
1 Coat, tropical worsted, khaki
1 Gloves, O's, dress, chamois, colour
1 Overcoat, field, O's
1 Overcoat, wool, doeskin, OD, O's, short style
2 Pyjamas
1 Slippers
1 Trousers, tropical worsted, khaki, O's

9.5 ATTACHED UNITS

We have studied all organic units, i.e., those assigned to the infantry division. At the beginning of the book, it was said that the division was supported by attached units (see chart 1). These will not be studied in volume 1 at length, but some notes concerning them are included in this section.

The major attachments to an infantry division were:

1 Tank Battalion (T/O&E 17-25)
1 Tank Destroyer Battalion (T/O&E 18-25)
1 Anti Aircraft Artillery Battalion, Automatic Weapons (T/O&E 44-25).

Dependent upon combat requirements the division could receive the support of units from the corps or the army, i.e.:

Engineer Combat Battalions, Corps
Engineer Treadway Bridge Company
Engineer Group
Field Artillery Battalions (155mm, 8″, towed or self-propelled, etc.)
Cavalry Reconnaissance Squadron (Army)
Chemical Company
etc.

Any type of unit could be attached to the infantry division as support. Units of another division could be attached to the division, if they were in its area or if they were needed for a specific task or operation. In the same manner, the division could detach some of its units to reinforce another division. An infantry regiment could be attached to a combat command from an armored division, for example.

Attachments to the 5th Infantry Division

By way of example, some units attached to the 5th Infantry Division, with the dates of attachment, are given below. This list is not exhaustive.

735th Tank Battalion	from 13/07/44 to 20/10/44
737th Tank Battalion	from 23/12/44 to 11/06/45
818th Tank Destroyer Battalion	from 13/07/44 to 20/12/44
803rd Tank Destroyer Battalion	from 25/12/44 to 13/06/45
449th AAA AW Bn	from 13/07/44 to 23/11/44
187th Field Artillery Bn (155mm)	from 30/07/44 to 01/08/44
150th Engineer Combat Bn	from 09/08/44 to 13/08/44
1st Plat, 994th Engineer Tdwy Br Co	from 09/08/44 to 13/08/44
537th Engineer Light Pont Co	from 09/08/44 to 13/08/44
204th Field Artillery Battalion	from 09/08/44 to 13/08/44
CCB, 7th Armored Division	from 09/09/44 to 15/09/44
3rd Cav Rcn Squadron	from 11/09/44 to 14/09/44
84th Chemical Company (SG)	from 12/02/45 to 28/02/45

Units of the 5th Infantry Division Detached Provisionally

This list is not exhaustive.

Division Artillery attached to the 95th Inf Div	from 23/11/44 to 27/11/44
10th Infantry Regiment attached to the 4th Inf Div	from 22/12/44 to 24/12/44
5th Cav Rcn Troop attached to the 4th Inf Div	from 23/12/44 to 24/12/44
11th Infantry Regiment attached to the 4th Armored Div	from 8/03/45 to 11/03/45.

U.S. ARMY RANKS

Enlisted men's ranks during the Second World War were noticeably different than those of today. Officer ranks are identical. Warrant officer ranks are not only different, but today four ranks exist instead of two during WWII.

Pay grades ranged from 1 to 7, with 1 being the highest (the opposite of today). Pay grade 7, private, did not wear insignia.

In 1941, the rank of first sergeant was rated pay grade 2, the same as that of technical sergeant. Technician ranks did not exist, and the only warrant officers ranks in the army were those of the Army Mine Planter Service (six grades).

Army Regulation AR 630-35, dated 4 September 1942, made effective the following changes:

warrant officer ranks were created for all arms other than for the Mine Planter Service

technicians ranks were created. There were three grades: 3rd, 4th and 5th, which corresponded to the pay grades of the enlisted men. The difference between the technician ranks and the other ranks related to a command, in that the other ranks were attached to a command, whereas technician ranks were without a command.

Army Regulation AR-600-35, dated 31 March 1944, made effective the following change:

the rank of first sergeant became grade 1, as with the rank of master sergeant, and was rated higher than that of technical sergeant.

ENLISTED MEN RANKS

Rank	Abbreviation	
	WWII	Modern
Private	Pvt	PVT
Private First Class	Pfc	PFC
Corporal	Cpl	CPL
Sergeant	Sgt	SGT
Staff Sergeant	S Sgt	SSG
Technical Sergeant	Tech Sgt	SFC†
First Sergeant	1st Sgt	1SG
Master Sergeant	Mr Sgt	MSG

† The rank of technical sergeant no longer exists. It has been replaced by that of sergeant first class (SFC), or platoon sergeant (PSG); these ranks have retained the wartime insignia of technical sergeant.

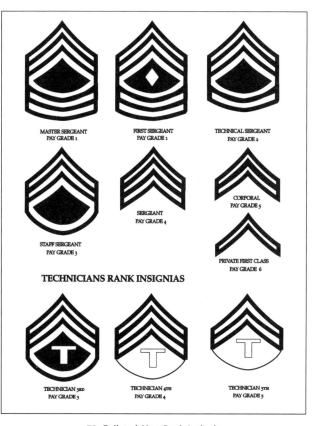

72. Enlisted Men Rank Insignia

OFFICER AND WARRANT OFFICER RANKS

Rank	Abbreviation	
	WWII	Modern
Chief Warrant Officer	CWO	CW (2/3/4)
Warrant Officer (Junior Grade)	WOJG	WO1

Warrant officer ranks were specialists' ranks, similar to technicians' ranks. A warrant officer did not have a command; he could supervise an administrative or technical section, under the control of an officer.

Rank	Abbreviation	
	WWII	Modern
Second Lieutenant	2nd Lt.	2LT
First Lieutenant	1st Lt.	1LT
Captain	Capt.	CPT
Major	Maj.	MAJ
Lieutenant Colonel	Lt. Col.	LTC
Colonel	Col.	COL
Brigadier general	Brig. Gen.	BG
Major general	Maj. Gen.	MG
Lieutenant general	Lt. Gen.	LTG
General	Gen.	GEN

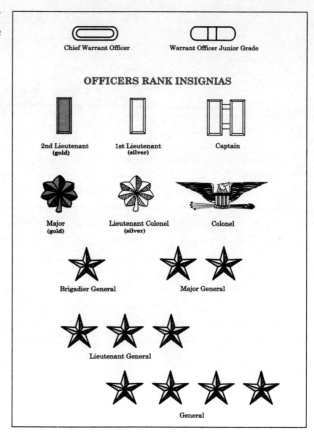

73. Officer and Warrant Officer Ranks

U.S. ARMY UNIT SYMBOLS

U.S.ARMY UNIT SYMBOLS

WWII	Today	WWII	Today
Unit		O Ordnance	
Infantry		Q Quartermaster	
Cavalry		MP Military Police	MP
E Engineers	⊓	Medical	
● Artillery	●	Tank, Armored	
S Signal		TD Tank Destroyer	
Antiaircraft Artillery		Band Band	

UNIT SIZE SYMBOLS

XXXX Army
XXX Army Corps
XX Division

III Regiment
II Battalion or Squadron*
I Company or Troop*

••• Platoon
•• Section
• Squad

X Brigade or Combat Command
Headquarters or small unit

* In Cavalry

74. Organization chart symbols

U.S. ARMY ABBREVIATIONS
SECOND WORLD WAR

AA	Anti-aircraft		CCA	Combat Command A
AAF	Army Air Forces		CCB	Combat Command B
AB	Airborne Division		CCR	Combat Command R
Abn	Airborne		CE	Corps of Engineers
AC	Air Corps		Cen	Center
AD	Armored Division		CG	Commanding General
Adj	Adjutant		Ch	Chaplain
Adm	Administration		Clk	Clerk
Adv	Advance		Clr	Clearing
AEB	Armored Engineer Bn		Cn	Cannon
AFAB	Armored Field Arty Bn		Co	Company
AG	Adjutant General		CO	Commanding Officer
AGF	Army Ground Forces		Col	Colonel
AIB	Armored Infantry Bn		COL	Colonel (modern)
Am	Ammunition		Coll	Collecting
AP	Airplane		Com	Communication
AR	Army Reserve		Comd	Command
Armd Div	Armored Division		Comdr	Commander
Armd	Armored		Comdt	Commandant
Armr	Armorer		Cons	Construction
Artif	Artificer		CP	Command Post
Arty	Artillery		Cpl	Corporal
ASF	Army Service Forces		Cptr	Carpenter
Asst	Assistant		CRS	Cavalry Reconnaissance Squadron
AT	Anti-tank		CSCG	Command and General Staff College
AUS	Army of the U.S.A		CSI	Combat Studies Institute
Auto	Automatic, Automobile (Automotive)		DA	Department of the Army (post-WWII)
AW	Automatic Weapons		DC	Dental Corps
BAR	Browning Automatic Rifle		Dent	Dental
Bde	Brigade		Det	Detachment
BG	Brigadier General (modern)		Div	Division
Bglr	Bugler		DOD	Department of Defense (post-WWII)
Bn	Battalion		DP	Distribution Point
Brig. Gen.	Brigadier General		Drftm	Draftsman
Bsc	Basic		DSC	Distinguished Service Cross
Btry	Battery		DSO	Distinguished Service Order
CofS	Chief of Staff		ECB	Engineer Combat Battalion
Cal.	Caliber		Ech	Echelon
CAPT	Captain (modern)		EM	Enlisted Man
Capt	Captain		Engr	Engineers
Carr	Carrier		Engr Cbt Bn	Engineer Combat Bn
Cav	Cavalry		ESB	Engineer Special Brigade
Cbt	Combat		ETO	European Theater of Operations

ETOUSA	European Theater of Operations U.S. Army		Maj.	Major
Ex-O	Executive Officer		Maj. Gen.	Major General
FA	Field Artillery		MC	Medical Corps
FA Bn	Field Artillery Battalion		Mech	Mechanic
Fld	Field		Mech	Mechanized (modern)
FM	Field Manual		Mecz	Mechanized
FO	Field orders		Med	Medical
FUSA	First US Army		Msgr	Messenger
FUSAG	First US Army Group		MG	Major General (modern)
Fwd	Forward		MG	Machine Gun
G-1	As S-1 but for a General Staff		MIA	Missing in Action
G-2	As S-2 but for a General Staff		MLR	Main Line of Resistance
G-3	As S-3 but for a General Staff		Mort	Mortar
G-4	As S-4 but for a General Staff		MOS	Military Occupational Specialty
Gen.	General (4 and 5 stars)		Mr Sgt	Master Sergeant
GEN	General (modern)		Msg	Message
Gen	General		Msg Cen	Message Center
GHQ	General Headquarters		Mtd	Mounted
Gldr	Glider		MTOUSA	Mediterranean Theater of Operations US Army
Gnr	Gunner		Mtr	Motor
Gp	Group		Mtz	Motorized
HB	Heavy Barrel (caliber .50, AA)		Mun	Munition
HE	High Explosive		NARA	National Archives and Record Administration
HHB	Headquarters and Headquarters Battery (modern)		NATO	North Africa Theater of Operations
HHC	Headquarters and Headquarters Company (modern)		NATOUSA	North Africa Theater of Operations US Army
			NCO	Non Commissioned Officer
HHD	Headquarters and Headquarters Detachment (modern)		NCS	Net Control Station
			NG	National Guard
Hosp	Hospital		NUSA	Ninth US Army
How	Howitzer		O	Officer, Order
Hq	Headquarters		O's	Officers, Orders
Hq&Hq Co	Headquarters and Headquarters Company		Obsvn	Observation
Hv	Heavy		Obsvr	Observer
ID	Infantry Division		OCMH	Office of the Chief of the Center of Military History, US Army
Inf	Infantry			
Instr	Instrument		OCS	Officer Candidate School
Int	Intelligence		Odly	Orderly
Intel	Intelligence (modern)		Off	Officer
IR	Infantry Regiment		OP	Observation Post
KIA	Killed in Action		Opns	Operations
LD	Line of Departure		Opr	Operator
Ldr	Leader		OR	Organized Reserves
LMG	Light Machine Gun		Ord	Ordnance
Lmn	Lineman		OSS	Office of Strategic Services
Ln O	Liaison Officer		PE	Port of Embarkation
Lt Col	Lieutenant Colonel		Pers	Personnel
Lt. Gen.	Lieutenant General		Pion	Pioneer
LTC	Lieutenant Colonel (modern)		Plat	Platoon
LTG	Lieutenant General (modern)		POL	Petrol Oil Lubricant
M	Model		Prcht	Parachute
MAC	Medical Administrative Corps		PTO	Pacific Theater of Operations
Maint	Maintenance		Pvt	Private
MAJ	Major (modern)		QM	Quartermaster

QMC	Quartermaster Corps		Sup	Supply
R	Rifle		Surg	Surgeon
RA	Regular Army		Sv	Service
Rad	Radio		SWP	South West Pacific
Rad Opr	Radio Operator		SWPA	South West Pacific Area (Command)
Rcd	Record		T	Transportation, Transport
Rcn	Reconnaissance		T/A	Table of Allowances
RCT	Regimental Combat Team		T/BA	Table of Basic Allowances
Recon	Reconnaissance (modern)		T/E	Table of Equipment
Regtl	Regimental		T/O	Table of Organization
Repl	Replacement		T/O&E	Table of Organization and Equipment
Ret	Retired		TBn	Tank Battalion
Rgt	Regiment		TC	Transportation Corps
ROTC	Replacement Officers' Training Center		TD	Tank Destroyer
Rr	Rear		Tech	Technical
RTC	Replacement Training Center		Techn	Technician
S Sgt	Staff Sergeant		TF	Task Force
S-1	Assistant Chief of Staff for Personnel		Tg	Telegraph
S-2	Assistant Chief of Staff for Intelligence		Tk	Tank
S-3	Assistant Chief of Staff for Operations and Training		TM	Technical Manual
			Tng	Training
S-4	Assistant Chief of Staff for Supply		TOT	Time Over Target
Sb	Switchboard		Tp	Telephone
SC	Signal Corps		Tr	Troop
SCR	Signal Corps Radio		Trans	Transportation
Sct	Scout		Trk	Truck
Sec	Section		Trl	Trailer
Sect	Section		TUSA	Third US Army
Serv	Service		US	United States
Sgt	Sergeant		USA	United States Army
Sgt Maj	Sergeant Major		USAFET	United States Army Forces European Theater
SHAEF	Supreme Headquarters Allied Expeditionary Forces		USFET	United States Forces European Theater (1945)
			USMHI	United States Army Military History Institute
Sig	Signal		Vis	Visual
SG	Smoke Generator		WAC	Women's Army Corps
SMG	Submachine Gun		WC	Weapons Carrier
Sn	Sanitary		WD	War Department
SNL	Standard Nomenclature List		WIA	Wounded in Action
SOP	Standing Operating Procedure		Wldr	Welder
SOS	Service of Supply		WO	Warrant Officer
SP	Self Propelled		WP	White Phosphorus (Willy Peter)
Sp	Special		Wpn	Weapons
Sqd	Squad		XO	Executive Officer (modern)
SSG	Staff Sergeant (modern)		1LT	First Lieutenant (modern)
SSN	Specification Serial Number		1st Lt	First Lieutenant
St	Staff		1st Sgt	First Sergeant
Sta	Station		2nd Lt	Second Lieutenant
Stf	Staff		2nd-in-Comd	Second in Command

EXAMPLE OF CASUALTIES AND REPLACEMENTS IN AN INFANTRY REGIMENT
– 10TH INFANTRY REGIMENT

Unit or standard T/O&E	Date	Replacements and returns from hospital	Losses	Officers	Warrant Officers	Enlisted Men
Inf Regt T/O&E	26/02/44			152	5	3100
10th Inf Regt	10/07/44			152	5	3029
	from 10/07/44 to 23/07/44		KIA	1		15
			WIA	2		81
			MIA			1
			non-combat			15
	from 14 to 23/07	Replacements				4
	25/07/44	Replacements				72
	from 26/07/44 to 29/07/44		KIA	1		77
			WIA	23		323
			MIA			35
	Total July		KIA	2		92
			WIA	25		398
			MIA			37
10th Inf Regt	31/07/44			130	5	2596
	31/07/44	Replacements		5		130
10th Inf Regt	01/08/44			135	5	2772
	10/08/44		KIA	1		16
			WIA	3		10
			MIA			6
	from 01/08/44 to 31/08/44		KIA	3		43
			WIA	10		230
			MIA			10
	31/08/44	Replacements		37	1	631
10th Inf Regt	31/08/44			151	4	2867
Inf Regt T/O&E	30/06/44			153	5	3049
	from 10 to 16/09	Casualties	Total	24		674
	from 17/09/44 to 23/09/44		KIA	8		35
			WIA	6		430
			MIA	12		250
			non-combat	8		211
	23/09/44	Returns from hospital		1		89
	09/44	Replacements		67		1775
10th Inf Regt	23/09/44			141	4	2659
	from 24/09/44 to 30/09/44		KIA	1		11
			WIA	8		90
			MIA			53
			non-combat	4		88
10th Inf Regt	30/09/44			153	4	3110
			KIA			13
			WIA	6		141
			MIA	2		88
	21/10/44	Replacements and returns from hospital		16		358

Unit or standard T/O&E	Date	Replacements and returns from hospital	Losses	Officers	Warrant Officers	Enlisted Men
10th Inf Regt	21/10/44			156	4	3057
	Recapitulation –		KIA	20		279
	from 14/07/44 to		WIA	66		1593
	21/10/44		MIA	11		400
			non-combat	21		613
10th Inf Regt	01/11/44			155	4	3051
	30/11/44		KIA	4		24
			WIA	13		377
			MIA	1		147
	30/11/44	Replacements		41		790
	30/11/44	Returns from hospital –387, included in above				
10th Inf Regt	30/11/44			161	4	2693
	31/12/44		KIA	4		72
			WIA	20		409
			MIA	4		83
	31/12/44	Replacements		31		1153
	31/12/44	Returns from hospital –306, included in above				
10th Inf Regt	31/12/44			160	4	3003
	31/01/45		KIA	2		43
			WIA	10		225
			MIA	3		75
		Replacements and returns from hospital	Total	256		
10th Inf Regt	31/01/45			154	4	2933
	End of February 1945		KIA	3		30
			WIA	12		286
			MIA			138
	End of March 1945		KIA	total	34	O+EM
			WIA	total	162	O+EM
			MIA	total	42	O+EM
	End of April 1945		KIA	total	13	O+EM
			WIA	total	58	O+EM
			MIA	total	19	O+EM
Total Casualties	from 14/07/44 to 08/05/45		KIA	30		667
			WIA	130		3088
			MIA	22		668
			Total	182		4423
			Total Combat	O+EM		4605
			non-combat	O+EM		2519
Grand Total of Casualties	from 14/07/44 to 08/05/45	combat and non-combat		O+EM		7124
	from 14/07/44 to 08/05/45	Total replacements		189		4223
	from 14/07/44 to 08/05/45	Total returns from hospital		80		2326

This table has been realized from data given in *History of the Tenth Infantry Regiment in WWII*, Public Relations Section, Tenth Infantry Regiment (The Battery Press, Nashville, TN). Some incongruities between the total strength by the month end and the monthly account of losses and replacements was noticed. However, it was preferred to keep the data as given in the unit history, as this certainly came from After Action Reports (AAR), rather than to modify them to give a perfect arithmetic result. The numbers for month ends, which are the official account of the regiment's strength from the AAR, are correct. From August to December the numbers were taken from the After Action Reports of the 10th Infantry Regiment.

APPENDIX V

ORGANIZATION OF THE 5TH INFANTRY DIVISION ON 6 JUNE 1944

Organization	T/O&E	Date	Change	Date
Cavalry Rcn Troop, Mecz	2-27	15 July 43	1	15 Sept 43
Engineer Combat Bn	5-15	15 July 43		
Hq & Hq & Sv Co, Engr Bn	5-16	15 July 43		
Engineer Combat Company	5-17	15 July 43		
Div Arty, Motor, Inf Div	6-10	15 July 43	1	9 Oct 43
	2	27 Jan 44		
Hq & Hq Btry, Div Arty	6-10-1	15 July 43	1	9 Oct 43
			2	27 Jan 44
			3	17 Mar 44
FA Bn, Motor, 105mm How	6-25	15 July 43	1	7 Oct 43
			2	4 Feb 44
Hq & Hq Btry, FA Bn, 105	6-26	15 July 43	2	4 Feb 44
			3	17 Mar 44
FA Btry, FA Bn, 105mm	6-27	15 July 43	1	20 Oct 43
			2	4 Nov 43
Serv Btry, FA Bn, 105mm	6-29	15 July 43	1	13 Oct 43
			2	4 Feb 44
FA Bn, Motor, 155mm How	6-335	3 July 43	1	14 Aug 43
			2	4 Dec 43
			3	18 Feb 44
Hq & Hq Btry, FA Bn, 155	6-36	15 July 43	1	14 Aug 43
			2	23 Oct 43
			3	29 Nov 43
			4	6 Feb 44
			5	17 Mar 44
FA Btry, FA Bn, 155mm	6-337	3 July 43	1	10 Dec 43
Serv Btry, FA Bn, 155mm	6-339	3 July 43	1	17 Dec 43
Infantry Division	7	15 July 43	1	3 Sept 43
Hq, Infantry Division	7-1	15 July 43	1	13 Oct 43
Hq Co, Infantry Division	7-2	15 July 43	1	25 Aug 43
			2	13 Oct 43
			3	5 Jan 44
Special Troops, Inf Div	7-3	15 July 43	1	25 Aug 43
			2	7 Sept 43
			3	13 Oct 43
			4	5 Jan 44
Infantry Regiment	7-11	26 Feb 44		
Hq & Hq Co, Inf Regt	7-12	26 Feb 44		
Service Co, Inf Regt	7-13	26 Feb 44		
Inf Cannon Co, Inf Regt	7-14	26 Feb 44		
Infantry Battalion	7-15	26 Feb 44		
Hq & Hq Co, Inf Bn	7-16	26 Feb 44		
Infantry Rifle Company	7-17	26 Feb 44		
Heavy Weapons Company	7-18	26 Feb 44		
Inf AT Co, 57mm gun	7-19	26 Feb 44		
Medical Battalion	8-15	15 July 43	1	3 Sept 43
Hq & Hq Det, Med Bn	8-16	15 July 43	1	3 Sept 43
			2	4 Dec 43
Collecting Co, Med Bn	8-17	15 July 43	1	3 Sept 43
			2	13 Sept 43

Organization	T/O&E	Date	Change	Date
Clearing Co, Med Bn	8-18	15 July 43	1	17 Jan 44
Ordnance LM Co, Inf Div	9-8	15 July 43	1	14 Oct 43
QM Co, Inf Div	10-17	19 Feb 44		
Signal Co, Inf Div	11-7	11 Dec 43		
MP Platoon, Inf Div	19-7	15 July 43	1	10 Dec 43
			2	10 Feb 44

Source: Headquarters 5th Infantry Division, APO 5, U.S. Army, 6 June 1944 (list of the T/O&Es under of which the 5th Infantry Division was organized at this date).

5TH INFANTRY DIVISION "RED DIAMOND" 1944–1945

5th INFANTRY DIVISION HEADQUARTERS

Division Commander
Maj Gen Stafford LeRoy Irwin (03/07/43)
Maj Gen Albert E. Brown (21/04/45)

Assistant Division Commander
Brig Gen Alan D. Warnock (20/11/42)

Chief of Staff
Col. Paul O. Franson

G-1
Lt Col Hugh J. Socks
Lt Col Clayton E. Crafts

Assistant G-1
Capt Bernard Fisher

G-2
Lt Col Donald W. Thackeray

Assistant G-2
Major Thomas C. McGuire

G-3
Lt Col Randolph C. Dickens

Assistant G-3
Lt Col George K. Moody
Major Paul H. Vanderheiden

Assistant (Air)
Capt Adolph D. Katz

G-4
Lt Col Richard L. McKee

Assistant G-4
Major Ralph L. Norling

Adjutant General
Lt Col Charles H. Conway

Assistant Adjutant General	Major Elmer L. Lawson
Chemical Officer	Lt Col Levin B. Cottingham
Quartermaster Officer	Lt Col Daniel R. Taylor
Assistant Quartermaster Officer	Capt Robert A. Bagley
Ordnance Officer	Lt Col Burns C. Cox
Assistant Ordnance Officer	Major Robert H. Dietz
Signal Officer	Lt Col David P. Gibba
	Major John T. Newman (20/02/45)
Assistant Signal Officer	Capt John F. Jenkins
Provost Marshal	Major James C. Couty
Divisional Surgeon	Lt Col Enos G. Walker
Judge Advocate	Lt Col Edward S. Hemphill
Finance Officer	Lt Col Arthur B. Dwinnell
Inspector General	Lt Col Dewey B. Gill
	Lt Col Clarence J. Nelson (20/02/45)
	Lt Col Robert F. Bates (24/03/45)
Military Government	Lt Col E. B. Peddy
Assistant Military Government	Major Henry N. Hooper
	Major John H. Hudspeth
	Major John H. Vincent
Medical Inspector	Major Marcus H. Sugarman
Dental Surgeon	Major William A. Kneedler
Neuro-Psychiatrist	Major Harry D. Nesmith
Special Service Officer	Major Robert J. Malcolm
Public Relations Officer	Capt Alexander B. Campbell (10/11/44)
Chaplain	Lt Col Clarence F. Golisch

5th SPECIAL TROOPS

DIVISION HEADQUARTERS COMPANY
Company Commander
Maj John C. Ohaver

5th QUARTERMASTER COMPANY
Company Commander
Capt Ralph F. Kubal

5th SIGNAL COMPANY
Company Commander
Capt Joseph W. Kohnstamm
Wire Officer
1st Lt Jack Morril

705th ORDNANCE COMPANY
Company Commander
Capt Sylvester W. Banaszak
1st Lt Robert P. Ritter (07/10/44)
Capt Max D. Thomason (07/11/44)
1st Lt Robert P. Ritter (16/05/45)

5th MILITARY POLICE PLATOON
Platoon Commander
Maj James C. Couty

5th DIVISION ARTILLERY

Division Artillery Commander
Brig Gen Harold A. Vanderveer (08/09/42)
Executive Officer
Col Samuel W. Horner II
General's Aide
Capt John Twist
S-3
Lt Col Otto (08/44)
Air Officer
Maj Strunk

19th FIELD ARTILLERY BATTALION
(Direct Support 11th Infantry)

Battalion Commander
Lt Col Charles J. Payne
Executive Officer
Maj Eldon B. Colegrove
S-3
Capt Frakes
Liaison Officers
Capt Eldon B. Colegrove
Capt Larson (LnO1)
Capt Spiller (LnO2)
Capt Schaibley (LnO3)
Forward Observers
1st Lt Brensen
1st Lt Reiss (B Btry)
1st Lt Neal Greer (C Btry)

MEDICAL DETACHMENT
Capt Frederick P. McIntyre, MD (TDY 09/44)

21ST FIELD ARTILLERY BATTALION
(General Support, 155mm)

Battalion Commander
Lt Col Robert L. Brunzell
Lt Col Charles P. Baerman (07/10/44)
Executive Officer
Lt Col Charles P. Baerman (→07/10/44)
S-3
Maj Marcus W. (Bill) Braatz

Forward Observers
2nd Lt Gordon S. Henry*
1st Lt Holden
Techn 4th George Bachman (Radio operator)
Liaison Pilot
1st Lt Sorenson (→03/45)

46TH FIELD ARTILLERY BATTALION
(Direct Support 10th Infantry)

Battalion Commander
Lt Col James R. Johnson
Lt Col Robert L. Brunzell (09/10/44)
Maj Charles R. Ballou (WIA 28/12/44)
Lt Col B. B. Blank (29/12/44)
Executive-Officer
Maj Conde (KIA 28/12/44)
Maj R. C. Canaday (29/12/44)
S-3
Capt Frank Woodin (11/44) (Maj)
Liaison Officer
Capt George S. Polich (LnO1)
Capt John L. Lynch (LnO2)
Forward Observer
1st Lt Chester E. Ball (SilS, BrzS&CL&V, PH&2CL)
1st Lt George Dutko (1st Bn/10th)
Capt Dale W. Baughman (3rd/10th)
1st Lt Dmohoski (WIA)
Techn 4th Melillo (Radio operator)
1st Lt Budziak (MIA)
Radio Sergeant
S Sgt Robert H. Duffy
Liaison Pilots
1st Lt Robert Tedd
1st Lt Thomas Thompson

"B" FIELD ARTILLERY BATTERY
Forward Observer
2nd Lt George G. Klein

MEDICAL DETACHMENT
Capt Frederick P. McIntyre, MD (11/44)

50TH FIELD ARTILLERY BATTALION
(Direct Support 2nd Infantry)

Battalion Commander
Lt Col William R. Calhoun*
Executive Officer
Maj Joseph P. Muliolis
Battalion Sergeant Major
Mr Sgt Herman

S-1	Capt Lacey
S-2	Capt Jean W. Christy
S-3	Capt Paul A. Rennord (Maj)
Asst S-3	Capt Frank Woodin (→11/44)*
S-4	Capt George Lentz
Asst S-4	WO Flummerfelt (Air Observer)

Liaison Officers
Capt Herman Jost (1/2nd Inf)
Capt David Shia (2/2nd Inf)
Capt Norbert Garrison (3/2nd Inf)

MEDICAL DETACHMENT
Battalion Surgeon
Capt Albert Sumner
Medical Officer
Capt Frederick P. McIntyre, MD (TDY, 09/44)

HQ BTRY, 50th FIELD ARTILLERY BN
Battery Commander
Capt Edsel Budahn*
1st Lt Baker (Capt)

1st Sergeant	1st Sgt Devries
Communication Sergeant	Tech Sgt Smooths

Liaison Pilots
1st Lt Gouchberg (KIA, 28/09/44)*
1st Lt William H. Chambers (20/08/45)
1st Lt Owens
1st Lt Walsh (KIA 03/45)*

2nd Lt John R. Staley, Jr (WIA, 07/02/45)

"A" FIELD ARTILLERY BATTERY

Battery Commander
Capt Thomas H. Cooper*
Executive Officer
1st Lt Anthony J. Osage
Forward Observers
1st Lt Robert M. Webb
1st Lt Woodrow Young
2nd Lt Anthony J. Osage (then Ex-O)
2nd Lt Robert Massonet (KIA 12/44)

"B" FIELD ARTILLERY BATTERY

Battery Commander
Capt Harry Grusin*
Executive Officer
1st Lt Troutman
Forward Observers
1st Lt Irving Logue
1st Lt Yanarella

2nd Lt Raymer (Air Observer)

"C" FIELD ARTILLERY BATTERY

Battery Commander
Capt Robert McCartney*
Executive Officer
1st Lt Chester Ball
1st Lt Victor L. Sitton
Chief of Firing Btry
S Sgt Clyde Devine
Forward Observer
1st Lt Chester E. Ball (SilS, BrzS&CL&V, PH&2CL)
1st Lt Victor L. Sitton
1st Lt Herbert T. Green
1st Lt Pisapia
1st Lt Mark Gaddie (Air Obsr, KIA 28/09/44)

SERVICE BATTERY

Battery Commander   Capt George Lentz*

2nd INFANTRY REGIMENT

Regimental Commander
Col Lawrence Mickel
Lt Col Paul T. Carrol (29/04/44)
Col A. Worrel Roffe (09/07/44)
Col Walter R. Graham (28/04/45)
Executive Officer
Lt Col William H. Blakefield (04/45)

S-1	Capt Matt A. Britten
S-2	Major Donald Acker
	Major Norman Beard
S-3	Capt Emile Bussolati
S-4	Major Frank Zebbs*
	Capt William H. Birbari

Chaplain
Capt Harold O. Prudell

MEDICAL DETACHMENT
Regimental Surgeon
Maj Alois R. Sintzel

HEADQUARTERS COMPANY, 2nd INF
Company Commander
Capt Robert Crannen (KIA)
Capt Emory Horn
Communication Platoon
Communication Officer, Plat Comdr
Capt Orris S. Hiestand
Assistant Com Officer   WO Gruissen
Intelligence & Reconnaissance Platoon
1st Lt Russell Hatch

SERVICE COMPANY, 2nd INFANTRY
Company Commander
Capt Lloyd L. Smith
Staff Section
Administration Group, Pers Off
Capt Matt A. Britten (BrzS, 06/44-19/08/44)
Capt John Livingston
Operations Group   WO P. T. O'Brien
Regimental Sergeant Major   Mr Sgt F. Gill

INFANTRY CANNON COMPANY, 2nd INF
Company Commander
Capt Austin Triplett*
1st Lt A. Grimm (KIA)
1st Lt Carl R. Cleve

ANTI-TANK COMPANY, 2nd INFANTRY
Company Commander
Capt Howard Searles
Capt Robert R. Gregorin

1st BATTALION / 2nd INFANTRY
Battalion Commander
Lt Col George W. Childs
Maj Horace E. Townsend (26/07/44)
Lt Col Paul T. Carrol (30/07/44)*
Maj William H. Blakefield (05/09/44)
Lt Col Beryel J. Pace (28/04/45)
Executive Officer
Maj Philip C. Staples (10/44)
Maj Robert C. Russell (12/44)

S-1	Capt Allen W. Head
S-2	1st Lt Garston W. Driver Jr
S-3	Capt Robert C. Russell (10/08/43→12/44)*
	Capt Louis N. Giroux
S-4	1st Lt Frank J. Mackey*
	1st Lt John W. Kriney
Battalion Surgeon	Capt Morris Greenberg
Communication Sergeant	S Sgt Robert J. Dunsirn

"A" RIFLE COMPANY
Company Commander
1st Lt Marvin King*
Capt Lennis Jones
Capt Dale V. Orff

"B" RIFLE COMPANY
Company Commander
Capt Tommy R. Gilliam*
Capt Norman J. Mecklem, Jr

Executive Officer
  1st Lt Raymond Leonard

1st Sgt	1st Sgt Thomas Miller*
1st Platoon	2d Lt Thomas Ewing*
2nd Platoon	1st Lt Lee Rothermel*
3rd Platoon	1st Lt John W. Kriney*
Weapons Platoon	1st Lt Joseph Roche*

"C" RIFLE COMPANY
Company Commander
  Capt Emil J. Bussolati*
  Capt Willis S. Bloom

"D" HEAVY WEAPONS COMPANY
Company Commander   ?

2nd BATTALION / 2nd INFANTRY
Battalion Commander
  Lt Col Leslie K. Ball
  Maj Horace E. Townsend (20/02/45)
  Maj Beryl C. Pace (11/03/45)
  Maj Horace E. Townsend (21/04/45)
Executive Officer
  Capt Draytford Richardson
Battalion Surgeon
  Capt Edward Stevenson
  Capt Richard Snipe (08/44)
  Capt Frederick P. McIntyre, MD (→09/44)
Battalion Medical Assistant
  Capt Harry Dion
  1st Lt Fred P. Body, MAC (08/44)

S-1	Capt Joseph M. Swantek
S-2	1st Lt Blaine Asher Jr
S-3	Capt Robert T. Russell (→12/44)
	Capt John J. Sullivan Jr
S-4	1st Lt Robert T. Fairey Jr

"E" RIFLE COMPANY
Company Commander
  Capt George C. Major (POW 07/44)
  Capt Joseph Fekete Jr
  Capt Robert W. Lefler

Platoon Leader	1st Lt Norman R. Hughes

"F" RIFLE COMPANY
Company Commander
  Capt Richard W. Stone (KIA 08/09/44)
  Capt John Savage (KIA)
  Capt Joseph Baranowski

"G" RIFLE COMPANY
Company Commander
  Capt Philip C. Staples*
  Capt Dave B. Hott

Platoon Leader	1st Lt Robert W. Dunn

"H" HEAVY WEAPONS COMPANY
Company Commander
  Capt William H. Birbari (then S-4)
  Capt James H. Bennett

3rd BATTALION / 2nd INFANTRY
Battalion Commander
  Lt Col J. Matthews
  Lt Col Thomas A. Lindley
  Lt Col Robert E. Connor (09/44)
Executive Officer
  Maj Robert E. Connor
  Maj Philip C. Staples (09/44)

S-1	Capt John A. Paul*
S-2	1st Lt F. Penny*
	1st Lt John H. Pohlman
S-3	Capt C. Nelson*
	Capt Frederic C. Thompson
S-4	1st Lt Vincent D'Imperio*

Communication Officer
  1st Lt Don R. Walin*
Battalion Surgeon
  Capt Arthur Romanski

"I" RIFLE COMPANY
Company Commander
  Capt E. Mackey (KIA)
  Capt G. Grafston (WIA)
  1st Lt R. Barnett
  1st Lt Karl Johnson

Squad Leader	S Sgt Leon Belardinellis

"K" RIFLE COMPANY
Company Commander
  Capt Johnson (WIA)
  Capt H. Pale

"L" RIFLE COMPANY
Company Commander
  Capt G. Breakstone
  1st Lt G. Doran
  1st Lt Powell
  Capt Eugene E. Slocum (WIA 24/12/44)

Platoon Leader	1st Lt Eugene E. Slocum (WIA 10/10/44)

"M" HEAVY WEAPONS COMPANY
Company Commander
  Capt George W. Welch*
  Capt Arthur A. Purcell

Platoon Leader	2nd Lt Marden C. Goodwin (01/12/44→07/02/45)

10th INFANTRY REGIMENT

Regimental Commander
  Col Robert P. Bell (24/05/42)*
Executive Officer
  Lt Col William M. Breckinridge*

S-1	Capt Henry Scharf
S-2	Maj Edward N. Marsh
S-3	Maj Harris C. Walker
S-4	?
Communication Officer	Capt Robert H. Phillips

HEADQUARTERS COMPANY, 10th INFANTRY
Company Commander
  ?

Intelligence & Reconnaissance Platoon
Platoon Leader	1st Lt Douglas W. Curtiss
	(WIA 22/08/44)

SERVICE COMPANY, 10th INFANTRY
Company Commander
  Capt George Hope, III

CANNON COMPANY, 10th INFANTRY
Company Commander
  Capt Ferris A. Kercher (15/01/45)*
  Capt Roland B. Greig (15/01/45)

ANTI-TANK COMPANY, 10th INFANTRY
Company Commander
  Capt Neil Jantz
AT Mine Platoon	1st Lt Frank M. Vinson, Jr

1st BATTALION / 10th INFANTRY
Battalion Commander
  Lt Col Frank V. Langfitt, Jr (WIA 08/09/44)
  Maj Wilfrid H. Haughey, Jr (08/09/44)
  Lt Col Frank V. Langfitt, Jr (07/12/44)
  Maj Stanley M. Hays (06/45)
Executive Officer
  Maj Wilfrid H. Haughey Jr
  Maj Ferris A. Kercher (15/01/45)
S-1 & HQ Company Commander	?
S-2	1st Lt Leo E. Harris
	Capt Bruce Bauer
S-3	Capt Manford C. Bear
S-4	?
Communication Sergeant	S Sgt Casper J. Alagna

"A" RIFLE COMPANY
Company Commander
  Capt Elias R. Vick Jr (KIA 10/09/44)
  1st Lt William H. Hallowell (10/09/44)
  1st Lt Charles K. Boughten (Rhin)
Executive Officer
  1st Lt William H. Hallowell
Platoon Leaders
  2nd Lt Kenneth C. Bresnen (1st Platoon, Rhine)
  2nd Lt Karl Greenberg (2nd Platoon, WIA 10/09/44)
  2nd Lt Warren G. Shaw

"B" RIFLE COMPANY
Company Commander
  1st Lt Robert W. Dunn

"C" RIFLE COMPANY
Company Commander
  Capt William B. Davis (KIA 10/09/44)
  1st Lt Eugene N. Dille (10/09/44)
  1st Lt Issac Storey (10/09/44)
Executive Officer
  1st Lt Eugene N. Dille (KIA 10/09/44)
Platoon Leaders
  1st Lt Carl E. Hansen (1st Platoon)
  1st Lt Issac H. Storey (2nd Platoon)
  1st Lt Ralph R. Cuppeli (3rd Platoon, WIA 10/09/44)

"D" HEAVY WEAPONS COMPANY
Company Commander
  Capt Robert E. Todd
Executive Officer
  1st Lt Francis L. Carr

2nd BATTALION / 10th INFANTRY
Battalion Commander
  Lt Col Julian H. Martin (WIA 30/07/44)
  Lt Col William H. Simpson (31/07/44)
  Lt Col Paul T. Carrol (18/09/44)
  Lt Col William H. Simpson (24/09/44)
  Lt Col Harris C. Walker (05/11/44)
Executive Officer
  Maj William H. Simpson (→31/07/44)
  Capt Roy W. Hancock
S-1 & Headquarters Company Commander
  Capt Edward Martin (→04/45)
  Capt Odvar Haug (04/45)
Motor Officer, Ex-O Hq Co
  1st Lt Odvar Haug
Message Center Chief
  Sgt Horace F. Lockwood
S-2	?
S-3	Capt Harry E. Arthars (→04/45)
S-4	1st Lt Hangus T. Brown
Medical Detachment
  Capt William S. Yocum, MD

"E" RIFLE COMPANY
Company Commander
  Capt John H. Lathrop

"F" RIFLE COMPANY
Company Commander
  Capt Eugene M. Witt
  Capt Theodore F. Kubarek (KIA)
  Capt Roy Crumrine
Executive Officer
  1st Lt Ralph J. Rooney
1st Platoon Leader
  Lt Leroy Jenks
2nd Platoon Leader
  Lt Francis Markey
3rd Platoon Leader
  Lt Joseph Bergman
Weapons Platoon Leader
  Lt Ladson A. Barnes
Platoon Leader	1st Lt Andrew H. Paulishen

"G" RIFLE COMPANY
Company Commander
  Capt Lewis R. Anderson
  Capt Whittington (PH, DSC)
Platoon Leader
  2nd Lt Charles J. Watkins

"H" HEAVY WEAPONS COMPANY
Company Commander
  1st Lt Hangus T. Brown
3rd Platoon (Mortar)
Squad Leader   Sgt William T. Hope

3rd BATTALION / 10th INFANTRY
Battalion Commander
  Maj Alden P. Shipley
  Maj Wilfrid H. Haughey Jr (Lt Col) (DSC, 09/02/45)
Executive Officer
  Maj Stanley M. Hays
  Maj John J. McCluskey (02/45)
S-1   ?
S-2   ?
S-3   Maj Charles W. McClean
S-4   Capt George W. Threlkeld
Communication Officer   1st Lt Richard A. Kramer

"I" RIFLE COMPANY
Company Commander
  Capt James C. Borror
  Capt John C. Dalton
Executive Officer
  1st Lt John D. Kennedy (08/44→09/44)*
Platoon Leader
  1st Lt John D. Kennedy (03/44→07/44)
  1st Lt Martin J. Gemoets (10/11/44→WIA 04 and 06/12/44)

"K" RIFLE COMPANY
Company Commander
  Capt John J. McCluskey (→02/45)
  Capt John C. Dalton
  Capt John D. Kennedy (10/44→12/45, PH, BrzS&CL, Croix de Guerre w/Palms)
Executive Officer
  1st Lt Martin J. Gemoets (20/12/44, BrzS, PH&CL)
1st Platoon
  Platoon Sergeant
  Technical Sergeant Dwight Cummings*
  Squad Leader
  Sgt James N. Arrington
2nd Platoon
  2nd Lt Ruric N. Williams
  Platoon Sergeant
  Technical Sergeant Branch*
3rd Platoon
  2nd Lt William E. Nowling (until KIA, 08/09/44, PH)
  Technical Sergeant William E. Griffith (08/09/44→WIA 08/22/44, SilS &V, PH)
  Platoon Sergeant
  Technical Sergeant William E. Griffith (→08/09/44)*
Weapons Platoon
  Platoon Sergeant
  Technical Sergeant Woodrow Combs*

"L" RIFLE COMPANY
Company Commander
  Capt Harold Bowers
1st Platoon   1st Lt Wilfred Longpre

"M" HEAVY WEAPONS COMPANY
Company Commander
  Capt Frank M. Bradley

11th INFANTRY REGIMENT

Regimental Commander
  Col Charles W. Yuill (→21/11/44, BrzS, Croix de Guerre)*
  Col Paul Black (21/11/44, BrzS&CL, Croix de Guerre, Red Star Order)
Executive Officer
  Lt Col Phillip W. Merrill (→22/02/45, BrzS&CL, SilS)*
  Lt Col Homer C. Ledbetter (22/02/45, BrzS&CL, Croix de Guerre)
Assistant Executive Officer
  Lt Col Homer C. Ledbetter (13/11/44→22/02/45)
S-1   Capt A. Bruce Campbell, Jr (01/09/44 became historian, 10/11/44, Division Public Relation Officer)*
                       Capt Elbert L. Cooper (01/09/44, BrzS&CL)
S-2   Maj Sigward A. E. Anderson (→07/08/44)
                       Maj Woodrow W. Morse (07/08/44, SilS, BrzS&CL, Air Medal)*
Assistant S-2   Capt Carl R. McFarland#
S-3   Maj Cornelius W. Coghill, Jr (→11/11/44, evacuated sick, BrzS&CL)*
                       Capt Robert H. Williams (TDY 11→14/11/44)
                       Lt Col Philip W. Merril (acting S-3, 14/11/44)
                       Maj Cornelius W. Coghill, Jr (16/11/44)
Assistant S-3   Capt Ferris A. Church (22/10/44→01/11/44, SilS, BrzS)
                       Capt Jack S. Gerrie (22/10/44→25/12/44) (accidentally killed on 29/12/44, DSC, BrzS, PH, Croix de Guerre)
                       Capt Robert D. Spencer (#, BrzS)
S-4   Maj Robert B. Shamblin (→01/09/44, assigned to Div G-4 Section)*
                       Maj Alfred Perry Teegarden (01/09/44, Capt, BrzS, PH)
Historian   Capt A. Bruce Campbell (01/09/44→09/11/44)
Combat Liaison Officers
  Capt Richard H. Durst (Regt Ln O, Div, 28/07/44→10/09/44)*
  Capt Harold S. Emerson#
  Capt Jack S. Gerrie# (accidentally killed on 29/12/44)
  1st Lt Oliver C. Yanco#

1st Lt Leonard A. Duston (#, BrzS&2CL, PH, SilS)

Chaplains
Capt Thomas P. Hennessey (#, BrzS)
Capt William S. Jones (#, BrzS&CL)
Capt James E. Parr#

HEADQUARTERS COMPANY, 11th INFANTRY
Company Commander
Capt Richard H. Durst (→28/07/44)
Capt Harold S. Emerson (08/08/44)*
Capt Leo H. Eberhardt (19/10/44, SilS, BrzS)
Executive Officer
1st Lt Dana S. Jones

Communication Officer	Capt Roy E. Hogan (BrzS, SilS)
Asst Communication Officer	CWO Joseph Stephens (BrzS)
Communication Chief	Mr Sgt Rudy F. Etley (BrzS)

First Sergeant
1st Sgt Charles B. Reeves (BrzS)
1st Sgt Douglas H. Wright
Security Officer (Gas Off)
1st Lt Eugene R. Webb (#, BrzS)
1st Lt William F. Hintz#

Intelligence & Reconnaissance Platoon
Platoon Leader
1st Lt Leo H. Eberhardt (→19/10/44)
1st Lt Dana S. Jones (19/10/44, BrzS, PH)
2nd Lt Leonard A. Duston, Jr (01/03/45)

Platoon Sergeant	Tech Sgt Leonard A. Duston, Jr [1]

SERVICE COMPANY, 11th INFANTRY
Company Commander
Capt Max B. McCaslin*
Capt Herbert V. Gawthrop (19/10/44, BrzS)
Capt Lt Andrew J. Hreha
Supply Officer, Administration
WOJG Eugene E. Stahl
Staff Section

Personnel Officer	Capt Kenneth C. Doty (BrzS)
Adjutant, Assistant S-1	WOJG Clarence E. Welsh
Special Service Officer	1st Lt Will M. Smith (2nd Lt #)

Supply Section

Munition Officer	Capt Lowell K. Tuttel (BrzS)
Munition Officer Assistant	WOJG Francis J. Flood

Transportation Platoon

Motor Transport Officer	Capt George W. Larson (SilS, BrzS)
Maintenance Officer	2nd Lt Frederick A. Coenen (#, PH)
Asst Motor Transport Officer	WOJG George W. Massey

Supply, Battalion S-4
1st Lt Franklin H. Drunagel#
1st Lt Russell E. Sprague#
1st Lt Doran R. Zwygart (1st Bn, 01/45→08/05/45, BrzS&CL) [2]

INFANTRY ANTI-TANK COMPANY, 11th INF
Company Commander
Capt Alfred Perry Teegarden (→01/09/44)*
1st Lt James M. Davis (01/09/44)
Capt Fairfield Rock (#, PH, BrzS)

Executive Officer
1st Lt Walter J. Constantine#
Reconnaissance Officer
2nd Lt John W. Morring#
First Sergeant
1st Sgt James H. Canter
Platoon Leaders
1st Lt Rocco J. Barbuto
1st Lt John A. Filbert (#, BrzS)
1st Lt Harold B. Mathauser (#, BrzS, PH)
1st Lt Leroy Van De Carr, Jr#
2nd Lt Victor J. Wirpsa

INFANTRY CANNON COMPANY, 11th INF
Company Commander
Capt Harry M. Smith (→22/10/44, SilS&CL, BrzS)*
1st Lt Joseph F. Schaech (22/10/44, BrzS, PH)
Capt Harry M. Smith (31/10/44→30/11/44)
1st Lt Henry T. Bass, Jr (31/01/45→KIA 14/03/45, BrzS, PH)
Executive Officer
1st Lt Stanley M. Anderson (15/03/45, KIA 15/03/45, PH)
First Sergeant
1st Sgt William M. Jones
Platoon Leaders
1st Lt Joseph H. Gallant (#, BrzS)
1st Lt Charles Roggenstein (#, BrzS, Capt)
2nd Lt John A. Bedell#
2nd Lt Jerome H. Glickman (#, PH, 1st Lt)
2nd Lt Elmer H. Graham (#, BrzS, 1st Lt)

MEDICAL DETACHMENT
Regimental Surgeon
Maj Bert H. Rightman, MD
Maj Rankin A. Nebinger, MD*
Dental Officer
Capt Clare B. Sauser, MD (SilS)
Capt Andrew E. Lobben, MD
Medical Officer
Capt Marcus M. Horenstein, MD#
Capt Paul A. Rothenberg, MD (#, BrzS)
Capt George P. Spence, MD#

1st BATTALION / 11th INFANTRY
Battalion Commander
Lt Col Homer C. Ledbetter (→13/11/44)*
Lt Col Herman R. Schell (14/11/44→08/05/45, BrzS, SilS, PH&CL&V, Croix de Guerre)
Executive Officer
Maj John T. Russell (→25/09/44, PH, BrzS)*
Maj Herman R. Schell (26/09/44→14/11/44)
Capt Jack S. Gerrie (14/11/44)
Maj Robert H. Williams (08/12/44→08/05/45, SilS, BrzS&CL&V, Croix de Guerre)
S-1 & Hq Company Commander
Capt Harold S. Emerson (→07/08/44, Regt Hq Co)
Capt Joseph H. Cox (07/08/44→12/09/44, PH, SilS)*
Capt Kenneth E. Hughes (22/10/44, BrzS)
1st Lt Christian E. Finkbeiner (31/01/45→08/05/45, SilS, BrzS&CL)

1. Technical Sergeant Leonard A. Duston was commissioned officer, 2nd Lieutenant, on 16/11/44.
2. The Supply Officer, S-4 of the Battalion, was assigned to the Service Company (see chapter 2, section 2.3). Knowing the battalion to which he was assigned, his name has been noted twice, in the Service Company and in the Battalion Staff.

Motor Transport Officer, 2nd-in-Comd, Hq Co
  1st Lt Christian E. Finkbeiner (31/12/44)
  1st Lt Rocco J. Barbuto#
  1st Lt Harry G. Rekemeier (→08/05/45, BrzS)
Reconnaissance Platoon
  S-2 Commanding Officer
Communication Platoon
Communication Officer
  1st Lt Harry G. Rekemeier (#, BrzS)
  2nd Lt Frank D. Pennybacker (→08/05/45)
Ammunition & Pioneer Platoon
Munition Officer   1st Lt Loren H. White
                              (31/01/45→08/05/45,
                              BrzS&Cl PH)
Anti-tank Platoon
  1st Lt James G. Collier, Jr (31/01/45→08/05/45, BrzS)
S-2
  1st Lt Jesse E. Truax (BrzS, SilS)
  1st Lt Robert V. Gray (→31/01/45, SilS, BrzS, PH)*
  Capt Carl R. McFarland
  1st Lt James N. Peck (→08/05/45, SilS&CL, BrzS, PH&CL)
S-3
  Capt Stanley R. Connor (→11/09/44, SilS)*
  Capt Robert D. Spencer (11/09/44, BrzS)
  Capt Forrest Porter Raley (10/12/44→21/04/45, BrzS&CL)
  1st Lt Robert V. Gray (→08/05/45)
S-4
  1st Lt Herbert V. Gawthrop (22/10/44)*
  1st Lt Christian E. Finkbeiner (19/10/44)
  1st Lt Doran R. Zwygart (01/45→08/05/45)

MEDICAL DETACHMENT, BN SEC
  Capt Thomas Seideman, MD (BrzS&CL)
  Capt Robert J. Scott, MD (BrzS)
  1st Lt Jim C. Kelly, MAC

"A" RIFLE COMPANY
Company Commander
  Capt Elbert L. Cooper (→01/09/44, BrzS&CL)*
  1st Lt Anthony J. Miketinac (01/09, WIA 09/09/44, PH)
  Capt Lt Harold J. Taylor (09/09/44→31/01/45, BrzS)
  1st Lt Harold F. Bryant (14/03/45→08/05/45, SilS, BrzS&CL)
Executive Officer
  1st Lt Harold F. Bryant (31/01/45→14/03/45)
  1st Lt Jesse E. Truax (→08/05/45, BrzS, SilS)
Platoon Leaders
  1st Lt Miketinac (→01/09/44)*
  1st Lt Harold F. Bryant (→31/01/45)
  1st Lt Charles F. Brauer (PH&CL)#
  1st Lt Robert L. Carlson#
  2nd Lt George W. Alsup (PH)#
  2nd Lt Lawrence W. Durance (PH)#
  2nd Lt Leonard A. Ganus (→08/05/45, BrzS&CL) 1st Platoon
  2nd Lt Stanley F. Rygiel (→08/05/45) 2nd Platoon
  2nd Lt John F. LaFave (→08/05/45, BrzS) 3rd Platoon
  2nd Lt Frederick M. Muller (→08/05/45, BrzS) Wpn Platoon
Platoon Sergeant
  Tech Sgt Brown
MG Section, Weapons Platoon
  S Sgt Marvin B. Simmons (03/45)

"B" RIFLE COMPANY
Company Commander
  Capt Harry R. Anderson (→05/11/44WIA, SilS, BrzS&CL, PH)*
  1st Lt William A. Randle (05/11/44→08/05/45, SilS,
    BrzS&CL, PH)
Executive Officer
  1st Lt Keith B. Liesch (SilS, BrzS)*
  1st Lt William A. Randle (→05/11/44, BrzS&CL, SilS, PH)
  1st Lt William H. Estey (05/11/44→12/44, BrzS)
  1st Lt Charles B. Vickers (01/45→08/05/45, BrzS&CL, PH)
First Sergeant
  1st Sgt Morris M. Boyer
1st Platoon
  1st Lt William H. Estey (→05/11/44)*
  2nd Lt Alfred B. Guernsey (BrzS, VE day)
2nd Platoon
  1st Lt James B. Van Horn (→02/10/44, KIA)*
  2nd Lt Philip G. Denbo (02/10/44, PH)
  1st Lt Stanley Maly, Jr (PH, VE day)
Platoon Sergeant
  S Sgt Foster Ferguson
3rd Platoon
  2nd Lt George W. Alsup (PH, 10/44))
  1st Lt Laurel M. Venters (03/45→08/05/45, PH&CL)
Platoon Sergeant
  S Sgt Charlie L. Houston (03/45)
Weapons Platoon
  Tech Sgt William V. Sapp (10/44)
  1st Lt Joseph T. Zawistowski (BrzS&CL, PH, VE day)
Platoon Leaders
  1st Lt William Eubanks (KIA 30/07/44, PH)
  1st Lt John King (KIA 30/07/44, PH)
  1st Lt George H. Crane (WIA 30/07/44, PH)
  2nd Lt Bruce L. Mack (KIA 22/08/44, PH)
  2nd Lt Abraham Badler (MIA 17/09/44, PH)
Platoon Sergeants
  S Sgt Charles Josephson (→15/09/44, WIA)*
  Tech Sgt Troy B. Key (03/45)

"C" RIFLE COMPANY
Company Commander
  Capt Forrest P. Raley (→10/12/44, BrzS&CL)*
  1st Lt Gordon V. Gorski
  1st Lt Lucien E. Levesque (03/45, BrzS, PH)
  Capt Keith B. Leisch (14/03/45→08/05/45, SilS, BrzS)
Executive Officer
  1st Lt Gordon V. Gorski
First Sergeant
  1st Sgt Virgil Ross
1st Platoon
  2nd Lt Frederick G. Welch (VE day)
2nd Platoon
  2nd Lt Richard E. Treter (VE day)
3rd Platoon
  1st Lt George W. Putney (SilS, BrzS)*
Platoon Leaders
  1st Lt Keith B. Liesch
  1st Lt Gordon V. Gorski
  1st Lt Ross W. Stanley (BrzS, SilS, PH)
  1st Lt Howard S. Warnock

"D" HEAVY WEAPONS COMPANY
Company Commander
1st Lt Johnny Hillyard (KIA, 09/09/44, PH)*
1st Lt William A. Powell (09/09/44, KIA 09/09/44, PH)
1st Lt Basil Jones, III (09/09/44→12/09/44, BrzS)
Capt Lt Robert B. Furman, Jr (12/09/44→08/05/45, SilS, BrzS&CL)
Executive Officer
1st Lt Harry O. Kaylor (03/45, BrzS&CL, PH, WIA)
1st Lt Robert F. Grampietro (VE day, SilS)
First Sergeant
1st Sgt Chap X. Osborn
1st Platoon (MG)
1st Lt Gordon F. Jacobsen (#, VE day, BrzS)
2nd Platoon (MG)
2nd Lt Quinto T. De Sieno (#, VE day, BrzS, PH)
3rd Platoon (Mortar)
2nd Lt Alfred Ullman, Jr (VE day)
Platoon Leaders
1st Lt Robert B. Furman, Jr (BrzS&Cl, SilS)*
2nd Lt Paul J. Hodgson (PH)#
Platoon Sergeants
Tech Sgt Guy Calhoun*
Tech Sgt Wilson D. Warren
MG Section Leaders
S Sgt Thomas C. McCrystal (03/45)
S Sgt Dexter Cunningham (03/45, WIA)

2nd BATTALION / 11th INFANTRY
Battalion Commander
Lt Col Kelley B. Lemmon, Jr (→19/09/44, DSC, BrzS)*
Capt Ferris A. Church (Temp, 20/09/44→25/09/44)
Lt Col John T. Russell (Maj 26/09/44→17/12/44 evac, BrzS, PH)
Maj Ferris A. Church (Capt 18/12/44→22/12/44)
Lt Col John N. Acuff, Jr (Maj 23/12/44, BrzS &CL, PH, Croix de Guerre)
Executive Officer
Maj Herman Schell (→09/09/44, WIA)*
Maj Ferris A. Church (09/09/44→22/10/44)
Maj Harry M. Smith (22/10/44→01/11/44)
Maj Ferris A. Church (01/11/44→18/12/44)
Maj Ferris A. Church (23/12/44, SilS, BrzS)
S-1 & Hq Company Commander
Capt Wilbur W. Wood (→02/45)*
S-2
1st Lt Verl L. Cameron (→07/08/44, BrzS, PH)
Capt Douglas C. Hargrave (07/08/44→09/09/44, PH)*
2nd Lt Felton (19/10/44)
2nd Lt Stanley R. Kuwik (24/01/45, BrzS)
S-3
1st Lt Charles P. Bartley (→30/07/44, WIA, PH&2CL)
Capt Page H. Brownfield
Capt Ferris A. Church (30/07/44→09/09/44)*
Capt Harry M. Smith (30/11/44→23/12/44, SilS&CL, BrzS)
Capt Basil Jones, III (24/01/45, BrzS)
Capt Robert D. Spencer (03/03/45)
Capt Forrest Porter Raley (21/04/45, BrzS&CL)

S-4   1st Lt Andrew J. Hreha
1st Lt Tyrus L. Mizer (19/10/44, BrzS)
2nd Lt Charles B. Camp (24/01/45, PH, 1st Lt)
Munition Officer   2nd Lt Charles B. Camp#
Anti-tank Platoon   2nd Lt Alvin A. Cutler#
First Sergeant, Hq Co   1st Sgt Orville R. Cheatham

MEDICAL DETACHMENT, BN SEC
Capt Emanuel Feldman (SilS)
Capt John M. Hoffman (SilS)
2nd Lt Edwin R. Pyle, MAC (DSC)

"E" RIFLE COMPANY
Company Commander
Capt Ferris A. Church (→30/07/44)
Capt Jack M. Brown (30/07/44→08/09/44, WIA, 1st Lt, BrzS, PH)
1st Lt Basil Jones III (08/09/44, WIA)
Capt Harold Taylor (09/09/44) (WIA)
Capt Basil Jones, III (19/10/44, 1st Lt, BrzS)
Capt Thomas G. Dodson (24/01/45, WIA)
1st Lt J. C. Shirley (14/02/45, PH)
Executive Officer
2nd Lt John A. Diersing (KIA, 02/10/44, PH)
1st Lt J. C. Shirley (→24/01/45, without assignment on 31/01/45)
1st Lt William E. Jackes (24/01/45, WIA, PH)
1st Lt Stanley M. Anderson (→14/03/45)
1st Sergeant
1st Sgt Claud W. Hembree
Platoon Leaders
1st Lt Thomas J. Cullison (MIA 10/09/44, BrzS, SilS)
1st Lt Edward A. Meierdiercks (19/11/44, WIA, BrzS&CL, PH)
1st Lt Stanley M. Anderson (15/03/45)
2nd Lt Arthur T. Welton (24/01/45)
1st Lt Clinton G. Hall (PH)
1st Lt J. C. Shirley
1st Platoon
1st Lt William E. Jackes
Platoon Sergeant
Tech Sgt Richard L. Marnell (03/03/45, WIA, DSC)
2nd Platoon
Tech Sgt Woodrow Stewart (03/03/45)
3rd Platoon
1st Lt Joe A. Rawls (03/03/45)

"F" RIFLE COMPANY
Company Commander
Capt Douglas C. Hargrave (→07/08/44, PH)
1st Lt Nathan F. Drake (07/08/44→KIA 08/09/44, PH)
1st Lt James M. Wright (08/09/44→MIA 10/09/44, SilS)
1st Lt Keith B. Liesch (11/09/44, SilS, BrzS)
1st Lt Jack M. Brown (24/01/45, BrzS, PH)
First Sergeant
1st Sgt Willard Cheek
Platoon Leaders
1st Lt Matthew Wirtz (MIA 10/09/44)
1st Lt George W. Darroch#
1st Lt Cedric E. Farmer (#, PH)
1st Lt Arthur W. Haney (#, PH)
1st Lt Harry C. Jordan, Jr (#, BrzS, PH&CL)
2nd Lt Darrel O. Connor# (KIA 02/03/45, PH)

"G" RIFLE COMPANY
Company Commander
Capt Jack S. Gerrie (→12/10/44, DSC, BrzS, PH, Croix de Guerre)*
Capt Richard H. Durst (13/10/44→WIA 08/02/45, PH, SilS)
Capt J. T. Watson (02/45)
1st Lt Lucien E. Levesque (15/03/45, BrzS, PH)
Executive Officer
1st Lt Stanley M. Anderson (→E Co)

Platoon Leaders
Capt J. T. Watson (attached, 31/01/45)
1st Lt Lucien E. Levesque#
1st Lt Stanley M. Anderson
Platoon Sergeants
S Sgt Kenneth E. Price
Sgt Dale B. Rex (KIA 18/12/44, DSC)
Tech Sgt James C. Jones (KIA 23/01/45, PH)
Squad Leaders
Sgt Andrew J. McGlynn
Sgt Kenneth Price (PH)

"H" HEAVY WEAPONS COMPANY
Company Commander
Capt Robert D. Spencer (→11/09/44, BrzS)*
Capt Stanley R. Connor (12/09/44, SilS)
Executive Officer
1st Lt Robert J. Bauschalt (24/01/45, BrzS)
Platoon Leaders
2nd Lt George G. Hutzler
1st Lt Ross W. Stanley (09/09/45)
1st Lt Tillman C. Faulkner (#, BrzS)
1st Lt Aulbry C. Hitchings (#, BrzS&2CL)
1st Lt Harold A. Phifer (#, SilS, PH)
1st Lt Elmon W. Holmes (#, BrzS)

3rd BATTALION / 11th INFANTRY
Battalion Commander
Lt Col William H. Birdsong, Jr (PH, BrzS&2CL, SilS, Croix de Guerre)*
Maj John N. Acuff (Temp, 25→27/11/44, BrzS&CL, PH, Croix de Guerre)
Executive Officer
Maj John N. Acuff (→22/12/44, Capt)*
Maj Harry M. Smith (23/12/44)
S-1 & Hq Company Commander
Capt Quintan B. Le Monte (BrzS)*
1st Lt Edward C. Melane (02/02/45, BrzS, PH)
S-2
1st Lt Earl C. Cameron (WIA 20/03/45)*
Capt Raymond W. Bitney (20/03/45, PH, BrzS)
S-3
Capt Page H. Brownfield
1st Lt Charles P. Bartley (01/08/44→10/09/44, PH&CL) *
Capt Richard H. Durst (10/09/44→13/10/44)
Capt Robert M. Gill (13/10/44, SilS, BrzS)
S-4   1st Lt Robert A. Kaiser
1st Lt Russell E. Sprague (22/10/44)
Motor Transport Officer, Ex-O, Hq Co
1st Lt Robert P. Genther (#, 2nd Lt, BrzS)
Communication Officer
1st Lt Frank A. Bishop, Jr # (WIA 22/03/45, BrzS, PH)
Munition Officer, A&P Platoon
2nd Lt Edward C. Melane # (KIA 23/03/45)
Platoon Sergeant, A&P Plat
S Sgt Robert E. Thrower
Anti-tank Platoon
1st Lt Mitchell J. Hazam (PH, BrzS&CL)
2nd Lt Harry H. Shields, Jr (PH)
1st Lt Eugene L. Goodrich# (23/03/45, BrzS, SilS)
Medical Detachment, Bn Sec
Capt Panfilo C. Di Loreto, MD (BrzS, SilS)
1st Lt T. H. Pritchett, MAC (WIA, SilS, PH&CL)

"I" RIFLE COMPANY
Company Commander
Capt Franklin Smith (→10/09/44, WIA, BrzS, SilS, PH)*
1st Lt Richard A. Marshall (10/09/44, WIA 10/09/44, SilS, PH&CL)
Capt Charles P. Bartley (12/09/44, Capt 16/09, WIA 16/09/44)
Capt Raymond W. Bitney (17/09/44→23/01/45, WIA)
1st Lt Edward Kosloski (24/01/45, PH, KIA 10/02/45, PH)
Capt Robert V. Link (01/03/45→08/05/45, BrzS, SilS, PH)
Executive Officer
1st Lt Stephen T. Lowry (→01/09/44, SilS, PH)*
1st Lt Richard A. Marshall (01/09→10/09/44, 17/09→WIA 18/09/44, SilS, PH&CL)
1st Lt Edward Kosloski (18/09/44→23/01/45)
Attached
Capt James T. Neely, Jr (WIA 23/01/45, BrzS, PH)
Platoon Leaders
1st Lt Christian J. Christoffels (#, PH&CL)
1st Lt Robert A. Emery (#, BrzS, PH)
2nd Lt Clifton R. Byrd#
Platoon Sergeants
Tech Sgt Fred Crawford (KIA 30/07/44)
Wpn Sec Leader
S Sgt Joseph A. Hartke

"K" RIFLE COMPANY
Company Commander
Capt Robert Altman (→01/09/44 WIA, BrzS, PH)
1st Lt Stephen T. Lowry (01/09/44→KIA 09/09/44, SilS, PH)
Capt Joseph H. Cox (10/09/44, SilS, PH, #)
Capt Basil Jones, III (BrzS)
Capt Charles P. Bartley (09/02/45→WIA 13/02/45, PH&CL)
1st Lt Irven F. Jacobs (03/03/45)
Executive Officer
1st Lt Johnny R. Hillyard (→KIA 10/09/44, PH)*
1st Lt Mitchell J. Hazam (# →11/02/45)
Platoon Leaders
1st Lt Mitchell J. Hazam
2nd Lt Marc S. Tartaglia (PH&CL)
1st Lt James G. Kerr, Jr#
2nd Lt John A. Mannow (22/03/45)
2nd Lt Alexander G. Booras (PW 23/03/45)
1st Lt Max E. Lett#
1st Platoon
2nd Lt William B. Belchee (23/03/45, SilS)
Platoon sergeant
Tech Sgt Heber L. Braley (PW 23/03/45)
2nd Platoon
1st Lt Ralph A. Hardee (→KIA 09/08/44, DSC, PH)*
3rd Platoon
1st Lt Robert A. Emery (BrzS, PH)*

"L" RIFLE COMPANY
Company Commander
Capt Robert H. Williams (→11/11/44, SilS, BrzS&2CL/V Croix de Guerre)*
1st Lt Thomas B. McCabe (11/11/44→KIA 14/11/44, PH)
Capt Robert H. Williams (14/11/44→08/12/44)
Capt Glen T. Elliot (08/12/44→KIA 23/01/45, PH)
1st Lt Robert A. Kaiser (23/01/45→WIA 11/02/45, PH)
1st Lt Mitchell J. Hazam (11/02/45, BrzS&CL, PH)
Capt Thomas G. Dodson (03/03/45, SilS, PH)

Executive Officer
  1st Lt Oliver C. Yanko (→15/08/44)*
  1st Lt Thomas B. McCabe (15/08/44→11/11/44, PH)
  1st Lt Robert A. Kaiser (14/10/44)
1st Sergeant
  1st Sgt Joseph Bryant*
Mess Sergeant
  S Sgt Joseph Hasslinger*
1st Platoon
  1st Lt Victor L. Schuman (BrzS&CL, PH&CL)
2nd Platoon
  1st Lt Andrew J. Keller (→KIA 08/08/44, SilS, PH)*
3rd Platoon
  1st Lt Lewis M. Dilwith (→23/04/45, BrzS)*
  1st Lt Walter Furay
  Lt Fortunato
  Platoon Sergeant
  Tech Sgt Barney Gassaway (→WIA 16/11/44, SilS, PH)*
Weapons Platoon
  1st Lt Thomas B. McCabe (→15/08/44)
  Tech Sgt Frederick M. Keppler (11/11/44)
  Platoon Sergeant
  Tech Sgt Frederick M. Keppler (→11/11/44)*
Platoon Leaders
  1st Lt Walter E. Anderson (BrzS)
  1st Lt James N. Broyles (#, BrzS, PH)
  1st Lt Charles G. Maier (#, PH&CL)
  2nd Lt Orlando J. Heinitz#
Attached
  Capt Glenn T. Elliot (16/11/44→08/12/44)
Squad Leaders
  S Sgt Arthur Kissinger
  S Sgt Elmer Porter
  S Sgt Ralph Sutter
  S Sgt Arnold Tank (3rd Platoon from Battle of the Bulge to the end of the war)
  S Sgt De Leon (3rd Platoon from Battle of the Bulge to the end of the war)
  S Sgt Teklinski (3rd Platoon from Battle of the Bulge to the end of the war)

"M" HEAVY WEAPONS COMPANY
Company Commander
  Capt Jack D. Jester*
  Capt Don M. Brown (19/10/44, BrzS, SilS)
  1st Lt Russell Y. Mitchell (05/45)
Executive Officer
  1st Lt Robert B. Furman (→10/09/44, BrzS&CL, SilS)*
  1st Lt Russell Y. Mitchell
Reconnaissance Officer
  1st Lt Irven F. Jacobs#
Platoon Leaders
  2nd Lt John R. King#
  2nd Lt Thomas J. Carney, Jr#
2nd Platoon
  1st Lt Russell Y. Mitchell (#, BrzS, SilS)*
  1st Lt William Handler
  Platoon Sergeant
  S Sgt Walter J. Obarzanck
  Squad Leaders
  Sgt Lloyd Stephans
  Sgt Walter Harness
  Sgt Earl L. Flickenger (BrzS, PH)
3rd Platoon
  2nd Lt William Handler (#, SilS, BrzS&CL, PH&CL)*
  2nd Lt Howard S. Singer
  1st Lt Walter E. Anderson (#, BrzS)
  Platoon Sergeant
  S Sgt Walter E. Bishop
  S Sgt James L. Hodges (BrzS, KIA)
Assignment to the 11th Infantry not known
  2nd Lt John D. Hammons (KIA 21/07/44, PH)
  2nd Lt Bruce L. Mack (KIA 22/08/44, PH)
  1st Lt Walter L. Tichenor (DOW 30/08/44, PH)
  2nd Lt Willard Bernhardt (KIA 10/09/44, PH, Croix de Guerre)
  2nd Lt Myler T. Parker (KIA 10/09/44, PH)
  2nd Lt Lewis S. Dillelo (KIA 04/10/44, PH)
  2nd Lt Neal L. Hubbard (KIA 18/10/44, PH)
  1st Lt Harold I. Stebbins (KIA 18/11/44, PH)
  2nd Lt Rudolph J. Kainz (KIA 20/12/44, PH)
  2nd Lt Alfred Scarigli (KIA 27/12/44, PH)
  1st Lt Murry L. Summers (KIA 28/12/44, BrzS, PH)
  2nd Lt Alvin A. Cutler (KIA 13/02/45, PH)

7th ENGINEER COMBAT BATTALION

Battalion Commander
  Lt Col Hugo J. Stark*

HQ & SERVICE COMPANY
Company Commander
  Capt Nick Pokrajac*
  Capt Robert J. Barlock (17/08/44)
  1st Lt James Evans (01/11/44)

"A" COMPANY
Company Commander
  Capt Charles H. Marks*

"B" COMPANY
Company Commander
  1st Lt T. G. Manos*
  1st Lt Ward Miller (01/04/45)

"C" COMPANY
Company Commander
  Capt Robert J. Barlock*
  Capt Nick Pokrajac (17/08/44)
  1st Lt William Rivers (21/12/44)
Platoon Leader
  1st Lt Olson (WIA, 29/07/44)

5th MEDICAL BATTALION

Battalion Commander
Lt Col Howard H. Bass (Croix de Guerre, BrzS+CL)*

HEADQUARTERS COMPANY
Company Commander
Capt Harold D. Johnson, MAC (27/04/43, BrzS)*
Warrant Officer, Supplies
WOJG Charles M. O'Boyle (BrzS)*

"A" COLLECTING COMPANY
Company Commander
Capt James J. Clements, MC (10/43, PH, BrzS)*

"B" COLLECTING COMPANY
Company Commander
Capt Harry D. Nesmith, MC (08/43→02/44)*
Capt Robert J. Brennan, MC (02/44, BrzS)

"C" COLLECTING COMPANY
Company Commander
Capt Francis Fox, MC (01/43, BrzS)*
Officers
1st Lt Paul Weaver

"D" CLEARING COMPANY
Company Commander
Capt Frank J. Anker (06/43, BrzS)*

5th CAVALRY RECONNAISSANCE TROOP

Troop Commander
Capt Theodore A. Twelmeyer*
Capt Donald E. Robinson (28/08/44)
Platoon Leaders
1st Lt Raymond W. Reed

1st Lt Norman Sterling
1st Lt Stanley A. Swieckowski
2nd Lt Howard H. Froment
2nd Lt John J. Wampler

5th INFANTRY DIVISION, BAND

WO Lionel G. Croteau
Tech Sgt John W. Golden
Tech Sgt Russel Anders

S Sgt Joe Davis
Sgt W. Kulebokeon

Symbols and abbreviations used:

→:	to	&CL (2CL)	with Cluster (Oak leaf cluster)
*:	liberation of Angers (from 8 to 10 August 1944)	/V	V-device for Valour
#:	listed on the roster of the 11th Infantry dated 31/01/45; date of assignment and of departure unknown	DSC	Distinguished Service Cross
		KIA	Killed in Action
		WIA	Wounded in Action
VE day:	listed on the roster dated 08/05/45; date of assignment and of departure unknown	DOW	Died of Wounds
		POW	Prisoner of War
SilS:	Silver Star	TDY	Temporary Duty, Temp
BrzS:	Bronze Star		
PH:	Purple Heart		

Information concerning decorations is principally given for the 11th Infantry Regiment; except for some names not listed in the *History of the Eleventh Infantry*, it is complete. For the other units, if nothing is noted, that is because no information was available.

This roster is not exhaustive because no complete listing exists. It was compiled using the following books:

Members, *2nd Infantry regiment, Fifth Infantry Division* (Army & Navy Publishing Company, 1946) (roster but without unit identification)

Public Relations Section, Tenth Infantry Regiment, *History of the Tenth Infantry Regiment in World War II* (The Battery Press, Nashville, TN) (without roster)

The 11th Infantry Regiment, *History of the Eleventh Infantry Regiment, 5th Infantry Division, European Theater* (Army & Navy Publishing Company, Baton Rouge, LA, 1945) (roster by units, very interesting, particularly for the names of the officers, many names in the text)

David Polk, *Fifth Infantry Division* (Turner Publishing Company, 1994)

Martin Blumenson, *Breakout and Pursuit* (The European Theater of Operations, U.S. Army in WWII, Center of Military History, U.S. Army, Washington, D.C., 1961)

Hugh M. Cole, *The Lorraine Campaign* (The European Theater of Operations, U.S. Army in WWII, Center of Military History, U.S. Army, Washington, D.C., 1950)

Charles B. MacDonald, *Arnaville, in Three Battles: Arnaville, Altuzzo, and Schmidt* (U.S. Army in WWII, Center of Military History, U.S. Army, Washington, D.C., 1952)

Historical Section, Hq 5th Infantry Division *The Fifth Infantry Division in The E.T.O.*, 1945 (The Battery Press, Nashvile, TN)

Robert H. Williams, Regimental Historian Emeritus, *Surviving Members of the Regiment, The Eleventh Infantry Regiment, Fifth Infantry Division, The European Theater of Operations, Supplement to the Regimental History-World War II* (Florida, 1994)

In addition, to complete the roster many veterans of the 5th Infantry Division were contacted:-

Manford C. Bear

Fred P. Body

Matt Britten

Jean W. Christy

Robert E. Connor

Thomas H. Cooper

Lewis M. Dilwith

Leo H. Eberhardt

Martin J. Gemoets

Tommy R. Gilliam

Odvar Haug

Wilfrid H. Haughey

Herman H. Jost

Ferris A. Kercher

Charles H. Marks

Chester E. Ball

George Bachman

William E. Griffith

James N. Arrington

George G. Klein

Richard D. Kramer (for his father Richard A. Kramer)

Special thanks for their researches to:

Richard H. Durst

Robert "Herb" Williams

COMMAND ROSTER OF THE 11TH INFANTRY REGIMENT ON 31 JANUARY 1945

REGIMENTAL HEADQUARTERS (01)

(TOE strength: 11 officers including the chaplains; actual strength: 12)

Regimental Commander	Col Paul J. Black (1542) [1]
Executive Officer	Lt Col Homer C. Ledbetter (1542)
S-1 Personnel Officer & Adjutant	Capt Elbert L. Cooper (2110)
S-2 Intelligence Officer	Major Woodrow W. Morse (9301)
Assistant S-2	Capt Carl R. McFarlan (9301)
S-3 Operation & Training Officer	Major Cornelius W. Coghill, Jr (2162)
Assistant S-3	Capt Robert D. Spencer (2162)
Combat Liaison Officer #1	Capt Harold S. Emerson (1930)
Combat Liaison Officer #2	1st Lt Oliver C. Yanko (1930)
Chaplain #1	Capt Thomas P. Hennessey (5310)
Chaplain #2	Capt William S. Jones (5310)
Chaplain #3	Capt James E. Parr (5310)

HEADQUARTERS COMPANY, INFANTRY REGIMENT (02)

(TOE strength: 4 officers; actual strength: 6; 1 WO)

Company Headquarters

Company Commander	1st Lt Leo H. Eberhardt (2900) (Capt)
Executive Officer	1st Lt Dana S. Jones (1542)
Security Officer	1st Lt Eugene R. Webb (1542)
	1st Lt William F. Hintz (1542)

Communication Platoon

Communication Officer, Plat Comdr	Capt Roy E. Hogan (0200)
Communication Officer, assistant	CWO Joseph Stephens (0200)

Intelligence & Reconnaissance Platoon

Platoon Commander	2nd Lt Leonard A. Duston, Jr (1542)

SERVICE COMPANY, INFANTRY REGIMENT (36)

(TOE strength: 11 officers; actual strength: 13; 4 WO)

Company Headquarters

Company Commander	Capt Herbert V. Gawthrop (2910)
(replaced by)	1st Lt Andrew J. Hreha (2910)
S-4, Supply Officer	Capt Alfred P. Teegarden (4010) (Maj)
(ex S-4)	Maj Robert B. Shamblin
Supply Officer, Administration	WOJG Eugene E. Stahl (4411)

Regimental Headquarters Platoon

Staff Section

Military Personnel Officer	Capt Kenneth C. Doty (2200)
Special Service Officer	2nd Lt Will M. Smith (5000)
Orientation, Assistant S-3	(No officer assigned) (5000)
Adjutant, Assistant S-1	WOJG Clarence E. Welsh (2110)

Supply Section

Munition Officer	Capt Lowell K. Tuttel (4510)
Munition Officer, assistant	WOJG Francis J. Flood (4510)

---

1. The number in parenthesis represents the Specification Serial Number (SSN). The duty of each officer listed represents the definition of the SSN except in the following cases:- 0200 Communication Officer, 0600 Motor Transport Officer, 1524 Anti-tank Unit Commander; 1542 Infantry Unit Commander; 1192 Infantry Cannon Unit Commander; 4010 Supply and Evacuation Staff Officer. The rank in parenthesis following the SSN corresponds to the rank one level higher.

Transportation Platoon
Platoon Headquarters

Motor Transport Officer	Capt George W. Larson (0600)
Maintenance Officer	2nd Lt Frederick A. Coenen (0605)

Battalion Sections

S-4, Supply Officer (Bn)	1st Lt Franklin H. Drunagel (4010)
S-4, Supply Officer (Bn) [2]	2nd Lt Glenn E. Alway (4010) (1st Lt)
S-4, Supply Officer (1st Bn)	1st Lt Doran R. Zwygart (4010)
S-4, Supply Officer (3rd Bn)	1st Lt Russell E. Sprague (4010)

Maintenance Section

Motor Transport Officer, assistant	WOJG George W. Massey (0600)

MEDICAL DETACHMENT, INFANTRY REGIMENT (32)

(TOE strength: 10 officers; actual strength: 11)

Headquarters Section

Detachment Commander	Major Rankin A. Nebinger (3500)
Dental Officer	Capt Andrew E. Lobben (3170)
Dental Officer	Capt Clare W. Sauser (3170)

Battalion Sections

Medical Officer, Gen Duty (3rd Bn) [3]	Capt Panfilo C. Di Loreto (3100)
Medical Officer, General Duty	Capt Marcus M. Horenstein (3100)
Medical Officer, General Duty	Capt Paul A. Rothenberg (3100)
Medical Officer, Gen Duty (1st Bn)	Capt Robert J. Scott (3100)
Medical Officer, General Duty	Capt George R. Spence (3100)
Administrative Asst, MAC (1st Bn)	1st Lt Jim C. Kelly (2600)
Administrative Asst, MAC (2nd Bn)	1st Lt T. H. Pritchett (2600)
Administrative Asst, MAC (3rd Bn)	1st Lt Edwin R. Pyle (2600)

INFANTRY ANTI-TANK COMPANY, INFANTRY REGIMENT (22)

(TOE strength: 7 officers; actual strength: 7)

Company Headquarters

Company Commander	Capt Fairfield Rock (1524)
Executive Officer	1st Lt Walter J. Constantine (1524)
Reconnaissance Officer	2nd Lt John W. Morring (9312)

Anti-tank Platoons

Platoon Commander	1st Lt John A. Filbert (1524)
Platoon Commander	1st Lt Harold B. Mathauser (1524)
Platoon Commander	1st Lt Leroy Van De Carr, Jr (1524)
Platoon Commander	2nd Lt Victor J. Wirpsa (1542)

INFANTRY CANNON COMPANY, INFANTRY REGIMENT (26)

(TOE strength: 5 officers; actual strength: 6)

Company Headquarters

Company Commander	1st Lt Henry T. Bass, Jr (1192) (KIA 15/03/45)
Reconnaissance Officer, Ex-O	(No officer assigned) (9312)

Cannon Platoons (× 3)

Platoon Commanders	1st Lt Joseph H. Gallant (1192)
	1st Lt Charles Roggenstein (1192) (Capt)
	2nd Lt Elmer H. Graham (1192)
	2nd Lt John A. Bedell (1192)
	2nd Lt Jerome H. Glickman (1192) (1st Lt)

2. One of the three Battalion S-4's was replaced during January 1945, although it is not known which.

3. Battalion Section Commander (*2-3), see chapter 2, section 2.6, Medical Detachment T/O&E 7-11. Each battalion section included a medical officer and a medical assistant, MAC. One of the medical officers was assigned to the headquarters section, but which is unknown.

1ST INFANTRY BATTALION, HEADQUARTERS (03)

(TOE strength: 4 officers; actual strength: 4)

Battalion Commander	Major Herman R. Schell (1542) (Lt Col)
Executive Officer	Capt Robert H. Williams (1542) (Maj)
S-2, Intelligence Officer	1st Lt Robert V. Gray (9301)
S-3, Operations & Training Officer	Capt Forrest P. Raley (2162)

HEADQUARTERS COMPANY, INFANTRY BATTALION (04)

(TOE strength: 5 officers; actual strength: 7)

Company Headquarters

S-1 Personnel Officer & Adjutant[4]	Capt Kenneth E. Hughes (2110)
	1st Lt Christian E. Finkbeiner (Capt)
Motor Transport Officer	1st Lt Rocco J. Barbuto (0600)

Communication Platoon

Communication Officer	1st Lt Harry G. Rekemeier (0200)

Ammunition & Pioneer Platoon

Munition Officer	2nd Lt James N. Peck (4510) (1st Lt)
	2nd Lt Loren H. White (4510) (1st Lt)

Anti-tank Platoon

Anti-tank Officer	2nd Lt James G. Collier, Jr (1542) (1st Lt)

A COMPANY (05) (TOE strength: 6 officers; actual strength: 6)

Company Commander	Capt Harold J. Taylor (1542)
Executive Officer	1st Lt Harold F. Bryant (1542)
Platoons Commanders:	1st Lt Charles F. Brauer (1542)
	1st Lt Robert L. Carlson (1542)
	2nd Lt George W. Alsup (1542)
	2nd Lt Lawrence W. Durance (1542)

B COMPANY (06) (TOE strength: 6 officers; actual strength: 5)

Company Commander		1st Lt Charles B. Vickers (1542)
Executive Officer		1st Lt William Randle (1542)
Platoon Commanders:	2nd Plat	2nd Lt Stanley Maly, Jr (1542) (1st Lt)
	3rd Plat	2nd Lt Laurel M. Venters (1542) (1st Lt)
	Wpn Plat	2nd Lt J. T. Zawistowski (1542) (1st Lt)

C COMPANY (07) (TOE strength: 6 officers; actual strength: 5)

Company Commander		1st Lt Gordon V. Gorski (1542)
Executive Officer & 4 Platoon Commanders:		
		1st Lt Keith B. Liesch (1542) (Capt)
	3rd Plat	1st Lt George W. Putney (1542)
		1st Lt Ross W. Stanley (1542)
		1st Lt Howard S. Warnock (1542)

D COMPANY (08) (TOE strength: 8 officers; actual strength: 5)

Company Commander		1st Lt Robert B. Furman, Jr (1542) (Capt)
Reconnaissance Officer		1st Lt Harry O. Kayler (1542)
Platoon Commanders:	1st Plat	2nd Lt Gordon F. Jacobsen (1542)
	2nd Plat	1st Lt Quinto T. De Sieno (1542)
		2nd Lt Paul J. Hodgson (1542)

2ND INFANTRY BATTALION, HEADQUARTERS (09)

(TOE strength: 4 officers; actual strength: 4)

Battalion Commander	Major John N. Acuff, Jr (1542) (Lt Col)
Executive Officer	Major Ferris A. Church (1542)
S-2, Intelligence Officer	2nd Lt Stanley R. Kuwik (9301) (1st Lt)
S-3 Operation & Training Officer	Capt Basil Jones III (2162)

---

4. Company commander, headquarters company, infantry battalion (*2-1), see chapter 3, section 3.1

HEADQUARTERS COMPANY, INFANTRY BATTALION (10)

(TOE strength: 5 officers; actual strength: 3)

Company Headquarters

S-1, Adjutant General, Co Cdr	Capt Wilbur W. Wood (2110)
Motor Transport Officer	

Communication Platoon

Communication Officer	

Ammunition & Pioneer Platoon

Munition Officer, Plat Comdr	2nd Lt Charles B. Camp (4510) (1st Lt)

Anti-tank Platoon

Platoon Commander	2nd Lt Alvin A. Cutler (1542) (KIA 13/02/45)

E COMPANY (11) (TOE strength: 6 officers; actual strength: 5)

Company Commander	Capt Thomas G. Dodson (1542)
Executive Officer	1st Lt J. C. Shirley (1542)
Platoon Commanders:	1st Lt William E. Jackes (1542)
	2nd Lt Joe A. Rawls (1542)(1st Lt)
	2nd Lt Arthur T. Welton (1542)

F COMPANY (12) (TOE strength: 6 officers; actual strength: 5)

Company Commander	Capt Jack M. Brown (1542)

Executive Officer & 4 Platoon Commanders:
1st Lt George W. Darroch (1542)
1st Lt Cedric E. Farmer (1542)
1st Lt Arthur W. Haney(1542)
1st Lt Harry C. Jordan, Jr (1542)

G COMPANY (13) (TOE strength: 6 officers; actual strength: 4)

Company Commander	Capt Richard H. Durst (1542)
Executive Officer	1st Lt Stanley M. Anderson (1542) (KIA 15/03/45)
Platoon Commanders:	Capt J. T. Watson (1542) (attached)
	1st Lt Lucien E. Levesque (1542)

H COMPANY (14) (TOE strength: 8 officers; actual strength: 6)

Company Commander	Capt Stanley R. Connor (1542)
Reconnaissance Officer	1st Lt Robert J. Bauschelt (1542)
Platoon Commanders:	1st Lt Tillman C. Faulkner (1542)
	1st Lt Aulbry C. Hitchings (1542) (1st Lt)
	1st Lt Harold A. Phifer (1542)
	2nd Lt Elmon W. Holmes (1542)

3RD INFANTRY BATTALION, HEADQUARTERS (15)

(TOE strength: 4 officers; actual strength: 4)

Battalion Commander	Lt Col William H. Birdsong, Jr (1542)
Executive Officer	Capt Harry M. Smith (1542) (Maj)
S-2, Intelligence Officer	1st Lt Earl C. Cameron (9301)
S-3, Operations & Training Officer	Capt Robert M. Gill (2162)

HEADQUARTERS COMPANY, INFANTRY BATTALION (16)

(TOE strength: 5 officers; actual strength: 6)

Company Headquarters

S-1, Battalion Adjutant, Co Cdr	Capt Quintan B. LeMonte (2110)
Motor Transport Officer	2nd Lt Robert P. Genther (0600) (1st Lt)

Communication Platoon

Communication Officer	1st Lt Frank A. Bishop, Jr (0200)

Ammunition & Pioneer Platoon

Munition Officer	2nd Lt Edward C. Melane (4510) (1st Lt)

Anti-tank Platoon

Platoon Commander	2nd Lt Eugene L. Goodrich(1524) (1st Lt)
Replacement	2nd Lt Harry H. Shields, Jr (1542)

I COMPANY (17) (TOE strength: 6 officers; actual strength: 4)

Company Commander	1st Lt Edward Koslosky (1542) (KIA 10/02/45)
Executive Officer &	1st Lt Christian J. Christoffels (1542)
Platoon Commanders:	1st Lt Robert A. Emery (1542)
	2nd Lt Clifton R. Byrd (1542)

K COMPANY (18) (TOE strength: 6 officers; actual strength: 4)

Company Commander	Capt Joseph H. Cox (1542)
Executive Officer	1st Lt Mitchell J. Hazam (1542)
Platoon Commanders:	1st Lt James G. Kerr, Jr (1542)
	1st Lt Max E. Lett (1542)

L COMPANY (19) (TOE strength: 6 officers; actual strength: 6)

Company Commander   1st Lt Robert A. Kaiser (1542)
Executive Officer & 4 Platoon Commanders:

	1st Lt James N. Broyles (1542)
	1st Lt Charles G. Maier (1542)
3rd Plat	1st Lt Lewis M. Dilwith (1542)
	1st Lt Walter E. Anderson (1542)
	2nd Lt Orlando J. Heinitz (1542)

M COMPANY (20) (TOE strength: 8 officers; actual strength: 6)

Company Commander	Capt Don M. Brown (1542)
Reconnaissance Officer, Ex-O	1st Lt Irven F. Jacobs (9312)
Platoon Commanders:	1st Lt Russel Y. Mitchell (1542)
	2nd Lt John R. King (1542)
	2nd Lt Thomas J. Carney, Jr (1542)
	2nd Lt William Handler (1542)

Strength of the 11th Infantry Regiment on 31 January 1945

Strength	T/O&E	Actual
Officers	153	146
Warrant Officers	5	5

Source: Personnel Roster, 31 January 1945, 5th Infantry Division, 11th Infantry Regiment, APO 5, NY, via Richard H. Durst.

BIBLIOGRAPHY

PRIMARY SOURCES

Tables of Organization and Equipment (T/O&E)

Series 2 Cavalry:
2-27, 15 July 43, C1, C2, C3; 16 June 45, C1, C2.

Series 5 Engineers:
5-15, 15 July 43; 13 March 44, C1, C2.
5-16, 15 July 43; 13 March 44, C1.
5-17, 15 July 43; 13 March 44.
5-192, 10 July 43 (not in the Infantry Division).

Series 6 Artillery:
6-10, 15 July 43, C1, C2; 26 February 44, C1; 27 September 44, C1.
6-10-1, 15 July 43, C1, C2, C3, C4, C5; 27 September 44, C1.
6-25, 15 July 43, C1, C2, C3, C4; 27 September 44, C1.
6-26, 15 July 43, C1, C2, C3, C4, C5, C6; 27 September 44, C1.
6-27, 15 July 43, C1, C2, C3, C4, C5, C6; 27 September 44, C1.
6-29, 15 July 43, C1, C2, C3, C4, C5; 27 September 44, C1, C2.
6-35, 15 July 43, C1, C2, C3.
6-36, 15 July 43, C1, C2, C3, C4, C5, C6, C7, C8; 27 September 44, C1, C2.
6-37, 15 July 43, C1, C2, C3, C4.
6-39, 15 July 43, C1, C2, C3, C4.
6-335, 3 July 43, C1, C2, C3, C4, C5; 27 September 44, C1.
6-337, 3 July 43, C1, C2, C3, C4, C5, C6; 27 September 44, C1, C2.
6-339, 3 July 43, C1, C2, C3, C4; 27 September 44, C1.

Series 7 Infantry:
7, 1 August 42; 15 July 43, C1; 24 January 45, C1, C2; 12 April 46.
7-1, 15 July 43, C1, C2, C3, C4; 13 January 45, C1, C2, C3, C4, C5.
7-2, 15 July 43, C1, C2, C3, C4, C5; 13 January 45, C1, C2, C3, C4, C5.
7-3, 15 July 43, C1, C2, C3, C4; 13 January 45, C1, C2.
7-11, 1 April 42; 15 July 43, C1, C2; 26 February, C1.
7-12, 15 July 43; 26 February 44, C1, C2.
7-13, 15 July 43, C1, C2; 26 February 44, C1, C2.
7-14, 15 July 43; 26 February 44, C1, C2, C3.
7-15, 15 July 43; 26 February 44, C1.
7-16, 15 July 43; 26 February 44, C1, C2.
7-17, 1 August 42, C1; 15 July 43; 26 February 44, C1, C2, C3.
7-18, 15 July 43; 26 February 44.
7-19, 15 July 43; 26 February 44, C1, C2, C3.

Series 8 Medical:
8-15, 15 July 43, C1, C2; 14 February 45, C1.
8-16, 15 July 43, C1, C2, C3, C4; 14 February 45, C1.
8-17, 15 July 43, C1, C2, C3; 14 February 45, C1.
8-18, 15 July 43, C1, C2; 14 February 45, C1.

Series 9 Ordnance:
9-8, 15 July 43, C1; 17 November 44.

Series 10 Quartermaster:
10-17, 15 July 43, C1, C2; 19 February 44, C1; 1 June 45.
10-57, 8 August 43, C1, C2, C3; 6 July 44, C1, C2 (not in the Infantry Division).

Series 11 Signal:
11-7, 15 July 43; 11 December 43, C1, C2, C3, C4.

Series 19 Military Police:
19-7, 15 July 43, C1, C2; 28 March 44, C1; 12 September 44, C1, C2.

241

Series 20 Miscellaneous:
20-107, 8 March 44, C1, C2.

Tables of Basic Allowances (T/BA)
2, 1 March 42, C1, C2, C3.
5, 1 December 42, C1, C2.
7, 20 June 42, C2; Supp No. 1, 15 September 42.

Tables of Allowances (T/A)
20, 5 April 44.

Archival Documents
Order of Battle of the United States Army Ground Forces in WWII, Pacific Theater of Operations, Office of the Chief of Military History, DA, Washington, D.C., 1959.

Order of Battle, U.S. Army, WWII, European Theater of Operations, Divisions, ETOUSA, Paris 1945 (Captain Robert J. Greenwald).

Preliminary report on "Standard Operating Procedure, 2nd Division", file 370.2, Hq 5th Division, Fort McClellan, Alabama, 3 March 1940.

Reorganization of the 5th Infantry Division, War Department, The Adjutant General's Office, Washington, to The Commanding General Second Army, AG 322, 14 February 1946.

Reorganization of the 5th Infantry Division, Hq Second Army, LTG Simpson, to Commanding General, 5th Infantry Division, Camp Campbell, Kentucky, 26 February 1946.

Reorganization of 5th Signal Company, General Orders No. 6, Hq 5th Infantry Division, 28 March 1944.

Reports from Triangular Divisions, War Department, The Adjutant General's Office, Washington, to The Commanding Generals of the 1st, 2nd, 3rd, 5th, 6th Divisions, AG 320.2, 18 December 1939.

Reports on Triangular Division, Hq 5th Division, Fort McClellan, Alabama, to All Division Staff Officers and Unit Commanders, AG 320.2, 19 January 1940.

Reports from Triangular Divisions, War Department, The Adjutant General's Office, Washington, to The Commanding Generals of the 1st, 2nd, 3rd, 5th, 6th Divisions, AG 320.2, 5 March 1940.

Report on the Triangular Division, Hq 5th Division, Fort Benning, Georgia, 16 April 1940.

Reports on the Triangular Division, Hq 5th Division, Office of the Assistant Chief of Staff, G-3, Fort Benning, Georgia, to Commanding General, 5th Division, 22 April 1940.

Standard Nomenclature list, SNL G-102, vol 4, 25 September 43, C1, C2.

Tables of Organization and Equipment, Hq 5th Infantry Division, APO 5, U.S. Army, 6 June 1944.

Williams, Robert "Herb" *War Diary* (unpublished, extracts sent by E-mail).

Government Publications
Army Regulations 320-5, *Military Terms Abbreviations and Symbols, Dictionary of United States Army Terms*, Hq, Department of the Army, 28 November 1958, Government Printing Office.

Conference course, Training Bulletin No. GT-20, *The Rifle Platoon and Squad in Offensive Combat. Part 2: The Attack.* Pictorial supplement to FM 7-10, The Infantry School, Fort Benning, Georgia, 15 May 1943

Conference course, Training Bulletin No. GT-20, *The Rifle Platoon and Squad in Offensive Combat. Part 3: Security Missions.* Pictorial Supplement to FM 7-10, The Infantry School, Fort Benning, Georgia, 30 June 1943.

Conference course, Training Bulletin No. GT-20, *The Rifle Platoon and Squad in Combat. Part 4: Defensive Combat.* Pictorial Supplement to FM 7-10, The Infantry School, Fort Benning, Georgia, 1 October 1943.

Conference course, Training Bulletin No. GT-1, Chapter 1, *Organization of the Infantry Regiment*, The Infantry School, Fort Benning, Georgia, 1 October 1943.

Field Manual, 5-6, *Operations of Engineer Field Units*, War Department, 23 April 1943 with changes, Government Printing Office.

Field Manual, 7-20, *Infantry Field Manual, Rifle Battalion*, September 28, 1942, War Department.

Field Manual, 11-10, *Signal Corps Field Manual, Organization and Operations in the Infantry Division*, 6 October 1941, with changes, War Department, Government Printing Office.

Field Manual, 100-5, *Field Service Regulations, Operations*, 22 May 1941, War Department, Government Printing Office.

Medical Supply Catalog, MED 3, 1 March 1944, Hq Army Service Forces, Government Printing Office.

Medical Department Supply Catalog, 1 January 1941, War Department, Government Printing Office.

Modern Reconnaissance: A Collection of Articles from The Cavalry Journal, The Military Service Publishing Company, Harrisburg, PA, 1944.

Quartermaster Supply Catalog, QM Sec. 1, August 1943, Hq Army Service Forces, Government Printing Office.

Quartermaster Supply Catalog, QM 3-1, May 1946, Hq Army Service Forces, Government Printing Office.

Quartermaster Supply Catalog, QM 3-4, 1945, Hq Army Service Forces, Government Printing Office.

Quartermaster Supply Catalog, QM 6, 31 January 1944, Hq Army Service Forces, Government Printing Office.

Quartermaster Supply Catalog, QM 6, April 1947, Hq Army Service Forces, Government Printing Office.

Correspondence with:
Chester E. Ball, Col. (Ret), 04/10/94
Manford C. Bear, 28/01/97
William H. Birdsong, Brigadier General (Ret), 11/10/93, 09/11/95
Fred P. Body, 17/10/95
Matt A. Britten, 10/11/96
Robert E. Connor, Brigadier General (Ret) 03/11/95
Thomas H. Cooper, 16/09/96

Lewis M. Dilwith, 14/12/92, 10/11/93, 16/05/96, 16/12/96

Richard H. Durst, Col. (Ret), 17/09/93, 07/10/95, 20/11/95, 07/03/96

Leo H. Eberhardt, Col. (Ret), 25/06/96

Martin J. Gemoets, Col. (AUS Ret), 16/01/97

Tommy R. Gilliam, Col. (Ret), 20/08/96

Odvar Haug, 08/01/97

Wilfrid H. Haughey, Jr, 04/11/95, 18/01/96

Stanley Hays, Col. (Ret), 06/05/96

Gordon S. Henry, 15/01/96

Herman H. Jost, Jr, 06/11/95

Ferris A. Kercher, 07/01/97

Kelley B. Lemmon, Jr, Major General (Ret), 30/10/95

Charles H. Marks, 11/08/96

Andrew G. McGlynn, 12/08/96, 25/09/96

Richard Nowling, 10/04/96

William Standfield, Major (Ret), 25/04/96

Joseph G. Rahie, 06/08/96, 23/09/96

Thomas S. Watson, 02/01/97

Robert "Herb" Williams, 28/03/94, E-mails: 08/01/97, 09/01/97, 14/01/97, 23/01/97, 30/01/97, 07/02/97.

Veterans met in Angers:

Major General (ret) William M. Breckinridge, Col (ret) Richard Durst, Col (ret) George W. Bachman, Col (ret) Chester E. Ball, Robert H. Williams, Franklin Smith, Lewis M. Dilwith, Marc S. Tartaglia, James A. Almond, Douglas C. Hargrave, Leon Belardinellis, Frank J. Forcinella, Earl Patton, Joseph Zanko, Herman R. Schell, Richard B. Nowling (36th Inf Div, 143rd Inf Regt).

SECONDARY SOURCES

Government Publications

Doubler, Captain Michael D. *Busting the Bocage: American Combined Arms Operations in France, 6 June-31 July 1944* (Fort Leavenworth, Ks: U.S. Army Command & General Staff College, Combat Studies Institute, 1989)

Drea, Edward J. *Unit Reconstitution, A Historical Perspective* (Fort Leavenworth, Ks.: U.S. Army Command & General Staff College, Combat Studies Institute, CSI Report No. 3, 1 December 1983).

House, Captain Jonathan M. *Toward Combined Arms Warfare: A Survey of 20th-Century Tactics, Doctrine, and Organization* (Fort Leavenworth, Ks.: U.S. Army Command & General Staff College, Research Survey No. 2, August 1984).

Books

Beck, Alfred M., Abe Bortz, Charles W. Lynch, Lida Mayo & Ralph F. Weld *The Corps of Engineers: The War Against Germany (The Technical Services, U.S. Army in WWII)* (Washington, D. C.: Center of Military History, United States Army, 1985).

Blumenson, Martin *Breakout and Pursuit (The European Theater of Operations, U.S. Army in WWII)* (Washington, D. C.: Center of Military History, United States Army, 1961).

Cole, Hugh M. *The Lorraine Campaign* (The European Theater of Operations, U.S. Army in WWII) (Washington, D.C.: Center of Military History, United States Army, 1950).

Coll, Blanche D., Jean E. Keith & Herbert H. Rosenthal *The Corps of Engineers: Troops and Equipment (The Technical Services, U.S. Army in WWII)* (Washington, D. C.: Center of Military History, United States Army, 1958).

Fowle, Barry W. (Ed.) *Builders and Fighters, U.S. Army Engineers in WWII* (Fort Belvoir, VA.: Office of History, U.S. Army Corps of Engineers, 1992).

Gabel, Christopher R. *The U.S. Army GHQ Maneuvers of 1941* (Washington, D.C.: Center of Military History, United States Army, 1991).

Gemoets, Martin J. *A Short Story of War -1944, In France and Germany* (N.p., New Mexico: Privately published, 1993).

Greenfield, Kent Robert, Robert R. Palmer & Bell I. Wiley *The Organization of Ground Combat Troops (The Army Ground Forces, U.S. Army in WWII)* (Washington, D.C.: Center of Military History, United States Army, 1947).

Jessup, Jr, John E. & Robert W. Coakley *A Guide to the Study and Use of Military History* (Washington, D.C.: Center of Military History, United States Army, 1980).

Katcher, Philip *The U.S. Army 1941-45* (London: Osprey Publishing Company, 1995).

Laughlin, Cameron P. & John P. Langellier *U.S. Army Uniforms, Europe 1944-1945* (London: Arms & Armour Press, 1986).

MacDonald, Charles B. *Company Commander* (New York: Ballantine Books, 1961, revised edition).

Members 2nd Infantry Regiment *Second Infantry Regiment, Fifth Infantry Division* (Baton Rouge, LA: Army & Navy Publishing Company, 1946).

Members 11th Infantry Regiment *History of the Eleventh Infantry in WWII* (Baton Rouge, LA: Army & Navy Publishing, 1946).

Palmer, Robert R., Bell I. Wiley & William R. Keast *The Procurement and Training of Ground Combat Troops (The Army Ground Forces, U.S. Army in WWII)* (Washington, D.C.: Center of Military History, United States Army, 1948).

Polk, David *Fifth Infantry Division* (Paducah, KY: Turner Publishing Company, 1994).

Public Relations Section, Tenth Infantry Regiment *History of Tenth Infantry Regiment in World War II* (Nashville, TN: Battery Press, n.d., reprint edn).

Roz, Firmin & Gabriel Louis Jarray *Tableau des Etats-Unis, de la crise de 1933, à la victoire de 1945* (N.p.: Editions SPID, 1946).

Stanton, Shelby S. *U.S. Army Uniforms of WWII* (Harrisburg, Pa: Stackpole Books, 1991).

Also available from Helion & Company Limited:

British & Commonwealth Armies 1939-43
Mark Bevis
96pp. Paperback. Helion Order of Battle series volume 1
ISBN 1-874622-80-9

Handbook of WWII German Military Symbols and Abbreviations 1943-45
Terrence Booth
128pp., 800 b/w symbols, over 1,200 German military terms translated. Paperback
ISBN 1-874622-85-X

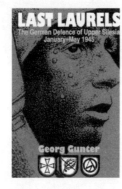

Last Laurels. The German Defence of Upper Silesia 1945
Georg Gunter
320pp., 170 b/w photos, 20 maps. Hardback
ISBN 1-874622-65-5

A selection of forthcoming titles:

British & Commonwealth Armies 1944-45 (Helion Order of Battle volume 2)
by Mark Bevis   ISBN 1-874622-90-6

Imperial German Army 1914-18 – Organisation, Structure, Orders of Battle
by Hermann Cron and Duncan Rogers   ISBN 1-874622-70-1

Rays of the Rising Sun. Japan's Asian Allies 1931-45 Volume 1 – China & Manchukuo
by Philip S. Jowett and John Berger   ISBN 1-874622-21-3

SOME ADDITIONAL SERVICES FROM HELION & COMPANY

BOOKSELLERS

- over 20,000 military books available
- four 100-page catalogues issued every year
- unrivalled stock of foreign language material, particularly German

BOOKSEARCH

- free professional booksearch service. No search fees, no obligation to buy

Want to find out more? Visit our website – www.helion.co.uk

Our website is the best place to learn more about Helion & Co. It features online book catalogues, special offers, complete information about our own books (including features on in-print and forthcoming titles, sample extracts and reviews), a shopping cart system and a secure server for credit card transactions, plus much more besides!

HELION & COMPANY
26 Willow Road, Solihull, West Midlands, B91 1UE, England
Tel 0121 705 3393   Fax 0121 711 4075
Email: publishing@helion.co.uk   Website: http://www.helion.co.uk